since
CUMORAH

since CUMORAH

THE BOOK OF MORMON IN THE MODERN WORLD

HUGH NIBLEY

Published by
DESERET BOOK COMPANY
44 East South Temple
Salt Lake City, Utah
1970

Library of Congress No. 67-21349

SBN No. 87747-240-8

Lithographed by

DESERET NEWS PRESS

in the United States of America

PREFACE

The purpose of this book is to call attention to some points on which the main hypothesis of the Book of Mormon may be tested. The hypothesis is that the Book of Mormon contains genuine history, and with it goes the corollary that the work was divinely inspired. Because of that corollary no serious attempt has been made to test the main hypothesis; for to test a theory means to take it seriously if only for a little while, to assume for the sake of argument that it may conceivably, however absurdly, be true after all. That is a concession no critic of the Book of Mormon has been willing to make.

Instead of the vigorous onslaught that the Book of Mormon hypothesis invites and deserves, it has elicited only a long monotonous drizzle of authoritarian denunciation, the off-hand opinions of impatient scholars whose intelligence and whose official standing will not allow them to waste a moment more than is necessary to write off an imposture so obviously deserving of contempt.

But today it is being pointed out in many quarters that authoritarianism is the very antithesis of true science, and that the best scientific theory is not the sane, cautious, non-committal one but the daring and revolutionary one. "A theory which asserts more," says Karl Popper, "and thus takes greater risks, is better testable than a theory which asserts very little,"[1] and he further notes that preference

---

[1]Karl R. Popper, "Science: Problems, Aims, Responsibilities," in *Federation Reports*, American Societies for Experimental Biology, Vol. 22 (1963), pp. 963f.

should always be given to the theory that makes more precise assertions than others, explains more facts in greater detail, invites more tests, suggests more new experiments and unifies more hitherto unrelated problems. On all these points the Book of Mormon scores high. It is the very extravagance of its claims that makes it so deserving of the respect which is denied it. The outrageous daring of its title page is the very thing that should whet the appetite of a real scholar: here is a book that is asking for a fight, so to speak, and if it is as flimsy as it looks at first glance any competent schoolman should have little trouble polishing it off in an hour or so.

But, strangely, through the years the challenge has had no takers. The learned have been peculiarly reluctant to tangle with this book. They have been willing enough to wave their credentials and state their opinions, but they have been adroit and determined in avoiding any serious discussion. To illustrate, Bernard De Voto once hailed an ambitious critic of Joseph Smith and the Book of Mormon as ". . . a detached, modern intelligence, grounded in naturalism, rejecting the supernatural." This is good news indeed for the Book of Mormon, for a confirmed naturalist who has made a study of the life of Joseph Smith is the very person best qualified to put Smith's supernaturalist claims to a severe test. "Observations or experiments can be accepted as supporting a theory," writes Popper,[2] "only if these observations or experiments may be described as severe tests of the theory . . . serious attempts to refute it." Today we read more and more in the journals about the importance of having a falsifiable rather than a verifiable theory. Anything can be verified, we are told, but a good scientific theory is one that can readily be falsified, that is, easily refuted if and where it is in error. And so it is fortunate that we have critics ready, willing, and able to

[2]Ibid., p. 964.

attack the historical claims of the Book of Mormon, for
that book is delightfully falsifiable.

But their attack to be effective must be met with the
strongest possible resistance: if it meets a half-hearted
defense it can never boast a real victory: "Since the method
of science is that of critical discussion (Popper again), it is
of great importance that the theories criticized should be
tenaciously defended . . ." That is, there must be a discussion, with the purpose of discovering by all possible
means every weakness in both positions. But that is not
the way Mr. DeVoto and his friends see it at all. For a
reliable defense they trust implicitly in the impartiality
and intelligence of the prosecution. They give the prize
to their champion not for bringing new life into the discussion but for effectively silencing all further discussion.
The last thing in the world they want is for the debate to
continue. In the impressive footnotes and credentials of
accepted authorities they see their own release from endless years of drudgery and research and from the risks and
uncertainties of an indefinitely prolonged debate with its
constant danger of new and disturbing revelations and its
frequent and humiliating disclosures of great gaps and
defects in the knowledge even of the foremost investigators. How much better to put the whole thing to bed
with the announcement that sound scholarship has at last
settled the issue once for all.

That this is the position that the experts take is perfectly apparent in their quick and angry reaction to any
word of criticism directed at the established oracles. Any
attempt to continue or renew the discussion by pointing
to the flaws and contradictions that swarm in their pages
meets with almost hysterical protests of prejudice, dis-
respect, and impertinence. By denying prejudice in their
own ranks, they deprive themselves of the one thing that
makes their work valuable. How could anyone "grounded

in naturalism, rejecting the supernatural" be anything but prejudiced in favor of naturalism and against the supernatural? And why not? How could anyone put up a halfway decent defense of the Book of Mormon without being prejudiced in its favor? There is nothing wrong with having and admitting two sides in a controversy. By definition every theory is controversial, and the better the theory the more highly controversial. There can be no more constructive approach to a controversial issue like this one than to have each side present the evidence which it finds most convincing, always bearing in mind that authority is not evidence and that name-dropping is as futile as name-calling. Sweeping statements and general impressions are sometimes useful in the process of getting one's bearings and taking up a position, but they cannot serve as evidence because they are expressions of personal impressions which are non-transferrable.

Which brings up an important point: we are not going to *prove* anything in this book. The evidence that will prove or disprove the Book of Mormon does not exist. When, indeed, is a thing proven? Only when an individual has accumulated in his own consciousness enough observations, impressions, reasonings and feelings to satisfy him personally that it is so. The same evidence which convinces one expert may leave another completely unsatisfied; the impressions that build up to definite proof are themselves non-transferrable. All we can do is to talk about the material at hand, hoping that in the course of the discussion every participant will privately and inwardly form, reform, change, or abandon his opinions about it and thereby move in the direction of greater light and knowledge. Some of the things in the pages that follow we think are quite impressive, but there is no guarantee at all that anybody else will think so. The whole thing may well impress some as disappointingly inconclusive, for we must insist that we have reached no final conclusions, even privately, and that all we can see ahead is more and ever more problems. But they are problems with a meaning, and it is our personal conviction that if the Book of Mormon were not a solid and genuine article we would long since have run out of such meaningful material, i.e., that there is much more behind all this than mere literary invention.

Some, impressed by the sheer mass and charge of the Book of Mormon, are now asking why it can't be seriously and respectfully treated as a myth. Lots of myths are today coming in for the most reverential treatment. But the book disdains such subterfuge, and never tires of reminding us that it is not myth but history and must stand or fall as such: ". . . I would that ye should remember that these sayings are true, and also that these records are true." (Mosiah 1:6.) ". . . we know our record to be true, for behold, it was a just man who did keep the record." (3 Nephi 8:1.) There may be mistakes in the record (3 Nephi 8:2), but there is no fraud or fiction: "And whoso receiveth this record, and shall not condemn it because of the imperfections which are in it, the same shall know of greater things" (Moroni 8:12.), for "if there be faults they be the faults of a man. But behold we know no fault . . . therefore, he that condemneth, let him be aware. . . ." (Moroni 8:17.) To call this record a myth is to condemn it as effectively as by calling it a fraud. We are going to approach the Book of Mormon as real history, in hopes that some reader may pick up a useful impression here or there.

HUGH NIBLEY

History is the record of the unpredictable. Old orders give way without perceiving their own passing. The religious world of early Christianity was just such an unstable age. Yet the most penetrating Roman historian, Tacitus, considered Christianity at the close of its apostolic ministry nothing but a disreputable superstition. This fact prompted today's leading private Bible translator of the Anglo-American world to ask whether the modern age might not have somewhere an unrecognized counterpart of the ancient ministry of inspired apostles. In his preface to his translation of Acts, J. B. Phillips considered, "It is perfectly possible that the unpublicised and almost unknown activities of the Spirit through His human agents to-day are of more permanent importance than all the news recorded in the whole of the popular Press."

The need of modern "activities of the spirit through His human agents" was hardly felt when Joseph Smith announced revelation to a Christian world firm in confident orthodoxy. Nearly a century and a half later, Christianity itself is in the crisis of a doctrinal revolution of such proportions that serious believers and leaders display the deepest anxiety. The president of Harvard University has recently challenged the lack of conviction of the teachers who train Christian ministers: "Men continue to scorn older formulations of belief . . . but now belief itself—professedly —is consciously eschewed. We have all become doubting Thomases." Now it is a question of what doctrines may survive when creeds are no longer valid statements of faith.

As never before, the claims of Joseph Smith to modern revelation demand the attention of serious men. The fact that a scholar of the stature of Hugh Nibley has found it productive to spend years on the question of the Book of Mormon shows that no easy dismissal of this work as an obvious imposture is possible. His research has examined Joseph Smith's claims at every point where historical scholarship possesses the tools to do so. Fortunately for this purpose, Joseph Smith "translated" an ancient American record of religious history roughly the size of the historical portions of the Old Testament. Anyone with slight experience with the Book of Mormon knows that its prophetic portions are only reached through chapter after chapter of historical detail—of migrations from the Near East, of religious traditions and practices, of unfamiliar names and strange *mores*, of economic, political and military affairs. The very existence of a purported history of this length is an open invitation to competent scholars to demolish the claim of its author that it is history. No other product of Joseph Smith's life shows such promise of giving unerring knowledge of whether he is a genuine prophet or a clever fraud.

Yet the main case against the Book of Mormon continues to be argued mainly on the ground that it is the inevitable product of the nineteenth century. In the first place, no one has so far offered this thesis who is in the slightest competent to say whether the Book of Mormon is more like the nineteenth century than the ancient world that it chronicles. A student of the nineteenth century may indeed find parallels in this period and the Book of Mormon, but without a knowledge of the world of antiquity, he simply is not equipped to make a judgment whether the Book of Mormon resembles more Joseph Smith's environment or the ancient culture it claims to represent. Professor Nibley is the only person now publishing on this question who is equipped to make valid observations. A

simple scanning of the table of contents will show him
dealing with the writings of the Christian fathers, the
writings of the Christian gnostics, Jewish literature and
traditions, Arabic literature and traditions, Near-Eastern
history and archaeology, not to speak of a half-dozen
assorted areas of special competence such as military tactics
and social disintegration. Professor Nibley has looked into
these areas at least enough to ask questions about them,
and that is all he does. But he asks odd questions.

The last century in the field of ancient studies is as
iconoclastic as the industrial revolution in the world of
practical concerns. The fact that the accuracy of the Book
of Mormon is more evident after new discoveries makes it
impossible now to be honest and simply ridicule this record.
These discoveries have done more than vindicate the Book
of Mormon. They have shown enough of its truth to put
a burden of investigation on anyone who is seriously interested in religious or historical reality. New evidence
demands a fresh look at the claim that the Book of Mormon
is a record of ancient religious history, sealed up for the
instruction and salvation of the modern world. Readers
of every level of education have in this book exciting and
provocative insights to God's purposes under the competent
guidance of a gifted scholar. Lack of answers to his evidence for the Book of Mormon over two decades is rapidly
forging the conviction that it is unanswerable.

Richard Lloyd Anderson
Professor of History and Religion
Brigham Young University

The publishers express appreciation to *The Improvement Era* for their consideration in allowing articles which appeared in their magazine under the title "Since Cumorah" to be reproduced in this volume.

CONTENTS

PART IV. THE REAL BACKGROUND OF THE BOOK OF MORMON

Chapter 9. SOME FAIRLY FOOLPROOF TEXTS

Chapter 10. PROPHETS IN THE WILDERNESS

Chapter 11. A RIGOROUS TEST: MILITARY HISTORY

PART V.   THE PROPHETIC BOOK OF MORMON

Chapter 12.   GOOD PEOPLE AND BAD PEOPLE

Chapter 13.
PROPHECY IN THE BOOK OF MORMON: THE THREE PERIODS

CONCLUSION

Part I.

The Book of Mormon as Scripture

"... there can be no more Bible."

Clutching at Straws:

The Classic Charges against the Book of Mormon

The first line of defense against the Book of Mormon, a barricade thrown up even before it had come from the printer, was the charge that since the Bible is the absolute, letter-perfect, flawless, and final Word of God, to designate any other writing as holy scripture could only be the height of blasphemy. It was an easy thing, however, for Orson Pratt and others "to expose this popular, though fatal error, invented by priestcraft in the early ages of the apostasy, and transferred to succeeding generations. . . ."[1] We need not repeat here the oft-published evidence that the writers of scripture have always thought of the setting forth of the word of God for men as an open-ended affair in which God is free to speak whenever he chooses, regardless of how reluctant men may be to allow him that privilege, since the proposition is readily conceded by leading Christian scholars today.[2]

The second mortal offense of the Book of Mormon was the admission on the title page that this record, translated "by the gift of God," might possibly contain mistakes.

[1]Orson Pratt, "Divine Authenticity of the Book of Mormon," Pamphlet (Liverpool, Oct. 1850), reprinted in *Orson Pratt's Works* (Salt Lake City: Deseret News Press, 1945), I, pp. 107ff.; quote is from p. 109.
[2]For a survey of the question, see W. C. Unnik, in *Vigiliae Christianae*, III (1949), pp. 32ff.

Mistakes? In a book revealed by the power of God? Another blasphemous conception. Yet today Bible scholars
accept this proposition as readily as they do the first, and
labor day and night to come up with a more correct text
of the Holy Bible than any at present available. The idea
that a book can contain many things that are true and of
God and at the same time many things that are false and
of men was one that Catholics and Protestants alike found
perfectly unthinkable in the days of Joseph Smith, though
most students of the Bible accept it today. And once the
possibility of human error is conceded, why should the
idea of a corrected edition of the Book of Mormon be
offensive? Revised and improved editions of the Bible
are constantly coming from the press, and the Mormons
have never believed in an infallible book or an infallible
anything in which men have had a hand. God allows
fallible humans to be co-workers with him on the road
to a far-distant perfection, but he expects them to make
lots of mistakes along the way.

        Why, then, have the critics been scandalized and de-
lighted to discover that the second edition of the Book
of Mormon corrected many mistakes in the first? For
years this writer used only the First Edition in his classes,
and it is still by far the best. It is full of mistakes, but
they are obvious ones. According to the printer, J. H. Gilbert, Joseph Smith told him to leave the grammar un-
altered, since "the Old Testament is ungrammatical. . . ."
As we shall see, recent studies of the Old Testament
prophets show that they often mix up their persons, numbers and tenses in impassioned discourse, just as Abinadi
does in the first edition of the Book of Mormon, pp. 182f.
On the other hand, the prophet gave Gilbert a free hand
with punctuation and spelling: "The manuscript," says
the printer, ". . . was one solid paragraph, without a punctuation mark, from beginning to end." Imagine six hundred pages of that! How is it to be explained except on

the assumption that the text was actually dictated word for word by one uneducated man to another? It was no ruse or trick, since nobody but the printer ever mentioned it, and he was authorized to correct the manuscript where he thought necessary. The original manuscript used by the printer is now in part available, and it shows that Mr. Gilbert did take liberties with the text. Are we to believe that Joseph Smith is responsible when we read in the first edition on page 69 five lines from the bottom, "For my soul deliteth in the Scriptures . . ." and just two lines below that, "Behold, my soul delighteth in the Scriptures"? Since by his own admission the printer was authorized to correct the spelling, isn't he to blame for putting in the fifth line from the bottom of page 280: ". . . Lamoni rehearst unto him . . ." and on the bottom line, ". . . now when Lamoni had rehearsed unto him. . . ." Or who is accountable for the "peeple" on page 127, after the word had been spelled properly a hundred times? If the printer was correcting Oliver Cowdery's spelling he should have corrected these mistakes; if not, Cowdery himself had obviously slipped up and any editor was not only free to correct the slip but bound to. Whether the printer chooses to use or omit a hyphen or a comma is a matter of punctuation and entirely up to him. "There were some printing errors," Joseph Smith wrote, and people still throw up their hands in horror, as if there are not printing errors to be found in almost any edition of the Bible.

An occasional printing error in a Bible disturbs no one, both because it is to be expected and is easy to correct. Changes in wording to clarify the English also cause little offense. "A-going" and "a-journeying" (first edition, p. 249) were perfectly accepted usage in Joseph Smith's time and place, but not any more: consequently we change them in today's editions lest they confuse the young, though to this writer "a-going" and "a-journeying" have a nice swing and color—his grandmother always spoke that way.

In your English Bible you will find many words in italics; these are all words *not* found in the original, and they vary from edition to edition: they are put there by the various translators in attempt to convey as clearly as possible what they thought the original writers had in mind. Thus you will find in the very second verse of your King James Bible the word "was" in italics—because in the Hebrew texts the word "was" is simply not there, but to make good *English* it *has* to be put in. If men can take such liberties with the Bible, while holding it to be an infallible book, why should we not be allowed the same freedom with the Book of Mormon, which nobody claims to be infallible?

If one examines the long list of changes in various editions of the Book of Mormon one will find not a single one that alters the meaning of any passage. In two places, it is true, words have been added in later editions: they should be in italics to show that they are there by way of explaining the text, *not* changing it. In the first edition Mary is referred to as "the mother of God, after the manner of the flesh," (1 Nephi 11:18); the insertion in later editions of *"the Son* of God . . ." is simply put in to make it clear that the second person of the godhead is meant, and thereby avoid confusion, since during the theological controversies of the early Middle Ages the expression "mother of God" took on a special connotation which it still has for many Christians.

Three verses beyond (1 Nephi 11:21) the declaration of the angel, ". . . behold the Lamb of God, yea, even the Eternal Father!" has been augmented in later editions to ". . . even the Son of the Eternal Father!" to avoid confusion: in this passage the Eternal Father is possibly in apposition not to "Lamb" but to "God"—he is the Lamb *of* God-the-Eternal-Father. But that might not be obvious to most readers, and so to avoid trouble, and without in the least changing the meaning of the text, the Lamb of God is made equivalent to the Son of the Eternal Father. Both ideas are quite correct, and there is no conflict between them. In the same way, the second edition adds the words ". . . or waters of baptism" to the term "waters of Judah" in the first edition (1 Nephi 20:1) by way of clarifying— not changing—what the writer had in mind.[3]

Sometimes the editors of later editions of the Book of Mormon have made "corrections" that were better left unmade. Thus one officious editor in his attempt to visualize and rationalize a practical system of ventilation for the Jaredite barges omitted a number of significant words from the first edition which if carefully analyzed seem to give a far better plan for air-conditioning than that found in Ether 2:17-20 of our present editions.[4] And was it necessary to change the name of Benjamin (in the first edition) to Mosiah in later editions of Ether 4:1? Probably not, for though it is certain that Mosiah kept the records in question, it is by no means certain that his father, Benjamin, did not also have a share in keeping them. It was Benjamin who displayed the zeal of a life-long book-lover in the keeping and studying of records; and after he handed over the throne to his son Mosiah he lived on and may well have spent many days among his beloved records. And among these records could have been the Jaredite plates, which were brought to Zarahemla early in the reign of Mosiah, when his father could have still been living. (Mos. 8:9ff.)

The first edition of the Book of Mormon, though the most readable, is not the standard version today. That is because it is hard to use, with its long chapters and lack of numbered verses, and the grammar is sometimes disturbing to us. Disturbing, but never misleading, that is the point. Much of the New Testament is in barbaric Greek,

---

[3]See below, p. 151.
[4]On this see H. Nibley, *An Approach to the Book of Mormon,* 2nd edition, (Salt Lake City: Deseret Book Company, 1964), pp. 276-7.

and the ancient pagans often jeered at the illiteracy and
bad grammar of the Disciples; yet in our English Bible
their grammar is meticulously correct. Is that an indication of skulduggery? No more than the poor grammar of
the ancient Apostles was proof that they were not inspired.
If anything, Joseph Smith's poor grammar serves the purpose of proving, as did theirs, that the inspired words of the
prophets were no product of the schools or the invention
of cunning and clever men.

The Book of Mormon claims to be written in "words
of plainness": its meaning is always clear. Joseph Smith
at the end of his life proclaimed it the correctest book on
earth. Correctest in what sense? The text of *Tom Sawyer*
is far better attested than that of the Bible, but does one
conclude from that that *Tom Sawyer* is a more "correct"
book? What is a "correct" book? One with properly
cut margins, appropriate binding, a useful index, accurately numbered pages? Not at all; these are mere mechanical details, as are also punctuation, spelling, and even
grammar—those matters about which the critics of the
Book of Mormon have made such a to-do. Perhaps only
a book of science can be really correct in the sense of conveying perfectly accurate information: only here we must
remember Karl Popper's warning: ". . . *every* scientific
statement must remain *tentative forever.*" So what is a
correct scientific statement today may not be correct to-
morrow. The correctest book in the world is the one that
will be found to contain the fewest untrue statements
after all the books in the world have been checked and
compared. Of course no one can know today which book
that will be, unless one knows it by revelation. But such
a statement made about the Book of Mormon by its translator invites the most searching examination. To such an
examination we intend to contribute.

To shore up the weakness of the total-Bible argument,
opponents of the Book of Mormon have always depended

heavily on vigorous declamations against the character of
Joseph Smith. The accepted procedure has been to argue
that since Smith was a rascal the Book of Mormon *must* be
a fraud, while resting the proof of his rascality squarely
on the fact that he produced the Book of Mormon.

Today we can no longer view the issues from the
vantage-point of those friends and enemies of Joseph
Smith, both of whom could claim to have known him
personally and intimately. We can indeed examine the
credentials of the various character witnesses, as we at-
tempted to do in *The Myth Makers*, but the whole question of Joseph Smith's character has become academic. On
the other hand, we now enjoy certain advantages in testing of the Book of Mormon which were denied to earlier
generations. The whole discussion has shifted ground
completely, though critics of the Book of Mormon are still
desperately determined to keep it in the old grooves. How
drastically things have changed can be illustrated by comparing the position taken by the clergy one hundred years
ago with the position they take on the same issues today.
At that time they argued that the Book of Mormon could
not be true because its existence refuted the most basic
tenets of the Christian faith. Today, those particular tenets
are all being revised as the churches begin to teach the
very things that so outraged them coming from the
Mormons.

Let us look in on a public discussion which was edifying the summer crowds at Boulogne-sur-Mer in a warm
July of the year 1850. The ministers of three leading de-
nominations had sent to Elder John Taylor and his three
companions laboring in the city a "respectful public challenge, to meet us in open and public debate," wherein they
intended to demonstrate 1) that Joseph Smith was "blasphemous and daring imposter," 2) that the Book of Mormon was "a stupid and ignorant farrago of nonsense," and
3) that the pretended divine calling of the Elders them-

selves was a fraud. Three more ministers acted as referees. The prosecution rested their case on the writings of the Reverend Henry Caswall, Professor Turner, and John C. Bennett. This put President Taylor at a peculiar advantage, since he was not only intimately acquainted with Joseph Smith, but had also known Caswall and Bennett personally, while his opponents had never set eyes on any of them.[5]

"Concerning Mr. Caswall," said Elder Taylor, "I was at Nauvoo during the time of his visit. He came for the purpose of looking for evil. . . . I saw Mr. Caswall in the printing office at Nauvoo." Here is news indeed; in examining Caswall's story some years ago, we were unable to find a witness to his visit, but here we have one. We even have a report of the Psalter episode: "He had with him an old manuscript and professed to be anxious to know what it was. I looked at it and told him that I believed it was a Greek manuscript. In his book he states that it was a Greek Psalter; but that none of the Mormons told him what it was. Herein is falsehood, for I told him." It is significant that in a later version of his story, published sometime after this discussion, Caswall changed his story and had Joseph Smith, who in his first version said "That ain't Greek . . ." say ". . . some of it is Greek." We showed in our study that there was indeed something very suspicious about Caswall's Psalter-story in which we detected a rather obvious trap to catch Joseph Smith, a trap that never worked, though the Reverend Caswall made devious and toilsome efforts to prove that it did.[6] And now we have interesting confirmation of our trap theory.

It was the third night of the great discussion. The ministers, who had put much store by Caswall's testimony,

---

[5]The minutes of the meeting are to be found in a pamphlet, "Three Nights' Public Discussion . . ." (Liverpool, 1850), reproduced in Orson Pratt, *A Series of Pamphlets*, (Liverpool, 1851).

[6]H. Nibley, *The Myth Makers*, (Salt Lake City; Bookcraft, 1961), pp. 216ff.

that night brought with them a manuscript to test *Taylor's* knowledge of Greek. That was irrelevant, of course, since President Taylor's claim was not that he had proven the Caswall manuscript to be Greek or that his identification was correct, but only that he had said he thought it was Greek. However, the reverend gentlemen put three sentences in strange writing before Taylor and asked him to tell them which of the three was Greek:

> Elder Taylor.—This, I think (pointing to the first).
> Mr. Cleeve.—There is not a letter of Greek in it; it is a verse of Japanese (laughter and confusion.)
> Elder Taylor.—That certainly has the appearance of Greek.
> Mr. Groves (another minister, not one of the three).—I declare it is much more like Hebrew. . . .
> A gentleman in the meeting.—Let me see it. I am a graduate of Oxford, and I declare that there are Greek characters in it, and that any person not familiar with the language could easily mistake it for Greek.—(Cries: "It is all a trick! Shame!" and much confusion.) . . . A second Gentleman.—"It is written to imitate Greek, and is evidently done so with an intention to deceive."
> Mr. Cleeve.—There is not a letter of Greek in it.
> First Gentleman.—I declare there is, sir, and I will not be contradicted.—(Confusion.)

To such desperate measures would men of the cloth resort to discredit the Book of Mormon. Here we have a plain enough demonstration of the sort of thing Caswall was up to. If the discussion resulted in nothing else, it did conclude with clear statements by both sides of the

positions they took. The contrasting viewpoints were thus
summed up by President Taylor:

> Now have they Apostles? No. They ridicule
> the idea of them. Have they Prophets? No.
> They tell us there is to be no more prophecy. Have
> they evangelists, pastors, and teachers, inspired
> men? No. They don't believe in inspiration, and
> tell us that the cause of inspiration has ceased.
> Do they speak in tongues? No. You have heard
> it turned to ridicule time and again (during the
> discussion). Do they have prophets among them
> that prophesy? No. This they call delusion. If
> any are sick, do they do as St. James says, "send
> for the elders of the church that they may pray
> for them, and anoint them with oil in the name of
> the Lord?" No.

In their rebuttals the ministers confirmed all these
points, with the referees joining in on their side. But what
would their position on these issues be today? Hesitant,
if they kept up with the times.

Aggiornamento. The Churches Give Ground:

Aggiornamento is a word favored by Pope Paul VI,
and he translates it as "up-dating." A new conception of
the church, and especially of its spiritual gifts is now running hand in hand with a new concept of the scriptures,
and that in turn throws the door wide open to a new look
at Mormonism and the Book of Mormon. What has
brought this strange state of affairs to pass? It has been
the discovery of ancient records, long forgotten by men,
but brought to light in the years since Cumorah, and
especially in our own generation, to make the Cumorah
story appear less and less fantastic and more and more
probable as the years go by and the documents accumu-

late. The compelling power of ancient voices speaking anew from the dust since Cumorah and especially since Qumran is today driving the whole Christian world along strange paths. "No one can deny," writes a Methodist scholar with strong Catholic leanings, "that something remarkable is going on in the formerly 'unchanging' Roman Catholic Church."[7] Nothing less than a thoroughgoing revamping of doctrines and ordinances is indicated. Restoration and revelation, forbidden words but a decade or so ago, have become the watchwords of a "renewed" Christianity, both Catholic and Protestant.

What is responsible for this astonishing revolution? A protestant and a Catholic scholar, co-authoring a new book on the liturgical movement, have shown that the initial impulse and continuing pressure behind the movement has been the progressive discovery of increasingly ancient documents opening up step by step new and strange vistas of an ancient church totally unlike anything that conventional Christianity had imagined.

R. P. Marshall, the Protestant minister, begins by noting that Protestants have been guilty of a systematic neglect of rites and ordinances; indeed, "only in recent years has worship been seriously considered by Protestants as a field for study. . . ."[8] On the other hand, the Catholic writer, M. J. Taylor, S. J., notes that the rites of the Roman Church have long since become all but meaningless for the people: "Men seem unable to leave well enough alone. They want to add to what tradition has given them." Such additions "made for a sense of spectacle. . . . In the liturgies where bishops and the popes were celebrants the chants became almost symphonic. . . . The people, unable to participate in the musical supports to these rites, surrendered their role to the choir."[9] That is, both Catholic

---

[7]R. P. Marshall with M. J. Taylor S. J., *Liturgy and Christian Unity* (Englewood Cliffs, N. J.: Prentice Hall, 1965), p. 43.

[8]*Ibid.*, p. 5.

[9]*Ibid.*, p. 110.

and Protestant authorities admit that their churches are today far removed from the original rites of the church, a return to which is the purpose of the so-called liturgical movement, "a practical effort . . . to renew the lives of all the faithful here and now through a revived liturgy."[10a] And this is where the voices from the dust come in, for the movement began with those "patristic and liturgical studies" which sought the true nature of the liturgy in the oldest available documents.[10a]

Dom Gueranger (1805-1875) of the monastery of Solesmes started the movement, but though he "thought it necessary to go back to the past . . . he lacked the historical documents" necessary to take him far enough. Hence, "his renewal went back to a time when the Roman liturgy was not at its best."[11]

The greatest advance was made in Germany at the Monastery of Maria Laach, which "made an immeasurable contribution to the liturgical movement in its scholarly liturgical studies" and "produced . . . ample historical justification for . . . reform."[12] In short the unearthing of old documents or "historical studies (doctrinal, liturgical, and pastoral) made it quite clear that our present liturgy was not in the best of health."[13] Without such documents none would have suspected the need of going "back to the earlier tradition, . . . a return to tradition to overcome defects of the present."[13] The same need is now felt by many Protestants, and for them too, "the liturgical movement has sought the aid of history and theology in the study of the rites." "Catholics and Protestants," Marshall concludes, "must recover what they have lost, and one cannot cast blame on the other."[14]

---

[10]*Ibid.*, p. 124.
[10a]Ibid., p. 124.
[11]*Ibid.*, 125.
[12]*Ibid.*, p. 128.
[13]*Ibid.*, p. 130.
[14]*Ibid.*, pp. 38, 10. Cf. p. 47: "Now we are seeking to recover the lost radiance of the Christian religion."

As everyone knows, the world was mightily offended
by the assertion of the Latter-day Saints that the Christians had lost many of the ancient rites and ordinances
and was scandalized and amused by their preoccupation
with rites and ordinances that they considered essential
to salvation.

Today the Christian world both admits serious losses
and seeks to fill the gap by going back to long-forgotten
writings, the oldest and most important of which have come
forth literally from the dust in our own time. This astonishing turn of things can be illustrated by utterances,
characteristically frank and scholarly, of the present pope,
Paul VI. "Now everything is new, surprising, changed,"
he writes of the liturgy; "even the ringing of the bells at
the Sanctus has been done away with."[15] *Everything* new
and changed! That is surprising indeed, but there is a
reason: "We are concerned," wrote the Pope in his First
Encyclical, "to restore to the church that ideal of perfection
and beauty that corresponds to its original image . . . [and
have] the desire of renewing the whole structure of the
church."[16]

When Mormons have spoken of a restoraton of the
gospel, other Christians have been quick to take offense
and demand in outraged tones, "Restoration? When was
it ever lost?" But now no less a person than the Pope of
Rome declares that there must be a restoration affecting
"the whole structure of the Church"! He speaks of "the
great spiritual renewal which the Second Vatican Council
hopes to promote" and champions "the Church's heroic
and impatient struggle for renewal: the struggle to correct
the flaws introduced by its members."[17] The church
"today . . . is examining herself and formulating the things
which Christ, her founder, thought and willed concerning

[15]Address by Pope Paul VI, delivered March 17, 1965, and printed in
The Pope Speaks, Vol. 10, No. 4 (1965), p. 343.
[16]Quoted in *The Pope Speaks*, same issue as footnote 15 above, p. 269.
Cf. p. 345, ". . . this new liturgy, this spiritual rebirth. . . ."
[17]*Ibid.*, pp. 51, 256, respectively.

her. . . . The church must now define her own nature. . . .
In this way the church will complete the doctrinal work
which the First Vatican Council intended to enunciate."[18]

To one familiar with the Catholic polemic of bygone
years with its pounding emphasis on the great, monolithic,
unchanging, universal, victorious church, all this sounds
very new, surprising, and changed indeed. Isn't it rather
late in the day to try to decide what the church is all
about? There must be some good reason for such a drastic
and abrupt change of viewpoint, and the cause is not far
to seek—new discoveries of old documents are confronting
the world with an image of the early church that is totally
different from all former imaginings, but an image to which
the present Christian world must somehow manage to adjust. That is not the whole story, but as in the liturgical
movement in general, it is undoubtedly the prime mover.

The voice of Qumran seems to echo in the terms by
which the present pope and the council choose to designate the church: "The People of God," "The New Israel,"
"The Wayfaring Church" elicit the image of Israel in the
desert, the small band of faithful saints that "sometimes
looks like a small flock."[19] "The church has turned a corner," writes the editor of the Catholic World. "Today we
belong to a church which has defined itself as the people
of God. . . . We live in an age of renewed attention to the
charismatic gifts of Holy Spirit bestowed on every baptized
person with the 'right and duty' to use these gifts for the
building up of the Body of Christ."[20]

Eduard Meyer noted long ago that one of the unique
aspects of Mormonism, setting it off completely from all
other religions, was the idea of a continuation of the
charismatic gifts as shared by all members.[21] The "right

---

[18]*Ibid.*, pp. 108-9.
[19]*Ibid.*, p. 365.
[20]R. M. Brown, editorial in *The Catholic World*, March 1966, p. 341.
[21]Ed. Meyer, *Ursprung und Geschichte der Mormonen* (Berlin, 1912),
pp. 80-81.

and duty" in our quotation refers to the new Catholic policy of "every member a missionary": "It pleases us that the text [of the Council schema] constantly demands that the entire church be missionary, and also that each member of the faithful, insofar as possible, become in spirit and in works a missionary."[22]

There is much talk now in both Protestant and Catholic journals of revelation and inspiration—need we remind the reader that from the beginning its claim to continuing revelation was considered to be the most obnoxious and dangerous aspect of Mormonism?[23] Father Latourelle notes that the Second Vatican Council is the very first time a council of the church has ever methodically considered the basic foundations of revelation, tradition, and inspiration.[24] And now we are told that "when either the Roman Pontiff or the body of bishops in conjunction with him defines a proposition, they propound it in connection with revelation," so that "all are bound to abide by, and conform to, this revelation. . . ."[25] Infallibility, we are told, "is co-extensive with the deposit of divine revelation," i.e., the words of the Bible as "propounded with the assistance of the Holy Spirit. . . ."

Reversing the argument of Tertullian, the Pope proves the presence of the Holy Spirit by the existence of the church, instead of *vice versa*: "But if the church is here, the Holy Spirit is also here, the Paraclete," so that "the church can never fail to give assent to these definitions because of the activity of the Holy Spirit."[26] The cornerstone of authority is now revelation and the Holy Spirit. But it was not always so. Whatever became of Scholastic Philosophy,

---

[22]In *The Pope Speaks*, 10 (1964), p. 2.
[23]See our "Mixed Voices" in *The Improvement Era*, Vol. 62 (1959), pp. 145ff, 185, 388-90, 501f.
[24]R. Latourelle, "La Revelation et sa transmission selon la Constitution 'Dei verbum,'" in *Gregorianum*, 47 (1966), p. 36.
[25]From the Dogmatic Constitution on the Church (De Ecclesia), published in *The Pope Speaks*, 10 (1965), p. 376.
[26]*The Pope Speaks*, 10 (1965), pp. 107, 376, 260. Cf. Tertullian *De pudicitia* xxi, in Migne, *Patrol. Lat.*, 2:1077-1080.

the proudest and greatest achievement of the Roman
Church, which up until now has been officially designated
as the one proper key to revelation, i.e., to the deposit of
the scriptures?[27] Now revelation itself is something more
than the word of God in the Bible, official statements are
now to be considered as made somehow "in connection
with revelation." Today scholasticism is out and direct
revelation is cautiously taking over. The present Pope
even refers to his predecessor, Pius XII, clearly but with
careful indirection, as a prophet, one who spoke in "solemn
tones like the voice of the prophet of God and the father
of the world."[28]

The role of new documentary discoveries in bringing
these strange changes about is evident from a number of
papal utterances. "The Pope recognizes that recent ex-
plorations, methods, diggings, texts, inscriptions, papyri,
codexes, ruins, etc., have *entirely changed* the problems of
Biblical exegesis in the last fifty years" (italics ours), and
he calls for intensified search for the original texts, and a
new scientific Catholic method of exegesis.[29] Noting that
"even such illustrious commentators as St. Jerome sometimes had relatively little success in explaining more difficult questions" of scripture, the present Pope suggests
"General Rules for the Exegete," requiring "appropriate
use of the new exegetical techniques, particularly those
advocated by the historical method taken as a whole . . .
relying on the help of textual criticism, literary criticism,
and linguistic knowledge." He emphasizes the importance
of "the sound findings of recent investigations," and allows
that "the Catholic exegete can and should be free to
exercise his own perspicacity and intelligence. Only in this

---

[27]See the discussion in M. Grabmann, *Geschichte der scholastischen
Method* (Graz., 1957), I, 4-28. The Dogmatic Constitution issued by the
First Vatican Council, April 24, 1870, declared scholasticism to be "for all
time the classic form of Catholic systematics." *Ibid.*, p. 21.
[28]In *The Pope Speaks*, 10 (1964), p. 31.
[29]Cit. A. Bea, in *Biblicia*, 24:315-316.

way will each person . . . contribute to the continuing progress of the sacred doctrine."[30]

Though this apparent freedom of investigation is actually to be under the strict surveillance of the "living magisterium" of the Church and "subject to the authority and jurisdiction of the Ordinances,"[31] still it is the scholars with their "diggings, texts, inscriptions," etc., who furnish the information necessary to decide what the teachings and rites of the church should be.

It is astonishing how many of the changes that are taking place in Catholic and Protestant doctrines and ordinances are in the direction of those very things that have heretofore been peculiar to Mormonism and that have always brought persecution and derision on the heads of the saints in the past. This may be shown by a glance at the *Dogmatic Constitution on the Church*, published by the Second Vatican Council on November 25, 1965.[32]

The first section is headed "The Father's Plan" and speaks of the gospel in terms of a plan going back to the pre-existence. The second chapter is entitled "The People of God," and in the section headed "A Chosen People," presents us with that new image of the church so startlingly different from the one that has been diligently cultivated since the Fathers of the fourth century, as it shows us "the new Israel, journeying in the present world . . . moving forward through temptations and trials. . . ."

The next section is headed "A Priestly People," and teaches that "the common priesthood of the faithful" is "in its own distinctive way a participation in the one priesthood of Christ. . . ." The next section announces that all must through the sacraments (ordinances) be "reborn as sons of God." Next we learn that "the Holy People of God also share in Christ's prophetic office by bearing

---

[30]See "General Guidelines for the Exegete," in *The Pope Speaks*, 10 (1964) pp. 87-89. Cf. *Ibid.*, 10 (1965), p. 261.
[31]*The Pope Speaks*, 10 (1964), pp. 90, 19-22.
[32]See above, Note 25.

living witness to Him." This calls (in the next section)
for the gifts of the spirit, which should be widely enjoyed
in the church. The next section calls upon all to be missionaries.

Chapter VII has a title that would have shocked any
church historian a few years back, when church and
eschatology were held to be diametrically opposed to each
other[33]: "The Eschatological Character of the Wayfaring
Church and its Union with the Heavenly Church." It was
just this sort of talk that St. Augustine and his contemporaries effectively put an end to; for him and his scholastic
successors (who hardly receive any notice at all in the
new order of things) the church on earth *was* the eschatological and heavenly church.[34] But now it is a different
story as we are whisked off to Qumran to see a little band
of "saints," scorned and rejected by the world, living in
expectation of the coming Lord at the end of the times:
"The final age of the world has already come upon us," the
chapter begins, informing us that "until the appearance of
new heavens and a new earth in which justice dwells, the
wayfaring church . . . wears the ephemeral look of this
world."

So now the universal church, militant and triumphant,
established once for all to remain (according to the formula
of the former Vatican Council) "firm and steadfast until
the end of the world" has taken on "the ephemeral look of
this world"! Nay, for all its resounding claims "the Cath-
olicity of the church is always enormously deficient."[35]

The Christian world cannot be wholly unaware of
moving in the direction of things that they mocked and
derided when voices first spoke from Cumorah. One indi-

---

[33]The "rediscovery of the importance of eschatology within the New
Testament" has taken place only in recent years. C. H. Dahl, in W. Davies
& D. Daube, *The Background of the New Testament and Its Eschatology*
(Cambridge University, 1956), p. 422.

[34]Discussed by Paul Tillich, in *Neue Zeitschrift für systematische Theologie*, 3 (1961), pp. 237-8.

[35]*The Pope Speaks*, 10 (1964), p. 80.

cation of this is the observation of one of the foremost Catholic authorities on the Dead Sea Scrolls, in one of the first and best books ever to appear on the subject, that the correct title for the community at Qumran should be Latter-day Saints, but that the title could not be used because unfortunately it had been preempted by a "so-called Christian sect."[36]

While Roman Catholics today concede that changes are being made and have been made in the past in the rites, customs, and administration of their church, some of them have taken pains to point out to this writer that the really important part of the heritage, the *doctrine* of the church, has remained unchanged, fixed in the inalterable formulas of the creeds. But this is a misunderstanding. The great councils of the church, including all the early ecumenical councils, were held primarily to discuss and decide on matters of doctrine; if the words of the creeds have remained unchanged, the interpretation of those words has been a theme of endless controversy that still goes on.[37] It is understandable that the Catholic clergy where they can take the position of Bousset that their church has never changed its fundamental doctrines; yet as Owen Chadwick has shown, the greatest changes in that church in modern as in ancient times have been doctrinal ones.[38]

---

[36]George Molin, *Die Söhne des Lichts* (Vienna: Harold, 1954), p. 146; see our summary in *An Approach to the Book of Mormon* (Salt Lake City: Deseret Book Company, 1964), pp. 153-4.

[37]H. Nibley, *The World and The Prophets*, pp. 43-47, 66-72.

[38]O. Chadwick, *From Bousset to Newman*. (Cambridge Univ. Press, 1956.)

CHAPTER 2

A New Age of Discovery

The Book of Mormon Describes the Bible

In three ways the Book of Mormon by implication rejected the conventional ideas of what the Bible is supposed to be: 1) by its mere existence it refuted the idea of a "once-for-all" word of God; 2) by allowing for the mistakes of men in the pages of scripture is rejected the idea of an infallible book; 3) and by its free and flexible quotations from the Bible is rejected the idea of a fixed, immutable, letter-perfect text.

But beyond that the Book of Mormon contains certain explicit statements about the Bible that are most enlightening. It claims that many precious things were anciently removed from the holy book, and that these things are to be restored in the due time of the Lord by the bringing forth of long-lost writings, specifically of holy writings that had been anciently hidden away "to come forth in their purity" in the last days. It describes the ancient and "original" state of both the Old and the New Testaments in terms that invite the closest inspection by biblical students. Fundamentalists and higher critics have been equally scandalized by the Book of Mormon, which on the one hand neither assumed that the Old Testament was a single book written without error by the very finger of God, nor on the other allowed the verdict of the higher critics, that it was only a thing of human shreds and

patches. Today both theories are being modified, with
the students of the past generation of higher critics reluctantly conceding the essential unity of the Old Testament, while the fundamentalist sects make a great to-do
about searching the "original" documents as if the true
meaning and the true text were still in doubt. The picture
of the original Old Testament that is beginning to emerge
is very much like that which confronts us in the pages of
the Book of Mormon. There Nephi, looking far into the
future, is shown a vision of the Gentiles bringing "a book"
to the remote descendants of his father in the New World,
and is told, "The book that thou beholdest is a record of
the Jews, which contains the covenants of the Lord, which
he hath made unto the house of Israel; and . . . also . . .
many of the prophecies of the holy prophets; . . ." (1 Nephi
13:23.)

This is our Old Testament, but such a book was quite
strange to Nephi, and the angel explains that ". . . it is a
record *like unto* the engravings which are upon the plates
of brass, save there are not so many; nevertheless, they contain the covenants of the Lord . . . unto the house of Israel;
wherefore, they are of great worth unto the Gentiles."
(*Idem.* Italics added.) The only scriptures Nephi knew
were a collection of writings, more extensive indeed than
what is contained in our Old Testament, but not conflicting with it.

When Lehi eagerly examined the plates which his
sons had brought down from Jerusalem, he discovered that
they contained (1) ". . . the five books of Moses, . . ." (2)
". . . the prophecies of the holy prophets, from the beginning, even down to the commencement of the reign of
Zedekiah; . . ." (3) "And also a record of the Jews from
the beginning, . . ." including a genealogy of the whole line
of Joseph, embracing Lehi's own forefathers. (1 Nephi
5:11-14.) These writings are designated in modern Jewish

terminology as the Tanach, i.e., the Torah, the Prophets, and the Historic and other writings.

These are the elements of Nephi's Bible, and of ours, which, he assures us, contains an authentic record as far as it goes, and "many of the prophecies of the holy prophets," but by no means all.

The New View of the Old Testament

The change of attitude toward the Old Testament in our day has come suddenly and surprisingly. Up until the present generation the Christian world enjoyed the conviction that it had pretty well taken the measure of the Bible, and that the future could hold little more than an indefinite repetition of familiar sermons and commentaries lubricated by the occasional addition of learnedly specialized and technical footnotes. If the fundamentalists had their "once-for-all" Bible, the higher critics were no less satisfied that their own interpretations were definitive. In the same year (1889) in which Westcott and Hort issued the first edition of what they fondly entitled "The New Testament in the Original Greek," thereby serving notice that the most formidable of all textual problems had been solved, "Robertson Smith expressed his belief that . . . nothing of vital importance for the study of the Old Testament remained uncertain."[1] As in so many other fields, the neat and easy rule of evolution, that greatest of time- and work-savers, explained everything: "Owing until recently to the lack of any real control of their views from external sources, biblical scholars have been forced to construct their systems in a historical vacuum," Professor Albright reminds us, and since they lacked solid information, "to redeem their constructions from pure subjectivity the ablest of them were forced to employ some philosophical scheme as a frame of reference." That was where evolution came in, a "unilateral evolution from the materialistic, sensuous, and dis-

---

[1] J. N. Schofield, in *Expository Times*, 71 (1960), p. 195.

orderly to the spiritual, the ideal, and the orderly," which "formed a bed of Procrustes into which all facts and generalizations had to be fitted."[2]

The sudden acquisition of vast amounts of solid factual information where only speculation was known before has left many scholars standing at the post: "Though Bible scholars live in an age of unprecedented discovery," Cyrus Gordon notes, "they stand in the shadow of 19th century higher criticism . . . even though archaeology has rendered it untenable."[3]

Specifically, what has been rendered untenable was the popular sport of cutting up every chapter in the Bible into sections each of which is ascribed to a different author. Instead of that we find today "a significant perception that beneath all its variety of forms and of ideas, the Old Testament has a deep unity." Important in this shift has been the new view of the prophets. It was the fashion "a generation ago . . . to suppose that in the Old Testament we have a dualism of two irreconcilable concepts of religion, the prophetic and the priestly," emphasizing "a contrast between bad priests and good prophets."[4] The evolutionary formula required that the prophets, being spiritually advanced, should have a deep antipathy to the primitive formalities of the Temple. But now we know that there is "no definite line of demarcation" between the various aspects of Old Testament religion, and "that the evolutionary view of the Old Testament prophets cannot be accepted . . . every stress must be laid on continuity."[5] That is to say, from the beginning Israel has had only one gospel.

By far the greatest influence in effecting a new reading of the Old Testament comes from the Dead Sea Scrolls.

---

[2]W. F. Albright, in *Cross Currents*, 9 (1959), p. 114.
[3]C. Gordon, in *Christianity Today*, 4 (Nov. 23, 1959), p. 131.
[4]H. H. Rowley, in S. Hooke, *op. cit.*, p. 260. A generation ago such a thing was unthinkable, H. Torczyner, in *Zeitschrift der Deutschen Morgenländischen Gesellschaft*, 85 (1931), pp. 287-324.
[5]H. H. Rowley, in *Expository Times*, 71 (1959), p. 98.

And the surprising thing that the Scrolls show us is that the text of the Bible has not been so much altered—for actually they show that it has been on the whole preserved with astonishing integrity—as mutilated by the removal of material from the original. As Professor Albright puts it, "Our Hebrew text has suffered much more from losses than from glosses." And he proceeds to illustrate the point from a number of books, showing that "future translations will have to expand the text substantially—including . . . some [passages] of great importance for their content."[6]

Which brings us back to our original proposition that "they have *taken away* . . . many parts . . . that were most precious . . ." and that these are to be restored by the bringing forth of "other books" and records. There is no better illustration of both these points to date than the Dead Sea Scrolls. By furnishing us with older texts of the Bible than any heretofore known, they show very clearly that present misunderstanding of the scriptures is not due to corruptions of the text but rather to serious omissions and deletions.

Nephi and the New Testament

Even more remarkable is what Nephi has to tell us about the *New* Testament. First, that its substance goes back to the *spoken* words of Jesus; that "when it proceeded forth from the mouth of a Jew it contained the plainness of the gospel." (1 Nephi 13:24.) Repeatedly (four times) Nephi uses the peculiar and vivid expression ". . . proceeded forth from the mouth of a Jew," or "proceedeth out of the mouth of a Jew." (1 Nephi 14:23.) It was word of mouth, or, to use the strictly literal equivalent, it was in the form of *logia.*

The most significant texts being discovered today are the lost *Logia,* or mouth-utterances, of Jesus, now recog-

---

[6]W. F. Albright and D. N. Freedman, in *Journal of Bible and Religion,* 31 (1963), pp. 111f.

nized as the oldest form and substance of the gospel message.[7] From these the Gospels were constructed.

Next, Nephi tells us, these things which were had
among the Jews in pure, simple, and understandable form
". . . go forth by the hand of the twelve apostles of the
Lamb, from the Jews unto the Gentiles, . . ." (1 Nephi
13:26.) In the hands of these last, and at an early date,
they suffered mutilation: ". . . they have taken away from
the gospel of the Lamb many parts which are plain and
most precious; and also many covenants of the Lord have
they taken away." (1 Nephi 13:26.) It is "the great and
abominable church" which is charged with this folly, and
here it is only fair to point out that 1 Nephi 22:13f designates *any* who fight against Israel by that unsavory title,
and that the damage to the scriptures was done by that
same great and abominable before the New Testament
went out into the world, possibly before it left Palestine:
"And *after* these plain and precious things were taken away
it goeth forth unto *all* the nations of the Gentiles; . . ." (1
Nephi 13:29. Italics added.) One of the important discoveries of modern "form criticism" has been that the
original word-of-mouth tradition was revamped (*neu
geformt*) by certain early Christian groups and in that
form "handed on" to the world; the revising took place
soon after the appearances of the Lord following the resurrection, and there is still a good deal of uncertainty as to
just who did it and why.[8]

In our day the experts have reached the reluctant
consensus that the Christian message has not come down to
us in its original form. "The present generation," writes a
leading authority on New Testament documents, "stands
at the beginning of a new cycle, in the search for the
original Greek New Testament." And it stands perplexed,

---

[7]W. Schneemelcher, *Neutestamentliche Apokryphen*, (Tübingen: Mohr,
1959), I, 9, 46, 262ff.)
    [8]*Ibid.*, I, 46-47.

not knowing which way to turn: "Any substantial effort to improve the basic critical test must 'mark time' until the whole complex of textual studies reveals a new integrating pattern . . . we know only that the traditional theory of the [New Testament] text is faulty but cannot yet see clearly to correct the fault. . . . The critic is sobered by the realization that the best critical text so far achieved now holds little assurance of being the original text."[9] "Thirty or forty years ago," wrote C. C. McCown, "there was much talk of the 'assured results' of literary-historical criticism. . . . Now . . . biblical scholarship . . . must fight for its life . . . in the light of new methods and new archaeological, textual, paleographical, and historical discoveries."[10]

Through the centuries that followed their loss, according to Nephi, ". . . because of these things which are taken away out of the gospel of the Lamb, an exceeding great many do stumble, . . ." (1 Nephi 13:29.) What word could more aptly express the situation of Bible readers down to the present day: they walk, but as they walk, they stumble— they do not agree on what they read, and they never have agreed, and today the whole scholarly world is by its own admission stumbling around in the dark, looking for some "new integrating pattern" and wondering what can possibly be "the point of the entire Johannine corpus." (C. H. Dodd) It is remarkable that Nephi does not mention corruptions or insertions in the text but keeps hammering away at that one fatal defect, the precious things which "they have taken away." Finally Nephi has good news—in his own due time the Lord is going to bring forth writings which were "sealed up to come forth in their purity," those writings of John which Nephi himself was forbidden to duplicate. (See 1 Nephi 14:26-27.)

---

[9]K. W. Clark, in W. D. Davies & D. Daube (editions), *The Background of The New Testament and Its Eschatology* (Cambridge University, 1956), pp. 30, 31, 42.

[10]C. C. McCown, in *Journal of Biblical Literature,* 75 (19....), pp. 12f.

But if we do not have the original texts, we are getting a pretty good idea of what happened to them. Here again Nephi "calls his shots" unerringly. Shown in a vision the life and ministry of Christ and the apostles, he was about to write down what he had seen but was prevented from doing so with the command, "But the things which thou shalt see hereafter thou shalt not write; . . ." (1 Nephi 14:25, 28.) It was explained to him that the recording of these things was reserved for "the apostle of the Lamb of God that he should write them" (1 Nephi 14:25), and he was told by the angel "that the name of the apostle of the Lamb was John." (1 Nephi 14:27.) John and not Nephi was to write all these things down, and after that they were not to be published but "sealed up to come forth in their purity . . . in the own due time of the Lord, unto the house of Israel." (1 Nephi 14:26.) We are now assured that the three Synoptic Gospels are not the original "Evangelion" at all, but are, to use Schneemelcher's expression, an *Ersatz*.[11] They come from another milieu entirely from that of John, with whose writing they are "completely unfamiliar."[12]

The fact that there are three Synoptic Gospels instead of one poses the greatest riddle of New Testament criticism: Why are there three, and why do they differ? The very "multiplicity of the Gospels," is adequate evidence that someone has been manipulating the records.[13]

Today the experts think they have a pretty good idea of the sort of people responsible. They were people who had received the gospel from the apostles, but immediately after the passing of the apostles proceeded to make basic alterations, deliberately disregarding some of the most im-

---

[11]Schneemelcher, op. cit., p. 339.

[12]C. L. Mitton, in *Expository Times*, 71 (1960), p. 240.

[13]Schneemelcher, *op. cit.*, I, 44f. The efforts of Marcion and Tatian to unite the three Gospels into one were based on the assumption (1) that the Gospels were apostolic, but (2) that they had been subjected to fallible human manipulation, *ibid.*, I, 11-12.

portant teachings.[14]   They were not the old Jewish-
Christian communities, but various local churches of gentile
composition, into whose hands the record came at an
early time (in the 70's and 80's AD),[15] and by whom the
alterations—especially deletions—were made.[16] The changes
consisted in new interpretations of the scriptures, *not* in
corruptions of the text, and in substantial omissions.[17]

Nephi's view of the New Testament, then, rests on
two basic propositions. Proposition number one is that
the Bible has come down to the world in a mutilated form:

". . . for behold, they have taken away from the gospel
of the Lamb many parts which are plain and most precious;
and also many covenants of the Lord have they taken
away. . . .

". . . because of these things which are taken away
out of the gospel of the Lamb, an exceeding great many do
stumble. . . ." (1 Nephi 13:26, 29.)

Proposition number two is that the Lord will put an
end to this state of things by the bringing forth of more
information:

". . . I will be merciful unto the Gentiles in that day,
insomuch that I will bring forth unto them, in mine own
power, much of my gospel, which shall be plain and
precious. . . ." (1 Nephi 13:34.)

This knowledge is to be imparted by written documents, including some of the writings of Nephi's own
descendants, "hid up to come forth unto the Gentiles."
(1 Nephi 13:35.)   But aside from them we are told of

[14]Eusebius, *Church History*, V, 25; Schneemelcher, *op. cit.*, I, 9. There
was at first a tendency to canonize anything written by the apostles, and then to
attribute to the apostles whatever one wanted to canonize, whether written
by them or not.
[15]*Ibid.*, I, 12: The canon grew up "slowly in the various collections of
the . . . separate Church provinces." By the middle of the second century
the four Gospels had by no means received general acceptance, *ibid.*, p. 11.
[16]*Ibid.*, I, 8: It was in the 70's and 80's that a written *Ersatz* took the
place of the original "oral utterances." The apostles themselves wrote little;
their testimony was fixed in writing only after their departure, *ibid.*, p. 9.
This agrees with Eusebius, *Church History*, III, 24.
[17]Irenaeus, *Adv. Haereses*, I, 27, 4. Eusebius, *loc. cit.*

"other books . . . these last records" (39-40, both in the *plural*) which are to come forth to and circulate among the Gentiles before their conversion to the gospel. Since it is made very clear throughout the chapter that the Gentiles referred to are *not* the Church, it would appear that the books and records which are "seen among the Gentiles" (40) may be other writings besides the Book of Mormon.[18] Not to labor the point, whether we see in 1 Nephi 13 reference to the Bible and the Book of Mormon only or to yet more records to come (as is clearly indicated in 14:26), we have at least the clear declaration that certain books and records apart from the Bible are to come forth and change men's view of the Bible itself, because of whose mutilation "an exceeding great many do stumble." (1 Nephi 13:29.)

Every step of Nephi's account of the New Testament writings can be discerned in the emerging pattern of New Testament studies today: (1) Its original form was the spoken word or *logia;* (2) clearly understood only in their original Jewish-Christian setting; (3) transmitted at an early time, "by the hand of the apostles" (i.e., in written form) to the Gentiles (see 1 Nephi 23:24-26); (4) who proceeded in the various churches to reinterpret and delete much of the record (v. 27). (5) After the damage was done the New Testament went forth "unto all the nations of the Gentiles." (v. 29.) It is a fact that while ancient manuscripts of the New Testament are found all over the Old World in many languages, they all represent the same mutilated families of texts. That is why we are still looking for the original. (6) Because of the deficiencies in the known writings the churchmen have never been able to understand them or agree about what they mean, and today they stand in as great perplexity as ever; in other words, they "stumble." (7) Finally we are assured that

---

[18]In 1 Nephi 13, verses, 3, 4, 10, 12, 14, 15, 16, 17, 19, 23, 29, 30, 31, 32, 33, 38. Mormon 8:12; Ether 4:8, 13.

there are unspoiled documents hidden away, awaiting that
time when they shall "come forth in their purity. . . ."

And indeed, for the first time in history, scholars are
in our own day beginning to put their hopes quite frankly
in the possible discovery of such documents. (8) To these
points we might add the peculiar role of John in Nephi's
account—the only New Testament character mentioned
in the Book of Mormon—since John is today by far the most
important as well as the most baffling and mysterious
figure in the search for the original Christian message.

"The Wretched Apocrypha"

One of the reasons for the initial neglect of the Dead
Sea Scrolls was that when they first came out, no one was
prepared to cope with them. For strictly speaking they are
Apocrypha, and few scholars were concerned with the
Apocrypha when by 1945 their study had "reached its
lowest ebb."[19]

What are the Apocrypha? They are a large body of
writings, Jewish and Christian, existing alongside the Bible,
each of which has at some time or other been accepted as
true revealed scripture by some Christian or Jewish group.
Where do they come from? The actual manuscripts are
as old as our Bible manuscripts and are sometimes written
by the same hands, but their contents betray widely scattered sources, some of which are orthodox and some of
which are not.

Then why bother about them? Because writers of
the Bible respect them and sometimes quote them, thus
including excerpts of the Apocrypha in our Bible, while
the fathers of the church in the first three centuries accept
many of them as genuine and quote them as scripture—
they cannot be lightly dismissed.[20]

---

[19]C. Torrey, *The Aprocryphal Literature* (New Haven: Yale University,
1945), p. 40.
[20]A list of 25 apocryphal passages found in our Bible is given by Torrey,
op. cit., p. 18.

Why are they not included in the Bible? Well, some
of them are: The Catholic Bible contains fourteen books
which are not found in Protestant versions of the Bible.
On the other hand, there are books in our Bible, such as
Revelation, Esther, Ruth, Ecclesiastes, and the Song of
Songs, which some of the most respected doctors of the
Jews and Christians, ancient and modern, think are really
Apocrypha and should not be in the Bible.[21] Then who
decides just what is scripture and what is not? That is just
the question: "Outside books?" cries Professor Torrey, "by
what authority? The authority was duly declared, but
it continued to be disputed . . . down even into the 19th
century."[22]

Consider the case of the Book of Enoch. "Nearly all
the writers of the New Testament were familiar with it. . . .
It is quoted as a genuine production of Enoch by St. Jude
[in the New Testament], and as scripture by St. Barnabas. . . . With the earlier fathers and apologists it had all
the weight of a canonical book." Yet, "from the fourth
century of our era onward it fell into discredit; and under
the ban of such authorities as Hilary, Jerome, and Augustine, it gradually passed out of circulation, and became
lost to the knowledge of Western Christendom."[23] By what
authority do Hilary, Jerome, and Augustine, who disagreed
widely among themselves on scriptural matters, put under
the ban a writing that the *early* church accepted and treas-
ured as scripture? Here we see that later church leaders,
none of whom claimed to be the head of the church,
actually removed "many precious things" from the record.

But if the authority of those who condemned various
"Apocrypha" is dubious, their reason for doing so is not

---

[21]Thus Athanasius or a contemporary rejects Ruth and Esther, Migne,
Patrologia Graeca, 28:289. Sulpicius Severus, *Historia Sacra* II, 31 says that
many Christians do not accept the Book of Revelation and Philastrius says
there is great disagreement in the Church over who wrote the various epistles
in the New Testament, Migne, *Patrologia Latina*, 12:1200-2.

[22]Torrey, *op. cit.*, p. 4.

[23]R. H. Charles, *The Book of Enoch* (Oxford, 1912), p. ix.

far to seek. For the basic premise of the Jewish and
Christian doctors alike from the fourth century on is that
prophecy and revelation have forever ceased.[24] In such
a case, the only hope of certitude lay in the possession of an
absolutely infallible book of scripture. This allows no place
for the proposition that a writing might be partly true and
partly false: every syllable of the word of God must be
absolutely perfect and above suspicion, for if it is not,
if one allows that there might be any inaccuracy whatever
in the Bible, then we are in the intolerable position of
never being exactly sure whether any particular verse of
the Bible is reliable or not. Such was the argument of St.
Augustine, and such has remained the position of Christendom since his day.

It follows that all the Apocrypha, not being scripture,
are full of uncertainties and therefore to be avoided as a
pernicious nuisance. As early as the second century it was
declared dangerous to allow any latitude whatever to "outside writings," and from the fourth century on that meant
the Apocrypha.[25] If, as St. Augustine puts it, "men of the
most outstanding piety and wisdom often disagree" about
the scriptures,[26] how can men receive guidance from lesser
works, including translations of the Bible? Since it was
officially declared that "the written fountain of all revelation is the Bible," that source had to be completely infallible.[27] The Reformers condemned the Apocrypha as the
doctors of the Church had; it was Karlstadt who first bound
a number of works of which he disapproved together in one
cover, gave them the name of "Apocrypha" and declared
them "worthless for Christian use."[28] The Synod of Dort
(1618-9) and the Westminster Confession alike agree with

[24]D. Flusser, in *Israel Exploration Journal*, 3 (1953), p. 39; K. Aland,
in *Journal of Theological Studies*, 12 (1961), p. 48, for Jewish and Christian
attitudes.
[25]*Apostolic Constitutions*, I, 6; Eusebius, *Church History*, IV, 8, 1.
[26]St. Augustine, in *Patrologia Latina*, 35:1536.
[27]H. J. Denzinger, *Enchiridion symbolorium definitionum* . . . (Rome,
1957), see references under *If* [p. (9)], in *Index Systematicus*.
[28]Torrey, *op. cit.*, p. 5.

Bishop Lightfoot that the "wretched Apocrypha" are but a
"patchery of human invention,"[29] and in 1816 the American
Bible Society condemned them all as "objectionable
books."[30]

Since the Christian world had for centuries taken a
uniform stand against the Apocrypha, is it any wonder that
Joseph Smith's double outrage of adding to the word of
God while proclaiming the possibility of error in it brought
the roof down on his head? The indiscretion of the Book of
Mormon was followed by a statement of principle regarding the Apocrypha which was received as a revelation in
1833: "Verily, thus saith the Lord unto you concerning
the Apocrypha—There are many things contained therein
that are true, and it is mostly translated correctly; there
are many things contained therein that are not true, which
are interpolations by the hands of men. . . . Therefore,
whoso readeth it, let him understand, for the Spirit mani-
festeth truth; and whoso is enlightened by the Spirit shall
obtain benefit therefrom; and whoso receiveth not the
Spirit, cannot be benefited." (See D&C 91.)

The first part of this revelation is a clear statement
of the very position taken by Christian scholars today not
only regarding the Apocrypha but the Bible as well. Now
we rub our eyes when we read in leading Protestant journals: "It needs to be repeated in the strongest possible
manner that the hope of absolute certainty based on an
Infallible Book . . . is a delusion,"[31] or that God's plan for
the human race obviously does not include what is called
an "infallible volume of scripture. . . . The Bible . . . was
never brought into complete harmony by any central authoritative 'Board of Editors' ";[32] or Father Herbert's
declaration that "the inadequacy of the doctrine of the
inerrance of scripture has demonstrated itself. It is too

[29]*Ibid.*, pp. 36-37.
[30]*Ibid.*, p. 40.
[31]V. Taylor, in *Expository Times*, 71 (1960), p. 72.
[32]L. Wallis, *The Bible and Modern Belief* (Duke University Press, 1949),
p. 32.

narrow to fit the facts; it cannot be followed through . . .
without special pleading . . ." ;[33] or E. C. Blackman's that
"That word of God is in the words of the Bible, but it is
not to be identified with them . . . but interpreted out of
them."[34]

Interpreted by whom? The most learned and devoted
men often disagree, as St. Augustine pointed out; who
then shall tell us what the Bible says? There is only one
way out, the way indicated in the second part of our
revelation, and that is revelation itself. It is not surprising
therefore that this upsetting recognition of the fallibility
of the Bible should be accompanied by much discussion
of the possibility of revelation—a theme that now fills the
theological journals. "The return to ideas of inspiration
and revelation may be put down as one of the marked
trends of our biblical scholarship of the last decade," said
S. V. McCasland in a presidential address to the Society of
Biblical Literature in 1953.[35] And G. W. Bromiley might
have been paraphrasing the Doctrine and Covenants when
he wrote in 1959: "But since the works are written in the
Spirit, they must also be read in the Spirit if they are to
accomplish their primary function. . . . In other words, the
minds and hearts of the readers must be enlightened by the
same Spirit by whom the writings themselves were inspired," though he hastens to add, "This enlightenment or
illumination is not properly inspiration itself."[36]

Nor is it surprising that there has been a rather sudden
recognition of the fact that ancient Christians did not for
a moment regard the scriptures as sealed and final, but
down to the middle of the third century were perfectly
willing to accept the proposition that more inspired writ-

[33]Father Herbert, cited in *Expository Times,* 70 (1958), p. 33. Cf. *The Catholic Biblical Quarterly,* 5 (1943), pp. 115-159.
[34]In H. Davies and D. Daube, *Eschatological Background of the New Testament* (Cambridge, 1956), pp. 18f.
[35]S. V. McCasland, *The Journal of Biblical Literature,* 73 (1954), p. 6.
[36]G. W. Bromiley, in *Christianity Today,* 4 (1959), p. 139.

ings might be forthcoming.[37] One of the first Christian
martyrs is reported as saying, "If there are ancient faith-
promoting books, why can't there be modern ones . . . or
why should the present have less authority than the past
because of some superstitious veneration of mere antiquity?"[38]

Section 91 also has a message for those Latter-day
Saints who wonder why the Church has not been forward
in officially recognizing and adopting such works as the
Dead Sea Scrolls. We do recognize them. Here it is explicitly declared that there is benefit to be derived from
the study of these works by those who are enlightened by
the Spirit. But on a purely intellectual basis, their study
can only lead, as it has, to endless squabbling and confusion. The Prophet was told to leave those who wanted the
Apocrypha to read them for themselves, with the distinct
understanding that they are full of precious things mingled
with interpolations by the hands of men. This today is the
recognized condition of the Apocrypha, and the policy of
the Church towards them has always been the same.

Serious and thorough study of the Apocrypha is, according to Professor Torrey, "a comparatively recent
need."[39] And even Professor Zeitlin, a bitter enemy of the
Scrolls, calls for a serious study of the Apocrypha, "which
had been thrown aside . . . by the Jews, but which should
now be reclaimed by them."[40] Because of the new manuscript finds, "the whole question of canonicity, and the
date and fixing of the canon, will have to be restudied.
. . ."[41] For we are now told that canonization may have
relegated to the Apocrypha a good deal of genuine scripture.[42] In 1957 Professor Riesenfeld "exploded a bombshell"
at the New Testament Congress at Oxford when he de-

---

[37]W. van Unnik, in *Vigiliae Christianae*, 3 (1949), pp. 1-4.
[38]Martyrdom of Perpetua and Felicitas, in *Patrologia Latina*, 3:15.
[39]Torrey, *op. cit.*, p. v.
[40]S. Zeitlin, in *Jewish Quarterly Review*, 37 (1946-7), p. 248.
[41]J. P. Hyatt, in *Journal of Biblical Literature*, 76 (1957), p. 6.
[42]H. Cadbury, in H. Davies and D. Daube, *op. cit.*, p. 319.

clared that some of the apocryphal deeds and sayings of Jesus are genuine, for until then "the opposite view has been held and in some circles has been exalted into the position of accepted doctrine."[43]

In short, the Apocrypha have been until recently an unexplored bog. To this day "there is no regularity, but utter confusion" in their classification.[44] It is now recognized that "literally speaking there are no apocrypha in Jewish literature,"[45] that the early Christians made no distinction whatever between canonical books and Apocrypha,[46] and that the Greek Orthodox Church never made "a formal and authoritative utterance" on the subject.[47]

The idea of Canon vs. Apocrypha is an invention or rather a convention of scholarship, the result of "one long process of cooling and hardening."[48] The conventional breakdown has been into canon (the books of the Bible), Apocrypha (books found in some Bibles), and Pseudepigrapha (books never qualified as biblical), but the classification is arbitrary and confusing. "A new terminology is needed," Professor Torrey announces; ". . . the current classification . . . as Apocrypha and Pseudepigrapha is outworn and misleading, supported neither by history nor by present fact."[49] "There is no real distinction between them," wrote M. Gaster of the Jewish holy writings, "and their treatment in the hands of the Jews has been precisely the same. They all belong to that vast literature . . . which fall under one head called Midrash or Midrash Agada."[50]

A leading Catholic scholar points out another reason

[43]*Expository Times*, 70 (1958), p. 129.

[44]Torrey, *op cit.*, p. 28. "No classification is possible," according to M. Oesterley, *An Introduction to the Books of the Apocrypha* (New York: Macmillan, 1935), p. 9.

[45]M. Gaster, *Studies* (1925), I, 280f.

[46]W. Schneemelcher & E. Hennecke, *Neutestamentliche Apokryphen* (Tübingen, 1959) I, 1-4, 8-10.

[47]Torrey, *op. cit.*, p. 34.

[48]G. A. Deissmann, *Light from the Ancient East* (New York, 1927), p. 251.

[49]Torrey, *op. cit.*, p. 10.

[50]Gaster, *op. cit.*, I, 281.

for rejecting the old distinction between Apocrypha and scripture, namely that there is between the two a class of writing which because of its high antiquity and prestige in the early Church cannot be relegated to the level of Apocrypha and which at the same time does not qualify as scripture simply because it never happened to get bound in with the other books of the Bible, "an intermediary class," he calls it, of which, however embarrassing, "it is impossible to deny the existence."[51]

The student who goes to encyclopedias and handbooks to learn about the Apocrypha is soon puzzled to discover that no two "official" lists are the same.[52] One authority will consider the subject of Apocrypha adequately treated with the discussion of the fourteen apocryphal books of the Bible, while another will list hundreds of interesting titles. Why is there no agreement? Because everything seems to overlap; all these works seem to be forever swapping the same basic ideas and expressions among themselves, so that once we have determined which of the writings are the oldest, we can pretty well rule all the others out as mere repetition. Only, since every apocryphal writing is a composite, no one knows for sure which is really the oldest and who is borrowing from whom. Take the case of the Book of Enoch, for example.

We have seen that the early Christian and patristic writers accepted this work as authentic scripture down to the fourth century, when the great doctors of the church

---

[51] J. Ruwet, in *Biblica*, 25 (1944), p. 334.

[52] Aside from articles on Apocrypha in almost any encyclopedia, representative lists of New Testament Apocrypha may be found in B. Altaner, *Patrology* (New York: Herder, 1960), and especially E. Hennecke & W. Schneemelcher, *Neutestamentliche Apokryphen* (Tübingen: J. C. B. Mohr, 1959), of which only vol. I has appeared. Lists of Old Testament Apocrypha are given by R. Travers, *Talmud and Apocrypha* (London: Soncino Press, 1933), pp. 173f.; H. H. Rowley, *Relevance of Apocalyptic* (London: Lutterworth, 1944); S. Zeitlin, in *Jewish Quarterly Review*, 37 (1946-7), pp. 218-248, and 40 (1949-50), pp. 223-250; A. Cronbach, in *Hebrew Union College Annual*, 18 (1944), pp. 119f. The "standard" collections of Apocrypha in English are R. H. Charles, *The Apocrypha and Pseudepigrapha of the Old Testament* (Oxford, 1913), 2 vols., and M. R. James, *The Apocryphal New Testament* (Oxford, 1953).

put it under the ban, and it disappeared completely.[53] The
eccentric Scotchman James Bruce brought to England from
his famous expedition to the headwaters of the Nile in 1773
an Ethiopian text of the Book of Enoch. This can be
checked against Greek fragments of Enoch, one of which,
acquired by the eccentric Irishman Chester Beatty in 1930
(Beatty made his money in Utah copper) is 1000 years
older than the Ethiopian documents. And now the Hebrew
sources of the Book of Enoch, centuries older than the
Greek fragments, have finally turned up in Cave IV at
Qumran.

Though "it comes from many writers and almost as
many periods," its value lies in the fact that "some of its
authors—and there were many—belonged to the true succession of the prophets."[54] How would such men dare to prophesy in the name of Enoch? They had to, according to R.
H. Charles, because the doctors of the Jews gave them no
alternative. The latter "could tolerate no fresh message
from God, and so, when men were moved by the Spirit of
God to make known their visions . . . they could not do so
openly, but were forced to resort to pseudonymous publi-
cations."[55] Even so, Charles himself recognized that part
of the book at least may well go back to very early times.[56]
After all, all the prophets do have much the same message,
and the now recognized practice of the prophets of giving
out the words of their predecessors as their own receives
its first clear statement and justification in the Book of
Mormon, wherein Nephi explains his policy: ". . . for I did
liken *all* scriptures unto us, that it might be for our profit
and learning." (1 Nephi 19:23. Italics added.) This peculiar and interesting attitude that viewed past events as

---

[53]Above, note 23.
[54]R. H. Charles, *The Book of Enoch*, p. x.
[55]R. H. Charles, *Apocrypha and Pseudepigrapha of the Old Testament*,
II, p. viii; cf. H. H. Rowley, *Relevance of Apocalyptic*, p. 38; D. Flusser, in
Israel Exploration Journal, 3 (1953), pp. 39f.
[56]See his article on Apocrypha in the eleventh edition of *Encyclopedia
Britannica*, II, 176 (XI edition).

living again in Israel's present experience is highly characteristic of the Dead Sea Scrolls, but was generally ignored
by scholars before their discovery.

The complexity of apocryphal works is thus by no
means a sign of fraud. The fact that "certain considerable
portions of the book (of Enoch) belonged originally not
to the Enoch literature at all, but to an earlier work," i.e.
the Book of Noah, adds to its value rather than lessening
it.[57] Along with the Book of Enoch, known as 1 Enoch and
written in Hebrew about 66 AD, we have also an Epistle
of Enoch, and a Book of the Secrets of Enoch, or 3 Enoch,
written in Palestine before 70 AD and best known as the
Slavic Book of Enoch.[58]

We cannot dismiss these other works with a smile,
because each book is a mixture of things, and they all overlap. One part of 1 Enoch, for example, sounds very Christian and had accordingly been given a title of its own,
The Similitudes of Enoch. "Many scholars have held that
the work has been interpolated by a Christian editor, and
in particular they have found references to the Son of Man
to be accretions, and have accordingly removed them."[59]
That is a good illustration of how the experts work, removing from the ancient texts whatever they think does not
belong there. First Enoch contains, for example, remarkable
parallels to the teachings of Paul.[60] Should these "many
precious things" be removed? It is the Dead Sea Scrolls

[57]Discussed at length by R. H. Charles, *The Book of Enoch*, pp. xlvi-lii.
Charles discusses the many conflicting conjectures about the nature of the
work, pp. xxx-xlvi.
[58]G. N. Bonwetsch (Ed.), in *Texte und Untersuchungen*, 3. Reihe, 14 Bd.,
Heft 2 (Leipzig, 1922), including the Slavic text. *The Epistle of Enoch* is
comprised in sections 97:6 to 98:3 of 1 Enoch. Some Greek fragments were
discovered at Akhmim in 1886-7 and published by U. Bouriant, in *Mission
Archeologique Francaise au Caire*, IX, Facsimile i, 1892, pp. 93-147. The
Hebrew version of 3 Enoch is edited by H. Odeberg, III Enoch (Cambridge
University, 1928), and there is a text in the *Jewish Quarterly Review*, 20
(1929f), pp. 77-85, and also W. R. Morfill, *The Book of the Secrets of Enoch*
(Oxford, 1896).
[59]H. H. Rowley, *Relevance of Apocalyptic*, pp. 56-57.
[60]B. Brinkmann, in *Biblica*, 13 (1932), pp. 315-334, 418-434. The early
churches, while rejecting even such established works as the Pastor of Hermas,
accepted Enoch as scripture, J. Ruwet, *op. cit.*, p. 333.

that have taken away the license of the learned to cut and
slash as they pleased, for they have shown that many concepts formerly held to be uniquely Christian were familiar
to Jews before the time of Christ.

Particularly close ties have been noted between 1
Enoch and a very old work called the Book of Jubilees,
known in one version as the Lepto-Genesis or Little Genesis, which scholars suggested years ago was the remnant
of a lost book of Abraham from which our own Genesis
accounts were taken.[61] Now among the first of the Dead
Sea Scrolls to be discovered was one that now goes by the
name of the Genesis Apocryphon, the largest part of which
is labeled by its editors as the Book of Abraham, the other
parts being books of Lamech and Noah. These books are
so close to Jubilees as to give "the impression of having
possibly been a source on which the writer of Jubilees
drew."[62] Jubilees itself is so full of Christian stuff that it
has been declared to be of all Jewish Apocrypha the one
presenting Christian apocalyptic ideas "in their most complete form."[63] The astonishing mixture and overlapping of
Jewish and Christian elements in the Enoch writings would
thus seem to be something far more fundamental than a
mere Christian re-editing of the texts.

A type of apocryphal literature that has recently come
to the fore thanks to new documentary discoveries is the
testament form. Jubilees has been called the Testament of
Moses, and we now have a Testament of Abraham (in
Arabic and Ethiopian, originally written in the first or
second century in Hebrew), a Testament of Isaac and
Jacob (in Arabic and Ethiopian), a Testament of Job
(written by a Jew in Greek in Egypt in the second century), a Testament of Solomon (in Hebrew), a recently
discovered Hebrew Testament of Naphtali, a Testament of

---

[61]S. Zeitlin, in *Jewish Quarterly Review*, 30 (1939f), pp. 1-31; A. Epstein,
in *Revue des Etude Juives*, 21 (1890), pp. 80-97, and 22 (1891), pp. 1-25.

[62]Y. Yadin, *A Genesis Apocryphon* (Jerusalem, 1956), p. 21.

[63]C. Clemen, *Primitive Christianity and Its Non-Jewish Sources* (Edin-
burgh, 1912), p. 118.

Isaac (the Coptic text first published in 1958), and the all-important Testament of the Twelve Patriarchs.[64] These writings are called testaments because in them a patriarch or prophet before his death addresses his children or his followers, giving them prophecies and blessings and foretelling what is to befall them individually and collectively. In every case there is an all-embracing revelation of the whole of human history, centering about a recent vision in which the old man was caught up to heaven and viewed the cosmos and the great plan of salvation in its fulness, including the council in heaven at the creation when it all began.[65]

What we wish to point out here is that the first section of Nephi's book is an abridgment of his father's writings. It is really Lehi's book, and it follows the testament form in every particular: The story of the patriarch's perplexities and wanderings, his journey to heaven and eschatological discourse, and his blessings and admonitions to each of his sons are thoroughly typical in every respect, so that it would be perfectly proper to distinguish the first part of 1 Nephi from that hero's account of his own "reign and ministry" by calling it "The Testament of Lehi," its being by Nephi's own account a separate work from his own. (1 Nephi 1:16-17.) Read along with the other old Jewish testaments, it gives an overpowering impression of authenticity, which may some day be demonstrated by the impartial verdict of an electronic computer.

Since part of every testament is an ascension, the works called testaments could be and sometimes are called Ascensions. We have already mentioned the peculiar ser-

---

[64]M. R. James, *The Testament of Abraham*, in *Texts and Studies*, II, 2; *Testament of Job*, text in *Jewish Quarterly Review*, 13 (1901), pp. 111-127; and 258ff.; *Testament of Solomon*, text in *Jewish Quarterly Review*, 11 (1898), pp. 1-45; *Testament of Levi*, texts in *Jewish Quarterly Review*, 12 (1900), pp. 651ff. The Greek text of the *Testament of the Twelve Patriarchs* may be found in *Patrologia Graeca*, 2:1027-1150. The newly found Coptic text of the *Testament of Isaac* is in *Jul. Theol. Stud.* 8 (1957), 228-237.

[65]For a list of the more important "Testaments" see H. Nibley, *The Vigiliae Christianae*, Vol. 20, (1966), p. 12, footnote 62.

vice of the Assumption (or Ascension) of Moses in determining the nature of the Dead Sea Scrolls deposit.[66] The testaments of Abraham and Isaac have also been labeled the Assumptions of Abraham and Isaac. Just to show how complicated things get, the Ascension of Moses begins with a section that also has been called the Testament of Moses, written in Hebrew at the very beginning of the first century. This is thrice quoted as scripture in the New Testament (Acts 7:36 and Jude 16, 18), and by early apocryphal writers and church fathers.[67] There is an Ascension of Isaiah (also called the Testament of Isaiah) which sounds so Christian that Torrey declared it to be "entirely a Christian composition," though admitting that it was very hard to tell whether such a writing is Christian or not.[68] Thanks to the Dead Sea Scrolls, however, Torrey's verdict must be repealed, and the Ascension of Isaiah must now be classified, according to Flusser, with Jubilees, the Book of Enoch, and the Twelve Patriarchs, which all fuse together.[69]

Since the prophecies found in the testaments are all apocalyptic in nature, these works could also be entitled Apocalypses—again a mere matter of convenience. The Apocalypse of Moses, the Apocalypse of Baruch, of Sophonia, of Daniel, of Abraham, and of Elijah (first known in 1899) were all first seriously considered at the turn of the century, but, as with the other Apocrypha, we are only just beginning to realize their true significance, the last two being especially important.[70] Related works

[66]See below, p. 61.

[67]H. H. Charles, *Apocrypha & Pseudepigrapha of the Old Testament,* II, 407.

[68]C. Torrey, *Apocryphal Literature,* p. 14.

[69]D. Flusser, *Israel Exploration Inl.,* 3 (1953), pp. 30-47.

[70]Apocalypse of Moses, text in *Jewish Quarterly Review,* 7 (1894), pp. 216-235; *Apocalypse of Elijah,* Coptic text ed. G. Steindorff, in *Texte u. Untersuchungen,* N. F. II (XVII), 1899, Heft 3a; Hebrew text, M. Butterweiser, *Die Hebraisch Elias-Apokalypse* (Leipzig, 1897) and S. Kraus, in *Jewish Quarterly Review,* 14 (1902), pp. 359ff.; *Apocalypse of Sophonia* text in *Texte u. Untersuchungen,* N. F. II, 3a, 1899 (ed. Steindorff). The Apocalypse of Abraham is translated in P. Reissler, *Altjüdisches Schrifttum* . . . (Heidelberg: Kerle, 1966), pp. 13-39.

are 3 Baruch, the Remains of Jeremiah (by a Jew in the second century or by a Christian in the third or fourth century),[71] a book of the Secrets of Moses, with commentary (Samarian), and a samaritan story of the death of Moses.[72] Important pseudo-historical works are the Book of the Lives of the Prophets, the Book of Melchizedek, the Prayer of Manasseh, the History of the Deportation of the Children of Israel (attributed to Jeremiah).[73] None of these can be condemned outright, but each must be judged on its merits as a whole and in parts. One never knows where an authentic and valuable item might turn up, as in the recently found Book of Joshua in Arabic, containing a good deal not found in our biblical Book of Joshua, but which can be checked against older sources.[74]

Of interest to Latter-day Saints is the Book of Jasher, one of the first English translations of which was published in Salt Lake City. "There can be little doubt that the Book of Jasher was a national epic," according to Cyrus Gordon; but how much of this particular book goes back to the original? "The time is ripe," he says, "for a fresh investigation of such genuine sources of scripture, particularly against the background of the Dead Sea Scrolls."[75]

A good illustration of the apocryphal problem is offered by the famous Testament of the Twelve Patriarchs. Completely neglected until very recently, this work was first brought to light by Robert Grosseteste, the Bishop of

---

[71]F. Stegmüller, *Repertorium Biblicum Medii Aevi* (Madrid, 1950ff.), I, No. 114.

[72]M. Gaster, *The Asatir, The Samaritan Book of the "Secrets of Moses"*, etc. (London: Royal Asiatic Society, 1927).

[73]Texts of the *Lives of the Prophets*, the *Book of Melchizedek*, and *The Prayer of Manasseh* may be found in *Patrologia Graeca*, 43:393-414, 28:525-530, and 1:646-9.

[74]M. Gaster, in *Journal of the Royal Asiatic Society*, 1930, pp. 567-599.

[75]C. Gordon, in *Christianity Today*, 4 (1959), p. 133. While there was in all probability a real Book of Jasher, "a larger more or less unified epic composition" of great age (see S. Mowinckel, in *Zt. f. Alttest. Wiss.*, 53 [1935], pp. 130-8), it has never been clear which of many later writings that bear the name really belong to it. The presence in Medieval "Books of Jasher" of passages paralleling parts of the *Testament of Judah* would indicate that not all their matter is late or forged. The book read by many Latter-day Saints still has to be examined line by line on the basis of D&C 91.

Lincoln, about 1242 A.D. He thought it was a Christian work and it was duly included in the pages of the *Patrologia*.[76] Recently two books appeared on the Twelve Patriarchs, one declaring it to be a Christian work that "may no longer be reckoned to the pseudographic literature of the Old Testament. They must be classified among the literary productions of the early Christian Church."[77] The other author reached the opposite conclusion, that the work is "free of any Christian interpolation of any importance,"[78] thus agreeing with Charles' earlier verdict, that it was a Jewish writing which had "much influence . . . upon the language of our Lord and of the New Testament."[79] This illustrates how the interpreter can edit a work to suit himself; in this case one group of experts accounts for the Christian material in the Twelve Patriarchs as a Christian *interpolation,* while the other with equal convictions explains that the Christians later borrowed it. The Dead Sea Scrolls would seem to favor the latter interpretation.

The Christian Apocrypha

In our short discussion of the Jewish Apocrypha we have imperceptibly moved into the area of Christian Apocrypha—another example of the ubiquitous overlapping from which we never escape; for the same old question, Is this Jewish or is it Christian? plagues the student of early Christian as much as of early Jewish writings. Lists of Christian apocryphal writings are even more confusing than the Jewish lists, since the latter at least include fourteen indisputably "biblical" Apocrypha (the taxonomists actually employ this oxymoron!), while among the Christian titles, nothing is certain.

---

[76]Migne, *Patrologia Graeca*, 2:1030-1150.

[77]M. De Jonge, *The Testament of the Twelve Patriarchs* (Assen, 1953), pp. 117f.

[78]M. Philonenko, *Les Interpolations chrétiennes des Testaments des Douze Patriarches et les Manuscrits de Qumran* (Paris: Presses Universitaires, 1960), pp. 59f.

[79]H. H. Rowley, *Relevance of Apocalyptic*, p. 63, n. 3.

In 1638 when Charles I of England received the great Alexandrian Codex of the New Testament as a present from the Patriarch of Constantinople, there came bound in the book with the canonical texts and obviously considered as scripture by the people who used the codex, two writings designated as letters of Clement to the Corinthians. These letters, though frequently quoted by early church writers, were at the time entirely unknown to Western scholars, the church having completely lost track of them.

These were the first of a special class of writings to which the Catholic theologian Cotelier in the seventeenth century gave the name of "Apostolic Fathers," it being assumed that the authors had known the apostles or at least their disciples. The title is not a satisfactory one, and the problem of classifying the Apostolic Fathers has been a difficult one, as they were "written, transmitted, interpolated, disregarded, recovered, and analyzed for theological and polemical purposes from the second century to the twentieth, and it seems unlikely that any impartial observer exists who can comprehend them apart from this history of debate."[80] The so-called Apostolic Fathers recognized today as being both ancient and orthodox are:

I Clement, Letter to the Corinthians, written c. 95/96 in Rome, of high authority in the early church but virtually unknown in later times.

II Clement's Letter, not a letter and not by Clement. Written probably by a priest in Corinth, c. 135-140 AD, contains some very old sayings of Jesus.

Letters of Ignatius, Bishop of Antioch, c. 110-115. Letters to Seven Churches, written on his way to martyrdom in Rome, are accepted as genuine, an equal number rejected.

Polycarp, Bishop of Smyrna, Letter to the Philippians. Polycarp died in 155.

---

[80]R. M. Grant, in *The Journal of Religion,* 39 (1960), p. 120.

Papias of Hierapolis, Sayings of Jesus, written c. 135-150.

The Didache, or Teachings of the Twelve Apostles, discovered at Constantinople in 1872. Written between 100 and 150 AD in Syria, Palestine, or Egypt.

The Shepherd of Hermas, written in Rome c. 140, by the layman Hermas; divided into Visions, Mandates, and Similitudes for the instruction of the church.[81]

As an example of the usual overlapping, an important discourse in the Didache on the doctrine of the Two Ways (i.e., the Way of Light and the Way of Darkness that lie open to all during this lifetime of probation) also turns up slightly altered in an Epistle of Barnabas (classed by some as an Apostolic Father), and it would now appear that both go back to a common pre-Christian teaching frequently referred to in the Dead Sea Scrolls.[82]

All the Apostolic Fathers are related, in fact, and although orthodox and Christian, they show many affinities with the Dead Sea Scrolls and quote other apocryphal works. This leads to the usual problems of classification: Some would still reject the Pastor of Hermas and for that matter parts of the New Testament as unorthodox;[83] and while Hennicke lists a hundred authentic Christian Apocrypha, J. Perier insists that "the canonical apocryphal literature of the primitive church is contained almost entirely in but seven works: "The Didache, the Didaschalia, the Apostolic Constitutions, the Greek Canons (i.e., rules for the Church, 84 or 85 of them), the Apostolic Canons (27 or 30 of them), the Canons of Hippolytus, and the 127 Canons of the Apostles," which Perier himself edited.[84] To all of these we refer below.

[81]Complete texts and discussions (except for the Didache) are supplied in A. R. M. Dressel, *Patrum Apostolicorum Opera* (Leipzig, 1863). For translations, E. Goodspeed, *The Apostolic Fathers, an American Translation* (New York: Harper, 1950).
[82]L. W. Barnard, in *Church Quarterly Review*, 1958, p. 229.
[83]E. Peterson, in *Vigiliae Christianae*, 8 (1954), p. 70.
[84]J. Perier, in *Patrologia Orientalia*, VIII, 553.

The sands of Egypt have yielded up papyrus fragments of unidentified gospels, sayings of Jesus, apocryphal
gospels (of the Nazarenes, Ebionites, Hebrews, and
Egyptians), conversations of Jesus with his disciples after
the resurrection, at least 40 "Gnostic" gospels, Infancy
Gospels, telling of the childhood of Jesus and some important collections of non-canonical stories about Jesus.[85]
Again, none of this material can be lightly dismissed, for it
all overlaps and much of it goes back to very early
times. The Gospel of the Twelve Apostles, for example,
found in 1913, is mentioned by Origen as authentic scripture in the Church of his day, and in his own opinion older
than the Gospel of Luke,[86] and has close ties, for example,
with all seven of the important works mentioned by Perier
above.

If we were merely to begin to point out the relationships between the hundreds of Apocrypha, nearly all of
them first brought to light *since Cumorah*, we should soon
find ourselves at sea. But it is no longer a shoreless sea,
for thanks to many recent studies, dim and distant but im-
posing islands have begun to take shape through the mists.

The most impressive of these is that corpus of writings
known as the Pseudo-Clementines. The *Patrologia Graeca*
attributes to Clement of Rome besides the two epistles,
letters to the Virgin and to James the Elder, twenty
homilies, a work on the acts of Peter, liturgical writings, and
the famous Clementine Recognitions, a novel which was
"a favorite piece of 'Sunday afternoon literature' " in the
church of the second century.[87] Since this Clement is supposed to have been the Bishop of Rome, the important
Apostolic Constitutions are also attributed to him as well
as certain decretals and episcopal letters, and even the so-

---

[85]All these are translated into German in E. Hennecke and W. Schneemelcher, *op. cit.*, Vol. I (1959).

[86]E. Revillout, in *Patrologia Orientalia*, II, 123-7.

[87]R. M. Grant, *Second Century Christianity* (London: SPCK, 1946),
p. 10.

called Cave of Treasures—the Pseudo-Ephraim or Book of Rolls.[88] Forty years ago the celebrated Eduard Schwartz declared that the Clementine writings "have no significance whatever for the study of early Judaism and Christianity."[89] But today, thanks again to the Dead Sea Scrolls, the position of the "Tuebingen School," which saw in the Clementine Recognitions the most valuable first-hand view of the primitive church, has been vindicated.

To trace but a single line, the Apostolic Constitutions, attributed to Clement, show very close affinities with a work published in the last year of the nineteenth century and given the title of "The Testament of Our Lord and Savior Jesus Christ." This work was also attributed by its ancient compiler to Clement, and purports to contain instructions given by the Lord to the apostles after the resurrection on matters of doctrine and organization.

Both these works in turn are closely related to a writing discovered in 1897, the Epistle of the Apostles or conversations of Jesus with His Disciples After the Resurrection. (The Ethiopian version was labeled, "The Testament in Galilee of Our Lord Jesus Christ.")[90] These works in turn are very close to another collection called the Didascalia, purported teachings of the Lord to the apostles after the resurrection. Parts of this are identical with the eighth book of the Apostolic Constitutions, but also very close to the canons of the Epistle of Peter attributed to Clement, above, and various other apostolic canons including the "127 Canons of the Apostles" first published in 1912, which claims to have been "composed by

[88]Stegmüller, op. cit., I, No. 76.

[89]E. Schwartz, in Zeitschrift fur die Neutestamentliche Wissenschaft, 31 (1932) pp. 151-199. Standard works on this much-discussed theme are by Rud. Knopf (1899), Hans Waitz (1904 and 1929), C. Schmidt (1905 and 1929), W. Heintze (1913f.), F. Gerke (1931), G. Rehm (1939), O. Cullmann (1954), H. J. Schoeps (1958f.), G. Streckes (1959), W. Ullman (1960).

[90]L. Guerrier and S. Brebaut (eds.) Le Testamente en Galilee de Notre-Seigneur J.-Christ, in Patrologia Orientalia, IX, 143-236.

our Fathers the holy Apostles and published by Clement the disciple of the Apostle Peter."[91]

Whatever one may think of these works today, many of them display "complete mastery" of the canonical materials and many are now accepted by most scholars as representing the authentic views of the early Christians,[92] to whom their teachings, especially about the return of the Lord after the resurrection were "of sovereign importance."[93]

When the Lord first met with the apostles after the resurrection, he rebuked them for their hardness of heart and slowness to believe; for they had thought it was all over with the crucifixion, and when reliable witnesses reported that Jesus had risen, they stubbornly refused to believe them. It was only when the Risen Christ himself took them in hand and for a period of forty days gave them instructions in "the things of the kingdom" that they were ready to go forth as missionaries to all the world. That post-resurrectional instruction made all the difference in the world to the apostles yet we find few words of that priceless instruction in the Bible! It is therefore more significant when the great *majority* of the earliest Christian writings to come into our hands announce that they are purveying those very lost teachings of Jesus which we miss so much—the words of the Lord to his disciples after the resurrection. And in this area a particular collection of recently discovered documents is the most valuable.

------

[91]E. Rahmani (ed.), *Testamentum Domini nostri Jesu Christi* (Mainz, 1899). The relationships are discussed at length by C. Schmidt, *Gespräche Jesu mit seinen Jüngern nach der Auferstehung*, Vol. VII (1919), of *Texte und Untersuchungen*, pp. 156-9, 162-4, 211-213, 230ff. A more recent study of the same is by H.-J. Schoeps, in *Studia Theologica*, 8 (1955), pp. 41ff. O. Perler, in *Rivista de Archeologia Christiana*, 25 (1949), p. 72, points to the dependency of I Clement on IV Maccabees. A text and discussion of the *127 Canons of the Apostles* is in the *Patrologia Orientalia*, VIII, 553-710, edited by J. and A. Perier. Quotation is from p. 567.
[92]C. Schmidt, *op. cit.*, pp. 213f.
[93]*Ibid.*, p. 245.

A Survey of Some Major Discoveries Since Cumorah

The great discoveries of our time were heralded by impressive preliminary rumblings. In 1886, according to Eduard Meyer "not a single document existed to attest the authenticity of the Old Testament as history." A year later the Amarna Tablets, a whole library of correspondence between the kings of Egypt and the princes of Palestine and Syria in the days of the Patriarchs, came forth.[94] But the great and revolutionary discoveries came with the finding of two other libraries, those of Ugarit and Qumran.[95] The former was first discovered at Ras Shamra ("Fennel Cape" on the Syrian coast) in 1928, but it is still yielding documents, thirty boxes of tablets, "a whole new archive," having been found in 1960.[96] Here is a temple archive from the fourteenth and fifteenth centuries B.C., kept by Israel's closest neighbors, the Canaanites. From these records we learn for the first time how close the ancient Hebrews were in culture and religion to those Canaanites and can appreciate the force of Lehi's remark to his sons that the one real difference between their own ancestors and the earlier inhabitants of the land was a moral one: "Do ye suppose that our fathers would have been more choice than they [the Canaanites] if they had been righteous? I say unto you, Nay." (1 Nephi 17:34.)

The Ras Shamra fragments opened up a whole new world to biblical study by putting Israel in a new world setting. "It is now realized that Israel was no more isolated in her language than she was in her religion and culture, and that Hebrew . . . borrowed freely from other languages."[97] Hence it can be "no longer assumed that if a Hebrew passage is unintelligible it must be corrupted."[98]

---

[94]Ed. Meyer, in *Sitzber. der Berliner Akad. d. Wissenschaft,* Hist.-Phil. Klasse, 1908, p. 153.

[95]T. Robinson, in *Zeitschrift für die alt testamentliche Wissenschaft,* 73 (1961), p. 265.

[96]W. F. Albright, in *Journal of Bible and Religion,* 31 (1963), p. 110.

[97]C. S. Rodd, in *Expository Times,* 71 (1959), p. 131.

[98]H. H. Rowley, in *Expository Times,* 71 (1959), p. 97.

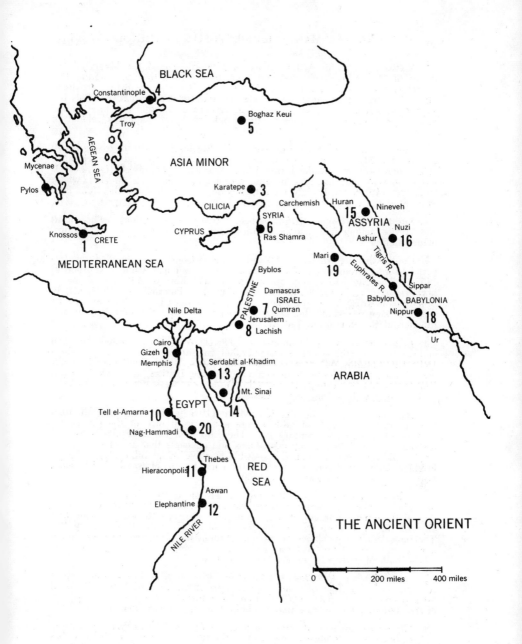

Some Important Manuscript Deposits.

(Explanation on following pages).

SOME IMPORTANT MANUSCRIPT DEPOSITS IN THE OLD WORLD

1 *Knossos,* where Sir Arthur Evans in 1900 discovered the library of the Palace of Minos, between 3,000 and 4,000 tablets from the 15th century BC, written in the Minoan Linear Script B. In the 1950's a young British architect, Michael Ventris, deciphered the writing and showed it to be Greek. This has altered the whole picture of ancient Near Eastern civilization and brought the Patriarchs of Israel into contact with people speaking languages related to our own.

2 Modern *Pylos* in Messenia, where C. Blegen in 1939 discovered 600 tablets of a Mycenaean palace archive. More tablets were discovered after 1952 when work was resumed after World War II. These tablets, in Linear B script, showed that the Mycenaeans were Greeks, and that Greeks (whose language is often surprisingly close to our own) were busy in the Near East as early as the times of the Patriarchs.

3 *Karatepe* where since 1946 have been discovered inscriptions in Phoenician and Hittite, telling how people migrated and founded cities in the century before Lehi.

4 *Constantinople,* where in 356 the Emperor Constantius founded the Imperial Library, from which a vast number of ancient mss. came to Europe in 1453ff. The city had a very ancient patriarchal library and many monastic libraries. There, in the library of the Jerusalem Patriarchate, the Greek P. Bryennius in 1872 discovered among many valuable early Christian Apocrypha the only known text of the *Didache,* which describes the organization and function of the church cir. 140 AD.

5 *Boghaz Keui,* where beginning in 1906 H. Winckler excavated the royal archives of the Hittites—more than 10,000 cuneiform tablets from the 14th and 13th centuries BC, mostly written in Hittite, a language related to our own. Scholars had formerly maintained that the Hittites, with whom Abraham has intimate dealings in the Old Testament, were either a myth or a scribal mistake—that they never existed!

6 *Ras Shamra* (ancient Ugarit), where C. Schaeffer beginning in 1929 brought forth thousands of tablets from a temple archive of the Canaanites going back to the 14th century BC. They are in a language closely related to Hebrew and contain many expressions and concepts that are close to those of the Old Testament, making it possible to solve many Bible mysteries and brightly illuminating certain phases of the early history of Israel. Thirty more boxes of tablets were excavated in 1960.

7 *Qumran* and the surrounding area, where since 1947 hundreds of caves have been explored, many of them yielding written documents comprising tens of thousands of fragments and more than 400 separate works. The most valuable of these were written by Jewish sectaries in the first century BC. The remarkable resemblance of their institutions and langauge to those found among the early Christians has called for a complete reevaluation of the nature both of early Christianity and of Judaism.

8 *Lachish,* where in 1935-6 J. L. Starkey discovered the first of the Lachish Letters, the office files of a military garrison of the time of Lehi. These 18 ostraca (writing on potsherds), written in Hebrew, give eyewitness accounts of the state of things in Palestine just before the fall of Jerusalem.

9 *Gizeh* near ancient Memphis, where the *Pyramid Texts* were discovered cut in the walls of tombs and passages of the kings of the V and VI Dynasties of Egypt (2600?-2200 BC). First collected and published by G. Maspero in 1881, they run in K. Sethe's edition to 712 spells and 1,048 pages. These writings are continued with new additions in the *Coffin Texts,* written on the inner sides of non-royal wooden coffins of the IX through XI Dynasties, and published by A. De Buck in 7 volumes. It is now realized that the frequent resemblance of these writings to the literature of Israel is not accidental.

10 *Tell el-Amarna,* where in 1887 two hundred cuneiform tablets were dug up by peasants, followed by hundreds of others, many of which were smashed and lost on the way to the dealers. In 1892 F. Petrie discovered the source of the documents, the royal archives of Ikhnaton at Amarna. The available collection consists of 358 cuneiform tablets, being the correspondence, in the Akkadian language (some of the letters are in Hittite), between the Egyptian court and the princes of Palestine and Syria, 1370-1348 BC, during the time of Israel's wanderings in the area.

11 *Hieraconpolis,* a prehistoric capital of Egypt, where in 1898 J. Quibell found a collection of predynastic Palettes containing very ancient ritual and historic texts. Just across the river in 1878 Mariette discovered the remains of a great royal library building, and to the north at Thebes where the documents now reproduced in the Pearl of Great Price were found was the great library of the Ramesseum.

12 *Elephantine,* where in 1906 A. Cowley and in 1911 E. Sachau discovered the business and law archives of a Jewish community of the fifth century BC. In 1953 more documents were located in Brooklyn, where they had lain unnoticed in a trunk for 50 years. In our opinion these letters, written in Aramaic to Persian officials and to important Jews in Jerusalem, supply the most valuable single commentary to the Book of Mormon.

13 *Serdabit al-Khadim,* ancient mines of the Pharaohs where people from Palestine were employed around 1500 BC and where they left some 30 rock inscriptions behind. These were discovered by Petrie in 1905, with important additions in 1948. They are written with Egyptian symbols but in Canaanitish dialect which has been identified as proto-Hebrew. They show the early Egyptianizing of the Semites and indicate much closer ties between the cultures of Egypt and Israel than have heretofore been conceded.

14 *Mt. Sinai,* at whose foot in the monastery of St. Catherine, K. Tischendorf in 1844 first spotted the manuscript of the Codex Sinaiticus in a wastebasket. The codex, which he finally acquired in 1859, contains valuable early Christian Apocrypha.

15 *Nineveh,* the third capital of Assyria, where in 1851 A. Layard discovered the huge library of Assurbanipal, founded by Sargon in the 8th century BC. Here was found what was long thought to be the original version of the flood story, and many documents illustrating and confirming the history of Israel.

16 *Nuzi,* where in 1925-26 Edward Cheira brought forth the great archives of the Hurrians, one tablet of which can be dated 1475 BC. These records contain accounts of men engaged in exactly the sort of activities as was Abraham and demonstrate the authenticity of the patriarchal age as depicted in the Old Testament.

17 *Sippar,* where a large temple library was discovered by H. Rassam in 1879 and P. Scheil in 1894. The ritual texts are important in constructing the over-all picture of Near Eastern religions in general, and of "patternism" in particular.

18 *Nippur,* where H. Hilprecht and others discovered a library of thousands of documents in 1889, including a flood story much older than the Nineveh version, and much closer to that of the Old Testament.

19 *Mari,* where in 1935-6 A. Parrot discovered a palace archive which had been destroyed by Hammurabi in the 18th century BC. Thousands of tablets, including correspondence with the king of Babylon, depict in great fulness the travels and business activities of important men in the days of Abraham and strikingly vindicate the biblical portrait of the patriarchs.

20 *Nag-Hammadi,* in which in the remains of an ancient Christian community was found in 1946(?) a collection of thirteen leather-bound volumes containing 49 separate writings (about 1000 pages). Though the books date from the 4th century, they contain Christian writings going back to the 2nd century of the church. By far the oldest Christian library known.

An example of puzzling Bible words explained by these records is the word *khashmal*, which is now known to mean "brass"—a word which this writer long thought to be an anachronism in the Book of Mormon.[99] Ideas and words go together, of course, and the Ugaritic ritual texts cast a flood of light on early Jewish cult practices, particularly the Year Rite and the Coronation patterns which today are "the centre of interest in the study of the relation between the religions of the Near East and the Old Testament."[100] The ritual picture that emerges conforms in detail to the long description of an Old World coronation rite that meets us in the pages of the book of Mosiah.[101]

It was the Ras Shamra texts more than anything else which showed that the Old Testament must be studied in an ever larger context to be properly understood. "The Bible strikes root into every ancient Near Eastern culture, and it cannot be understood until we can see its relationship to its sources in true perspective," according to Albright.[102] "One hundred years ago," writes A. Parrot, "in Mesopotamia was discovered that history lies behind the Old Testament. . . . Today the Old Testament itself is being discovered," to wit, in the Ras Shamra documents, in the Mari Tablets (a huge collection of tablets discovered on the upper Euphrates by Parrot himself), and in the Nuzi Tablets, vast private archives which "make frequent mention of the Habiri," and the Dawidum, and even tell of the use of fire-signals by the Benjaminites as described in the Old Testament.[103]

"The beginnings of Israel are rooted in a highly cul-

[99]T. Robinson, *op. cit.*, p. 267.

[100]J. Schofield, *Expository Times*, 71, p. 196.

[101]Compare the latest summary, S. Hooke, Ed., *Myth, Ritual, and Kingship* (Oxford, 1958), with our discussion in *An Approach to the Book of Mormon* (Salt Lake City: Deseret Book Co., 1964), Ch. 23 (pp. 256-268.)

[102]W. F. Albright, in *Journal of the American Oriental Society*, 64 (1944) p. 148.

[103]A. Parrot, in *Revue de l'Historie et de Philosophie Religieuses*, 1950, pp. 1-9. Cf. W. F. Albright, *The Biblical Period from Abraham to Ezra* (New York: Harper & Row, 1963), pp. 2-9.

tural Canaan," where we now know "Mesopotamians, Egyptians and branches of the Indo-Europeans [our own ancestors] mingled their cultures and their blood"—as we learn from our own book of Abraham. Hence "the notion that early Israelite religion and society were primitive is completely false."[104]

If the Book of Mormon reflects the culture of the whole Near East of its day, so does the Bible.[105] Cyrus Gordon would now even bring the Greeks into the Hebrew picture (as we did in the portrait of Lehi), by showing that "the people of ancient Greece and Israel have a common Semitic heritage based on the flow of Phoenician culture. . . . We were brought up to believe that the Jews gave us ethics and religion, that the Greeks willed us science and philosophy. Yet, we now see a similar tradition running through both cultures, and we can't be sure which culture gave us what."[106]

It was the Ugaritic texts that put the brakes on the higher critics, to use Speiser's expression, by demonstrating the futility of their favorite game, namely cutting every book of the Bible up into numerous separate sections which they claimed were the work of various interpolaters and commentators.[107] Whenever a scholar thought he could discern within a book of the Bible the slightest peculiarity of language or change of mood, outlook, or attitude, he would proudly announce the discovery of a new author or corrupter of the text. "A generation ago," writes H. H. Rowley, "we could speak of 'critical' as over against "traditional orthodoxy' . . . we knew exactly where one 'document' ended and another began. . . ."[108] True, "the unedifying conclusion of all such study is," as Gordon notes,

[104]C. Gordon, op. cit., pp. 133-4.
[105]For the Book of Mormon, H. Nibley, Approach to the Book of Mormon, Chapters 3-7.
[106]C. Gordon, Before the Bible, (New York: Harper & Row, 1962), pp. 32ff.
[107]E. A. Speiser, in Contemporary Review, IV, pp. 214-5.
[108]H. H. Rowley, op. cit., p. 97.

"that nothing is authentic"; but this loss of reality was
compensated for by the warm satisfaction of all playing
the same game and wearing the same "badge of inter-
confessional academic respectability."[109] But today numerous texts on closer examination show that it was common
practice in the East to introduce a variety of styles and
even dialects into a single composition.[110] "No Egyptologist
(or other Orientalist in parallel disciplines) is such a fool,"
writes K. A. Kitchen, "as to see 'sources' behind such texts
. . . or to scissor up these stone stele" as Bible students
have scissored up the Bible every time an author hits a
change of pace.[111] So now the trend of higher criticism has
been reversed, and there is "a growing emphasis on the
unity of the Old Testament . . . a significant perception
that beneath all its variety of forms and of ideas, the Old
Testament has a deep unity."[112]

The Patriarchs Come to Life

"One of the remarkable results of archaeological research during the period between the two wars," G. E.
Wright informs us, "was the sudden emergence of the
Patriarchal Age" as real history.[113] The kind of world described in the pages of Genesis really existed, and was
therefore not, as the higher critics had assumed, the invention of men writing many centuries after the times they are

------

[109]C. Gordon, *op. cit.*, pp. 134, 131.

[110]"No one questions that Hammurabi's Code is a single composition in
spite of the fact that the prologue and epilogue are not only written in poetry
(as against the prose of the laws) but in a different dialect from the laws,
because the poetry calls not only for a different style but even for different
grammatical forms." C. Gordon, *Ugaritic Literature* (Rome: Pontifical Biblical
Institute, 1949), pp. 6-7, discussing other cases as well. Cf. his article in
Christianity Today, 4 (1959), p. 132.

[111]K. A. Kitchen, in *Faith and Thought,* 91 (1959), p. 190. It has been
shown that varieties of style occur within single Egyptian documents as
well as Babylonian, *ibid.*, pp. 188f. Cf. S. Mowinckel, *Prophecy and Tradition* No. 3 (Oslo, Norse Academy of Science, 1946), pp. 7-8.

[112]H. H. Rowley, in S. Hooke, (ed.) *Ritual and Kingship* (Oxford, 1958),
p. 260. A generation ago such a thing was unthinkable, H. Torcgyner, in
Zeitschr. der Dt. Morgenland. Ges., 85 (1931), pp. 287-324.

[113]G. E. Wright, in *Expository Times,* 71 (1960), p. 292.

supposed to be describing; the Old Testament gives a vivid and accurate picture of the very world in which the patriarchs are said to have moved, and of no other.[114] Eduard Meyer and Ed. König were right when they insisted that the Old Testament narratives, unlike the dry annals of the Babylonians or the fairy stories of the Egyptians, were real history: ". . . this respect for fact and historical perspective in the records of the race finds no parallel in the whole literature of the ancient Near East until the time of Herodotus."[115]

The theory that Genesis was not intended as history but as "poetic media for the conveyance of divine truth," must now be discarded.[116] For "none of the Pentateuchal and other early historical sources of the Old Testament invented its material . . . [they] cannot be charged with any kind of fabrication."[117] And not long ago it was thought to be *all* fabrication! "It is clear," writes Albright, "that the substantial historicity of biblical tradition has been vindicated to an extent which few unprejudiced bystanders could have deemed possible a generation ago."[118] In commenting on this, Albright observes that the peculiar genius of the Jewish and Christian religions, as over against all other religions, is the total involvement of their teachings with a real historical background; he also notes that this background has been largely lost today, but has its clearest

---

[114]W. F. Albright, *Biblical Period from Abraham to Ezra*, p. 5: ". . . the patriarchs come alive with a vividness unknown to a single extra-biblical character in the whole vast literature of the ancient Near East." For discussions of the discovery of the Patriarchal Age, J. Reider, in *The Jewish Quarterly Review*, 27 (1937), p. 349; J. C. L. Gibson in *Journal of Semitic Studies*, 7 (1962), pp. 44ff; R. de Vaux, in *Revue Biblique*, 53 (1946), pp. 321-348; G. E. Wright, in *Expository Times*, 71 (1960) pp. 292-6, and *ibid.*, 72 (1961), pp. 213-6; A. Parrot, *op. cit.*, pp. 1-10.

[115]J. Gray, in *Vetus Testamentum*, Suppl. Vol. V (1957), p. 218. Cf. Ed. Meyer, *Die Israeliten und ihre Nachbarstämme* (Halle, 1906), p. 484, and *Geschichte des Alterums*, I, i, 131; and Ed. König, in *Historische Zeitschrift*, 132 (1925), pp. 290ff.

[116]T. C. Mitchell, in *Faith and Thought*, 91 (1959), p. 48.

[117]E. A. Speiser, *op. cit.*, p. 214.

[118]W. F. Albright, in *Cross Currents*, 9 (1959), p. 117. Cf. G. von Rad, in *Expository Times*, 72 (1961), p. 216; H. H. Rowley, *ibid.*, 71 (1960), p. 97.

expression in the Book of Mormon, which commits the
Mormons, whether they like it or not, to a literal and historical interpretation of the story of salvation.[119]

When a hundred years ago late Babylonian parallels
to the Hebrew flood story were discovered in the library of
Assur-bani-pal at Nineveh (first of the great library discoveries), it was instantly concluded that the Old Testament version had been lifted from this Babylonian
"original." But as still older versions of the flood story were
found in Mesopotamia, they were noted to be more like the
Genesis story the older they were, indicating that the Bible
story might be the oldest one after all.[120] From recent
studies of the Atra-khasis Epic, in fact, it would now
appear that the old Babylonian flood story, long accepted
as the original source of all the other flood stories,
including that in Genesis, is really secondary and "has
been wrenched from its context," which now appears for
the first time, offering "proof . . . that the whole framework
of Hebrew tradition in Genesis I-X, and not just the episode of the flood, has its counterpart in Sumero-Babylonian
legend."[121]

A perhaps even more striking vindication of the possible priority of much Bible material over the sources from
which it is supposed to have come is the discovery by
Drioton that a famous monument of Egyptian Wisdom
literature, which is supposed to have been the source and
inspiration of Hebrew Wisdom literature, "is actually an
indifferent Egyptian translation from a Semitic—Hebrew—
original. . . . This would be the 'Words of the Wise' on
which Proverbs also subsequently drew."[122] The idea that
the Babylonians and Egyptians might be dependent on the
Hebrews for ideas found in the Bible instead of the other
way round is indeed a revolutionary one.

----

[119]Albright, *op. cit.*, p. 111.
[120]Discussed by H. Nibley, in *A Book of Mormon Treasury* (Salt Lake
City: Bookcraft, 1959), p. 135.
[121]W. Lambert, in *Journal of Semitic Studies*, 5 (1960), p. 116.
[122]E. Drioton, in *Faith and Thought*, 91 (1959), pp. 191-3.

It is interesting that the ancient Hebrew remains, though not scarce, do not have the impact that the foreign materials do.[123] The Lachish Letters, containing eyewitness accounts of the desperate state of things in the land of Jerusalem in Lehi's day,[124] have excited far less comment than the Elephantine Papyri which show us a Jewish community living far up the Nile, whither they had fled for safety, possibly at the destruction of Jerusalem in Lehi's day.[125] In 1954 some of these records, the Brooklyn Aramaic Papyri, were discovered in a trunk, where they had been overlooked for fifty years.[126] Perhaps the most surprising discovery about these Jews settled so far from home, was their program for building a temple in their new home.[127] Not long ago learned divines were fond of pointing out that Nephi's idea of building a temple in the New World was quite sufficient in itself to prove once and for all the fraudulence of the Book of Mormon, since, it was argued, no real Jew would ever dream of having a temple anywhere but in Jerusalem. So the Elephantine Papyri score another point for the Book of Mormon.

The same year (1954) saw the publication of part of an actual record kept at an important Egyptian prison in what is usually thought to be the time of Joseph. It includes a list of seventy-five prisoners' names, of which forty are of West Semitic origin, by which "the genuine antiquity of some patriarchal names is . . . brightly illumined."[128]

[123]For a summary of important Hebrew finds, S. Moscati, *L'Epigrafia Ebraica Antica*, in *Biblica et Orientalia*, No. 15 (1951), discussing the Gezer Calendar (pp. 8ff), the Samarian Ostraca (27ff), the Siloam Inscription (40ff), the Ofel Ostracon (40ff), the seals (47ff), bulla and jar-handles (72ff), inscribed weights (99ff), the Samarian Ivories (106f), and newly found inscriptions (111ff).
[124]H. Nibley, *Lehi in the Desert*, etc., (Salt Lake City: Bookcraft, 1952), pp. 8f, 109.
[125]M. L. Margolis, in *Jewish Quarterly Review*, 2 (1911-2), pp. 419f.
[126]C. Torrey, in *Journal of Near Eastern Studies*, 13 (1954), pp. 149-53. For the complete text, E. G. Kraeling, *The Brooklyn Museum Aramaic Papyri* (New Haven: Yale Univ., 1953).
[127]Margolis, *op. cit.*, pp. 430-435.
[128]K. A. Kitchen, in *Faith and Thought*, 91 (1959), pp. 180-4.

Which reminds us that in 1938 Nelson Glueck first showed
Lehi to be an authentic West Semitic name, at home in
the borders near the Red Sea.[129] In 1958 the same authority
was able to trace part of Abraham's route through the
desert "into the wilderness of Zin from Palestine to Egypt
and back again. . . . After having discovered these
Abra(ha)mitic sites," he reports, "the chapters in the Bible
describing the journeys of Abraham and his people . . .
become clear to us."[130]

Within a stone's throw of Jerusalem (less than fifteen
miles away on the average), is a land that had been examined with care by Christian antiquarians since the days of
Origen and Jerome. Hundreds of caves containing thousands of written fragments had escaped detection through
the centuries until the desert suddenly came to life in the
early 1950's. "Discoveries tread on the heels of discoveries," cried Professor Cross. "The antique riches of this
land seem limitless."[131] By 1960 over 230 caves had been
explored, and writings had been discovered in many of
them.[132] The documents that interest us consist of more
than 400 manuscripts covering a span of 300 years—from
the end of the third century BC until 68 AD. They include "the first major biblical manuscript of great
antiquity,"[133] letters of the great leader Simon Bar Kochbah
(now read Kosiba) written by himself,[134] the "first known
Hebrew documents from the early Rabbinic period,"[135] and
above all the records and teachings of a pre-Christian
"Church in the Wilderness."[136]

------

[129]See The Improvement Era, March 1956, p. 152.

[130]N. Glueck, in Proceedings of the American Philosophical Society, 100 (1956), pp. 150-5.

[131]F. M. Cross, in The Biblical Archaeologist, February 1954, p. 17.

[132]G. Kuhn, in Theologische Literaturzeitung, 85 (1960), p. 651. For the latest list of new texts, R. Meyer, ibid., 88 (1963), pp. 19ff.

[133]F. M. Cross, op. cit., p. 2.

[134]Ibid., p. 11. C. Raphael, in Atlantic Monthly, May, 1967, pp. 91-97.

[135]R. Brownlee, in The Biblical Archaeologist, September 1951, p. 54.

[136]We have treated this theme at length in An Approach to the Book of Mormon, pp. 133-162 (Chapters 13-15).

More than a decade ago this writer, following a clue from an apocryphal work called the Assumption of Moses, suggested in the pages of *The Improvement Era* that the documents from the caves of Qumran had not been hastily buried by their owners to preserve them from the ravages of a Roman army but had rather been deliberately buried and sealed up to come forth in a later "dispensation."[137] Since then, the discovery of a fragment of the Assumption of Moses itself in one of the caves has put scholars on the track of investigation which now leads them to the conclusion that the Scrolls actually were buried "in a solemn communal interment" with the hope of their discovery in a later and better age.[138]

In this connection, one find in particular should be mentioned, namely the now famous Copper Scroll from Cave IV. It is a document of first importance: ". . . there is hardly an aspect of Near Eastern Archaeology, history, and religion that [it] does not in some way illuminate."[139] Originally it consisted of copper plates, but these have been riveted together so that they could be rolled up in imitation of a sacred leather scroll.[140] Why copper? Because this record was more valuable than any of the other Scrolls, being nothing less than a catalog of all the buried treasures of the society. If this record should perish, many if not all of their possessions—all dedicated to the Lord— would be irretrievably lost. Hence it had to be written on an enduring substance and carefully hidden away.[141] Consider some items from the Copper Scroll:

Item 4: ". . . tithe vessels, consisting of log vessels and amphorae, all of tithe and stored Seven-Year produce and

[137]*The Improvement Era*, 57 (February 1954), p. 89.
[138]M. Black, *The Scrolls and Christian Origins* (New York: Scribner, 1961), p. 12.
[139]J. M. Allegro, *The Treasure of the Copper Scroll* (New York: Doubleday, 1960), p. 25.
[140]*Ibid.*, p. 27; A. Dupont-Sommer, in *Revue de l'Histoire des Religions*, 151 (1957), p. 25.
[141]Allegro, *op. cit.*, p. 62.

Second Tithe . . . in the bottom of the water conduit, six cubits from the north towards the hewn immersion pool."

Item 26: ". . . buried at three cubits, (hidden) there is a pitcher, in it, one scroll, under it 42 talents."

Item 34: "In the (drain) pipe which is in the eastern path to the Treasury, which is beside the Entrance: tithe jars and scrolls in among the jars."[142]

All these were sacred treasures and could only be used for religious purposes.[143]   Note that along with the money are sacred writings, one of them in a clay vessel such as the Dead Sea Scrolls were found in, others packed in among the jars.   The "immersion pool" refers to "a ritual bath" according to Allegro's note, and the "Seventh-Year produce" reminds one of the custom, referred to casually in the Book of Mormon, of the people's bringing a seven years' supply to a great gathering.[144]

Pre-Christian baptism and seventh-year produce thus ring familiar bells to the student of the Book of Mormon. But what is of particular interest, of course, is the nature and use of the copper plates.   By both precept and example they proclaim for the first time clearly and unequivocally that it was indeed an ancient Jewish custom to conceal sacred records, including records kept on metal plates prized for their durability.   The business of writing on such plates was hard and distasteful work: "The scribe, not without reason, appears to have tired toward the end, and the last lines of writing are badly formed and rather small. One can almost hear his sigh of relief as he punched out the last two words in the middle of the final line."[145]   How clearly this recalls the protests and explanations of our Book of Mormon writers, ". . . and I cannot write but little of my words, because of the difficulty of engraving our words

---

[142]Translated by Allegro, with reproductions of text, on pp. 33, 43, 47.
[143]"To use such goods for non-religious purposes was a heinous sin." ibid., p. 61.
[144]3 Nephi 4:4.
[145]Allegro, op. cit., p. 27.

upon plates" (Jacob 4:1) and ". . . I would write it also if I had room on the plates, but I have not. . . ." (Mormon 8:5.) Writing on plates requires a cramped and abbreviated script, Moroni explains (Mormon 9:32), and Allegro also notes that writing on copper plates actually produces a new kind of writing that is peculiarly difficult to read, characterized by mixing forms of letters, ignoring the proper spacing between words, "running-over from one line to the next in the middle of a word," and general neglect of vowels.[146]

"A greater deficiency lies in ourselves," Allegro concludes, "we simply do not possess a sufficiently comprehensive technical Hebrew vocabulary to deal with a text of this kind."[146] This should have a sobering effect on those people who fondly suppose that if we could only discover some Nephite plates, the translation could be left to them: this sort of thing needs a Urim and Thummim indeed.

Since the past few decades have brought forth numerous exemplars of ancient writing on metal plates, of which Exhibit A are the gold and silver Darius plates— sacred history deposited in a special stone box by a near-contemporary of Lehi[147]—it is only too easy to forget that nothing in the coming forth of the Book of Mormon excited louder howls of derision than the fantastic idea of a sacred history being written on gold plates and then buried in the ground. The Copper Scroll and its message, compared carefully with what the Book of Mormon itself has to say about the recording and storing of bronze and gold plates, should give pause to the most skeptical critic of the Book of Mormon.

------

[146]*Ibid.*, pp. 28-30.
[147]There is a reproduction of these along with a discussion of "Ancient Records on Metal Plates," in Franklin S. Harris, Jr., *The Book of Mormon Message and Evidences* (Salt Lake City: Deseret News Press, 1953), pp. 95-105.

Cause for Alarm

In the Melchizedek Priesthood Manual for 1957 this writer included a chapter entitled "Unwelcome Voices from the Dust." This called forth some protest at the time, but the ensuing decade with its increasingly cool reception of new scrolls from Qumran has more than vindicated our position; it was just in 1957, in fact, that publication on the Scrolls suddenly cut down to a trickle and has remained at that low level ever since, as was pointed out by Professor Allegro in a rather sensational article in *Harper's Magazine* for August, 1966. Allegro's article caused quite a flurry and has led to much confusion by linking together two propositions which do not necessarily belong together. The first proposition was that the Dead Sea Scrolls had not proven popular with scholars at all, and are now receiving the deep-freeze treatment. With this proposition we agree.

The discovery of the Dead Sea Scrolls is "a marvelous story" in which it is not too hard to see the hand of the Lord.[148] It quickly produced "a whole cascade of revolutions."[149] Christian scholars, especially Roman Catholic, were at first alarmed at the threat to the "originality" of their version of Christianity and tried to minimize the importance of the Scrolls,[150] while Jewish experts viewed the new discoveries as a threat to Halachic, "normative," Judaism and in some cases with great severity denounced

---

[148]See A. Dupont-Sommer, in *Numen*, II/3 (1955), pp. 168ff.

[149]A Dupont-Sommer, *The Dead Sea Scrolls* (New York: Macmillan, 1952), p. 96. F. M. Cross uses almost the identical words: ". . . a cascade of revolutionary advances," in *Christian Century*, August 3, 1955, p. 889. "The little world of biblical scholarship has been turned topsy-turvy by the discoveries, to say the least . . ." Cross, in *The Biblical Archaeologist*, February 1954, p. 4.

[150]G. Graystone, in *The Catholic World*, 183 (April, 1956), pp. 11-15; A. Metzger, in *Biblica*, 1955, p. 481; G. Molin, *Die Sohne des Lichts* (Vienna: Herold, 1954), p. 186. "That the work of Christ is a recent development is a question that we do not intend to discuss here. Essentially, in fact, it is devoid of interest . . ." *The Pope Speaks*, 1955, p. 212. See J. M. Allegro, "The Untold Story of the Scrolls," in *Harper's* 233 (Aug. 1966), p. 46ff.

them as a fraud.[151] There was real consternation at what the Scrolls were doing to our accepted Bible text, and conservative scholars still try to brush them aside as of little consequence.[152] But in 1954 the Jews, who had once been cool towards the Scrolls, were glad to pay $250,000 for just four of them,[153] and Christian scholars now assure us that "All of us . . . should be proud to claim as part of our heritage that people whom we now know as Judean Covenanters or Essenes."[154]

Persistent denial has only called attention to the fact that vested interests have influenced the study of the Scrolls from the first and that their discovery has not been greeted with cries of unalloyed delight by Christian and Jewish scholars. "It is as a potential threat to Christianity, its claims and its doctrines, that the Scrolls have caught the imagination of laymen and clergy," wrote K. Stendahl.[155] It is not surprising that the Russians forthwith put forth the claim "that the Qumran discoveries conclusively prove that Jesus never lived."[156] But it is somewhat disturbing that after the Russians have seen their error and changed their position, our American intellectuals still accept Edmund Wilson's verdict "that the rise of Christianity should,

---

[151]J. M. Baumgarten, in *Tradition*, 1 (1958), pp. 209-226; S. Zeitlin, in *Jewish Quarterly Review*, 42 (1952), p. 150; 46 (1955-6), p. 215, and often in this journal of which he is editor, denounces the fraudulence of the Scrolls. T. Wechsler, in *Jewish Quarterly Review*, 43 (1952), p. 139, claims that the Scrolls are Kurdish composition of the twelfth century A.D.! "The initial reaction of most people" to the Copper Scroll "was to dismiss the scroll as a fairy tale," according to J. M. Allegro, *The Treasure of the Copper Scroll* (New York: Doubleday, 1960), p. 56.

[152]"The Isaiah Scroll was received with consternation in some circles," and when other Old Testament texts were read "the results were shocking," F. M. Cross, in *Christian Century*, August 10, 1955, pp. 920-1. "There is still a partial boycott of the Dead Sea Scrolls on the part of New Testament Scholars . . . ," W. F. Albright, in *Journal of Bible and Religion*, 31 (1961), p. 112. The Genesis Apocryphon "for seven years . . . was shifted about from place to place, without any particular care being devoted to it," Y. Yadin, *A Genesis Apocryphon*, (Jerusalem, 1956), p. 12.

[153]Yadin, *op. cit.*, p. 7.

[154]J. P. Hyatt, in *Journal of Biblical Literature*, 76 (1957), p. 11.

[155]K. Stendahl, *The Scrolls and the New Testament* (N.Y.: Harpers, 1957), p. 1.

[156]Bruce, *op. cit.*, p. 138.

at last, be generally understood as simply an episode of human history rather than propagated as dogma and divine revelation.[157] That "at last" clearly announces the vindication of a preconceived notion.

Actually the new documentary finds are a blow to conventional Christianity, which, as Stendahl points out, takes the position of the famous heretic Marcion: "He wanted Christianity to be a new religion, just as it is to us. Whereas the New Testament sees Jesus as the fulfilment of prophecies, we are apt to see him as the founder of a new religion. . . . Our pattern of thought is that of natural science: Jesus is the inventor of Christianity and the church is the guardian of his patent and copyright. In the New Testament the major concern is the diametrically opposite one: to make clear that all is 'old,' in accordance with the expectations of the prophets."[158] If this fact had been recognized, all the fuss and alarm about the threat to the "originality" of Christ (especially among Catholic scholars) would have been unnecessary. "If Dupont-Sommer is correct in this approach," wrote R. K. Harrison, who felt on the whole that he *was* correct, "the very foundations of the Christian faith might well be shaken by the realization that a hitherto unknown pre-Christian Jewish religious community had possessed similar beliefs and practices. On such a view Christianity would have to abandon its claim to uniqueness."[159]

But the Christian scriptures make no such claim to uniqueness, as Stendahl reminds us, and the Christian doctors should have known better since, as Bruce observes, "it has long been known that some kind of parallel can be found in the Talmud to practically every element in the ethical teaching of Jesus."[160] The men in the seminaries

---

[157]Edmund Wilson, *The Scrolls from the Dead Sea* (N.Y.: Oxford University Press, 1955), p. 108.
[158]Stendahl, *op. cit.*, p. 6.
[159]R. K. Harrison, *The Dead Sea Scrolls, an Introduction* (Harper Torchbook, 1961), p. 102.
[160]Bruce, *op. cit.*, p. 144.

have known for years about all kinds of such parallels, but they have never made "a thorough attempt to come to grips with the basic problem of what such parallels actually mean"; instead they have been quietly swept under the rug, with the result, as Stendahl notes, that the Christian world was "badly prepared to receive the good news from the Qumran Scrolls."[161] And it is precisely on these presuppositions, in particular that of the absolute uniqueness of the New Testament and the finality of the accepted scripture, that all criticism of the Book of Mormon has been based in the past. The new discoveries thus cut the ground away from all such criticism.

Which brings us to Allegro's second point, which is that the unpopularity of the Scrolls with Christian scholars must be due to the way in which they prove Christianity a fraud. Here he makes the mistake of identifying modern with ancient Christianity, assuming, as people commonly do, that there has only been one Christianity just as there has always been one Judaism though Prof. Goodenough has shown that rabbinical Halachic, "horizontal" Judaism is quite a different thing from the old "vertical" Judaism of another day, just so it can now be shown that what people label Christianity today is totally different from the ancient article. It is true that the Scrolls are very hard on conventional Judaism and conventional Christianity alike, and have been condemned by leaders of both religions. And they have been condemned for the very same reason that the Book of Mormon was condemned, for presenting a picture of ancient faith which was totally different from what modern Jews and Christians have always assumed it should have been.

What Yadin wrote eleven years ago still applies: "Any attempt at this stage of research to identify the Dead Sea sect with any other sect of the time is more likely to be based on assumptions than on facts"; but one thing we can

---

[161]Stendahl, op. cit., p. 2.

be sure, that "the commonplaces of scholarship are up for re-examination in the light of the new material offered by the scrolls."[162] And one of those commonplaces, long accepted but completely untested, has been the status of the Book of Mormon. "Scholars may disagree violently with each other's interpretations," writes F. F. Bruce, "and engage vigorously in debate; far more progress will be achieved in this way than by a mute agreement to differ."[163] Unfortunately, there has been no disagreement or debate about the Book of Mormon among those qualified to undertake a comparative investigation, but only a mute agreement to ignore: the apotropaic power of its title page has been insurmountable. But in view of the wonderful combination of circumstances that has been necessary to bring present-day students to a serious consideration of hundreds of valuable and neglected apocryphal writings, the neglect of the Book of Mormon should be anything but a surprise.

------

[162]Y. Yadin, *The Message of the Scrolls* (N.Y.: Simon & Schuster, 1957), p. 188.

[163]F. F. Bruce, *Second Thoughts on the Dead Sea Scrolls* (Grand Rapids: W. B. Eerdmans, 1961), p. 141.

CHAPTER 3

The Illusive Primitive Church

Qumran's Egyptian Twin

Twenty years ago a knowledge of the Coptic languages was limited to a forlorn handful of hopeless specialists. Today any serious study of the Early Church and its teachings is virtually impossible without Coptic. This is largely the result of the discovery of the Nag Hammadi library, a find whose importance is rivaled only by that of the Dead Sea Scrolls.[1] It is a most remarkable coincidence that in the same year in which the Arabs of Palestine started bringing to the markets mysterious writings from what turned out to be the oldest *Jewish* library yet known, the Arabs of Egypt, far up the Nile, started bringing in equally mysterious writings from what proved to be the oldest *Christian* library yet known. They were found on the site of an ancient religious community between sixty and seventy miles north of Luxor, and consisted of thirteen leather-bound volumes (books, not scrolls) representing forty-four different writings comprising "about a thousand large leaves, nearly eight hundred of them in good condition."[2] Although the library itself dates from the fourth century, "a number of these texts are from the second

---

[1] For a complete catalogue, see M. Krause, "Das koptische Handschriftfund bei Nag Hammadi," in *Mitteil d. Dt. Archaeol. Inst. zu Kairo,* 18 (1962), pp. 124-130.

[2] W. C. van Unnik, *Newly Discovered Gnostic Writings* (SCM Press, 1960, No. 30 of *Studies in Biblical Theology*), p. 8.

Nag Hammadi Books.

century," one important writing, for example, coming "from a small village-church not yet affected by gnosticism (i.e., by the Apostasy) between 125 and 150 AD."[3] As in Palestine also, the coming forth of the wonderful treasures was accompanied by all sorts of mystery and intrigue, with knotty problems of ownership presenting a formidable obstacle to publication.[4]

In 1956 an Egyptian scholar, Pahor Labib, himself a Copt, published a volume of photographs of the newly found texts, including complete photos of the Gospels of Philip and Thomas, the Apocryphon of John, a work called The Hypostasis of the Aeons (on the nature of authority), and a work on the creation.[5] Then nothing happened for several years, but recently the Germans have made a number of very valuable documents available.[6] A collection of 100 pages was secretly bought by a rich Swiss and taken to Zurich in 1952; it was named the Jung Codex after the famous psychologist C. J. Jung and contained the Gospel of Truth, the Apocryphon of James, a second century Apocryphon of John, a treatise on the Three Natures ("a mythical and theological exposition of vast dimensions and great detail"), and a work on the resurrection called the Letter to Rheginos.[7] So far, the Gospels of Thomas and Philip and the Gospel of Truth have been made available

---

[3]This was the *Apocryphon of James;* the quotation is from W. C. van Unnik, in *Vigiliae Christianae,* 10 (1956), p. 156.

[4]Van Unnik, *Newly Discovered Gnostic Writings,* p. 11.

[5]P. Labib, *Coptic Gnostic Papyri in the Coptic Museum at Old Cairo,* Fol. I (Government Press, Cairo, 1956).

[6]Such are the *Evanglium Mariae,* ed. W. Till, in *Texte u. Unters.* 60 (1955), pp. 62-77; the *Sophia Jesu Christi, ibid.,* pp. 194-295; the *Hypostasis of the Archons.* (Labib #133-145), transl. and discussed by H. M. Schenke. in *Theolog. Literaturzeitung,* 1958, pp. 663-669; the *Untitled Coptic-Gnost. Work* on the creation, edited by A. Böhlig & P. Labib, in Dt. Akad. A. Wiss. zu Berlin, Inst. f. Orientforschung, No. 58 (Akademie-Verlag, Berlin, 1962); trsl. & discussion by H. M. Schenke, in *Theol. Lit. Zeitung,* 1959, pp. 248-256, *Apocryphon of John,* ed. W. Till in *Texte u. Unters.,* 60 (1955), pp. 78-193; *Apocryphon of James* I & II, in *Kopt.-Gnost. Apokalypsen,* herausg. A. Böhlig & P. Labib (Halle-Wittenberg, 1963); which also contains the *Acta Pauli,* also translated & discussed by W. Schneemelcher, in *Theol. Lit. Zt.,* 89 (1964), pp. 241-254.

[7]See Introduction of N. Malmaine *Evangelium Veritatis,* (1956); and in *Vigiliae Christianae,* 9 (1955), pp. 66-102, analyzing the *Apocryphon of John.*

in English. To a Latter-day Saint some of the other writings
should prove far more interesting.[8]

Along with these Coptic finds should be mentioned
some very old and valuable Christian texts in Greek, the
Bodmer Papyri. These third century papyri are the oldest
copies extant (the original dates from 175-200 AD) and
the only exemplars in the original language of an apocryphal correspondence between Paul and the Corinthians, of
which later texts in other languages have been known. They
were found in Egypt and first published in 1958 and 1959.[9]
Together with them was discovered the first *Greek* text of
the famous Odes of Solomon, which deserves our attention
as a notable link between our *Coptic* Nag Hammadi text
and the *Hebrew* Dead Sea Scrolls. The Odes and Psalms
of Solomon were first discovered in 1906 on the site of
an ancient Christian community on the Tigris. They were
written in Syriac, and now in Bodmer Papyrus No. XI we
have the eleventh of these Odes in Greek on paper at least
three centuries older than our Syriac texts. The *Psalms* of
Solomon, written between 80 and 40 BC, are, of course,

------

[8]Note 6 above for original texts. For translations, R. M. Wilson, *The
Gospel of Philip* (New York: Harper and Row, 1962); M. Malinine, et al.,
Evangelium Veritatis (Zürich: Rascher, 1956): There is a German translation
by H.-M. Schenke of a newly discovered Coptic writing "On the Creation" in
Theologische Literaturzeitung, 1959, No. 4, pp. 245-256, and another (with
original text in A. Böhlig u. P. Labib (eds.), *Die Koptisch-Gnostische Schrift
ohne Titel aus Codex II von Nag Hammadi* (Berlin: Akad. Verlag, 1962).
There is a German translation of the important "Hypostasis of the Archons"
in the *Theol Literaturzeitung*, 1958, No. 10, pp. 661-671. Walter Till translates
the extremely important "Apocryphon of John" in *Texte und Untersuchungen*,
60 (1955), pp. 79-193, and the "Sophia of Jesus Christ," *ibid.*, pp. 195-293;
and "The Gospel of Mary," *ibid.*, pp. 63-77. The 1st and 2nd "Books of Jeu"
and the so-called "Second Coptic-Gnostic Work" are translated by C. Schmidt,
in *Texte und Untersuchungen*, 8 (1892). "The Apocalypse of Adam," "The
Apocalypse of Paul", and two "Apocalypses of James" are given in A. Böhlig
& P. Labib, eds., *Koptisch-Gnostische Apokalypsen aus Codex V von Nag
Hammadi* (Halle-Wittenberg: Wissensch. Ztschr. der Martin-Luther Univ.,
1963), Sonderband. There is an English translation of "The Apocalypse of
Elias" by H. P. Houghton in *Aegyptus*, 1960, pp. 179-210, and English, French
and German translations of "The Gospel of Truth" in M. Malinine et al.,
Evangelium Veritatis (Zürich: Rascher Verlag, 1956). M. Krause & P. Labib,
Die Drei Versionen des Apokryphon des Johannes (Wiesbaden: O. Harraso-
witz, 1962).

[9]M. Testuz (ed.) *Papyrus Bodmer X-XII* (Cologne-Geneve: Bibliotheca
Bodmeriana. 1959).

Jewish, while the usual debate has taken place over the Odes (100-150 AD), which Harris believed were written by one who "while not a Jew, was a member of a community of Christians, who were for the most part of Jewish extraction" and probably lived originally at Pella as Judaeo-Christian refugees from the fall of Jerusalem.[10] This, before the Dead Sea Scrolls were known, brought the Odes and Psalms right into their orbit, and the discussions of the Odes of Solomon of fifty years ago with their talk of the Roman invaders, Jewish sectaries, and flight into the desert read just like the Scrolls discussions of the past decade.

Some scholars long insisted that the Odes and the Psalms were a single composition, while others claimed the former Christian and the latter Jewish, and Harnack insisted that they were both Jewish, though with interpolations that were very close to the Johannine writings.[11] This is interesting, because one of the first things noted about the Dead Sea Scrolls was how close they were to John. Battifol saw a particularly close tie-in between the Odes and a Coptic work called the *Pistis Sophia*, the first part of which "tells how Jesus spent twelve years after the resurrection teaching his disciples the mysteries of the heavenly 'places.' "[12] This in turn is equally close to the newly found Psalms of Thomas (a Syriac work not to be confused with the Gospel of Thomas), which contains a very old didactic hymn on the pre-existence known as The Pearl.[13] The discovery came with a distinct jolt, that one of the Psalms of Solomon, which had been completely brushed aside in preference for the Odes because of their small literary

---

[10]J. R. Harris, *The Odes and Psalms of Solomon* (Cambridge University, 1909), pp. 87, 55. The Psalms were known before the Odes and were published by O. V. Gebhardt in *Texte und Untersuchungen*, XIII (1895), Heft 2.

[11]P. Batiffol, in *Revue Biblique*, N. S. 8 (1911), pp. 22-28, discussing various theories. W. Bauer, in *Kleine Texte*, No. 64 (1933), holds that the Odes are very close to Ignatius of Antioch and come from the end of the first century.

[12]G. Homer, *Pistis Sophia* (London: SPCK, 1924), pp. xv-xvi. For the text and a discussion of it, see C. Schmidt, *Pistis Sophia* (Hauniae, 1925).

[13]A. Adam, *Die Psalmen des Thomas und das Perlenlied* . . . Beiheft 24 (1959) of *Zeitschrift für die Neutestamentliche Wissenschaft*.

worth, contained what seemed to be a direct reference to
the Qumran community that produced the Scrolls.[14] And
so, far to the east in an old Christian community on the
Tigris were discovered a collection of Syriac writings which
actually belong in the same cover with the Dead Sea Scrolls
of the Judaean desert and the Nag Hammadi Library of
Egypt.

The Sayings of Jesus

The most sensational aspect of the newly found Coptic
papyri is the presence in them of the many statements
attributed to Jesus himself and not found in the Bible. Just
as the detection of dimly recalled and vaguely familiar
themes and phrases in the new Jewish and Christian texts
sent students back to search through long-neglected
apocryphal writings, so the present findings of many sayings of Jesus come as a reminder that many such sayings
have been lying around for many years now, almost completely ignored.[15] Now we must recognize the distinct
possibility that some if not many of these sayings may be
genuine, and in that case of the greatest importance. These
have long been known as the *Logia* (Sayings) or *Agrapha*
(Unwritten Things) of Jesus. They are found (a) in the
New Testament itself, (b) in variant readings of the New
Testament, (c) in many of the church writers down to St.
Augustine, and (d) today in the sands of Egypt.[16] As an
example of the second type, M. R. James gives the following additions to Mark 16:3, found in some early texts: "In
the third hour of the day there came darkness throughout
all the globe of the earth, and angels came down from the

---

[14]This was *Psalm 17* (or *Ode 60* [59]).
    [15]H. Köster, in *Zeitschrift für die Neutestamentliche Wissenschaft*, 48
(1957), p. 221. Collections of Agrapha may be found in *Patrologia Orientalia*,
IV, 151-182; XIII, 335-431; XIX, 531-624; J. H. Ropes, in *Texte und Untersuchungen*, No. IXV (1896), Heft 2 (154 Sayings of Jesus); also in *Kleine
Texte*, No. 11; A. Resch, *Agrapha*, in *Texte und Untersuchungen*, N. F. 15
(1906), Heft 3/4 (426 pages. Twelve medieval "Letters from Heaven" are
supposed to contain words of Jesus, F. Stegmüller, *Repertorium*, I, No. 148.
    [16]*Expository Times*, 69 (1958), p. 97; Köster, *op. cit.*, p. 223.

heavens. . . ."[17] Here is an interesting commentary on
the great darkness of the Book of Mormon, as well as
significant evidence (whether we accept it as scripture
or not) that the early Christians were quite aware that
the earth is round. It will be recalled that Origen's argument for the roundness of the earth was that the first
Christians taught that God had covenant people on the
other side of the world—the Antichthonians.[18]

The *Logia* or Sayings of Jesus as found in the early
Fathers have suffered unmerited neglect through the years,
the result of the thesis that our present Bible contains all
there is to know. ("A Bible! A Bible! we have got a Bible,
and there cannot be any more Bible." 2 Nephi 29:3.) It is
unmerited because all the words of Jesus in the Bible can
be read *in half an hour,* though Jesus' actual sermons often
lasted for many hours: What good Christian would be such
a fool as to walk out on the Lord while he was speaking?
It is also unwarranted because the purported words of
Jesus are found in the church writers of the early period.
If such men insist on quoting sayings which they actually
believe were uttered by the Master, what greater folly can
there be than refusing to give them serious attention? Yet
it was not until another great papyrus find in Egypt at the
turn of the century that serious attention was given to the
Agrapha.

The collection was the Oxyrhynchus, found in 1885,
125 miles south of Cairo and eighteen miles west of the
Nile, and includes among eighteen published volumes of
papyri the Behnesa Papyrus known as the "Sayings of Our
Lord."[19] Ten of these sayings have been treated with particular respect because they are also quoted by Origen,
the first and greatest of Christian theologians.[20] And now
from the sands of Nag Hammadi, still farther up the Nile,

---

[17]M. R. James, *Apocryphal New Testament* (1925 ed.), p. 33.
[18]Origen, *Peri Archon,* II, iii, 6, in *Patrologia Graeca* 11:194.
[19]Grenfell and A. S. Hunt, *Sayings of Our Lord* (London, 1897). See the
discussion by P. Batiffol, in *Revue Biblique,* N. S. 6 (1909), pp. 501-515.
[20]L. E. Wright, in *Journal of Biblical Literature,* 65 (1946), pp. 175ff.

comes another library with more Sayings of Jesus, most
but not all of them, being found in the Gospel of Thomas,
among the 114 *Logia* of which are found one-fifth of the
Oxyrhynchus sayings.[21] In 1896 Alfred Resch regarded
thirty-six of the more than two hundred Sayings of Jesus
which he had collected as genuine.[22] Today, viewing the
recently enlarged collection, scholars are prone to accept
at least ten of the Sayings as authentic, and another ten
as very probably so.[23] On what grounds do they judge?
On external grounds, answering the question, "Is the saying
quoted in an early and reliable source?" and on internal
grounds, asking "Is it broadly consonant in style and content with the mind of Jesus as we know it from the
canonical gospels?"[24]

It is the second point, of course, which has been the
franchise of theologians and scholars from the beginning,
since it amounts to asking simply, "Is this what *I* think
Jesus would have said?" The question has become rather
a hollow one, however, since the whole message of the
new discoveries is that there are many things that no scholar
left to himself would have thought possible. We must be
prepared for surprises and guard against the natural tendency to make every new text say what we think it should.
If external evidence shows that a saying like Logion No. 2
in the Gospel of Thomas, attributed to Jesus in the ancient
papyri from Oxyrhynchus and Nag Hammadi, also turns
up in the writings of Origen, Clement of Alexandria, and
the lost Gospel of the Hebrews, the scholar who will put it
aside because it does not represent *his* idea of what Jesus
would say is being very bold indeed.[25]

---

[21]R. Roques, in *Revue de l'Histoire des Religions*, 157 (1960), p. 195,
and G. Garitte, in *Museon*, 73 (1960), pp. 151-172.

[22]H. Koster, *op. cit.*, p. 221.

[23]*Loc. cit.*, and *Expository Times*, 69 (1958), pp. 97-99. J. H. Ropes,
J. Jeremias, and W. Kümmel all disagree, but not widely.

[24]*Expository Times*, 69 (1958), p. 97.

[25]R. Roques, *op. cit.*, p. 197.

The Gnostic Merry-go-round

The hitherto despised and outcast sectaries of the deserts now stand at the door and knock for admission into the company of the orthodox. At the same time the back-door by which fastidious scholars have in the past been able to avoid associating with such disreputable people is being effectively blocked as a way of escape. That door was the easy dodge of designating as *Gnostic* anything Jewish or Christian that one didn't happen to like.

Of the Jewish Apocrypha, Gaster writes: "Almost every sect which did not conform strictly to the tenets of the orthodox church of the first centuries, which used mystic or allegorical terms and evolved an independent system of cosmology, eschatology and soteriology was indiscriminately described as Gnostic."[26] "Nothing is easier," writes R. M. Wilson, "than to draw up a schematic outline of belief, be it orthodox, Gnostic or Jewish-Christian, and apply it to the texts. . . ."[27] The trouble is that there is no agreement on what is meant by the term "Gnostic," as F. C. Baur noted over a hundred years ago.[28] Discussions of Gnosticism still remain futile "as long as 'gnosticism' is not a clearly defined concept having certain definite sources. . . . Without a critical historical method it is impossible to advance further."[29]

We are now told that "to the Jew . . . Christianity must have appeared an eccentrically Gentile Gnosis, while to the Gentile it must have seemed an eccentrically Jewish one."[30] Whatever we find eccentric, we simply call Gnostic. This is a modern practice, however: ". . . this term describes not an ancient but a modern historical category and its fluctu-

---

[26]M. Gaster, in *Studies*, I, 369.
[27]R. M. Wilson, *The Gospel of Philip*, p. 15.
[28]F. C. Baur, *Die Christliche Gnosis oder die Christliche Religions-Philosophie* (Tübingen, 1835), p. 10.
[29]J. Munck, in *Studia Theologica*, 15 (1961), p. 195.
[30]R. P. Casey, in H. Davies and D. Daube (eds.), *Eschatological Background of the New Testament*, p. 56.

ating use has often confused issues."[31] It was not in fact until the eighteenth century that "Gnostic" became a term of censure.[32] The present discussions of Gnosticism are simply a "sham battle," Schoeps notes, "since everyone obviously understands something different by 'Gnosis.'"[33]

To the Patristic writers and to the church historians of a century ago, the Gnosis was simply the invasion of Christian theology by Greek philosophy.[34] However, long ago Mosheim noted the strongly Oriental flavor of the Gnostic teachings, and accordingly it was viewed by many as an Oriental intrusion.[35] But since both Greek and Oriental elements were apparent, and since both had notably fused in the Hellenistic world, a general consensus soon considered Gnosticism as a syncretism or synthesis of the two elements, usually thought to have taken place in Egypt.[36] Today the theory is being put forth that the Gnosis came from the bosom of heterodox Judaism where it arose independently though, of course, subject to some influence of Hellenistic and Oriental religious thought. Some even see in the Dead Sea Scrolls the first Gnostic writings![37] So here we go again with our usual overlapping and confusion: "Gnosticism," writes Van Unnik, is "a many-headed hydra . . . the sheer number of speculations and the bizarre patterns which they usually assume are enough

---

[31]*Ibid.*, p. 76. W. R. Schoedel entitles his study, "The Rediscovery of the Gnosis," in *Interpretation*, 16 (1962), pp. 387-401.

[32]M. Bouyer, in *Journal of Theological Studies*, N.S. 4 (1953), pp. 188-203.

[33]H. J. Schoeps, *Urgemeinde, Judentum, Gnosis*, p. 30.

[34]So. J. Matter, *Histoire Critique du Gnosticisme* (Paris, 1828), I, 45; R. A. Lepsius, *Der Gnosticismus* . . . (Leipzig, 1896), pp. 20, 22f., 25, E. Buonaiuti, *Lo Gnosticismo* (Rome, 1907), p. 11. On the Church Fathers, H. Leisegang, *Die Gnosis* (1924), p. 3.

[35]F. C. Baur, *op. cit.*, pp. 3ff. (on Mosheim). The Oriental theory is held by C. W. King, *The Gnostics and their Remains* (London, 1887), p. 3; W. Bousset, *Hauptprobleme der Gnosis* (Göttingen, 1907), p. 5; A. Altmann, in *Essays in Honor of J. H. Hertz* (I. Epstein *et al.* eds. London: Goldston, 1942), p. 19; G. Widengren, in *Zeitschrift für Religion und Geistesgeschichte*, 4 (1952), pp. 97-115.

[36]R. Reitzenstein, *Poimandres* (Leipzig, 1904); H. Leisegang, *op. cit.*, p. 5; H. J. Schoeps, *op. cit.*, pp. 31-34; F. Lexa, in *Egyptian Religion*, 1 (1933), pp. 106-116, even traces Gnostic teachings back to archaic Egypt.

[37]So Schubert, cited by Schoeps, *op. cit.*, p. 31.

to make anyone feel dizzy!"[38] There was much talk recently of a pre-Christian Gnosis which "goes back to heterodox Jewish conception . . . and to pre-Asiatic syncretism in general. In its origins Gnosis [this theory held] is Jewish-Near Eastern occultism, Oriental mysticism."[39] That covers a lot of ground, but it is only the beginning. For Cullmann the Clementine writings to which we have so often referred "attach themselves" to a "particular current of *gnostic* Judaism," best illustrated by the Dead Sea Scrolls, "a sort of Jewish gnosticism . . . which one can consider as the cradle of Christianity."[40]

So here we have early Christianity and the Jewish sectaries all mixed up in a common Gnostic milieu. For H. J. Schoeps this is sheer nonsense: "Gnosis was never anything but pagan Gnosis," he insists, the pseudo-Clementine writings being actually a vigorous assault *against* Gnosticism.[41] Some find the Odes of Solomon a Gnostic work closely related to the Pistis Sophia and to an "unofficial Judaism" which Batiffol designates as Gnostic, though noting that the Christology of the Odes is "entirely independent of any Gnostic speculation";[42] others say they are Gnostic in a peculiarly Christian sense,[43] and Klijn now concludes that they are "a genuine Christian work."[44] If they are Gnostic, R. Harris decided, "we can only say, 'Would God all the Lord's people were Gnostics.' "[45]

From the moment they became known, the Nag Hammadi texts were advertised as Gnostic writings, but right away the usual questions arose. Puech and Quispel, for example, after careful study conclude that the new Apoc-

---

[38]Van Unnik, *op. cit.*, p. 22.
[39]G. Quispel, *The Jung Codex*, pp. 76f.
[40]O. Cullmann, in *New Testament Studies*, 5 (1959), p. 166.
[41]Schoeps, *op. cit.*, pp. 39f., 61f.
[42]P. Batiffol, in *Revue Biblique*, N.S. 8 (1911), pp. 39f., 177.
[43]R. Abramowski, in *Zeitschrift für die Neutestamentliche Wissenschaft*, 35 (1936), pp. 44-46: "It is 'Christian-Gnostic,' but not the Gnosticism of mythological speculation."
[44]A. F. J. Klijn, *The Acts of Thomas* (Leiden: Brill, 1962), p. 47.
[45]R. Harris, *Odes and Psalms of Solomon*, pp. 12-16, 20.

ryphon of James "is perhaps Gnostic and probably Valen-
tinian,"[46] while Van Unnick declares that it "originated from
a small village-church not yet affected by gnosticism, between 125-150. . . ."[47] Most scholars believe the Epistle of
the Apostles is orthodox, but G. Bardy believes it is Gnostic.[48] The Gnostic Gospel of Thomas exhibits much that
deviates from Gnosticism, much that comes closer to the
doctrines of the "great Church";[49] how shall we classify it?

If we attempt to classify a document by its teachings
we run into a hopeless situation for half the Gnostic teachings—the pre-existent plan, this world as a place of probation, eternal progression, the spiritual creation, the withholding of certain teachings from the world, the divine
parentage of man, the pre-existent glory of Adam, etc.—
were held by the Primitive Church,[50] and the other half—
the unknowable and ineffable nature of God, the free use
of allegory in interpreting scripture, the appeal of philosophy as a theological foundation, the antithesis of matter
which is evil and spirit which is good, the search for God
in the mystic way, etc.[51]—were adopted by the later church,
so that there are no strictly peculiar Gnostic doctrines to
set Gnosticism apart from orthodox Christian views. For
some, the very essence of Gnosticism was belief in direct
revelation; for others, it was denial of direct revelation.[52]

How can one talk about a Gnostic religion? Irenaeus
says that no two or three Gnostics believed the same.[53]

---

[46]In *Vigiliae Christianae*, 8 (1954), p. 22.
[47]Van Unnik, *op. cit.*, p. 87.
[48]Peuch and Quispel, in *Vigiliae Christianae*, 8 (1954), p. 9.
[49]Van Unnik, *op. cit.*, p. 57.
[50]For a general discussion, see R. M. Grant, *The Secret Sayings of Jesus*
(New York: Doubleday, 1960).
[51]For the basic Gnostic teachings, see G. Quispel, in J. H. Waszink *et al.*,
Het Oudste Christendom (Haarlem: H. D. Tjeenk, 1951), I, 156ff., 162-5.
[52]". . . the knowledge professed by the Gnostic teachers . . . was a
knowledge designed to subordinate the revelation of Christ to the speculations
of human philosophy," H. L. Mansel, *The Gnostic Heresies of the First and
Second Centuries* (London, 1875), p. 8. The opposite view is taken by A.
Harnack, *Dogmengeschichte*, I, 254, and a middle ground by W. Volker, *Der
wahre Gnostiker nach Clemens Alexandrinus* (Berlin, 1952), pp. 365ff., 281.
[53]Irenaeus, *Contra haereses*, I, 11, 1.

"Gnosis," Bultmann concludes, "is the expression of various mythological and philosophical traditions and therefore may be characterized as a syncretistic phenomenon."[54] With their doctrines and practices coming from a dozen different sources, was there anything that all the Gnostics had in common? Some scholars have insisted that Gnosticism was actually a single religion, "a world-religion *sui generis,* which not only influences Neoplatonism and Christianity, but actually competed with them for supremacy."[55] It was, we are told, "a vast independent movement, an authentic mystery-religion whose roots reach back into the religious soil of the Hellenized Orient, its main doctrinal sources being the Greek Pseudo-Zoroaster and Hermes Trismegistus."[56] But others ask, who were the founders and leaders, the saints of this Pre-Christian Gnostic church? Who were its members aside from Christian and Jewish eccentrics? Where were its headquarters? Why do no contemporary writers seem aware of it? Why do we have "no clear documentary evidence for anything resembling a Gnosis prior to the Christian era?"[57]

The oldest use of the word "Gnosis" would seem to be by the Mandaeans, for *Manda* means Gnosis. These people were also called Dositheans, a Samaritan word that goes back possibly to the exile of 721 B.C.[58] Theirs is hailed as the purest and oldest system of Gnosticism, yet the Dositheans were the first and strongest *anti*-Gnostics, according to some, and they took their rise "on the soil of Palestine" and were "intimately connected with the movement whose

---

[54]R. Bultmann, *Das Urchristentum im Rahmen der antiken Religionen* (Zürich, 1949), p. 181.
    [55]G. Quispel, in *Het Oudste Christendom,* I, 152.
    [56]J. Doresse, in *Bulletin de l'Institut Egyptologique,* 31, p. 409; J. P. Steffes, *Das Wesen des Gnosticismus* (Paderborn, 1922), Ch. I (pp. 34-45); H. Gunkel, *Zum religionsgeschichtlichen Verständnis des Neuen Testaments* (Göttingen, 1903), p. 36.
    [57]R. M. Wilson, *The Gospel of Philip,* p. 16, and in *Vigiliae Christianae,* 9, p. 211.
    [58]A. Adam, in *Zeitschrift für die Neutestamentliche Wissenschaft,* Beiheft 24, p. 77.

outstanding protagonist was John the Baptist. . . ."[59] We
have noted elsewhere that these people are also thought
to have been the descendants of that Jonadab ben Rechab
who fled from Jerusalem in the days of Lehi, and for the
same reason Lehi did—to escape the machinations of the
wicked "Jews at Jerusalem" and to live the law in its purity
in the desert.[60]

Amidst all this confusion the reader may begin to
suspect that we have run into something akin to the peculiar fusion of Christian and Jewish elements in the Book of
Mormon.

The Real Gnosis

Every scholar has his own solution of the Gnostic
equations, but not one of them has succeeded in the eyes
of his fellows in balancing his equation. One factor in particular is consistently ignored, and that is the clear and
repeated pronouncement of all the earliest church writers
on the subject, that *there was a true Gnosis*. The word
"Gnosis" occurs twenty-seven times in the New Testament
and always refers to knowledge that comes by revelation.[61]
The oldest Christian definition of the Gnosis (and one consistently ignored by students of Gnosticism) is that it was
that knowledge the Lord imparted secretly to Peter,
James, and John after the Resurrection, and which they in
turn transmitted to the others of the Twelve and to the
Seventy.[62] There is no record of its having gone any
farther. Irenaeus, who calls this "the true Gnosis," insists
that it was handed down by the apostles to the bishops
and hence to the churchmen of his own day.[63]

But earlier and better informed writers tell another
story: ". . . when the holy chorus of the apostles had ended

---

[59]M. Black, *The Scrolls and Christian Origins*, p. 63.
[60]*An Approach to the Book of Mormon*, pp. 127f.
[61]H. Nibley, *The World and the Prophets* (Salt Lake City: Deseret Book
Co.), pp. 58f.
[62]Eusebius, *Church History*, II, 1, 3-4.
[63]Irenaeus. *Contra haereses*. IV. 33. 8. in *Patrologia Graeca*. 7:1077.

their lives in various ways, and that generation passed away of those who had heard the divine wisdom with their own ears, at that moment the conspiracy of godless error took its rise through the deception of false teachers, who, as soon as the last apostle had departed, first came out openly and henceforward undertook to match the teaching of the truth with what they *falsely* styled *Gnosis.*"[64] Overnight the church swarmed with the pretenders who claimed to have the knowledge that the Lord had given the apostles in private; they sprang up like mushrooms, and before long most of the people were following them.[65] The early writers are always careful to specify that they were the "false Gnostics," "Gnostics-so-called," "self-styled Gnostics," and thereby preserve a careful distinction between the false and the true Gnosis.[66] Each of the swarming imposters did everything he could to make the world believe that his and his alone was the true, ancient, and sole surviving heir of the original church and that he alone possessed the secret knowledge imparted to the apostles after the resurrection; and the smashing success that greeted many of them is a plain indication of how hungry the Christian world was for that very knowledge.

Some today suggest that Gnosticism was really a state of mind and accept W. Köhler's definition of it as "an impersonal religious mass movement."[67] It was a general groping for something everybody felt the church *should* have but obviously no longer did have; Gnosticism was before all else a vacuum phenomenon. The Gnosis rushed in to fill an empty space which did not exist as long as the

[64]Eusebius, *Church History,* III, 32, 7-8.
[65]H. Nibley, in *Church History,* 30 (1961), pp. 10-11.
[66]Eusebius, *loc. cit.;* Epiphanius says they called *themselves* Gnostics, in *Patrologia Graeca,* 41:329. They are false prophets, false apostles, and false teachers, according to *Clementine Recognitions,* IV, 35, in *Patrologia Graeca,* 1:1330. Eusebius begins his history by announcing his intention of refuting "the bearers of what they falsely called the Gnosis," (*Church History,* I, 1, 1). "They want to be called Gnostics, but they are not really Gnostics," writes Epiphanius, in *Patrologia Graeca,* 41:1012.
[67]Discussed by H. J. Schoeps, *op. cit.,* pp. 34f.

apostles were still alive; it "recognized a real mental want";[68] the Christian Gnostics felt that their teaching "supplied that which was lacking to complete the great synthesis to which religious thought was tending."[69] Hadn't Christ and the apostles supplied that? Exactly, *after* the resurrection, and that was the knowledge that people were missing—the Gnosis, "something extra which remained a secret for the uninitiated. . . ."[70]

The trouble with the Gnostics-so-called is not that they claimed to possess the wonderful post-resurrection revelations but that they did *not* possess them—they were only faking or wishfully thinking; they didn't have the Gnosis at all, and when the time came to deliver the goods, as it soon did, since they all challenged each other's exclusive claims, they were caught empty-handed—they *had* to come up with something: hence the feverish and irresponsible borrowing of any odds and ends of Oriental lore they could lay their hands on; hence the solemn and impressive appeal to philosophy—especially the recondite and mysterious gospel of Neo-Platonism—hence the willingness to make full use of genuine or spurious holy writings or even to forge new ones outright. What has made the study of Gnosticism so infinitely complex and hopelessly confusing is the willingness of the Gnostics in their need to throw anything into the hopper.

It was easy to demonstrate the folly of the Gnostic claims, but what had anybody else to put in their place? Nothing. Gnosticism "was defeated only at the price of substantial concessions still plainly visible in the structure of Christian theology."[71] "The main church had no choice," wrote C. Schmidt, "but to follow along the same path."[72] "In Catholicism," says Harnack, "Gnosticism won half a

[68]P. Neander, *Antignostikus* (Berlin, 1825), Introduction.
[69]C. H. Dodd, *The Bible and the Greeks* (London, 1935), p. 248.
[70]Van Unnik, *Newly Discovered Gnostic Writings*, p. 43.
[71]J. Morris, in *Past and Present*, 3 (1953), p. 9.
[72]C. Schmidt, *Gespräche Jesu mit seinen Jüngern*, p. 204.

victory."[73] In fact Harnack believed that the Gnostics were simply "the Christian theologians of the first centuries of the church," the only real difference between them and the later doctors being that they thrust on the church abruptly a theology which the latter accepted only gradually.[74] In the early period, "it is dangerous," we are warned, "to treat the Gnostics, the Apologists and others as distinct and separate groups," and since "the Gnostics remained fairly close to the 'orthodox' Church down to about 180 . . . it is indeed an open question how far we can really make use of such terms as 'orthodox' and 'heretical' at this stage."[75]

Quispel has shown how the great Neo-Platonic, Gnostic, and "Orthodox" teachers were all "educated in the same intellectual milieu, were all born in Egypt, all attended the same university at Alexandria where all became imbued with the same eclectic Platonism," and he asks us, "What could the term 'heretic' have meant at so early a time?"[76] We must bear in mind that "hitherto, the history of Christian Gnosticism has been written by its enemies," and in view of the new findings it would now appear that "Valentinianism (the most representative form of Gnosticism) was more 'Christian' than most of its adversaries would like us to think."[77] A common charge against the Gnostics is that they claimed to know the answers to the great questions of life, but what religion does not? After all, these are the questions "which perpetually excite mankind."[78] There is not a Gnostic teaching that some Gnostic did not reject or some orthodox Christian did not accept.

But what do we mean by "orthodox" Christians? If we knew that, we would have no trouble identifying heretics and Gnostics simply as those who disagreed with the "Main Church." But "Main Church" is strictly a modern term, in-

---

[73]A. Harnack, *Dogmengeschichte*, I, 250 (1931 ed.).
[74]*Ibid.*, I, 246, 250f.
[75]R. M. Wilson, *op. cit.*, p. 4.
[76]In *Het Oudste Christendom*, I, 152f.
[77]Van Unnik, *op. cit.*
[78]Van Unnik, *op. cit.*, p. 23.

vented to describe something for which the ancients had no
word and of which accordingly they had no concept. The
distinction was made only after the business had been
settled—not by a formal council or decree, but imperceptibly in a long series of compromises. Until then the
Christian church during the great crisis was like the Jewish
church, a swarm of sects, each claiming to be the one
original but none able to prove its case.[79] But when a
winner emerged—that party which got the sympathy and
armed might of the emperor on its side—the winning party
got to work and completely obliterated every trace of its
former rivals: "The beaten ones were not only covered
with green sod," as Schoeps puts it, "but with a great
silence as well," so that their rediscovery in our time has
come as the greatest surprise.[80]

But why are well-known orthodox Christian works
including the writings of John and Paul, the Odes of Solomon, and the Clementine Recognitions so full of Gnostic
expressions? Not because they are Gnostic, as has been
commonly assumed, Schoeps points out, but precisely
because they are fighting the Gnostics, to do which most
effectively they must employ the familiar jargon of the
Gnostics themselves.[81] And just as the anti-Gnostic writers
are thus an authentic guide to Gnosticism, so the teachings
and practices of the false Gnostics are a reliable guide to
the nature of the *true* Gnosis which they were counterfeit-
ing. If "Simon Magus (the arch-Gnostic) promised a baptism to eternal life,"[82] it does not follow that there was no
genuine ancient Christian baptism or that the Gnostics
invented the idea of baptism which is thus a later interpolation in the source; if the Marcosians faked a sacrament
with chemicals that made water seem to turn to blood, it
does not follow that there was no early Christian sacrament

---

[79]Schoeps, *op. cit.*, pp. 35f., 44f.; H. Nibley, in *Church History*, 30
(1961), pp. 10f.
[80]Schoeps, *op. cit.*, pp. 44f.
[81]*Ibid.*, p. 41.
[82]Eusebius, *Church History*, III, 26, 2.

but only a borrowing from the Gnostics; if the Valentinians had a parody of prophetic inspiration stimulated by the taking of drugs and potions or if they staged their own quaint version of celestial marriage, it does not follow that prophecy and marriage ordinances did not exist in the early church.[83] The peculiarly pernicious thing about the pretenders, as Irenaeus pointed out, was that they mixed everything up, "making convincing noises . . . taking liberties with the logia of the Lord, having become bad interpreters of the good and correct word . . . persuading many that they have the Gnosis. . . . They argue very convincingly . . . making truth and falsehood indistinguishable . . . making whatever they say seem truer than truth itself. . . ."[84] It is no wonder that men have remained hopelessly confused about the Gnostic ever since—confusion was their business.

To return to our newly found texts, Christian and Jewish, one of the odd things about them was that while they were often labeled Gnostic because of the Gnostic ideas and expressions in them, their teachings were overwhelmingly *anti*-Gnostic—indeed the most important of them were manifestly written as anti-Gnostic tracts.[85] We have seen the way in which that fact actually explains the presence in them of many Gnostic expressions. The Dositheans, often called the first Gnostics, taught extreme millennialism, resurrection of the flesh, baptism, and scriptural literalism—all teachings detested by the real Gnostics! We are told that the Gnostics "threw the whole eschatological complex of ideas overboard,"[86] yet all the writings we have been talking about were thoroughly eschatological; how can one call them Gnostic? The Odes of Solomon are "as Gnostic as the New Testament, no more and no less,"

---

[83]For these points, H. Nibley, in *Vigiliae Christianae*, 20:11f, n. 61.
[84]Irenaeus, *Contra haereses*, Preface, 1-2, 1; cf. Eusebius, *Church History*, IV, 7.
[85]C. Schmidt, *op. cit.*, pp. 169, 202, 204, 229, 374.
[86]*Ibid.*, p. 336.

writes Harris.[87]   Again, "the Gnostic heretics used the
Gospel of Thomas," but that does not mean that they wrote
it, R. E. Taylor observes.[88]   If Paul and John seem to talk
like later Gnostics it is not because they adopted Gnostic
ideas but the other way around; their words were twisted
to Gnostic ends because ". . . second century Gnosticism
. . . is the product of a defective exegesis of the New Testament."[89]   The Apocryphon of James can easily be given a
Gnostic interpretation, Van Unnik reminds us, but then so
can the Bible.[90]

It is H. J. Schoeps's final explanation of the Gnostic
anomalies that brings this reader back to the Book of
Mormon almost with a jolt.   When the false Gnostics
started making their claims, the only people who stood up
to them, according to Schoeps, were the Ebionites, "the
descendants of the original Church of Jesus," whose coun-
terblast is still preserved in the pages of the Clementine
Recognitions.[91]   This work is full of Gnostic jargon but
employed strictly to discredit the Gnostic so-called.   Actually, all the main points of Ebionite theology correspond
to the teachings of the Dead Sea Scrolls.[92]   Why should
Christians appeal to such a source?   They didn't; it just
happened that those teachings were the same as theirs,
though of course that was no accident. Now, the doctrines
embraced loosely under the general title of Essene go right
back, according to Schoeps, to the Rechabites, of the time
of Lehi. "Again and again new groups had gone out into
the desert to realize the chassidut"—the true way of life
of the covenant people, their ideas meeting us in the Enoch

---

[87]R. Harris, *Odes of Solomon,* p. 13.

[88]R. E. Taylor, in *Christianity Today,* 4 (1960), p. 3; Van Unnik, *op. cit.,*
p. 42, notes that the Gnostics often "dragged in" non-Gnostic material "to
support their interpertation"; henceforth it would be easy to suspect such
material of being Gnostic, because of its suspicious associations.

[89]R. M. Wilson, *op. cit.,* p. 16.

[90]Van Unnik, in *Vigiliae Christianae,* 10 (1956), p. 152.

[91]Schoeps, *op. cit.,* pp. 41-43, 61.

[92]*Ibid.,* pp. 77-85.

literature, Jubilees, and the Twelve Patriarchs.[93] It was by the "immigration of dissenting Jewish groups" from time to time that the societies which went back to the days of the nomadic Rechabites "were constantly renewed and regenerated."[94] Lehi's party was just such a group of dissenters, about the time of Jonadab ben Rechab, seeking a permanent settlement away from Jerusalem—at that time they never dreamed of sailing the seas. (1 Nephi 17).

One Big Book

We have often noted in the foregoing survey how very frequently the documents of one time and place will overlap in their ideas and expressions with those of other times and places. Herein we have an excellent means of testing the Book of Mormon. The sectaries of the desert were exceedingly conservative in their ways and tenacious in preserving the customs and teachings of their fathers. Lehi's was not the earliest offshoot, and since older communities than his have handed down writings through the long centuries which still reveal obvious affinities with the scriptures of later communities, we have every right to expect the Book of Mormon to have a lot in common with the whole body of writings.

The newly-found libraries seem to reach out and establish connections in every direction, from the Nile to the Tigris, and from the days of Adam to the Middle Ages. "The Qumran covenanters," writes Bruce, "bound themselves by a new covenant, but it was not so new as they thought; it was . . . a reaffirmation of the old covenant of Moses's day."[95] But no one knew that better than the covenanters themselves, the opening lines of whose *Manual of Discipline* declare the object of the society to be the carrying out of all "that has been commanded by the hand of Moses and by the hand of all His servants the prophets."

---

[93]*Ibid.*, p. 85. Cf. 80-84.
[94]*Ibid.*, p. 85. Cf. 80-84.
[95]Bruce, *Second Thoughts*, p. 147.

They were quite aware of the need to preserve intact the ways that went clear back to Moses. The Nag Hammadi books are just as insistent in tracing all their teachings and ordinances back to the ancients, even back to Adam himself.

"There is something unusual and coincidental," wrote the skeptical C. F. Potter, "almost what once was called 'providential,' in the fact that the 'Dead Sea Scrolls' . . .and the Gnostic codices . . . were both discovered in the same year."[96] Both raised the curtain on a background of the church that no living man dreamed of. It is a background of great breadth and depth, going back many centuries in time and covering vast areas of the Old World.

We have noted, for example, that the work called the Gospel of the Twelve Apostles, which was discovered in 1912 and which Origen claimed to be older than the Gospel of Luke, belongs to a group of writings reporting the Lord's teachings after the resurrection. And if we turn to the newly found Nag Hammadi texts, we find that the first one ever published (The Gospel of Thomas) begins with the words: "These are the secret teachings which the Lord who was dead and liveth (i.e., the risen Savior) spoke to Judas-Thomas. . . ."[97] Next we learn that the New Testament quotations in this work (which was written down about 140 AD) are "very similar to a collection used by the writer of I Clement."[98] But we have also noted that the Gospel of the Twelve Apostles is also very close to Clement, and H. J. Schoeps has shown that no writings are closer to the Dead Sea Scrolls than the Pseudo-Clementines![99] On top of that, Oscar Cullmann finds that this "jumbled mixture of old traditions" in the Gospel of Thomas indicates an

---

[96]C. F. Potter, *The Lost Years of Jesus* (Hyde Park: University Books, 1963), p. 148.
[97]A. Guillaumont, H.-Ch. Peuch, G. Quispel, W. Till, and Y. 'abd al Masih, *The Gospel According to Thomas* (New York: Harpers, 1959), p. 3.
[98]W. Frend, in *Antiquity*, 34 (1960), p. 263.
[99]H.-J Schoeps, *Urgemeinde, Juden-christentum, Gnosis* (Tübingen: J. C. B. Mohr, 1956), pp. 69-86.

origin in "the vicinity of Eastern Jordan where the Christian Jews settled after the fall of Jerusalem, in the year 70 AD,"[100] which takes us from the distant reaches of the Nile right into the desert communities of the Dead Sea Scrolls, where our two libraries, Jewish and Christian, seem to have a common origin.

When the scrolls were first examined, Brownlee classed as having "striking affinities" with each other, the religions of Qumran, the Covenants of Damascus, the Essenes, the Therapeutae of Egypt, and the John-the-Baptist movement, noting significantly, "to this list I would have added primitive Christianity. . . ."[101] Long ago R. H. Charles had suggested that when "a great company of the priests [became] obedient to the faith" (Acts 6:7) it was actually one of these sectarian groups joining the Church, and Brownlee specifically suggests the Qumran brethren.[102] The common motifs in sectarian Jewish and early Christian writings show "that the Essene sectaries were a fruitful field of evangelization [Christian missionary work]," according to professor Cross, "and that they in turn had influence on the formation of institutions of the apostolic and sub-apostolic church."[103]

Since the new researches have been made among the sectaries, Essenism is commonly used in a free and general sense as a sort of "over-all name or borderline concept for heterodox Judaism."[104] In the fourth century Epiphanius classed the desert sects of the Dead Sea and Jordan together as having common beliefs and practices but possibly for that very reason feuding fiercely among themselves. "The Sampsaeans or Elkesaites," he writes, "still survive in Arabia, living around and beyond the Dead

---

[100]O. Cullmann, in *Hibbert Journal*, 60 (1961), p. 121; cf. by the same writer, in *New Testament Studies*, 5 (1959), p. 166.

[101]W. Brownlee, in *The Biblical Archaeologist*, September 1960, p. 50

[102]R. H. Charles, *Apocrypha and Pseudepigrapha of the Old Testament*, II, 786.

[103]F. M. Cross, in *The Christian Century*, 72 (August 17, 1955), p. 944.

[104]H. J. Schoeps, *op. cit.*, pp. 68f.

Sea. The followers of a false prophet . . . they resemble
the Ebionites very closely in everything," the latter being
almost exactly like the Cerinthians and the Nazoraeans,
who claim to be true Israel, and also like the Gorgethoi
who are called Essenses, and who are practically the same
as the Dositheans, and so on.[105] Orthodox, Jewish-Christian, Gnostic, ". . . were these three streams so clearly distinct in the earlier stages of church history," asks R. M.
Wilson, "or should we not rather expect to find a certain
interpenetration of thought, a gradual hardening into lines
of cleaveage?"[106]

Whenever an important document of the past is discovered, students immediately begin comparing it with
every other document that might conceivably have any
connection with it. This is not necessarily wishful thinking
or "parallelomania"; it is the only way by which an unknown work can be assigned a likely place among the
records of the race. "From the most diverse scientific
areas," writes Dupont-Sommer of the Dead Sea Scrolls,
"studies are beginning to accumulate and converge ever
closer towards the solution of the comparative problem."[107]
Recently this writer called attention to a large number of
resemblances between the community of Qumran and an
ancient religious society described by certain commentators
in the Koran. Whether the parallels are significant or not
remains to be seen, but the writer was entirely within his
rights in calling attention to them.[108] It is also entirely in
order for him to point out resemblances between the Book
of Mormon and other religious writings. The most arresting
and disturbing thing about the Dead Sea writings is the
way they have of reminding the reader of everything else
he has ever read in Jewish *and* Christian sources. Here we

---

[105]Epiphanius, *Adv. Haeres,* in *Patrologia Graeca,* 41:236, 256-7, 284,
405, etc.
[106]R. M. Wilson, *op. cit.,* p. 15.
[107]A. Dupont-Sommer, *Nouveaux Aperçus sur les Manuscrits de la Mer
Morte* (Paris, 1953), p. 200.
[108]Hugh Nibley, in *Revue de Qumran,* 5 (1965), pp. 177-199.

find the oldest and purest Old Testament readings known, written by the hands of Jews living long before the time of Christ,[109] and along with them written by the same hands, many ideas and phrases which have heretofore been thought peculiar to the New Testament, including characteristic expressions of John and Paul! The same pages swarm also with things that we have long associated with the Jewish and Christian apocryphal writings, as well as teachings attributed to various ancient sectarian groups, from the pre-Christian Therapeutae of Egypt to the ninth century Karaites of Mesopotamia. And as if to atone for going so far astray, the same documents present sayings that are later to turn up in the writings of the most venerated and orthodox Fathers of the Christian Church and rabbis of the Jews! At the same time these people seem to be particularly close to the Hassidic Jews, who, unlike the rabbis, believed in continuing revelation, and displayed affinities with the medieval Catharian sects and other early forerunners of the Protestant movement, to say nothing of the Moslems.[110]

Though the overwhelming consensus of the experts is that these people were pre-Christian Jews, their teachings are so very Christian that as eminent an authority as Professor Teicher of Cambridge still maintains that they can only have been a Christian sect! It will hardly be necessary to point out to the reader that this surprising mixture of a strange kind of Judaism with a strange kind of Christianity ("the Church of Anticipation," Cross called it) is one of the things that has in the past so amused and offended the critics of the Book of Mormon.

The newly found *Logia* are particularly close to those pseudo-Clementine writings that represent the earliest postbiblical teachings of the Christian Church, and at the

---

[109]M. Greenbert in *Journal of the American Oriental Society*, 76 (1956), pp. 57-167.
[110]Most of the connections are treated below. For the Karaite affinities, see W. Wiedner, in *Jewish Quarterly Review*, 47 (1956-7), pp. 96-103.

same time they present the closest affinity to the milieu
of the Dead Sea Scrolls—that is to say, all these documents
teach the same things in the same words.[111] The Sayings
from various sources exhibit considerable variety and ample
evidence of alteration and adaptation; some are abbreviated
and some are expanded versions of the Lord's words in
the New Testament; some combine elements and episodes
that are separate and disconnected in the Bible (compare
3 Nephi!); others mix New Testament material with extra-
canonical material; while some are completely different
from anything in the gospels.[112] The *Logia* as a whole do
not follow any consistent doctrinal pattern, but seem just
thrown together, as if jotted down at different times and
places as the Lord spoke them.[113] In fact, H. Köster insists
that the important thing is not that a Logion may really
have been uttered by Jesus, but that it was accepted as
authentic by the early Saints and so leads us into the midst
of the first church, showing us what they believed and
practised.[114]

It was the heretic hunters of later ages who destroyed
the early image by suppressing every Saying which did
not agree with their concept of orthodoxy.[115] Here we see
the literal fulfilment of Nephi's prophecy that many precious things that proceeded out of the mouth of the Jew
would be taken away from the Book of the Lamb. Nephi's
peculiar and repeated expression, ". . . proceeded forth
from the mouth of a Jew; . . ." (1 Nephi 13:24) is a
clear reference to *Logia*, "utterances of the mouth," and
his statement that the apostles "bear record" of these
things in writing points to the thesis now propounded "in
the light of the recently discovered documents" that there

---

[111]On their closeness to the Clementines, G. Quispel in *Vigiliae Christianae*,
12 (1958), p. 195; O. Cullmann, in *Hibberts Journal* 60 (1961f.), p. 121;
R. Roques, *op. cit.*, pp. 202, 204.
[112]R. Roques, *op. cit.*, pp. 196, 205f.; H. Köster, *op. cit.*, pp. 226, 233;
L. Guerrier, in *Patrologia Orientalia*, IX, 148f.
[113]R. Roques, *op. cit.*, p. 206.
[114]H. Köster, *op. cit.*, pp. 221, 236-7.
[115]*Ibid.*, p. 223.

were "collections of sayings of Jesus before our canonical gospels were written" and that the Gospels were originally based on such collections.[116]

Aside from documents coming forth from old Christian and Jewish centers, we may not ignore those of more exotic origin, for the ancient Saints were driven and persecuted, and one can never tell where their footprints or writings may turn up; for example, in 1909 a Saying of Jesus ("Jesus said: Life is a bridge—do not linger on it, but hurry over it") was found inscribed in Arabic over two different gates of a palace mosque of a long-ruined Mogul city in northern India. Subsequent documentary discoveries indicate that this may well be an authentic saying of the Lord, in spite of its surprising provenance.[117]

And what shall we make of the Mandaean writings, with their ancient doctrines and ordinances that are at once Jewish and Christian?[118] Though discovered far to the east, they are viewed today as representing "perhaps a late version of the North Israelite-Samaritan tradition," a tradition older than the days of Lehi; and part of that tradition, "entirely independent of Christian influence," was the keeping of "Sunday as a holy day."[119]

---

[116]O. Cullmann, *op. cit.*, p. 121.

[117]J. Jeremias, in *Expository Times*, 69 (1957), pp. 7-9.

[118]R. Eisler, *Iesous Basileus ou Basileusas* (Heidelberg, 1930), II, 18, 21f., 356f., 699. The most important of the recently discovered Mandaean texts are E. S. Drower, *The Thousand and Twelve Questions* (Berlin: Akademische Verlag, 1960), and *The Canonical Prayerbook of the Mandaeans* (Leiden: Brill, 1959); R. Bultmann, "Die neuerschlossenen mandäischen und manichäischen Quellen," in *Ztsch. f. N.T. Wiss.*, 24 (1925), pp. 104-139; M. Lidzbarski, *Das Johannesbuch der Mandäer* (Giessen: A. Töpelmann, 1905); and *Ginza*, Important Manichaean sources in C. Schmidt (ed.) *Manichäische Handschriften der staatlichen Museen Berlin* (Stuttgart: W. Kohlhammer, 1940), Bd. I. Kephalia; C. R. C. Allberry, *A Manichaean Psalm-book*, in *Manichaean Mss. in the Chester Beatty Collection, Vol. II* (Stuttgart, 1938); H. J. Polotsky, *Manichäische Homilien*, Bd. I of *Manich. Handschriften der Sammlung A. Chester Beatty* (Stuttgart, 1934).

[119]A. Adam, in *Zeitschrift für die Neutestamentliche Wissenschaft*, Beiheft 24, p. 79.

"...but unto them it is not given"

How Things Get Lost

When Eusebius, early in the fourth century, set his hand to the work which was to earn him the title "The Father of Church History," he was appalled at the dearth of materials available to work with. He found himself, so he says, walking an untrodden path in an empty desert; the voices of the ancient church came to him, as he puts it, feebly and fitfully over a vast empty gulf.[1] A century earlier when Origen, the greatest theologian of the church, sought to present a clear and unequivocal explanation of the first principles of the gospel to his perplexed and wrangling generation, he had to confess that he could discover no authoritative statement of *any* of those principles in the literature of the church.[2]

From such sad cases it would appear that the early church either kept no records or else that they were lost. Today we know what happened: The early literature of the church was entirely lost and in its place another literature was substituted. As a result of recent discoveries, the student is now confronted with two quite distinct bodies of early Christian teaching. Just as pilgrims to the Holy Land have for many generations accepted Ommiad and Norman buildings and sixteenth century Turkish walls and

---

[1]Eusebius, *Church History*, I, 1, 3-5.
[2]Origen, *Peri Archon*, I, 2, 4, 6-10.

gates as the authentic settings of biblical history, since the
originals had long since ceased to exist, so the Christian
world as a whole has long accepted as the voice of the
original church, documents which have nothing to do with
that church, but are later substitutes for a literature that
disappeared at an early date. "The original literature,"
writes Schneemelcher, "was supplanted [*abgelöst*] by
another literature very strongly influenced by the non-
Christian environment."[3]

Why so? Because the original literature was a strange
and disturbing thing that the world could not stomach:
"Early Christian literature had no predecessors and no successors, but appears as a completely alien intrusion into
the classical tradition, an incongruous and unwelcome in-
terruption, an indigestible lump which, however, disap-
pears as suddenly as it came, leaving the schoolmen to
resume operations as if nothing had happened."[4] By the
time "classical" Christian literature of the schoolmen was
just beginning, all the forms of the original old Christian
literature, according to Overbeck, had ceased to exist.[5]
The transition took place roughly in three steps. Our
Synoptic Gospels are a product of the first of these steps.
The fact that there are three gospels instead of one and
that each of these is full of variant readings in the earliest
texts shows that we have here not the original New Testament but the results of "altering, eliminating . . . expanding"
of earlier texts.[6] Until the middle of the fourth century
other gospels, such as those of the Hebrews and Egyptians,
were accepted by the churches on an equal footing with
those writings which later became canonical; that is to say,
our synoptic gospels have behind them a still older Chris-

---

[3]W. Schneemelcher, *Neutestamentliche Apokryphen* (1959), I, 33.
[4]H. Nibley, in *Church History*, 30 (1961), p. 13, following A. Norden.
[5]F. Overbeck, *Ueber die Anfänge der patristischen Literatur* (Basel, 1954), pp. 23f.
[6]Schneemelcher, *op. cit.*, I, 14, 32f., 43, 47.

tian background literature which became lost, but today is being rediscovered.[7]

The second step away from the original Christian literature was the systematic corruption of the record by the so-called Gnostics. These people made a practice of claiming to be the unique and secret possessors of the earliest Christian writings. To make good their claims, they did not hesitate to practise forgery, and they borrowed freely from any available source. Available sources included some genuine old Christian writings along with all the other stuff, and so it happens that while the Gnostic writings are patently fraudulent, they nonetheless preserve a good deal of valuable material. The sifting of the wheat from the chaff in the Gnostic writings is a process that may go on for years to come.[8]

In the third phase of displacement, caution was thrown to the winds as Christian writers adopted the principle that any story that was edifying, whether true or not, could be safely treated as if it were true. Pseudoacts and pseudo-gospels were mass-produced by borrowing freely from popular pagan myths and legends, while the earlier Apocrypha were supplanted by new and sensational miracle-tales.[9] At every step of the development, the process was the same, namely the elimination of certain elements followed by the introduction of others to take their place. The impoverishment of the early heritage was quickly corrected by the process of "enriching" the remainder through a transfusion of new but very different material, which from then on was represented as the old original Christian heritage but was in reality what Schneemelcher calls "a literary

---

[7]J. Leipoldt, in *Religionsgeschichte des Orients in der Zeit der Welt-religionen* (Leiden: Brill, 1961), pp. 6-7.

[8]See *The Improvement Era*, 68 (January 1965), pp. 35ff.

[9]Schneemelcher, *op. cit.*, I, 51. Even the older Apocrypha were "forced out by the new popular literature of edification." *Ibid.*, pp. 34f.

fiction in the service of propaganda."[10] One is reminded of the enterprise which removes certain vitamins from flour by one process and replaces them by another; only in this case instead of the original value being restored, something very different was substituted in its place, so that Christian literature from the third century can rightly be designated as an "Ersatz."[10]

In the second century, Clement of Alexandria commented on the ways in which teachings of the early Church unavoidably and inevitably became lost. First of all, he says, things were lost through failure to write them down. Clement is aware, as Eusebius is, that the ancient apostles didn't need to write everything down because "the blessed men of old possessed a marvelous power," but, significantly enough, this power is no longer had in the church, and so what is not written is lost. Tradition preserves such things for a time, but not indefinitely: ". . . things there are which though not noted down still remained for a while, but they are now being lost. Some of these things are now completely extinguished, having faded away in the mind from sheer neglect and lack of exercise."

But even things which are written down and carefully transmitted get lost, "for they undergo a process of constant change," and have to be continually interpreted. Interpreted by whom? "Either by the one who wrote the scripture," says Clement, "or by another who has followed in his footsteps."[11] But where do we find such a one? Clement notes that there are things in his own writings which different readers are bound to interpret in different ways, making him say things he never intended—and there is nothing he can do about it.[12] Accordingly, Clement himself intends to play safe in high and holy matters by simply refusing to write what he knows, "fearing to write down

---

[10]*Ibid.*, I, 14, 33, 51.
[11]All these quotes from Clement of Alexandria, *Stromatum*, I, i, in J.-P. Migne, *Patrologia Graeca*, VIII, 704.
[12]*Ibid.*, 705.

the things I have kept myself from speaking; not that I
begrudge anything—for that would not be right—but simply
that I am afraid they might fall into the wrong hands and
lead people into further error: it would be as the proverb
has it, 'like giving a sword to a baby,' that is, we might
well be guilty of inciting them."[13]

The Secrets of the Kingdom

The deliberate reticence of the early Fathers is the
continuation of a policy observed by the Lord and the
Apostles before them. It has significant implications, for
it not only shows us how precious things could be lost, but
refutes the stock argument of the churchmen that God
simply would not permit really serious losses to take place.
On the contrary, it was by his command that the most
precious teachings were withheld from the post-apostolic
ages.

A conspicuous aspect of most of the recently discovered Christian writings, as well as of the early Apocrypha
in general, is the frequent insistence in them on secrecy.
At present anthropologists are becoming increasingly aware
that the deliberate suppression of information by the native
peoples among whom they work is far more general, far-
reaching, and significant than they hitherto have been
willing to admit. As a recent study points out, there are
two main kinds of reticence: ". . . a whole body of material
was secret in the sense that it was to be kept from the
outsider . . . the non-Aborigine. There was also secret
information which was to be kept from the uninitiated.
. . . I refer to the former as dissembled culture."[14]

Latter-day Saint missionaries laboring among native
peoples have long noted the existence among them of both
genuine secrets, that is, things too sacred to be mentioned
to anybody outside of a particular time, place, and religious

---

[13]*Ibid.*, 704.
[14]R. Hausfeld, in *Mankind,* 6 (November 1963), p. 50.

occasion, and on the other hand of an extensive daily dissembling to keep unqualified outsiders from meddling with things they would not understand or appreciate. Both types of reticence are conspicuous in the early Jewish and Christian literature. In the Dead Sea Scrolls the people of the community are instructed not to discuss their doctrines and doings with "the people of the pit," i.e., the outside world;[15] but aside from that they are put under specific oaths of secrecy regarding certain specific things.[16]

When Jesus instructed Peter, James, and John to tell no man of what they had seen on the Mount of the Transfiguration, he was withholding sacred things from the uninitiated,[17] when on the other hand he parried tricky questions of the Pharisees by asking them counter questions and then telling them that if they could not answer him he would not answer them, he was simply evading them.[18] In the Clementine *Recognitions,* when Peter refuses to tell Clement about salvation for the dead until Clement himself has received certain ordinances, he is withholding secret teachings,[19] but when he refuses to discuss the nature of the Godhead with Simon Magus, he explains that he is deliberately evading the man because he has no real desire to learn about the Godhead and only wants to cause trouble.[20]

Recently Professor Goodenough of Yale, after long years of searching among the earliest archaeological remains of Judaism, has been able to show that there has existed through the centuries not one but two distinct types of Judaism, the one following what he calls "the horizontal path," the other "the vertical path."[21] The former type, variously designated as rabbinic, halachic, normative, or

---

[15]IQS (Serekh Scroll), IX, 21-22.
[16]*Ibid.,* IV, 5-6; VIII, 11-12.
[17]Matt. 17:9; Mark 9:9; Luke 9:36.
[18]Mark 11:33.
[19]*Clementine Recognitions,* I, 52.
[20]*Ibid.,* II, 4.
[21]E. R. Goodenough, *Jewish Symbols in the Greco-Roman Period* (New York: Bollingen Foundation, 1953), I, 18-19.

Talmudic Judaism, is the only Judaism known to our his-
tories today. This is because its representatives have, by
years of determined struggle, either stamped its rival out
entirely where they could, or forced it underground. "The
final victory of rabbinic Judaism over its ancient mystic
rival," writes Goodenough, "makes it hard to convince
modern Jews of mystical tradition."[22]

The old submerged Judaism has been called Hasidic,
cabbalistic, ma'asimic, and Karaitic, but none of these
terms is very satisfactory since each designates only some
particular underground movement in Judaism. Seeking an
overall term, Goodenough refers to the "vertical" tradition
(i.e., seeking direct as against historical contact with heaven), and cautiously uses the word "mystic" to describe it.
It is not surprising that, in order to survive, "later teachers
of this tradition developed a 'secret teaching' (I dare not
say mystery) . . . characterized by a succession of heavens,
thrones of triumph, blessed meals with the Messiah. . . ."[23]
This preliminary glimpse should suffice to indicate that
what all "vertical" Jews had in common was secrecy and
emphasis on Messianic and prophetic teachings—teachings
which the doctors of the schools (the "horizontal" tradition) disliked intensely and opposed with all their might.

Just as Goodenough distinguished between two conflicting traditions of Judaism on the basis of recent
archaeological findings, so H. J. Schoeps, on the basis of
new manuscript discoveries, distinguished between two
like levels of Christianity and even goes so far as to suggest
that the old original Christianity was actually stamped out
by the latter type,[24] which was intellectually orientated
and strongly opposed to the old Messianic-millennialist
tradition.[25] The resemblance between the corresponding
schools of Jewish and Christian thought is not accidental.

---

[22]*Ibid.*, p. 21.
[23]*Ibid.*, p. 19.
[24]H. J. Schoeps, in W. D. Davies and D. Daube (eds.), *The Background
of the New Testament and Its Eschatology* (Cambridge, 1956), p. 123.
[25]H. Nibley, in *Jewish Quarterly Review*, 50 (1959), pp. 99f.

The Christian doctors got their doctrine and philosophy from the same Alexandrian fount from which the Jewish doctors got theirs, both being dedicated to the allegorical interpretation of the scriptures and the basic proposition that revelation and prophecy had forever ceased. Students have long been aware that primitive Christianity was a carrying forward of the old "vertical" Jewish tradition, from which it inherited the apocryphal writings which were so despised by the Jewish and Christian doctors alike.[26] "Legalistic Pharisaism," wrote R. H. Charles many years ago, "in time drove out almost wholly the apocalyptic, i.e., prophetic, element . . . and became the parent of Talmudic Judaism," whereupon Judaism became "almost wholly bereft of the apocalyptic wing which had passed over into Christianity."[27] It was because it represented that other tradition, as Professor Torrey has shown, that early Christianity was so intensely unpopular with the Jewish scribes and Pharisees; everything in the Christian teaching suggested to their minds the old vertical Messianic Judaism—Justin Martyr insists on bringing the identity of the two to the attention of the resentful Jew Trypho again and again.

"If we had only the traditions of the Jews themselves," Goodenough assures us, "we should hardly have suspected the existence of the whole body of apocryphal and pseudepigraphical literature, for these, I repeat, have survived thanks only to Christian copyists."[28] But these writings which the Jewish doctors had rejected and the early Christians accepted were in time rejected by the Christian doctors also,[29] and so were lost both to the Jewish and the Christian worlds, their very existence denied by "official" Judaism and Christianity, and sank out of sight until their rediscovery in our own day.

---

[26]C. C. Torrey, *The Apocryphal Literature* (London: H. Milford, 1945),
[27]R. H. Charles, *Apocrypha and Pseudepigrapha of the Old Testament* (Oxford, 1913), I, vii.
[28]Goodenough, *op. cit.,* p. 9.
[29]H. Nibley, in *Church History,* 30 (1961), pp. 12f.

The recognition of the "underground" nature of vertical Judaism and Jewish Christianity supplies the student
with valuable clues to understanding the real background
of the Bible, of which one begins to think now more than
ever in terms of hidden treasures. Only consider the illusive
nature of the Bible through the ages: why has it ever been
a subject of the widest disagreement, as St. Augustine notes
with sorrow, among even the most pious, devout, and
learned men? If such men cannot agree, Origen pointed
out in the third century, lesser men such as ourselves can
never be perfectly sure of what the Bible means.[30]

The Policy of Reticence

In all the scriptures and apocryphal writings one finds
frequent indication of the careful rationing out of the
teaching as people were able to receive it. It was not a
matter of secrecy. The word "secrecy" has connotations
which can be misleading here. There is nothing whatever
in the secret teachings of the early Christians which seeks
to beguile or mystify, nor is there the hush-hush and top-
secret mentality of the later Gnostics.

On the contrary, the rationing of information by and
among the early saints was in accordance with a clearly
stated policy by which no one was to be denied any teaching which he was ready to receive. And when was one
ready to receive information? As soon as one sincerely
sought and asked for it. When the Lord warned the
disciples against giving their treasures to those who, like
domestic animals, would not know how to appreciate them
or what to do with them, he immediately added instructions
as to who *should* receive, namely, *"every one* that asketh."
(Matt. 7:6-8.) A more magnanimous policy could not be
imagined, giving freely to all who ask and withholding
only from those who do not want holy things and would
accordingly be harmed by them.

----

[30]Origen, *contra Celsum,* in Migne, *Patrol. Graec.,* XI, 933.

The policy is familiar from the early Jewish writings as well. The so-called *Manual of Discipline* warns the faithful: "Do not give these things to the Children of the Pit, *because* they do not study them, neither do they seek them."[31] There is no snobbishness here: Israel has lost the secret things, the Dead Sea Scrolls repeatedly observe, because Israel has fallen away and lost interest in them. Likewise, these things are secrets kept from the world simply because the world will not receive them. Neither the early sectarians nor the Christians wanted or expected high and holy things to become the property of a humanity that remained recalcitrant and unregenerate. "The belief in secret lore entrusted only to the few initiated was persistently maintained throughout the centuries," according to Kohler.[32] The Scrolls constantly speak of the knowledge possessed by the saints as "the secret counsel" or "the secret plan of God" kept secret because only faithful Israel was worthy or able to receive it, and in the Scrolls faithful Israel is but a small remnant.[33] It has long been known that the terms Nasoraean, Zaddikim (also Zadokites, sons of Zadok), and Hasidim all refer to "those who keep the secret" or "those who abide by the covenant," the two concepts being virtually identical.[34]

A few well-known quotations from the New Testament should be enough to establish the reality of reticence as an essential principle of the gospel teaching. Consider such phrases as the following:

"... it is given unto you to know the mysteries of the kingdom of heaven, but to them it is not given."

---

[31]*Manual of Discipline* (IQS), V, 11.
[32]K. Kohler, *Jewish Quarterly Review,* NS XI (1920), p. 147.
[33]Typical expressions are in the *Zadokite Fragment,* III, 13-15; the *Battle Scroll* (Milhama), XVII, 8-9; *Manual of Discipline,* IV, 6; V, 10; VIII, 11f.; IX, 16-17; XI, 5, 19; Talmud, *Sab.* IX, 3-4.
[34]H. Zimmern, in *Zeitschrift d. deut. Morgenländ, Ges.,* 74 (1920), p. 433; M. Black, *The Scrolls and Christian Origins* (New York, Scribner's 1961), pp. 67-71; R. Eisler, *Jesuous Basileus* (Heidelberg, 1930), II, 21f., 698f.; Talmud, *Erub.* VI, 11.

"... they have ears to hear, and hear not: ..."

"... as they did not *like* to retain God in their knowledge, God gave them over to a reprobate mind, ..."
(Italics added.)

"All men cannot receive this saying, save they to whom
it is given."

"... he taught them many things by parables, ...
as they were able to hear it."

"And they understood none of these things: and this
saying was hid from them, ..."

"If I tell you, ye will not believe:"

"If I have told you earthly things, and ye believe not,
how shall ye believe, if I tell you of heavenly things?"

"This is an hard saying; who can hear it? ... Doth
this offend you?"

"Why do ye not understand my speech? even because
ye cannot hear my word."

"My sheep hear my voice, ..."

"I have yet many things to say unto you, but ye cannot
bear them now."

"... we cannot tell what he saith."

"... the time cometh, when I shall no more speak
unto you in proverbs, but I shall shew you plainly of the
Father."

"... the light shineth in darkness; and the darkness
comprehendeth it not."

"... as yet they knew not the scripture, ..."

He appeared "not to all the people, but unto witnesses
chosen ..."

"... they ... were forbidden of the Holy Ghost to
preach the word in Asia."

"Hearing ye shall hear, and shall not understand;"

"... I ... could not speak unto you as unto spiritual,
... I have fed you with milk, and not with meat; ..."

"... unspeakable words, which it is not lawful for
a man to utter."

". . . by revelation he made known unto me the mystery; . . . Which in other ages was not made known. . . ."

". . . the mystery which hath been hid from ages and from generations, but now is made manifest to his saints:"

". . . many things . . . hard to be uttered, seeing ye are dull of hearing."

". . . many things . . . I would not write with paper and ink; but I . . . come unto you and speak face to face, . . ."

In each of these sayings (and there are many others) it is apparent that something is being withheld, and it is also apparent that it is being held back not arbitrarily but for a good reason, namely, that people are not ready to receive it. It is also apparent that people are to be given knowledge as they are able to receive it, so that the mysteries of the kingdom are imparted by degrees. There are, as it were, automatic safeguards built into the teaching to protect sacred things from common misunderstanding and to protect the unworthy from damaging themselves with them. God, according to Justin Martyr, has hidden the truth from the smartest doctors of the Jews whose own warped minds render them incapable of grasping it.[35] When John the Baptist was hailed before the Jewish doctors, according to Josephus, he told them: "I will not reveal to you the secret that is among you, *because you have not desired it.*"[36] (Italics added.) One receives as one is able to receive.

An interesting variation of this theme is the teaching that Jesus appears in different ways to different people. Origen knows the doctrine, but it is more fully developed in ancient *Logia* and the newly discovered Gospel of Philip, which tells us that to angels Jesus appears as an angel but to men as a man, since everyone "comprehends" only

---

[35]Justin, *Dialogue*, 55:3, 120:5.
[36]From the *Slavic Halosis*, text in R. Eisler, *op. cit.*, II, 9.

what he is like.[37] Hence, another early writing reminds us,
we can understand God only to the degree to which we
are like God.[38] This is close to the teaching of the apostles,
that the time shall come when we shall see God as he is,
for we shall be like him,[39] and to the doctrine of eternal
progression: As God is, man may become. The fullest
exposition of the doctrine, however, is to be found in the
19th chapter of 3 Nephi, which is closely matched by the
14th and 15th chapters of John.

Techniques of Concealment

The earliest Christian Apocrypha, especially those
dealing with the Lord's teachings after the resurrection,
are represented as extremely secret, but always with the
understanding that they are to be given without hesitation
to those who really want them. Thus in an early text Peter
explains his policy in dealing with Simon Magus, who
wants to discuss the mysteries with him: "It is important
to have some knowledge of the man . . . if he remains
wrapped up and polluted in obvious sins, it is not proper
for me to speak to him at all of the more secret and sacred
things of divine knowledge, but rather to protest and
confront him, that he cease from sin, and cleanse his actions
from vice. But if he insinuates himself, and leads us on
to speak what he, as long as he acts improperly, ought not
to hear, it will be our part to parry him cautiously."[40]

Simon is to be told nothing until he has learned
repentance. This, it will be recalled, was the policy of
John the Baptist in dealing with the men who came out
from the schools to heckle him and of Jesus when the

---

[37]Gospel of Philip, 105:28ff., 106:1. ". . . he revealed himself as they
would be able to see him . . . to the great as great . . . to the small as small;
to angels as an angel, to men as a man . . ." So also in the very early *Epistle
of the Apostles* (Aethiop.) c. 14 (25); (Coptic) c. VII; and Origen, *Against
Celsus*, VI, 77, in *Patrologia Graeca* XI, 1416; the *Odes of Solomon*, No. 3;
the *Thanksgiving Hymns.*
[38]So the *Gospel of Truth*, p. 21, (f XIr), a common Gnostic teaching.
[39]I John 3:2; I Cor. 13:12.
[40]*Clementine Recognitions*, II, 4.

schoolmen laid clever traps for him.[41] Accordingly, when
Simon Magus insists on discussing the mysteries of the
godhead, Peter remarks, "You seem to me not to know what
a father and a God is: but I could tell you both whence
souls are, and when and how they were made; only it is
not permitted to me now to disclose these things to you."[42]
Peter explains that because of the wickedness of men, "God
has concealed his mind from men," and that the Christians
are under obligation "to honor with silence the very highest
teachings."[43] Even when the sincere investigator Clement
asks Peter about the fate of his parents who never heard
the gospel, Peter remarks, "Now, Clement, you are forcing
me to discuss things we are not allowed to talk about," but
offers to explain things "so far as it is allowed,"[44] with the
understanding that "with the passing of time the more
secret things will be disclosed to you."[45] When Clement
later ventures a bit of learned speculation about the anointing of Adam to be a high priest, Peter becomes angry and
rebukes him "for thinking we can know everything before
the proper time."[46]

A well attested *Logion* preserved in the Clementine
writings quotes Peter as saying, "Let us remember that
the Lord commanded us saying, 'Guard those secret things
[*mysteria*] which belong to me and the sons of my
house.' "[47] A variation of this, "keep my secret, ye who are
kept by it!" was often quoted by the church fathers and
is found in the very early Odes of Solomon.[48] Commenting
on it, Lactantius wrote, "We do not make a practice of
defending and discussing this thing publicly, because, with
the help of God, we quietly keep his secret to ourselves in

---

[41]Matt. 3:9f.; Luke 3:9; Matt. 21:23f.; Mark 11:28-33; Luke 20:2-8; etc.
[42]*Clementine Recognitions*, II, 60.
[43]*Ibid.*, I, 15, 23.
[44]*Ibid.*, I, 52.
[45]*Ibid.*, VI, 25.
[46]*Ibid.*, I, 47-48.
[47]*Clementine Homily*, XIX, 20, in *Patrologia Graeca* II, 441.
[48]Discussed by R. Harris, *The Odes and Psalms of Solomon* (Cambridge
University, 1909), p. 101.

silence . . . for it is proper to withhold and conceal the mystery with all possible care—especially so for us who bear the name of believers."[49] We have cited the Clementine Peter here as representative of all the early apocryphal teachings regarding the secrecy and reticence of the preaching. "Nothing is harder," he says to Clement, "than to reason about the truth in the presence of a mixed multitude of people. . . . I try for the most part, by using a certain circumlocution, to avoid publishing the chief knowledge concerning the Supreme Divinity to unworthy ears."[50] This recalls the Lord's admonitory introduction to teachings of particularly momentous import: "Who hath ears to hear, let him hear."[51] "The Mysteries of the Faith," says Clement of Alexandria, "are not to be disclosed indiscriminately to everyone, since not all are ready to receive the truth."[52]

There is a sound pedagogical principle involved here: "The teaching of all doctrine," says Peter in the *Recognitions*, "has a certain order: there are some things which must be delivered first, others in the second place, and others in the third, and so on, everything in its order. If these things be delivered in their order they become plain; but if they be brought forward out of order, they will seem to be spoken against reason."[53] That is why he rebuked the youthful Clement for wanting "to know everything ahead of time." Elsewhere he explains that the Lord "has commanded us to go forth to preach, and to invite you to the supper of the heavenly king . . . and to give you your wedding garments, that is to say, the privilege of being baptized. . . . you are to regard this as the first step of three, which step brings forth thirty commandments, as the second step does sixty and the third one hundred, as

---

[49]Lactantius, *Divine Institutes*, VIII, 26, cit. Harris *l.c.*
[50]*Clementine Recognitions*, III, 1.
[51]Discussed by M. Peuch, in *Vigiliae Christianae*, 12 (1958), pp. 186f.
[52]Clement of Alexandria, *Stromat.*, I, xii, in *Patrologia Graeca* VIII, 753.
[53]*Clementine Recognitions*, III, 34.

we shall explain to you more fully at another time."[54] This reminds one of Paul's rationing of the teaching to the saints,[55] but the three steps are significant. Papias says that the apostles taught that the 30, 60, and 100 "are the gradation and arrangement of those that are saved, and that they advance through steps of this nature," referring definitely to three degrees of glory.[56] The very early *Testament of Our Lord Jesus Christ* opens with the admonition that the document is to come into the hands "only of proven saints who dwell in the third order (or level) next to the mansion of my Father who sent me."[57] Here we see the teachings rationed with respect not merely to outsiders but within the Church itself. At the beginning of the second century, Ignatius wrote to the Saints at Tralles who had asked him for a letter about the mysteries: "I would like to write to you of heavenly things (or of things more full of mystery), but I fear to do so, lest I should inflict injury on you who are but babes . . . you would be strangled by such things."[58] In the same spirit Clement of Alexandria, as we have seen, refused to commit certain things to writing because giving them to the churches of his day would be like giving a sword to a baby.

Nearly all the earliest Christian writings are addressed "to secret societies of initiates," usually with strict instructions that their circulation be carefully limited.[59] Typical is the newly found *Apocryphon of James*, which begins: "Since you have asked me to send you a secret book of revelation, which was given to me and to Peter by the Lord, I cannot refuse or be silent. . . . But I . . . send it to

---

[54]*Ibid.*, IV, 35.
[55]Acts 15:23, 29; discussed in the ancient *Apostolic Constitutions* (a Clementine writing), VI, 12, in *Patrologia Graeca*, I, 941ff.
[56]Cited in Irenaeus, *Adv. Haereses*, V. 36. Papias is one of the earliest of all church Fathers.
[57]*Test. Dom. n. J. Christi*, Rahmani, ed., I, xviii (pp. 22f.). The Syriac word is equivalent to the Greek *taxis* and the Latin *ordo*, and refers, according to Rahmani, to the third heaven. Cf. the *Gospel of Truth*, 21:4-6, where "only the living who are in the Book of Life" are to receive these teachings.
[58]Ignatius, *Epist. ad Tralles*, c. 5.
[59]P. Batiffol, in *Revue Biblique*, 1911, p. 32.

you and to you alone. . . . Take care not to let this book
of the Lord be communicated to many. The Savior did not
want it transmitted to all the Twelve."[60] In one Clementine
writing, Clement is ordered by Peter "to hide this revelation
in a box, so that foolish men may not see it."[61] And in a
Clementine epistle, Peter writes to James: "Please do not
give over any of the writings I send to you to the gentiles;
transmit them only to those who have been tried and
proven:" specifically they are to be given to "the seventy-
two" just as Moses shared his revelations with a like
number of elders. This is interesting because Eusebius
quotes an authentic statement of Clement, that the Lord
after the resurrection gave the Gnosis only to Peter, James,
and John, who in turn passed it down "to the other
Apostles, who in turn transmitted it to the Seventy."[62]

The circulation of early teachings was further limited
by the difficulty of the idiom in which they were originally
written as Chrysostom noted long ago.[63] But to make
things still more difficult, they were often written in a
special jargon, a "special language," in fact, which is now
coming in for a good deal of attention.[64] Persecuted minorities have a way of shutting themselves in and developing
a secret idiom of their own to circumvent the watchful
malice of their oppressors.[65] Some of the writings in the
Dead Sea Scrolls, for example, "may be said, with some
slight exaggeration, to have been written in code," just
as were such important Jewish Apocrypha as Daniel,

---

[60]*Apocryphon of James,* 1:8-25, M. Peuch, trans., in *Vigiliae Christianae,*
8 (1954).
[61]M. R. James, *Apocryphal New Testament,* p. 520.
[62]*Clement, Epistle* in *Patrologia Graeca,* II, 25, 28-32; cf. Eusebius,
Church History, II, 1, 4.
[63]John Chrysostom, *De obscuritate prophetarum,* ii, in *Patrologia Graeca*
56:178, notes that since it is impossible to translate perfectly from one language
to another, there always must be an element of obscurity in the teaching of
scriptures.
[64]B. J. Knott, "The Christian 'Special Language' in the Inscriptions," in
Vigiliae Christianae, 10 (1956), 65-79.
[65]The early Christians like the Jewish sectaries of the desert were an
"underground" movement, J. Jeremias, in *Zeitschrift für Neutestamente Wissenschaft,* 42 (1949), 184-194.

Enoch, the Testament of the Twelve Patriarchs, and the Sibylline Oracles.[66] The important Odes of Solomon have been described by one of their editors as "a cipher within a cipher"![67] Indeed, the original meaning of "Apocrypha" is secret writing—writing too holy to be divulged to a cynical and unbelieving world: "An apocryphal book," writes M. R. James, "was—originally—one too sacred and *secret* to be in every one's hands: it must be reserved for the initiate, the inner circle of believers."[68] The theory was that "all these things were hidden from ordinary mortals; they were known to the great national heroes of the past, Enoch, Noah, Abraham, Moses, and others, having been revealed to them by angels. . . ."[69]

A. D. Nock finds in the New Testament itself "writings by men of esoteric piety addressed only to their spiritual brethren,"[70] and Riesenfeld now maintains that the Gospel of John consists largely of Jesus's "meditations" uttered confidentially in the circle of his apostles.[71] "When we open the Septuagint and the New Testament," writes Nock, "we find at once a strange vocabulary . . . the product of an enclosed world living its own life, a ghetto culturally and linguistically; they belong to a literature written entirely for the initiated."[72] It is this which has rendered "the strange world of the New Testament" so "baffling" and "exotic," according to Professor Cross.[73] The peculiarity consists not in the invention of new words but in the use

---

[66]J. Teicher, *The Habakkuk Scroll,* p. 47.
[67]R. Harris, *Odes and Psalms of Solomon,* p. 121.
[68]M. R. James, *op. cit.,* p. xiv.
[69]M. Oesterley, *Introduction to the Books of the Apocrypha* (New York, Macmillan, 1935), p. 71.
[70]A. D. Nock, in *Journal of Biblical Literature,* 52 (1933), p. 132.
[71]Cited by R. Marle, in *Etudes,* 302 (1959), p. 71.
[72]Nock notes that the former explanation of the peculiar language of the New Testament as being simply vulgar Greek no longer holds, since there is in the Koine "nothing corresponding to the Semitic flavor of the early Christian writers. Nothing could be less like the Pauline letters than the majority of documents" collected by Deissman to illustrate the prevailing Greek idiom of the day. *Op. cit.,* p. 138.
[73]F. Cross, in *Christian Century,* August 24, 1955, p. 971.

of familiar words in a new and unfamiliar context, "to express a new category" of things.[74] An exact parallel to
this is the Latter-day Saint adoption of such legal and
specialized words as testimony, endowment, sacrament,
conference, sealing, etc., in contexts which the outside
world does not understand.[75]

The special interpretation which the sectaries and the
early Christians put on familiar words must not be confused with the later practice of allegorical interpretation,
Cullmann reminds us. John's writings especially, he points
out, are full of double meanings, but in John this is no
mere literary conceit but the conveying of information to
those who have ears to hear.[76] A recent find illustrates
this principle by the best-known of all parables, that of
the Good Samaritan. To an outsider this is a story of the
loftiest humanitarian and moral purpose, completely satisfying in itself. Yet it would now appear that no early
Christian could possibly have missed the real significance
of the wine and the oil that heal the wounded man as
standing for the sacrament and the anointing that restore
the ailing human soul to a healthy state, thanks to the
intervention of the Lord, who is the Good Samaritan.[77]

The newly discovered apocryphal writings, both Jewish and Christian, refer with surprising frequency to the
plan of salvation as a hidden or buried treasure. They
accept the doctrine, as expressed by Lactantius, that "God
has hidden the treasure of wisdom and of truth," so that
the wise men of the earth have never been able to find it
by their own efforts.[78] Down through the ages God has
opened his treasury to the faithful few who have proven
true to the covenant and permitted them to share the secret

---

[74]Nock, op. cit., p. 132.
[75]Justin, Dialogue 100, gives a list of such words, as does Nock, op. cit.,
pp. 134f., and H. Gressman, Ursprung der Gnosis, p. 335.
[76]O. Cullmann, Urchristentum und Gottesdienst (Zürich, 1950), pp. 51f.
[77]Gospel of Philip, 126.
[78]Lactantius, Divine Institutes in Patrologia Latina, 6:452; so Tatian,
Orat. 6; this is the "Treasure of Light," e.g. in Second Book of Jeu, C. Schmidt,
ed., in Texte u. Unters., VIII, 196.

knowledge of his plans: "The treasury of the holy King is flung open, and they who worthily partake of the good things therein do rest, and resting they shall reign."[79] In the *Recognitions*, Peter explains that God has always concealed the kingdom, like a rich treasure, "yet he has caused the report of it, under various names and opinions, to be spread abroad through the successive generations, to the hearing of all." All men, that is, have at some time or other received some inducement to take at least a preliminary step in the direction of searching for the gospel; all men are accordingly under obligation to look further— none is without some report of the treasure, no matter how distant, ". . . so that whoever should be lovers of what is good, hearing the report, might be led to inquire."[80] The parallel to Alma 32 is striking. It is Christ who moves men to seek, according to Peter, and it is to him directly that they should turn for guidance in their search, being moved ". . . not from themselves, but from Him who has hidden it, so they should pray that the success and the way of knowledge might be given to them: which way is open only to those who love truth above all the good things of this world; and on no other condition can anyone even begin to understand it. . . ."[80] Again the free and liberal access to all men, and again the foolproof built-in controls against those who do not seek with pure intent. A famous *Logion* of Jesus, now attested in the Gospel of Thomas, enjoins all to be diligent seekers: "Let not him who seeks the Father cease until he finds him; and having found him, let him be amazed; and being amazed he shall reign, and reigning he shall rest."[81]

---

[79]*Acta Thomae*, Bonnet, ed., (p. 243). The theme is developed at length in the very early hymn called "The Pearl." These are the "pearls" and "treasures" of the New Testament, G. Quispel, in *Vigilae Christianae*, 12 (1958), 186f.

[80]*Clementine Recognitions*, III, 53-58.

[81]*Oxyrhynchus Logion* No. 9 (2); *Gospel of Thomas, Logion* No. 2, cf. Nos. 81, 88, 96; *Gospel of Truth*, 17:3ff.

Denial of Loss

As soon as the restraining influence of living Apostles was withdrawn from the Church, large numbers of quacks and pretenders began to capitalize on the secrecy of the early teachings, each one pretending that he alone had the Gnosis which the Lord imparted secretly to the disciples after the resurrection.[82] The simplest refutation of such claims was to insist that there never had been any secret teaching or any holding back of any doctrine whatever. Such is the position that Irenaeus takes, but even for him it proves quite untenable, and later fathers of the church agree that there was indeed a *disciplina arcana* or secret unwritten teaching of the apostles handed down to certain leaders of the church.[83] However, the easy and convenient abuse of the tradition of reticence by unprincipled individuals has made it possible for churchmen down to the present to label as misleading and spurious the very idea that there ever was any secret teaching.[84]

The doctors have welcomed this way out and made the most of it, for the idea that any Christian teaching might have escaped them both alarms and puzzles them. It alarms them because unless the information available to theologians is complete and final, they are forced to live with an element of uncertainty which is intolerable to their vanity and fatal to the finality and neatness which theological systems prize above all else. And it puzzles them because, like the schoolman Celsus in the second century, they cannot understand "why, if Jesus was sent to give a message he insisted on concealing the message." To Celsus, Origen replied that Jesus did not conceal his message from those who sincerely sought it,[85] but Celsus is not satisfied

---

[82]See above, pp. 82-83.
[83]Irenaeus, *adversus Haereses*, III, iv, in *Patrologia Graeca* 7:855; cf. 885-9 for his feeble arguments. Rules for dealing with arcane teachings were set forth by Innocent III, in *Patrologia Latina* 214:696.
[84]It was not until about 400 AD that the doctors of the church, to discredit all secret teachings, gave to the word "Apocrypha" a bad meaning, according to W. Schneemelcher, *N. T. Apocryphen*, I, 5.
[85]Origen, *Contra Celsum*, II, 70, in *Patrologia Graeca* 11:905.

and asks why Jesus showed himself to so few people after
the resurrection, when he had a wonderful chance of con-
verting the world and proving the resurrection by appearing to those who had put him to death. This forbearance
of the Lord has always puzzled the doctors of the church.[86]
The great Catholic scholar J. P. Migne was greatly
puzzled that the Lord should insist on keeping his true
mission and his true identity a secret from the world which
he was sent to redeem.[87] This is "the Messianic secret"
which has always perplexed scholars of Judaism and Christianity. In our own day Albert Schweitzer notes that while
it cannot be denied that Jesus insisted on making important
aspects of his ministry a secret, one is at a loss to explain
why he did it.[88]

At the present time Roman Catholic scholars are laying
considerable emphasis on the phrase "from the housetops,"
which signifies, according to them, that there was to be
nothing whatever kept secret or held back from the public
in the teachings of Jesus.[89] In the face of innumerable
indications to the contrary, it is hard to see how such an
interpretation can be put on a passage which is a mysterious
one to begin with: The Lord had just told the apostles
that their teaching would receive no better reception than
his had. (Matt. 10:25.) Then he adds that they should
not be afraid, ". . . for there is nothing covered, that shall
not be revealed; and hid, that shall not be known." (*Ibid.*,
10:26) Isn't he talking about the machinations of the
enemy here? Jesus continues: "What I tell you in darkness,
that speak ye in light; and what ye hear in the ear, that
preach ye upon the housetops." (*Ibid.*, 10:27.) The pecu-

---

[86]John Chrysostom, *Homily on Acts* I, 4, in *Patrologia Graeca* 60:19, gives
an amazing explanation for it, which was officially adopted by other churchmen, e.g., Oecumenius, *Comment on Acts*, I, 3, in *Patrologia Graeca* 118:45.

[87]J. P. Migne, *Scripturae Sacrae Cursus Completus* (Paris, 1840) 21:823-4.

[88]A. Schweitzer, *Geschichte der Lebenjesu Forschung*, I, 396. C. A. Bugge,
in *Zeitschrift für Neutestamentliche Wissenschaft* 7 (1906), p. 97, says we
cannot even be sure whether there was a Messianic secret or not.

[89]So J. de Manasce, in *The Mysteries* (Bollingen Series XXX, 2, [New
York, 1955]), pp. 139f., and H. Rahner, *ibid.*, pp. 357ff.

liar phrase "in the ear" is explained by a newly discovered
Logion of Jesus: "What you hear in the *other* ear preach
from the housetops."[90] This is akin to another Logion:
"These teachings are only for the tried and worthy: preach
other words to the churches."[91] There is thus no contradiction between a command to preach from the housetops
and the injunction to keep holy things from unworthy ears:
some things were to be divulged generally, others not.

"These things preach openly," says 4 Ezra, "but these
things keep secret," explaining that there are twenty-four
sacred books for public teaching but seventy others which
are reserved only "for the wise among thy people."[92] "Paul
did not divulge all his revelations," says Chrysostom, "but
concealed the greater part of them; and though he did not
tell everything, neither was he silent about everything, lest
he leave an opening for the teachings of false apostles."[93]
J. Jeremias has recently shown how such a policy explains
the apparent contradiction in ordering the apostles to
preach in all the world while at the same time commanding
them not to go outside of Israel: the general preaching,
Jeremias explains, was for a later dispensation, the limited
preaching for the present time.[94] Jesus' order, "What I
tell you in darkness, that speak ye in light," plainly refers
to such a double preaching. Granted that some things *are*
to be preached from the housetops, there is nowhere even
the vaguest indication that *all* things are to be so broadcast,
as the Catholic scholars now maintain. Such a concept
would be contrary to the basic principle that to those who
have, more will be given (Matt. 13:12) and to the progressive steps of enlightenment that are basic in the Christian
teaching.[95] "We believe," wrote Tertullian, "that the

---

[90]*Gospel of Thomas* 87:10-12.
[91]*Testament of Our Lord Jesus Christ*, (ed. Rahmani), p. xviii.
[92]4 Ezra 14:6f., 44-46.
[93]John Chrysostom, *De laudibus S. Pauli, Homil V,* in *Patrologia Graeca*
50:500.
[94]J. Jeremias, *Jesu Verheissung für die Völker* (Stuttgart, 1956), 15f., 61f.
[95]John 1:5, 10-12 illustrates the principle of reciprocity—God gives only
as man receives.

apostles were ignorant of nothing, but that they did *not* transmit everything they knew, and were *not* willing to reveal everything to everybody. They did not preach everywhere nor promiscuously . . . but taught one thing about the nature of Christ in public and another in secret: some things about the resurrection they taught to everyone, but some things they taught only to a few."[96]

There is a type of secrecy which the churchmen condone and practice. It is that air of mystery and aloofness which St. Augustine describes as such an important part of higher education in his day.[97] Paul of Samosata and Simon Magus are classical examples of schoolmen seeking to heighten their prestige, overawe the general public, beguile and intrigue the youth, silence criticism, abash the insolent, and attract an audience and a following by cultivating an atmosphere of recondite, even supernatural, learning and an attitude of lofty superiority to the ignorant masses. This is still the secret of success in most graduate schools throughout the land. But this was not the kind of secrecy practiced by the Christians, a thing which the learned men of their day simply could not understand.

Learned Romans like Caecilius, Celsus, Pliny, and Tacitus were convinced that the Christians kept their doctrines and ordinances secret because they were ashamed of them; they note that this secrecy only causes misunderstanding and arouses the worst suspicions and wildest speculations—why do the Christians insist on spoiling their case by clinging to it?[98] It is significant that the Christians never deny this secrecy, but defend themselves by replying that other religions and even the schools of philosophy all have their secrets, and, as is well known they were willing even to suffer death rather than betray it.[99]

---

[96]Tertullian, *De praesriptionibus*, c. 25f.

[97]St. Augustine, *Confessions*, I, 3.

[98]The fullest discussion is in Minucius Felix, *Octavius*, pp. 8-11; cf. P. C. Tacitus, *History*, XV, 44; Pliny, *Epistle to Trajan*, X, 34; Origen, *Contra Celsum*, I, 1, 1ff.

[99]Origen, *op. cit.*, I, 7, 12, 14, in *Patrologia Graeca* 11:667, 677, 685f. Tatian, *Adv. Graecos*, c. 27.

The Unwritten Tradition

Recently Roman Catholic scholars have pointed out that however much knowledge and wisdom their church may have acquired through the centuries, the fact remains that the apostles, who were nearer to the Lord in every way than any other men could ever be, possessed a knowledge of Christ and his teachings which was necessarily unique and unequalled in following ages.[100] If that is so, who can deny that something vital and important was lost with the passing of the apostles? Along with that we must consider the idea of the *disciplina arcana,* the existence in the church of an *unwritten* tradition handed down from the time of the apostles.[101] Certain fathers of the church laid great stress on this, especially St. Basil. Where in the scriptures, he asks, do you find the prayer on the sacrament? Where do you find a description of the baptismal rite? Where do you find such tokens as the sign of the cross? "Do not all these things come from the unpublicized and unutterable (secret) teaching which our fathers preserved for us in silence?"[102] Why in silence? Why unwritten? To keep them from falling into the hands of the unworthy by assuring the strictest secrecy of transmission.[103] As late as the fourth century, Athanasius warns, "One must not recite the mysteries to the uninitiated, lest outsiders who do not understand them make fun of them while they perplex and scandalize investigators."[104]

Basil calls this "the secret tradition" and insists that the written and the unwritten traditions must go together and be treated with equal respect since the one cannot be

---

[100]R. Latourelle, S. J., in *Gregorianum,* 44 (1963), pp. 256-260.

[101]Even the *Clementine Recognitions,* I, 21 speaks of "things which were clearly spoken, but were not clearly written down. . . ."

[102]Basil, *De Spiritu Sancto,* c. 27, in *Patrologia Graeca* 32:188.

[103]"Why have you dared to repeat what is not written?" says a very early apocryphon, The Revelation to Peter, in *Zeitschrift f. die N.T. Wissenschaft,* 23 (1924), p. 12.

[104]Athanasius, Apol. *contra Arianos,* c. 11, in *Patrologia Graeca* 31:677.

understood without the other.[105] Noted theologians through the centuries have not been averse to abetting their prestige by claiming the possession of such knowledge, and indeed there is no objection whatever to admitting the existence of secret, unwritten teachings going back to the apostles, provided only that we credit the church with possessing them—as long as they are the property of the churchmen, the churchmen are willing to admit their existence. The only trouble here is that when those who claim these treasures are asked to produce them, they can only do as the ancient Gnostics did under like circumstances: instead of producing the genuine old Christian or Jewish teachings, they simply fob off on the public the philosophy of the schools dressed up in a little reverential jargon. Basilides, for example, claimed that he had been secretly instructed by the Apostle Matthew in things which that disciple in turn had received in confidence from the Savior, but when he tried to produce some of this marvelous teaching, all he could come up with was the borrowed Categories of Aristotle.[106] Just so, the schoolmen of the Middle Ages thought they were delving to the heart of the Christian mystery when they were expounding scholastic philosophy.[107] They admitted the existence of the mystery, and they diligently sought for it, but they never came anywhere near it.

To explain the existence of an "arcane discipline" in the church while insisting at the same time that the Lord commanded that nothing be held back from the public, it has been found convenient to argue that there was indeed a secret teaching but that it was first introduced into the church by the catechetical schools of the third century.[108]

------

[105]His position is discussed by D. Thomasius, *Dogmentgeschichte der alten Kirche* (Erlangen, 1886), I, 209, 297f.

[106]Hippolytus, *Philosophoumena*, VII, 20.

[107]M. Grabmann, *Geschichte der scholastischen Methode* (Graz, 1957), II, 94f., 97-100.

[108]So H. Rahner, in *The Mysteries*, pp. 354f.; J. H. Barnard, *Odes of Solomon*, (Cambridge University, 1912), pp. 23, 25.

If, however, we consult the men responsible for introducing
it into these schools, we learn from them that they were
not inventing the thing at all, but consciously and carefully
following what they believed to be the old apostolic secret
teaching that went back to the beginning of the church.
Clement of Alexandria explains that in concealing certain
things from the general public, he is merely following the
practice and instruction of the apostles themselves.[109] And
indeed, there is no shortage of examples of secrecy in the
church *before* the third century. The vast majority of examples, in fact, come from the earlier period. We have
quoted a number of them above.[110]

To the argument that the Lord enjoined secrecy upon
the apostles only until the resurrection should have taken
place, we have the reply of the scriptures and of the large
"forty-day" apocryphal literature, i.e., the earliest of all
Christian literature, that the emphasis on secrecy after the
resurrection was if anything even greater than before.[111]

No one has ever denied that the basic rites and ordinances of the early church—baptism and the Lord's Supper
—were originally secret ordinances from which the general
public was rigidly excluded.[112] So secret were they, in fact,
that no certain knowledge of them has come down to the
Christian world, whose ritual and liturgy had to be devised
accordingly at a later date. As early as the fourth century,
Basil noted that no written account had come down from

---

[109]Clement of Alexandria, *Stromat,* V, x, 94ff.; IV, 161, 3; *In Levit.
Homil.* 13:3f.

[110]Thus of Peter, in the *Clementine Recognitions,* III, 74: "During the
whole three months which he spent at Caesarea for the sake of teaching,
whatever he discoursed of in the presence of the people in the daytime, he
explained more fully and perfectly in the night, in private, to us, as more
faithful and approved by him."

[111]R. Eisler, *op. cit.,* II, 157, notes that the injunction to secrecy (e.g.
Mark 9:1) was to be observed until the *general* resurrection, i.e., "until the
second coming of the Redeemer *in glory.*" Origen notes that the Lord's activities and teachings after the resurrection are "the deep and hidden teachings
of the church," *Contra Celsum* in *Patrologia Graeca* 11:1029ff.

[112]A. D. Nock, in *Mnemosyne,* Ser. IV, Vol. V (1952), pp. 185f., 192,
199f.; H. V. Soden in *Zeitschrift für die N.T. Wissenschaft* 12 (1911),
188-227.

ancient times prescribing how any ordinances should be performed.[113] Today even the Roman church is making drastic changes in rites and ordinances hitherto believed by most Catholics to have been the original, pristine Christian rites, descended without change or alteration from the time of the Apostles.

Why should the Roman church have taken this dangerous and unprecedented step? It is partly because the discovery of ancient documents in our own day has forced the Christian world to recognize that the practices of ancient times were really quite different from what they have heretofore been taught. We now see that in Origen, Hippolytus, Clement, Justin, and the Didache, we have brief and tantalizing glimpses of *"a later forgotten* aspect of the early Christian sacrament."[114] Scholars are just beginning to realize, for example, to what an extent the early Christians were attached to the temple, as when the Gospel of Philip says that the Christians are instructed by "hidden types and images that are behind the veil," so that "by these despised symbols we enter into a knowledge of salvation."[115] Christian scholars are rightly exercised to know what it is talking about.

The Last the Best?

Implicit and explicit in the concept of a gospel taught by degrees instead of all at once—"precept upon precept; . . . line upon line; here a little, and there a little"—is the idea that the most important, the highest, and the holiest teachings come *last.*[116] This is the exact opposite of the reasoning of the Christian world today, that the most

---

[113]See above, note 102.

[114]A. Adam, in *Theologische Literaturzeitung,* 88 (1963), pp. 10f.

[115]*Gospel of Philip* 132:20-25; 133:15. A. Adam, *op. cit.,* p. 16, says that the real source of the Christian sacrament was the temple and not the pagan mysteries, this fact being concealed by the extreme secrecy of the temple ordinances.

[116]Discussed by C. Schmidt, *Geschpraeche Jesu mit seinen Jungern,* . . . Vol. 43 of *Texte und Untersuchungen,* 1919, pp. 201ff.

important teachings must have come *first,* so that everything essential is known, while anything that may have
escaped is not really vital. Few would dispute that the
higher and holier a teaching is, the fewer are qualified to
hear it: One need only recall the Lord's practice of discussing "the mysteries of the kingdom of heaven" only with
his disciples behind closed doors, and of selecting only a
few chosen apostles to share in the still greater mysteries
such as the transfiguration. All Christians, indeed, agree
that the most glorious manifestations are reserved for the
end. But the importance of a teaching is not measured by
its depth and wonder but by the particular need of the
person receiving it. God does give people at all times what
are *for them* the most important teachings that could possibly be given.

For an unbaptized person nothing could be more important than baptism; for a sinful world repentance is a
teaching of transcendent importance. The Catholic theologians are quite right in saying that the Christian world
today possesses all that is essential for it to know, for what
is essential is simply that which is sufficient to lead men
to the next step. Such essentials and fundamentals have
always been available to the human race, but they are not,
on grounds of their importance, to be confused with great
and glorious things promised as the reward of faith in
ages and worlds to come. John Chrysostom constantly
explained to his perplexed congregations that they should
not be upset because the church no longer had spiritual
gifts and powers as it did in the days of the apostles,
because the important thing was not to heal the sick and
speak in tongues, etc., but to live an upright life. Thus by
deliberately confusing what is *important* with what is high
and holy, he beclouded the issue and made it seem that
nothing important had been lost after all. "Are we today
not just as good as the apostles?" he asks. ". . . But they
had signs and wonders, you say. But that was not what
made them great. How long will we go on excusing our

own indifference by appealing to their signs and wonders?"[117] This sensible argument still does not explain away
the lack of those spiritual manifestations which were the
glory of the early church.[118] "The more exalted, glorious
teachings of the gospel," writes Origen, "have always been
kept from the vulgar."[119]

To illustrate: We have in the New Testament only the
teachings given by the Lord to the apostles before the
resurrection. Yet we are emphatically told that these
teachings had not been enough to give these men faith
or understanding of the resurrection, so that they flatly
refused to believe the report of the resurrection when it
was given to them by reliable persons, and when the Lord
himself appeared to them, they tried to run away in terror.
Now, if we possess only a very small part of the words of
Jesus to the disciples before his death, how can we from
them alone acquire a faith and understanding which the
apostles failed to get from the Lord himself? The standard
explanation is that the apostles reread the things they had
not understood at first, which now in the light of the
resurrection and the effusion of the spirit became clear:
These teachings "they now transmitted to the church—the
words and deeds of Christ, plus the intelligence which
they had received through the illuminating action of the
Spirit."[120] That sounds nice, but it is not what the record
reports. The mere fact of the resurrection, though it made
everything appear in a new light, was apparently not sufficient to give the apostles what they needed. In an instant
the doubting Thomas accepted the resurrection, as the
others had at an earlier meeting, and yet the Lord had to
spend forty days off and on teaching the disciples "the
things of the kingdom" before they were ready to go out

------

[117]Chrysostom, *In Matth. Homil.*, 46, in *Patrologia Graeca* 58:479.
[118]Nibley, *The World and the Prophets* (Salt Lake City: Deseret Book
Company, 1957), pp. 3-5.
[119]Origen, *Contra Celsum*, V, 19, in *Patrologia Graeca* 11:1208-9.
[120]Latourelle, *op. cit.*, p. 257.

on their missions.[121] What he taught them was not, as is commonly maintained, simply a repetition of what they had heard before—far from it. All are agreed that at that time the apostles heard very secret things which they had never heard before; they asked questions which they had never dared ask before and cried in wonder, "These things are more marvellous than what we were taught before." Now for the first time they learned "the ultimate secrets," "the highest knowledge."[122] "Now," they cried, "he teaches us things which we had not known before, great, amazing, and real things."[123]

What were these things? If the story of Christ's return after the resurrection were only a myth or wishful thinking, we would find either total silence on the matter or else the usual gnostic-philosophic claptrap masquerading as deep mysteries. Instead of that, we find, if we bring the records together, a remarkably consistent exposition of doctrines heretofore unrecognized by the Christian world.

---

[121]Acts 1:3. ". . . the apostles . . . understood the Master only gradually and slowly," Bo Reicke, in *Interpretation*, 16 (1962), p. 160. An extreme case is in the *Apocryphon of James* 7:8, 10; 8:30; 11:6, where the Lord must prolong his post-resurrectional stay for eighteen days because the apostles simply cannot learn their lesson.

[122]*Apocryphon of James*, 2:33-39; *Apocryphon of John*, 19-22; *Acts of Thomas*, c. 47; *Evang. Barthol.* (fragment), in *Revue Biblique*, 10 (1913), p. 185. Jerome, *Adv. Pelag.* 2:15, says that the apostles after the resurrection asked the Lord to tell them what he had not told them before. So also in the *127 Canons of the Apostles*, Canon No. 12; *The Discourse on the Abbaton*, Sec. 480; the *Gospel of the Twelve Apostles*, in *Patrologia Orientalia* 2:135, 160f.

[123]*Epistle of the Apostles*, 3 (14), 5 (16), 11 (22).

CHAPTER 5

The Bible in the Book of Mormon

Pilfered Passages

By providing a great number of scriptural passages in versions far older than any others hitherto known, the newly discovered manuscripts fully demonstrate that peculiar flexibility of ancient scriptures which appear so clearly in the Book of Mormon. Mark Twain accuses Joseph Smith of having in composing the Book of Mormon "smouched from the New Testament, and no credit given."[1] But since the Book of Mormon was written to be read by people who knew and believed the Bible—indeed one cannot possibly believe the Book of Mormon without believing the Bible—it is hard to see why a deceiver would strew the broadest clues to his pilfering all through a record he claimed was his own. But of course what Mark Twain did not know was that ancient writing is *formulaic*, and that no writer was expected to cite chapter and verse for the word-for-word quotations and set expressions which made up his composition. For one thing, there would be no point to citing one's immediate source for an idea or expression, since that writer in turn was merely borrowing it from another. That was no more pilfering to the ancient mind than taking words out of the dictionary or thesaurus would be for a modern author. This should be obvious to anyone

---

[1]S. L. Clemens, *Roughing It*, Definitive Edition (New York, 1922), III, 110.

who has read much of ancient authors in the original—
translation of course completely effaces the original expressions and makes this kind of investigation clumsy and
dubious if not impossible. And yet though it is obvious, it
is only recently that biblical scholars have begun to realize
the extent to which it applies in the Bible. Take Paul, for
example. Paul has been hailed as the most original of
all the biblical writers. But just how original is he? Expressions regarded as characteristically Pauline turn out on
investigation to be actual quotations from the classical
writers, from the orators, the drama, the law courts, the
stadium, the boxing ring, the ancient religious rites even.[2]
His classical education was surpassed however by his
Jewish training, and we can never be sure that his ideas
and expressions do not belong to that tradition.[3] Thus a
number of scholars have independently shown the really
ancient background—traced by some even to Babylonian
times—of the well-known "Pauline" formula, "faith, hope,
and love," the appearance of which in the Book of Mormon
(where it is quoted by a diligent student of the ancient
records) has often been taken as absolute proof of fraud.[4]

Not long ago an eminent Protestant journal noted that
the Book of Mormon was "generously sprinkled with passages lifted bodily from the King James Version."[5] That
is the equivalent of accusing the New Testament of being
"generously sprinkled with passages lifted bodily from the
Septuagint." Whenever the scriptures are quoted, in the
Bible or elsewhere, it is always in some accepted human
version, for as far as can be determined it has been a very
long time since anyone has seen the Urtext. Even more

---

[2]E. Howells, in *Expository Times,* 71 (196), pp. 330ff.
[3]I. Levi, in *Revue des Etudes Juives,* 82 (1926), pp. 161-3, shows that
I Corinthians 2:9, is being quoted from an old Jewish apocryphal writing.
[4]R. Reitzenstein, in *Nachrichter v. d. kgl. Ges. d. Wiss. zu Göttingen,*
1916, pp. 362, 416, and 1917 Heft 1, pp. 130-151, and *Historische Zeitschrift,*
116 (   ), pp. 189-202. A. von Harnack, in *Journal of Biblical Literature,*
50 (1931), pp. 266ff.; cf. Alf. Resch, *Der Paulinismus u. die Logia Jesu,* in
Texte u. Untersuchungen. N.F. XII (1904).
[5]W. P. Walters, in *Christianity Today,* Dec. 19, 1960, p. 8 (p. 228).

shocking, it would seem that the verses are always delivered in the language of the person being addressed, no
matter what the original language of the particular scripture may have been. It is always the *audience* which de-
termines in what language God shall speak to men—the
experience of Pentecost should make that clear—and also
through what version or edition of the Scriptures he shall
speak. The edition is naturally the one which is both
understood and accepted by the hearer; in short, as missionaries know, people are always preached to *from their
own Bible*. To the world to which the English translation
of the Book of Mormon was addressed there was only one
acceptable Bible, the King James translation. And so the
Book of Mormon follows that. But no edition or translation
is perfect and the Book of Mormon does not follow the
King James version slavishly by any means—that is a thing
which the critics studiously overlook. As long as the King
James version conveys the correct meaning it is naturally
the text to follow; but the quotations from it in the Book
of Mormon are full of changes. Are they significant? Let
us see.

Nephi's Independent Sources

Towards the close of his book, Nephi quotes two
chapters of Isaiah (48 and 49) in full. This would indeed
be a daring thing for a forger to do—to include whole pages
of the Bible in a work designed to fool the Bible-reading
public. Still worse, the language is, without any attempt
at disguise, that of the King James version. If the author
of the Book of Mormon were an imposter, his attempts to
deceive are prodigiously artless.

But the Book of Mormon follows the language of the
King James Bible only as far as the latter conveys the
correct meaning of the original. So far is Nephi's translation
from being a slavish repetition of our Bible that there is
hardly a single verse that is identical in the two transla-

tions! Granting that Nephi was reading a text of Isaiah
barely a hundred years old, one would naturally expect
some discrepancies between it and the manuscripts available to us. But how would they differ? Here a forger
would be on dangerous ground indeed, and one approaches
the Book of Mormon demonstration with considerable
interest.

If we underline in red every word in the Book of
Mormon text of Isaiah 48 and 49 that is not found in the
King James Bible and vice versa we get a surprising display
of color, especially in the Book of Mormon. Most of the
differences are quite minor ones, such as an extra "nevertheless," "yea," "but," "behold," etc., but there are four
passages that stand out spectacularly in almost solid red.
They are 48:1, 14, and 49:1, 13. Now one of the important
results of recent Dead Sea Scrolls investigations is the
recognition that the text of the Septuagint (the Greek
translation of the Old Testament done in the third century
B.C.) opens the door to very old and valuable texts of the
Old Testament that differ quite markedly from the Masoretic text on which our King James translation is based.[6]
Unfortunately both the Dead Sea (Cave I) text of Isaiah
and the Septuagint text happen to be inferior articles, the
former "rather an anticlimax" to the hopes of scholars,
and the latter "among the poorest [texts] in the Greek
Bible."[7]

But even if we do not find the clear-cut contrasts
that so gratify the student who compares other books of
the Old Testament in the Qumran, Septuagint, and Masoretic versions, the case is far from hopeless, for we do find
significant variations when we compare chapters 48 and 49
of Isaiah in the King James (Masorete) Bible and the
Septuagint. Again we compare the red markings, and
again just four passages stand out, to wit, 48:1, 14, and

---

[6]F. M. Cross, Jr., *The Ancient Library of Qumran and Modern Biblical Studies* (New York: Doubleday, 1958), pp. 128-144.
[7]*Ibid.*, p. 132.

49:1, 13, that is, the Book of Mormon conflicts with the
King James Bible in the *same* verses in which the Septuagint and the Masoretic texts conflict! Of course a very sly
and thorough operator even a hundred years ago could
discover the discrepancies, since both texts were available
at that time, and exploit them. But there was no exploitation. Aside from the fact that such a clever person would
not run the risk of competing with the Bible in the first
place, one must recognize that the coincidence was never
pointed out or apparently even noticed by anybody. Moreover, in these four verses the Book of Mormon does *not*
follow any other known text. This too is significant, since
all available manuscripts are far removed from the
original,[8] their disagreements showing not what the original
said, but only that in these particular verses something is
seriously wrong. If Nephi's version (1 Nephi 20-21) is
correct, it should differ from both the King James and the
Septuagint and it does. Here is how they compare:

Isaiah 48:1

King James (Masoretic):

Hear ye this, O house of Jacob, which are called by
the name of Israel, and are come forth out of the waters
of Judah, which swear by the name of the Lord, and make
mention of the God of Israel, but not in truth, nor in
righteousness.

Septuagint:

Hear these things, house of Jacob, who are called by
the name of Israel and who came forth out of Judah, who
swear by the name of [the] Lord God of Israel, remember-
ing [him] neither in truth nor in justice.

Book of Mormon:

Hearken and hear this, O house of Jacob, who are
called by the name of Israel, and are come forth out of

---

[8]*Ibid.*, pp. 135, 133.

the waters of Judah, or out of the waters of baptism, who
swear by the name of the Lord, and make mention of the
God of Israel, yet they swear not in truth nor in righteousness.

Isaiah 48:14

King James:

All ye, assemble yourselves, and hear; which among
them hath declared these things? The Lord hath loved
him: he will do his pleasure on Babylon, and his arm shall
be on the Chaldeans.

Septuagint:

And they shall all be gathered together and shall hear.
Who announced these things to them? Loving thee I have
done what thou desirest concerning Babylon to the taking
away of the seed of the Chaldeans.

Book of Mormon:

All ye, assemble yourselves, and hear; who among
them hath declared these things unto them? The Lord
hath loved him; yea, and he will fulfill his word which
he hath declared by them; and he will do his pleasure on
Babylon; and his arm shall come upon the Chaldeans.

Isaiah 49:1

King James:

Listen, O isles, unto me; and hearken, ye people, from
afar; The Lord hath called me from the womb; from the
bowels of my mother hath he made mention of my name.

Septuagint:

Hear ye, islands, and give attention nations [or Gen-
tiles]. 'For a long time shall he stand,' saith the Lord.
From the womb of my mother [or since I was born] he
called my name.

Book of Mormon:

And again: Hearken, O ye house of Israel, all ye that are broken off and are driven out, because of the wickedness of the pastors of my people; yea, all ye that are broken off, that are scattered abroad, who are of my people, O house of Israel. Listen, O isles, unto me, . . . [The rest is like the King James.]

Isaiah 49:13

King James:

Sing, O heavens; and be joyful, O earth; and break forth into singing, O mountains: for the Lord hath comforted his people, and will have mercy upon his afflicted.

Septuagint:

Rejoice, [O] heavens, and celebrate O earth, let the mountains break [out] in jubilation and the hills in righteousness; because God hath had mercy upon his people and the humble of his people he has forgiven.

Book of Mormon:

Sing, O heavens; and be joyful, O earth; for the feet of those who are in the east shall be established; and break forth into singing, O mountains; for they shall be smitten no more; for the Lord hath comforted his people and will have mercy upon his afflicted.

In each of these passages there is a substantial difference between the three readings. In the first, the Septuagint omits all mention of the waters of Judah; the King James mentions waters of Judah but not "waters of baptism," found only in the Book of Mormon (though not in the first edition). In the second, the persons and numbers differ between the King James and the Septuagint, while the latter alone makes mention of removing the seed of the Chaldeans; the Book of Mormon and the Septuagint agree against the King James in adding "unto them" to the first sentence, while the Book of Mormon prefaces the sentence with the words, "yea, and he will fulfill his word, which he hath declared by them," not found in either of the other texts. The dropping out of this passage would explain the obvious confusion in the other two texts.

In the third passage the Book of Mormon has an introduction that is missing from both the King James and the Septuagint. Since it is a denunciation of the "wickedness of the pastors of my people," who are held responsible for the scattering of Israel, it is obvious why it is ignored by the doctors of the schools who made both the Septuagint and the Masora. Justin Martyr accused the Jewish doctors of removing passages which they found distasteful. The Septuagint interprets the people in distant places as gentiles and introduces a direct utterance of the Lord not found in the King James. In the fourth passage the sense of the Septuagint is quite different from that of the King James, explaining that the Lord will forgive his people if they humble themselves. The Book of Mormon adds a phrase found in neither of the other sources, obviously addressed to people possessing more information than we do: ". . . for the feet of those who are in the east shall be established."

This brief and superficial glance at three books is merely meant to indicate that there is something going on here that deserves more careful investigation. The way in which the Book of Mormon fits into the Old Testament picture is, to say the least, remarkable.

"Proof Texts"

The many quotations from the Old Testament in the Book of Mormon are almost all given as "proof texts." They belong to a type of Bible exegesis the significance of which was not appreciated until seen to supply the explanation to a baffling phenomenon that emerged in the study of the Dead Sea Scrolls. Various scholars had no difficulty at all matching up the historical situation as described in the Scrolls with the actual historical conditions known to have prevailed in Palestine during Byzantine, Roman, Greek, Babylonian, Persian, or Assyrian conquests and occupations. The only trouble was that since the tribulations of war and defeat are much the same at any time the experts could not agree on just which enemy the writers of the Scrolls had in mind. The solution was, that the persecuted sectaries had a way of comparing their present situation with *any* parallel situation in Israel's past: they were Israel in the wilderness, receiving the laws as they dwelt in their tents; the community in arms was the host of heaven overthrowing Belial in the beginning, or the victorious troops of David, or the Sons of Light overthrowing the Sons of Darkness in the last great conflict; their persecutors were the Kittim—of Rome or Macedon or Egypt or Assyria; their doctrinal opponents were "the house of Absolom" or "the house of Peleg"; the locale of events was designated by names of the geographical sites of great events in the history of Israel which they wished to compare with their own history. "There is no need to take such references literally," writes T. H. Gaster, ". . . it is quite futile to go casting around among the records of the Hellenistic or Roman periods for a particular villain . . ."[9] The most important borrowing of the Christians from Qumran, in the opinion of A. R. C. Leaney, who is determined to minimize any connection whatever between the Scrolls and the New Testament, was a special kind of scriptural exegesis, "the interpretation of contemporary events in the light of prophecy through a typological or allegorical method, a method not to be confused with that of the schools but peculiar to these people, "arising out of the desire to see prophecy fulfilled in contemporary events."[10] Along with this goes the use of "proof-texts" by which all

[9]T. H. Gaster, *The Dead Sea Scriptures* (Garden City: Doubleday Anchor Books, 1957), p. 25.
[10]A. R. C. Leaney, *Guide to the Scrolls*, pp. 69-70.

the ancient prophets are called upon to furnish explanation
or illustrations to a present doctrine or situation: "It is
evident that the Qumran community was using many of
the Christian church's proof-texts before the Christians
used them."[10]

The Book of Mormon opens with Nephi teaching his
people in the desert by reading the old books to them and
comparing their present situation with that of Israel in the
wilderness: ". . . I, Nephi, did teach my brethren these
things . . . I did read many things to them which were
written in the book of Moses . . . I did read unto them
that which was written by the prophet Isaiah; for I did
liken ALL scriptures unto us, that it might be for our profit
and learning." (1 Nephi 19:22-23.) Forever after the
Nephites on great public occasions of rejoicing or tribula-
tion were called upon to remember like blessings or sufferings of their ancestors, as the books were read to them and
the parallel situation pointed out to them. Thus when Alma
went to preach in the sticks to some Zoramite outcasts
who had been barred from the holy places because of their
poverty he took as his text the short autobiographical hymn
of the prophet Zenos, in which that Old World hero told
how he too had been banished from the religious community and wandered in the desert as a despised outcast
but still could call upon God wherever he was until God
finally vindicated him and punished his enemies. (Alma
33:3-11.) It was the most natural thing in the world for
the Nephites to name places in the New World after places
they had known in the old—a common practice among
colonists everywhere; if there was a Bountiful in the old
country we should not be surprised to learn that there was
a Bountiful in the New World, even as there is one in
Utah today. "And now I say, is there not a type in this
thing?" (Alma 37:45.) Thanks to the discovery of the
Dead Sea Scrolls it is now apparent that the ancient Jews
were much more concerned with types of things than has
hitherto been suspected.

The Isaiah Scroll.

"The Isaiah Question"

In view of the newly discovered insights into the nature of ancient scriptures, it is getting harder and harder to find really serious objections to the Book of Mormon, and today there is a tendency to fall back on the one point of attack that seems to have held up in the past, the so-called Isaiah question. Since this has been in capable hands in the past, we have directed our attention elsewhere; but constant prodding from non-Mormons who are not just attacking the Book of Mormon but apparently really want to know, combined with some very recent and important studies that put things in a new and surprising light, constrain us to undertake a brief discussion of this important point. This is especially in order since of recent years Isaiah has come in for far more attention and study than any other book of the Bible: in a period of ten years more than 30 studies were published on Isaiah 7:10-17 alone, and more than a hundred books and articles on the "Servant" passages.[11]

The Book of Mormon Explains Isaiah

Away back in the 12th century Ibn Ezra, a Jewish scholar, declared that chapters 40 to 66 of Isaiah seemed to form a literary unity, distinct in style and content from the rest of the book. To explain this, it was assumed that this part of the book was written not by Isaiah but by another person and at another time, presumably some 200 years later.

Since 1789 this hypothetical author has been referred to as the Second Isaiah or Deutero-Isaiah. But once the dual authorship of Isaiah was generally accepted, it soon became apparent that there was no need to stop at two Isaiahs. By applying exactly the same reasoning that split the original Isaiah in two, it was possible to break up the two main sections into a number of separate packages, each of which in turn readily yielded to the fragmentation process to produce scores of independent compositions, all going under the name of Isaiah.[12] First, chapters 40-66 broke up into separate books, 40-55 being by one author and 56-66 by another, duly labelled Trito-Isaiah. Chapters 36-39 were recognized as a separate book on the grounds of their resemblance to 2 Kings 18:13-20:19. The earlier Isaiah, chapters 1-35, became a swarm of separate sayings glued together, according to one school, from a large number of smaller or medium-sized collections or, according to another school, gathered as minor additions to a central main work. Some scholars agreed that chapters 1-12 and

---

[11]A. Fohrer, in *Theologischer Rundschau,* 28 (1963), p. 243. This study is a complete survey of Isaiah literature between 1953 and 1963.

[12]"The more the authorship of the Book of Isaiah has been investigated, the more complicated has the question appeared." Finally "there remained very few long passages of unchallenged authority. . . . It seemed that the entire book was best described as an anthology of the work of many writers . . . a confused amalgam of greater or smaller fragments from many sources." J. Eaton, in *Vetus Testamentum,* 9 (1960), pp. 138f.

13-23 represented separate collections, though each had his own theory as to how, when, where, and by whom such collections were made.[13] There is no point to going into the subject in detail. Typical is the present dating of the so-called Trito-Isaiah, which is variously placed in the 3rd, 4th, 5th, 6th, 7th, and 8th centuries B. C.[14]

The most recent survey of the whole Isaiah problem reaches the conclusion that because of its "very long and complicated prehistory" it will "never be possible to achieve a completely satisfying and thoroughly convincing analysis" of the original book of Isaiah.[15]

But our immediate concern is not with the unity of Isaiah but with the dating of the Deutero-Isaiah, since the charge against the Book of Mormon is that it quotes from that work, which did not exist at the time Lehi left Jerusalem. The dating of Deutero-Isaiah rests on three things: (1) the mention of Cyrus (44:28), who lived 200 years after Isaiah and long after Lehi, (2) the threats against Babylon (47:1, 48:14), which became the oppressor of Judah after the days of Isaiah, and (3) the general language and setting of the text which suggest a historical background commonly associated with a later period than that of Isaiah.[16]

The late date of Deutero-Isaiah is one of those things that has been taken for granted by everybody for years, so that today it would be hard to find a scholar who could really explain it and impossible to find one who could prove it. The Isaiah question belongs pre-eminently to that "large part of the questions about the history and prehistory of the Old Testament" which, as J. A. Soggin has recently noted, "were formulated at a time when men possessed a different concept of historical study and a much smaller

---

[13]The process is described in the latest extensive survey of the problem, Otto Eissfeldt, *Einleitung in das Alte Testament* (3rd ed., Tübingen: Morh, 1964), pp. 408-412.
[14]*Ibid.*, p. 460.
[15]*Ibid.*, p. 413.
[16]*Ibid.*, p. 408.

knowledge of the ancient East" than they do today.[17] Until
recently, Soggin observes, biblical scholarship was dominated by "the dream of the completely objective investigator, or at least by the belief that such an ideal was
attainable."[18] But with the passing of authoritarian abso-
lutes in scholarship, the interpretation of Isaiah has become
increasingly fluid. Thus, Eissfeldt can now tell us that
references to Cyrus or Babylon do not necessarily date the
chapters or even the verses in which they appear, the
passages being so typically "Isaian" that the names may
well be later substitutions.[19] He notes that Isaiah always
preached the restoration as well as the destruction of Jerusalem (he named his first child "The Returning Remnant"!), and that the threat and the promise go necessarily
and inseparably together, so that the optimism of Deutero-
Isaiah is no sign of separate authorship.[20] He notes that
there has never been any agreement among the experts as
to what are "characteristically Isaiah" thoughts and expressions,[21] and that while one group of scholars sees carefully
planned organization and development in the arrangement
of the writings, another cannot detect the slightest trace
of either.[22] Finally he concludes with pointing out that
there is a very close overall resemblance among all the
chapters of Isaiah and that if there is no chapter that
does not contain genuine utterances of the prophet, neither
is there a chapter that does not contain unauthentic passages.[23]

The trouble with dating any part of Isaiah, as Eissfeldt points out, is that we have nothing really definite to

[17]J. A. Soggin, "Geschichte, Historie und Heilsgeschichte im Alten Testament," in *Theologische Literaturzeitung*, 89 (1964), p. 724.
[18]*Ibid.*, p. 723.
[19]Eissfeldt, *op. cit.*, p. 420.
[20]*Ibid.*, pp. 416, 424. Likewise, the hymns of praise and the satiric verses,
though completely opposite in tone, belong together and do not indicate
separate authorship, p. 457.
[21]*Ibid.*, pp. 431f. and *passim.*
[22]*Ibid.*, pp. 452-3.
[23]*Ibid.*, pp. 461, 466.

go on; fixing dates or places with reference to "any religious or spiritual concepts is very uncertain. . . . all we have to go by is general impressions, and we must be satisfied at best with mere possibilities."[24] In the past, scholars have put great confidence in their ability to assign origins to documents on the evidence of the general language and setting of the text. A classic example is the impassioned utterance of Isaiah against the wicked nations, plainly the cry of an afflicted people to be avenged on their enemies, plainly an eschatological yearning that breathes the spirit of the exile, which therefore must have been written during the exile and by one of the exiles, long after Isaiah's day. And so we can identify Deutero-Isaiah. But, as Eissfeldt now points out, there is no reason why the imprecations against the nations should not have been uttered against the Assyrian army and empire in Isaiah's curse embracing as they did all the nations in their sinister host.[25] Nor, as other scholars note, is there any reason why one must be an exile to write about the exile; how far can we trust the insight of the experts when each can tell us that it is obvious to him that the exile passages were written in Babylon (Volz), Palestine (Mowinckel), Egypt (Marti), or Lebanon (Duhm)?[26]

The most telling dichotomy between Isaiah and Deutero-Isaiah in time is the emphasis of the latter on the apocalypse of bliss—the return of the exiles and the rebuilding of the holy city and temple, as against the grim apocalypse of woe that prevails in earlier Isaiah. But again, we are now being reminded that the two conceptions always form an indivisible whole in the thinking of Isaiah— you can't think of a gathering unless there has been a scattering and vice versa: they do not represent two different concepts of history at all, but one and the same doctrine that is basic to all the prophets and much older than Isaiah.

---

[24]*Ibid.*, pp. 464-5.
[25]*Ibid.*, p. 421.
[26]*Ibid.*, p. 447.

This is a thing that is being increasingly emphasized today in the light of comparative studies which show that the idea of a cyclic concept of things, of alternate periods of suffering and defeat followed by victory and prosperity, is attested very early in the Egyptian and Babylonian literature and seems to have been a fundamental part of the ritual patterns of the ancient East from very early times.[27] Because the eschatological and apocalyptic element dominates in the later apocrypha, it was long assumed to be a *later* religious development, but the comparative study of ancient ritual texts and monuments and their discovery in constantly increasing numbers is definitely changing the picture.

Turning now to the Book of Mormon, we find that the most widely accepted of all the divisions of Isaiah is the three-fold classification, following Isaiah's own designation, of the Words of Isaiah (ch. 1-35), the "Accounts" (*Berichte,* 36-39), and again the "Words" (40-66).[28] That the titles are authentic is implied in the designation of sections of the Book of Mormon by their ancient titles as The *Words* of Mormon, "An *account* of the sons of Mosiah . . . according to the record of Alma," and "the *account* of the people of Nephi . . . according to the record of Helaman. . . ." This is the sort of complexity that scholars discover everywhere in Isaiah, where certain words may serve as key words or signatures, denoting the beginning or ending of an independent writing that has been inserted into the text. If anything, the Book of Mormon attests the busy reshuffling and re-editing of separate parts of sacred writings that often go under the name of a single prophet.

It is further significant that the only passages from Isaiah quoted in the Book of Mormon are chapters 2-14 and 48-54. This corresponds surprisingly to the major

---

[27]One of the most useful collections of texts on this subject is that of A. von Gall, *Basileia tou Theou* (Heidelberg, Winter, 1926). For a more recent survey, see our "Expanding Gospel," in *BYU Studies,* 7 (1966), pp. 3-27.

[28]Eissfeldt, p. 408.

divisions of Isaiah on which the scholars have most widely
agreed, i.e., chapters 1-13 as the original Isaiah collection
and 49-55 as the authentic Deutero-Isaiah. Only these two
sections are quoted in the Book of Mormon. Why does
Nephi, the passionate devotee, as he proclaims himself, of
the writings of Isaiah, quote only from these two blocks
of those writings? Can it be that they represent what
pretty well *was* the writing of Isaiah in Lehi's time? The
failure to quote from the first chapter, the most famous of
all, suggests the theory of some scholars that that chapter
is actually a general summary of the whole work and may
have been added after.[29] But we are playing the same
game as the others, and it is time to return to firmer
ground.

The Transmission of the Record

If others than Isaiah wrote about half the words in
his book, why do we not know their names? The answer is,
because of the way in which they worked. They were
(as it is now explained) Isaiah's own disciples or students,
collecting and explaining his sayings with no desire to be
original; always they kept the master's teachings foremost
in mind. What we have in Isaiah is a lot of genuine words
of the prophet intermingled with other stuff by his well-
meaning followers.[30] Every chapter, including those in
Deutero- and Trito- Isaiah, contains genuine words of
Isaiah; and every chapter including all those in the early
part of the book, contains words that are not his. As Eissfeldt sums it up, in spite of all differences there are "very
strong stylistic and historical resemblances between 40-55
and 56-66," and yet "the relationship between chapters
1-39 and 40-55 is just as close . . . and the resemblances

---

[29]"This is the programmatic introduction presenting all the main themes
which will dominate the handling and expansion of Isaiah's oracles. . . ."
D. Jones, in *Zeitschrift für Alt-testamentliche Wissenschaft*, 67 (1955), p. 238.
L. G. Rignell has argued that Ch. I is definitely *older* than the rest of Isaiah,
to which it is an obvious addition; see G. Fohrer, *op. cit.*, p. 68.

[30]J. Eaton, in *Vetus Testamentum*, 9 (1960), pp. 138-141, 149.

include even peculiarities of speech."[31] With the spirit
and the words of the true Isaiah thus pervading and
dominating the whole work, the items that depart from the
standard can be readily explained on one theory or another.

Significantly enough, the Book of Mormon itself proclaims the re-editings and manipulations of the Isaiah text
all over the place. Every one of the 21 chapters extensively
quoted in the Book of Mormon appears in that work with
an impressive number of additions, deletions, alterations,
and transpositions. On the testimony of the Book of Mormon, the standard texts of Isaiah that have reached us
have indeed suffered in the process of transmission. That
process has recently been the subject of a significant study
by Douglas Jones, which may be profitably perused in conjunction with the very extensive statements contained in
the Book of Mormon explaining the peculiar customs of
preserving and transmitting the record among the Nephites.

Jones begins by noting that a special technique of
prophetic transmission was employed among the ancient
Jews. This is exemplified by the cases of Isaiah and Jeremiah. The latter, when he wishes to convey the word of
prophecy to men of a future time, (1) makes an abridgement of his past prophecies in order to "summarize the
message of twenty years into a concentrate suitable for a
single, uninterrupted reading"; (2) this he writes down on
a specially prepared document, and (3) in the presence of
witnesses (4) he seals it carefully and (5) lays the writings
away in a clay jar "that they may continue many days."[32]
This, Jones observes, "was a quite ordinary business trans-
action," but where the document is no ordinary business
paper but the word of prophecy, "every word of the narra-
tive breathes prophetic significance."[33]

----

[31]Eissfeldt, op. cit., p. 466.
[32]Douglas Jones, "The Tradition of the Oracles of Isaiah in Jerusalem,"
it Zt. f. N.T. Wiss., 67 (1955), pp. 227-8.
[33]Ibid., p. 231. The three witnesses were Uriah, Zechariah, and Isaiah
himself. Isa. 8:2.

Two centuries earlier Isaiah operated in the same way. He wrote an abridgement of his longer writings on a *gillayon*, "possibly a tablet of polished metal," according to Jones, which he sealed up in the presence of three witnesses and laid away "that they might live for future generations." Both prophets "write down a number of oracles in condensed form that they might also stand as a witness when the day comes, that Yahweh had declared before hand,"[34] both transmitting "a single symbolic prediction made to contemporaries but also written down and witnessed that people of a later time might see its fulfillment as Yahweh's work." For this it is necessary to seal the record "that it will not be tampered with" and to bury it or entrust it only to faithful disciples.[35]

At once the example of the Book of Mormon springs to mind, rooted as it is in the Old World practices current in the days of these very prophets: like their works it is an abridgement of much more extensive writings, put down on tablets of metal, witnessed, sealed, and buried to come forth as a witness for God in the later time.

Jones explains the present state of our Isaiah text by attributing it largely to the three successive transmissions by which it has come down to us. The first *traditio*, as he calls it, was the work of Isaiah himself, who prepared his metal plates or whatever they were and sealed them up to be a witness at a later time; the second was the bringing forth of this record hundreds of years later "by disciples of the period following the fall of Jerusalem." The third *traditio* is marked by the commentary of "the greatest of all Isaiah's disciples, whose work is now shown over and over again to reveal close knowledge of the teaching of Isaiah of Jerusalem." Desiring only to transmit the master's work in the clearest possible form, this disciple adds

---

[34]*Ibid.*, p. 237.

[35]*Ibid.*, pp. 228f., 236. Isaiah 30:8 is another "permanent record of Isaiah's oracles to stand as a witness that his plan had been declared of old."

his "reflexion on the marvellous way in which the divine word has been fulfilled."[36]

Compare these three steps in the long process of transmission with what we see happening over and over again in the Book of Mormon. Take the longest tradition, for example. In protohistoric times the Lord told the brother of Jared (as he is reported to have told Enoch and others of the Adamic and Patriarchal ages): "Write these things and seal them up; and I will show them in mine own due time unto the children of men." (Eth. 3:27.) The patriarch did as he was told, and in due time his writings came into the hands of Ether, who "went forth, and beheld that the words of the Lord had all been fulfilled," and then added his part to the writing, "and he finished his record . . . and he hid them in a manner that the people of Limhi did find them." (Eth. 15:33.) Next the writings were brought to King Mosiah, who translated them but was commanded to hide them up until a later generation. (Eth. 4:1.) Hundreds of years later Moroni got them, made a stringent abridgement of them ("and the hundredth part I have not written," 15:33), adding all kinds of commentaries and explanations of his own, after which, he reports, "he commanded me that I should seal them up; and . . . that I should seal up the interpretation thereof" (4:5), and finally, "I am commanded that I should hide them up again in the earth." (4:3.)

In our own dispensation they were brought forth again with the stipulation: "And unto three witnesses shall they be shown. . . . And in the mouth of three witnesses shall these things be established; . . . and all this shall stand as a testimony against the world at the last day." (Eth. 5:3-4.) After this they were removed again with the understanding that many parts of them still remain to be made known in future manifestations.

The whole process is identical with that now attributed

---

[36]*Ibid.*, p. 245.

to the transmission of Isaiah's text. The important thing
to note is that each transmitter did not merely hand the
records intact to the next one. Every one of the successive
editors *did* something to them—abridging, annotating, explaining, translating, doing what he could to make the
ancient words more comprehensible to his own age and
the people who should come after. Thus a large part of
the book of Ether consists of Moroni's own "reflexion on
the marvellous way in which the divine word has been
fulfilled," making Moroni Ether's "Deutero-Isaiah," yet for
all that it is still the book of *Ether*.[37] Why then should
we not recognize the same process of transmission with
periodic re-editings when Mr. Jones points it out to us
in Isaiah? The presence of such additions and changes no
more disqualifies it as the work of Isaiah than Mormon's
redoing of the plates of Nephi impugn the authorship of
Nephi.

The transmitters of Isaiah, we are told, "adapted the
words of the master to contemporary situations, expanding
them and adding further oracles."[38] And that is exactly
what the writers of the Book of Mormon do, beginning
with Nephi, who abridges his father's writings, brings all
the prophets, and especially Isaiah, up to date. (". . . for I
did liken *all* the scriptures unto *us*. . . ." (1 Nephi 19:22-23.
Italics added.) He explains that without a radical re-
interpretation by him his people could not even begin to
comprehend what the prophets were talking about: ". . . the
words of Isaiah are *not plain unto you*," he tells them
frankly (2 Nephi 25:4; italics added), being written in a

[37]Fohrer, *op. cit.*, pp. 64-65, notes that the increasingly accepted idea of
the book of Isaiah as the work of a "school" is actually an approach to the old
idea of single authorship, since all composition was undertaken with strict and
devout adherence to the teachings of one master. The concept is very conspicuous in the Book of Mormon, in which every longer book, though bearing
the name of its original writer, is the work of much editing by later hands.
[38]Jones, *op. cit.*, pp. 240-244, shows how this is done. The disciples felt
free to update the names of cities and individuals to make their preaching more
intelligible to contemporary hearers. Fohrer, *op. cit.*, pp. 73, 240.

special idiom that only the Jews understand (v. 5), and that Nephi understands because he knows their cultural and historical setting: ". . . I, of myself, have dwelt at Jerusalem, wherefore I know concerning the regions round about." (v. 6.)

If the process of transmission from the brother of Jared to Moroni seems fabulously long, there is evidence that the system was a very old and persistent one in the Old World as well as in the New. It has been shown that the identical system used by Isaiah was used by Jeremiah 200 years later. Twelve years ago we showed in *The Improvement Era* what others of more authority have since confirmed: that the sealing and laying away of some of the Dead Sea Scrolls consciously carried on the same tradition and used the same techniques, in the same confidence that the record would come forth as a witness in a later time.[39] Thus the tradition and practice survived from the time of Isaiah right down to the end of the Jewish nation. And in the other direction it goes back to ages long before Isaiah, when the Torah itself was deposited in the ark for the very purpose of providing a written witness for later ages. In Israel the transmission of the sacred records went hand in hand with the transmission of the crown itself, "just as Joash is handed the '*eduth* with his crown when he is made king," the '*eduth* being "the covenant or the tablets or the book as something deposited and therefore palpably present to be a witness" and not merely by an intangible teaching or tradition.[40] The transmission of the records with the crown is established procedure in the Book of Mormon. (Alma 37; Omni 11, 19-20; Moroni 10, etc.)

In explaining Isaiah to his people, Nephi makes some important points. Much remains of Isaiah's words to be fulfilled, he tells them, and in whatever age a fulfillment

---

[39]*The Improvement Era*, February 1954, p. 89.
[40]Jones, *op. cit.*, p. 234.

takes place his words stand as a witness, each fulfillment guaranteeing the validity of the prophecies whose fulfillment yet remains (2 Nephi 25:7); hence his writings are of peculiar "worth unto the children of men" in general. (v. 8.) We are concerned here with a repeating process: ". . . they have been destroyed from generation to generation," but never without warning (v. 9); Nephi confirms the destruction in his day that Isaiah had foretold long before (v. 10), foretells the restoration to follow (v. 11), only to lead to another catastrophe when "Jerusalem shall be destroyed again" (v. 14), to be gathered again, however, "after many generations" (v. 16) in much the same manner as Israel was brought out of Egypt—for the Exodus is another installment of this repeating story (v. 20) to which a long line of written reports bears witness as they too pass down "from generation to generation" (v. 22).

Hence Nephi is witness to the same things that Isaiah himself is: "And the words which I have spoken shall stand as a testimony against you. . . ." (v. 28.) He joins his words to those of Isaiah in a common declaration, "for *he* verily saw my Redeemer, even as *I* have seen him" (2 Nephi 11:2; italics added), and makes the remarkable announcement that since his brother Jacob "also has seen him as I have seen him" (v. 3), Nephi, Jacob, and Isaiah stand as three witnesses to their common teaching—they are contemporary, for all teach the same thing— ". . . all things which have been given of God from the beginning of the world, unto man, are the typifying of him." (v. 4.)

All the prophets teach the same thing; that is why the pious Jarom says he need not bother to write down anything: ". . . I shall not write the things of my prophesying, nor of my revelations. For what could I write more than my fathers have written? For have not they revealed the plan of salvation?" (Jarom 2.) We have to do here with a story already told, with a history of characteristic and repeating events recounted in a formulaic language of set terms and expressions that cannot be limited to any time or place.

When Jesus himself finally came to the Nephites, he again re-edited the whole corpus, recommended the words of Isaiah (3 Nephi 23:1), filled in the gaps of the record (vss. 8-13), corrected all defects (vss. 4, 6), brought the Nephite scriptures up to date (3 Nephi 24:1), and then "expounded *all* the scriptures *in one,*" as a single, unified work. (3 Nephi 23:14, 6. Italics added.) Just so, in the New Testament, when the Lord appears to the disciples after the resurrection, "he opened . . . the scriptures" to them. (Luke 24:32.) "And he said unto them, These are the words which I spake unto you, while I was yet with you, that all things must be fulfilled, which were written in the law of Moses, and in the prophets, and in the psalms, concerning me. Then opened he their understanding, that they might understand the scriptures." (Luke 24:44-45.)

It has often been objected that a plan that is already agreed on and a story that is already told are more depressing and repellent to the eager and inquiring mind than the thrill of exploring the unknown. But is a journey any less interesting because we have a map to go by? On the contrary, the scouts with the map not only learn more but have a more exciting time.

Since all the prophets tell the same story (2 Nephi 9:2), any prophet is free to contribute anything to the written record that will make that message clear and intelligible. The principle is illustrated throughout the Book of Mormon, and indeed by the very existence of the book itself—a book that shocked the world with its revolutionary concept of scripture as an open-ended production susceptible to the errors of men and amenable to correction by the spirit of prophecy. But the classic illustration of this principle is to be found in Isaiah's own writings. ". . . in 1880," writes H. Wildberger, "there was hardly a scholar alive who did not believe that Isaiah lifted the passage (Isaiah 2:2-4) from Micah (4:1-3), "the two being almost word for word the same. But now it would appear that both prophets are quoting "archaic ritual texts."[41] Isaiah is simply exercising his prophet's prerogative of clothing his own message in the inspired words of his predecessors when those words suit his purpose.

The very first Isaiah passage cited in the Book of Mormon (1 Nephi 20:1) differs radically as we have seen, from both the Masoretic and the LXX versions, which by their own disagreements show that the original text had been corrupted.[42] But that is not all, for the second edition of the Book of Mormon contains an addition not found in the first: ". . . out of the waters of Judah, *or out of the waters of baptism.*" It is said that Parley P. Pratt suggested the phrase, and certainly Joseph Smith approved it, for it stands in all the early editions after the first. Those added words are not only permissible—they are necessary. If a translation is, as Wilamowitz-Moellendorff defined it, "a statement in the translator's own words of what he thinks the author had in mind," then surely that phrase about baptism cannot be omitted. Isaiah did not have to tell his ancient hearers that he had the waters of baptism in mind, but it is necessary to tell it to the modern reader who without such an explanation would miss the point—for him the translation would be a misleading one without that specification. Where continued revelation is accepted and where all the prophets are speaking the same piece, this sort of thing makes no difficulty at all.

We have spent too long on an issue that will probably remain unsettled in our generation, but the net result of our little filibuster is not without justification. The indications are that a thorough study of the rapidly changing Isaiah problem may well leave the Book of Mormon in a

---

[41]H. Wildberger, in *Vetus Testamentum*, 7 (1957), p. 65.
[42]See above, pp. 131-3.

very strong position indeed. The dating of either the whole or any part of the Deutero-Isaiah must remain uncertain as long as there is no agreement among the experts as to the relationship of the parts to each other or as to the nature, authorship, or background of the whole. And as long as no one has or can produce irrefutable proof that any single Isaiah verse quoted in the Book of Mormon *could not* have been written before 600 B.C., or indeed has not been defended by reputable scholars as the product of a much earlier time, the chronological question remains wide open.

On the other hand, impressive positive results have been gained. We have discovered that the Book of Mormon is actually way out in front in proclaiming the unity and explaining the diversity of scripture in general and of Isaiah in particular. We have discovered that the peculiar practices employed in the transmission of inspired writings in the Book of Mormon, as well as the theory and purpose behind those practices, are the very ones that prevailed in Palestine at the time Lehi lived there. We have come across a great tradition of prophetic unity that made it possible for inspired men in every age to translate, abridge, expand, explain, and update the writings of their predecessors without changing a particle of the intended meaning or in any way jeopardizing the earlier rights to authorship. Isaiah remains Isaiah no matter how many prophets repeat his words or how many other prophets he is repeating. The Book of Mormon explains how this can be so, and its explanations would seem to be the solution to the Isaiah problem toward which the scholars are at present moving.[43]

---

[43]An exhaustive survey by C. Lindhagen (1953/4) shows that the present trend in Isaiah studies is toward (1) a more conservative and less arbitrary treatment of the text; (2) a tendency to reconcile what had appeared as conflicting ideas in Isaiah; *e.g.,* the Suffering Servant can stand for a number of different individuals and groups; (3) increasing recognition of the influence of the temple ordinances in Isaiah's teachings; G. Fohrer, *op. cit.*, p. 243.

Part II.

Philological Notes

CHAPTER 6

Strange Things Strangely Told

A Unique Document

Philologically speaking, the most wonderful thing about the Book of Mormon is that there is anything to discuss at all. Massive literary forgeries are very easily detected by those not determined to be taken in, and can be thoroughly discredited to any willing to listen to the evidence. Nothing could be easier than to expose the vast and detailed history of the Book of Mormon as fraudulent if it were such. Just to brush it aside is not enough—one can brush anything aside—but to ignore the Book of Mormon after the claims it has made, the influence it has exercised, and the opportunities it has offered the critics to expose it, is to run away from it. If the Book of Mormon is a fabrication, any ten pages of it should be quite sufficient to enable the student of ancient documents not only to reject it but to show the world exactly why he finds it fraudulent. This, strangely enough, no scholar has ever done, though many eminent scholars have put themselves confidently to the task of performing that easy and rewarding public service.

There are three possible explanations for the origin of the Book of Mormon. One is that it is a product of spontaneous generation. Another is that it came into existence in the way Joseph Smith said it did, by special messengers and gifts from God. The third is the hypothesis

that Joseph Smith or some other party or parties simply
made it all up. No experiments have ever been carried out
for testing any of these theories. The first has not even
been considered, the second has been dismissed with a
contemptuous wave of the hand, and the third has been
accepted without question or hesitation.

And yet the third theory is quite as extravagant as
the other two, demanding unlimited gullibility and the
suspension of all critical judgment in any who would accept
it. It is based on the simple proposition that since people
have written books somebody, namely Smith or a contemporary, wrote this one. But to make this thesis stick
is to show not only that people have written big books,
but that somebody has been able to produce a big book
like this one. But no other such book exists. Where will
you find another work remotely approaching the Book of
Mormon in scope and daring? It appears suddenly out of
nothing—not an accumulation of 25 years like the Koran,
but a single staggering performance, bursting on a shocked
and scandalized world like an explosion, the full-blown
history of an ancient people, following them through all
the trials, triumphs, and vicissitudes of a thousand years
without a break, telling how a civilization originated, rose
to momentary greatness, and passed away, giving due
attention to every phase of civilized history in a densely
compact and rapidly moving story that interweaves dozens
of plots with an inexhaustible fertility of invention and an
uncanny consistency that is never caught in a slip or contradiction. We respectfully solicit the name of any student
or professor in the world who could come within ten thousand miles of such a performance. As a sheer tour-de-force
there is nothing like it. The theory that Joseph Smith wrote
the Book of Mormon simply will not stand examination.
What kind of a book is it?

The Book of Mormon is a colossal structure. Considered purely as fiction, it is a performance without parallel.

What other volume can approach this wealth of detail and tight-woven complexity, this factual precision combined with simple open lucidity? Any book we choose is feeble by comparison: some of them have one quality and some another, but like Matthew Arnold's Homer, the Book of Mormon combines these usually incompatible qualities in a structure of flawless consistency. Our American literature is full of big, bumbling, rambling, brooding, preaching, mouthing books, spinning out a writer's personal (usually adolescent) reminiscences and impressions at great and unoriginal lengths. But this terse, compact religious history of a thousand years is something utterly beyond the scope of creative writing. To check this assertion, let the skeptical reader think of a number, any number between 10 and 30; then beginning with page one of the Book of Mormon, let him turn to every page in the book which is a multiple of that number and see what he finds there. Or let him think offhand of 50 or so numbers between one and 500—any numbers—and then consult those pages of the Book of Mormon. The point here is that we are choosing a large number of items from the Book of Mormon and choosing them completely at random. What a staggering wealth of detail we discover! What boundless prodigality of invention! Take every twentieth page, for example:

Page 1: A colophon explaining who wrote the book, his background, his sources of information, his reliability, his culture, the language he is writing in, an account of the time and setting of his story, the peculiar conditions prevailing, the worries and travels of Lehi—all this and more in the first five verses.

Page 20: Interprets a dream about a large and spacious building; Nephi sees in vision the wars, tribulations, and ultimate extermination of his descendants, great destructions upon the land, and a visit of the Savior to the survivors.

Page 40: Dissension and trouble on shipboard; Nephi

is bound and the ship almost founders in a typhoon; the people arrive in the New World and continue their Old World ways of farming and pastoral nomadism; they domesticate animals and search out precious metals.

Page 60: The ending of a thanksgiving hymn by Nephi, astonishingly like the Thanksgiving Hymn of the Dead Sea Scrolls. (Some have called this a psalm, but strictly speaking a psalm is a ritual hymn connected with the rites of the Temple.) Nephi's brothers charge him with royal ambition and plan to do away with him. He continues to migrate, taking along all who are willing. There is a description of the way in which civilizations are suffused through virgin lands.

Page 80: Entirely taken up with quotations from Isaiah; we have already seen some indication of how daring and ingenious these Isaiah translations can be.

Page 100: A discourse by Nephi on Satan's *modus operandi* in this world; he prophesies the final gathering of Israel and describes the conditions under which it is to take place.

To save space let us skip from the first hundred to the last hundred pages. Page 420: Describes the aftermath of a major, and very accurately depicted earthquake, which we hope to discuss later on.

Page 440: Here Jesus himself is addressing the people to whom he has appeared after the resurrection, showing them how all the prophets spoke of him.

Page 460: The ten-year-old Mormon receives instructions on the care of sacred records in the bad times ahead. A year later he goes with his father to Zarahemla and is overwhelmed by the sight of the place. A complicated local war is raging at the time.

Page 480: Takes us back thousands of years to the great dispersion from the Tower, describing in some detail the nature of those protohistoric migrations.

Page 500: The odd customs of Jaredite kings are described—how they spend their days in captivity. Prophets, including Ether, go forth among the people.

Page 520: Moroni, having finished his sad history, finds time on his hands; he prescribes an acid test for the truth of his book and discourses on the various gifts of the Spirit.

But enough, the reader can continue the game for himself. Here we have selected at random less than 2% of the pages of the Book of Mormon and from each have taken just an item or two. This sort of exercise is a good way of calling attention to the dense compactness of the book's contents, the remarkably even distribution of material, the easy, competent, confident, unencumbered handling of vast and complicated detail. Where else will one find such inexhaustible invention combined with such unerring accuracy and consistency? To put it facetiously but not unfairly, the artist must not only balance a bowl of goldfish and three lighted candles on the end of a broomstick while fighting off a swarm of gadflies, but he must at the same time be carving an immortal piece of statuary from a lump of solid diorite. In an undertaking like this, merely to avoid total confusion and complete disaster would be a super-human achievement. But that is not the assignment; that is only a coincidental detail to the main business at hand, which is, with all this consummately skillful handling of mere technical detail, to have something significant to say; not merely significant, but profound and moving, and so relevant to the peculiar conditions of our own day as to speak to our ears with a voice of thunder.

One stands aghast at the presumption of those journalists, professors, and hack-writers who through the years have made merry over the quaint language and unfamiliar subject matter of the Book of Mormon while choosing to ignore its unparalleled scope and mastery. One is amazed by the easy effrontery of those who still assure us that anyone with a little time on his hands and an open Bible at his elbow could produce a Book of Mormon.

The very least the candid student can do is to admit that we are up against a problem here—there are things about the production of the Book of Mormon which we simply do not understand. This was frankly admitted in Joseph Smith's day,[1] and the whole corpus of literature devoted to exposing the Book of Mormon succeeds only in exposing the confusion of its authors.[2] Students of the Bible now find themselves in the same situation. Thirty years ago every seminarist was convinced that he knew just where the Bible—*and* the Book of Mormon—came from. Those were the days when they knew all the answers, but today new tests are being applied to the Bible text, and we suggest the same tests for the Book of Mormon.

Problems of Testing

A forgery is defined by specialists in ancient documents as "any document which was not produced in the time, place, and manner claimed by it or its publisher." (Wilrich.) The Book of Mormon obligingly gives full information regarding the time, place, and manner of its production. All we have to do is to check these claims. How? Against what evidence? By the same methods and using the same evidence now employed to investigate the Bible. For the two books belong to the same universe of discourse, not only spiritually but also culturally and historically.

If the Book of Mormon were a work on mathematics, it should be submitted before all to mathematicians for intelligent criticism; if it were a book on chemistry, chemists should be called in; if it were about primitive races and customs, anthropologists might with caution be consulted; if it claimed to be a work on philosophy, we might submit it to the examination of philosophers; if it were put forth

---

[1]F. Kirkham, *A New Witness for Christ in America* (Independence, Mo.: Zions' Printing and Publishing Company, 1947), pp. 129-137.

[2]See our "Mixed Voices" in *The Improvement Era*, 62 (1959), pp. 145ff., and subsequent issues.

as a masterpiece of American literature, the English department might be invited to comment.

But it claims to be none of these, and as we have seen, the authenticity of an ancient writing can be judged only in terms of what it claims for itself, never of what others may claim *for* it. Otherwise one might begin by assuming that the Book of Mormon was written by an Eskimo hunter, a Portuguese fisherman, or a New York farmer, and from there proceed to seek out anything and everything in its pages that might confirm the theory. That won't do, because literary evidence can always be contrived, even unconsciously, by an ingenious and dedicated interpreter. What, then, is the Book of Mormon about by its own assertion?

First of all, the Book of Mormon is *not* a history of the Lost Ten Tribes, as many supposedly able critics have assumed; it is *not* a history of the Indians, but only of some very remote relatives of theirs living in a distant age with a totally different culture; it does *not* describe or designate any *known* ancient people, civilization, or individual in the Western Hemisphere, nor does it designate any recognized place, city, or territory in the New World—even Cumorah receives only limited recognition and only by Latter-day Saints. Strangely enough, nearly all Book of Mormon criticism in the past, whether favorable or unfavorable, has rested on one or more of these false assumptions. All have expended their powers in examining not what the Book of Mormon claims for itself, but only what others have claimed for it.

On the other hand, the book does designate *known* cities and territories in the Old World—there is no dispute as to where Jerusalem or the Red Sea is; it does supply specific dates in terms of absolute chronology—a tremendous aid to any serious investigation; it does designate well-known individuals, peoples, and civilizations in the Old World; it does explain fully the Old World cultural background of its authors, describing how that culture was transplanted into a new land with certain resulting changes; it does indicate the literary and linguistic traditions of its authors, and tells how the migrants viewed their own situation, zealously preserving their traditions and always conscious of the central, perennial, Near Eastern core-culture from which they sprang.

The authors of the Book of Mormon carefully explain that they are writing a very specialized history, confining their attention to the doings of one particular and numerically very minor religious group, whose peculiar traditions they trace back to a long line of Messianic prophets who used to seek refuge along with their followers in the deserts of Judaea.

To whom, then, should the Book of Mormon be submitted for criticism? Plainly to those who today are at grips with the documents that hold the keys to both Jewish and Christian history.

Recently a Protestant journal of wide circulation reported with obvious satisfaction that there is "no non-Mormon archaeologist who holds that the Indians descended from the Jews, or that Christianity was known in the New World before Columbus."[3] That is hardly surprising. For years we have pointed out that such results are only to be expected as long as people insist on looking for the wrong things in the wrong places. How could an archaeologist, of all people, hope to prove "that the Indians descended from the Jews, or that Christianity was known in the New World before Columbus"? As one of the world's foremost archaeologists recently wrote, "The first thing that must be remembered is the fact . . . that material evidence will give material results. You cannot, from archaeological evidence, inform yourself on man's ideas, beliefs, fears or aspirations. You cannot understand what his works of art or craftsmanship signified to him . . . with-

---

[3]*Christianity Today,* 8 (August 28, 1964), p. 42.

out a written word, and one in some detail, you can have no knowledge of social or political systems, of ethical or legal codes. . . ."[4] In a word, it is to the written word that we must turn if we would test the Book of Mormon, specifically to that very literature from whose common background it purports to have sprung.

And here we find ourselves in an awkward situation. The geologist can impart edifying information to the most ignorant audience by showing them a piece of rock and talking about it; a botanist can tell us something important about a plant we have never seen before; even sophisticated mathematical ideas can be conveyed by an able teacher to the mathematically ignorant, and one can learn something basic about the stars the very first time one hears an astronomer talk about them. But an ancient manuscript means *nothing whatever* to a person who has not already laid a broad and solid foundation in its language.

It is for this reason that the study of the documents has steadily lost ground in the 20th century in competition with more readily acquired sciences, until many have come to think of those ancient written records, which contain the lab notes and field-notes for the entire history of the human race, as only dusty papers with nothing to say. It is as if one were to try to reconstruct the life of Lord Chesterfield by the careful examination of his bones, his clothes, the house he lived in, the food he ate, etc.,—all of which are important—while throwing aside the man's daily journal, which tells us in his own handwriting where he was, what he saw and heard and did, and even what he thought and felt. This should be at least as instructive as the measurement of his bones.

The fond hopes of a few years ago that we would soon have electronic translators have today been dismissed by

---

[4]S. Piggott, *The Dawn of Civilization* (New York: McGraw-Hill, 1961), p. 15.

one who is generally regarded as the world's foremost
authority on machine translation. Yehoshua Bar-Hillel
states: "The machine will never be able to deliver flawless
translation of scientific or technical works [by far the
easiest to translate], if only because the relationships between a language and the ideas it seeks to express are by
no means simple and direct. . . . The precise meaning of
a sentence is often only apparent in its context, which the
reader must understand, and which a machine can never
understand. . . . The sooner we realize that the perfect
translation machine is an illusion, the sooner we can turn
our attention to pursuing a real improvement in linguistic
communication."

More recently the same authority has stated that
"The human translator . . . is often obliged to make use
of extralinguistic knowledge which sometimes has to be
of considerable breadth and depth."[5] This rules the
machine out either as a serious assistant or competitor,
for every word of an ancient religious text is loaded
with extra-linguistic associations. If anyone had ever
produced such a thing as a perfect translation, then
we might design a machine to duplicate the process. But
it has never been done, because we cannot even imagine
a perfect translation—the very concept eludes us.

A perfect translation would have to convey, imply,
suggest, hint, recall, and suppress the same things (no more
and no less) in the mind of its reader that the original
does to a reader of the original; it would have to bring
identical images to the minds of the two readers. But the
only reason we have a translation in the first place is that
the two readers do not live in the same world and therefore
do not have the same images. A word designating even as
simple a thing as a house or a tree suggests quite different
pictures to people living in different parts of the world,
and it is the genius of a language to bring to mind the

----

[5]Quoted by R. See, in *Science*, May 8, 1964, p. 621.

peculiar images, situations, moods, and memories of the culture that produced it, and of no other. A language produces almost automatically a photographic likeness of just one culture.[6] If we try to switch or substitute photographs, all kinds of explanations and clarifications are necessary, and that is why every translation that strives to be exact must fall back continually on elaborate explanatory notes. So we learn a language not in order to translate, but because there is so much in that language that can never be translated.

Every scholar in reading an ancient document for the first time constantly asks himself where its ideas and the expressions come from. Even the most original writer is influenced by somebody, and with the ancients originality was by no means the highest virtue in a composition; as a result, every ancient composition is a composite of concepts and expressions handed down from earlier times, each period having its own characteristic emphasis and preferences. This makes it possible to test the derivation and hence the authenticity of ancient texts. What makes the comparison of the New Testament and the Dead Sea Scrolls really significant, for example, is the fact that they "draw from a common reservoir of terminology and ideas."[7] When we are told that "echoes of New Testament thoughts and phraseology are clear in the scrolls, especially those having apocalyptic associations,"[8] we are brought to realize that in this field of study "key words and phrases are an index to thought."[9] Translation destroys all the clues.

In a field surrounded by language barriers proficiency in language can itself be a pitfall, since the superior linguist, lording it over his fellows, can easily forget that any degree of proficiency attainable in a human lifetime is still pitifully inadequate. Every scholar in considering the

---

[6]C. S. Coon, *The Story of Man* (New York: Knopf, 1962), pp. 18-19.
[7]W. Albright, in Davies and Daube, *op. cit.*, p. 169.
[8]J. Roberts, *Zeitschrift für alttestamentliche Wissenschaft*, 62 (1950), p. 241.
[9]L. J. Liebreich, in *Jewish Quarterly Review*, 46, p. 273.

possible background of a text he is examining is naturally limited to the consideration of texts he already knows about. Hence a researcher who knows Sanskrit but not Chinese might declare a document of Sanskrit origin because of the many points of relationship he finds between it and the literature he has studied, but be quite unaware that the same document might well contain three times as many references to Chinese sources. Literary critics of the Book of Mormon in the past have nearly all been ornaments of the English Department, who naturally detect in the Book of Mormon many things reminiscent of 19th Century American literature, which is not surprising since it was written in 19th Century America and since any two large collections of writings are bound to present many parallels. And so they have announced that they have quite definitely discovered the real origin of the Book of Mormon.

But the shock and horror with which the Book of Mormon was received in 19th Century America, the scandal and the hilarity of it all, should be quite enough to show that this was by no means a typical product of the times. If the critics had been able to look around more widely they would soon have discovered parallels to the Book of Mormon everywhere, and might have come to suspect that their source criticism was suffering from a serious shortage of sources. But will just any sources do for comparative purposes? By no means; the *first* rule of textual criticism is always to assume that a document is genuine and test it first of all against its purported background: if it does not fit into that, then its claims are indeed questionable; but if it shows any tendency to be at home in that setting then it deserves a careful and respectful examination. Unfortunately this is *not* the way in which critics have dealt with the Book of Mormon.

Two tests are important here, a literary and a cultural, since a writing betrays its origin both by its language—style, vocabulary, imagery, etc.,—and by the things it talks

about and describes, which inevitably betray something
of its real background. The first test is, broadly speaking,
Source History or Source Criticism (*Quellengeschichte*)
looking around for the possible written sources on which
the ancient writer drew; and the second is Form Criticism
(*Formgeschichte*), which seeks to reconstruct the kind of
setting in which a passage was written from the tone and
content of the passage itself. Once employed by rival
schools, these two formidable tools are now combined to
explore the background of the Bible. But their effectiveness
is by no means limited to that book—indeed biblical scholars
have borrowed their tools largely from Classical scholarship; one cannot imagine a more perfect subject for the
source critic and the form critic than the Book of Mormon,
for if ever there was a book crying for investigation this
is it; and if any other writing can match its wealth of
literary oddities and its exotic *Sitz im Leben* we have yet
to hear of it. Here then is an eminently testable document
whose author all his days asked nothing better of the
learned world than to subject it to the severest tests they
could devise.

Some Peculiarities of Composition

In matters of language and composition the Book of
Mormon from the first presented a welcome target to the
critics: here was something that even a child could see
was fraudulent, something that no intelligent person, let
alone a clever deceiver would dream of— " . . . from the
reformed Egyptian!!!" screamed Alexander Campbell, with
three exclamation points.[10] Nobody knew anything about
reformed Egyptian then. The word Demotic had not yet
come into general use. Lacking that, "Reformed Egyptian"
is as good a term as any to describe that peculiar and
remarkably abbreviated style of "cursive writing developed

---

[10]Cited in F. Kirkham, *New Witness for Christ in America,* II, 106.

"Ammon"

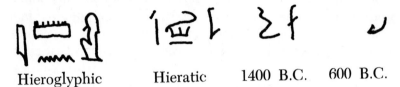

Hieroglyphic   Hieratic   1400 B.C.   600 B.C.

. . . my letter"

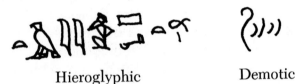

Hieroglyphic   Demotic

Styles of Egyptian writing. What could be more "Reformed"? (After Erman)

out of the Hieratic by systematic abbreviation from the 8th to the 4th centuries," which enjoyed the heyday of its international popularity in Lehi's own time.[11] We pointed out long ago that that peculiar type of writing known as Meroitic a baffling and still largely undeciphered Egyptian script which developed out of Demotic under circumstances remarkably paralleling the purported development of Nephite writing, has the most striking affinities to the characters on the so-called Anthon Transcript, which is thought to be Joseph Smith's own copying of a sample of the writing on the plates. The point is that there was such writing.[12]

---

[11]W. Spiegelberg, "Zur Definition des 'Demotischen'", *Ztschr. f. "Agypt. Sprache*, 37 (1899), p. 19.

[12]Another script that resembles that of the Anthon Transcript, and is still largely undeciphered is that of the Rifaud Papyrus, discussed by S. Sauneron and J. Yoyotte in *Bulletin de l'Institut Francais de'Archaeologie Orientale*, 50 (1952), pp. 107-117.

"It came to pass . . ."

Nothing delighted the critics more than the monotonous repetition of "it came to pass" at the beginning of thousands of sentences in the Book of Mormon. Here again is something that Western tradition found completely unfamiliar. Instead of punctuation the original manuscript of the Book of Mormon divides up its phrases by introducing each by an "and," "behold," "now," or "It came to pass . . ." Simply outrageous—as English literature, but it is standard Egyptian practice. Egyptian historical texts, Grapow points out, "begin in monotonous fashion" always with the same stock words; at some periods every speech is introduced with the unnecessary "I opened my mouth . . ."[13] Dramatic texts are held together by the constant repetition of Khpr-n, "It happened that . . ." or "It came to pass . . ."[14] In Egyptian these expressions were not merely adornments, as Grapow points out, they are a grammatical necessity and may not be omitted.[15] P. Humbert has traced the origin of prophetic biblical expressions to archaic oracular formulas.[16] At any rate they are much commoner in Egyptian than in the Bible, just as they are much commoner in the Book of Mormon. However bad they are in English, they are nothing to be laughed at as Egyptian.

Bad Grammar

The occasional change of person or number in the middle of a sentence or speech in the Book of Mormon is bad English grammar, but quite characteristic of ancient composition. How can we tell whether it is just a blunder here or the faithful—too faithful—rendering of the original? We can't, but there is an interesting coincidence to consider. J. Sperber has shown that "Personenwechsel" is characteristic of the more emotional passages of the Old

---

[13]H. Grapow, *Das Hieroglyphensystem*, pp. 23-25.
[14]*Ibid.*, p. 25.
[15]*Ibid.*, p. 31.
[16]P. Humbert, in *Archiv für Orientforschung*, 10 (1935/6), pp. 77-80.

Testament (not the New Testament), especially the inspired utterances of the prophets, and is most particularly
characteristic of Isaiah.[17] Perhaps the best example of
this in the Book of Mormon is in the impassioned speech
of the prophet Abinadi on pages 182-3 of the first edition.
One might profitably examine the distribution of such slips
in the first edition—perhaps they are more than a mere
coincidence. At least they are by no means contrary to
ancient usage.

The Colophons

The major writings of the Book of Mormon are introduced and concluded by "colophons," which have the purpose of acquainting the reader with the source of the
material given and informing him of the authorship of the
particular manuscript. Such colophons are found at 1 Nephi
1:1-3, 22:30-31, Jacob 1:2, 7:27, Jarom 1-2, Omni 1, 3-4,
Words of Mormon 9, Mosiah 1:4, 9:1, Helaman 16:25.
In his opening colophon Nephi refers to the excellence of
his parents, the good education his father has given him,
tells how he has been blessed of heaven, describes the
nature of the record he is writing and the sources from
which he is taking it including personal experience—"a
record of my proceedings in my days"—and the important
information that he can vouch for the truth of the record
having written it with his own hand. This complacent
advertising of one's own virtues, in particular one's reliability, is a correct and indeed a required fixture of any
properly composed Egyptian autobiography of Nephi's
time—a time at which the writing of autobiographies was
very fashionable. The colophon of the famous Bremer-
Rhind Papyrus contains "(1) the date (2) titles of Nasmin
(the author), the names of his parents" . . . his father's
prophetic calling and virtues, and a curse against "any

---

[17]J. Sperber, in *Zeitschr. für Assyriologie*, 32 (1918), pp. 23-33.

foreigner who shall take the book away from him" into whose hands it comes legitimately.[18] One colophon, which occurs at the end of no less than four famous Egyptian writings (Sinuhe, the Prisse Papyrus, the Man Weary of Life, and the Shipwrecked Sailor) reads (in the Shipwrecked Sailor version): "The account from beginning to end as found in a writing of . . . a scribe reliable of fingers, Amoni the son of Amonah, may he live, prosper and be healthy." The note on the reliability of the writer's fingers is matched by Nephi's ". . . and I make it with mine own hand." The interesting pair of names, Amoni and Amonah should catch the eye of any reader of the Book of Mormon.

Literary Genres

We have discussed elsewhere the surprising presence in the pages of the Book of Mormon of a full-blown *Qasida* or primitive desert poem, recited under exactly the proper circumstances and in exactly the proper form by Father Lehi.[19] His son Nephi shows a no less impressive familiarity with the accepted forms of literary composition and imagery as we shall soon see.

The first part of the Book of Mormon is Nephi's *autobiography*, in which he has included large parts of his father's autobiography. It so happens that in Nephi's day the autobiography was the most popular form of composition in Egyptian, the main purpose of such an exercise being, as J. Janssen pointed out, to acquire a good name with men and gods and pass on edifying and pious instructions to one's successors.[20] Such is plainly Nephi's purpose as stated in his colophons.

It should also be noted that with all its pious and

----

[18]R. O. Faulkner, in *Journal of Egyptian Archaeology*, 23 (1937), p. 10.
[19]H. Nibley, *An Approach to the Book of Mormon*, (Salt Lake City, 1964), pp. 225-228.
[20]J. Janssen, discussed in *Revue Biblique*, 1947, p. 136.

didactic tendencies, the Book of Mormon is completely devoid of proverbs—this is a peculiarity of Egyptian literature at all times,[21] while the completely historical orientation of the book is a peculiarity of Hebraic scripture;[22] the one oddity reflects "the language of the Egyptians," the other "the learning of the Jews." (1 Nephi 1:2). One prophet in the Book of Mormon indulges in withering irony and sarcasm; that is Abinadi, who happened to be a diligent student of the Hebrew prophets, whose style of irony he displays. The point here is that the irony has only been recognized by recent critics.[23] Such literary details deserve closer attention than they have received; but they are not likely to get it from a generation of scholars who spend more time at air terminals than in libraries.

Peculiar Imagery

The Book of Mormon is full of rather odd imagery, not found in the Bible and quite out of place in the world of Joseph Smith, but well attested in the documentary discoveries and researches of recent years. To take a few examples:

1. *The Star.* Nephi in a vision saw certain heavenly beings, whose "brightness did exceed that of the stars in the firmament. "And they came down and went forth upon the face of the earth. . . ." (1 Nephi 1:9-11.)

Now we all know that Lucifer fell "as a star from heaven," and the *Book of Enoch* says that that prophet "saw many stars descend and cast themselves down from heaven to that first star."[24] There is in fact a great deal in the early Apocrypha about the coming down of fallen

---

[21]H. Grapow, *Die bildlichen Ausdrücke der Aegypter* (Leipzig, 1924), p. 17.
[22]G. Holscher, *Hebräische Geschichtsschreibung,* p. 5.
[23]W. L. Holladay, "Style, Irony, and Authenticity in Jeremiah," in *Journal of Biblical Literature,* 81 (1962), pp. 44-54. Cf. Mosiah 11:11.
[24]*I Enoch,* 86:3.

stars from heaven to circulate among men upon the earth.[25]
But this is matched in the same writings by the other
side of the picture, the coming down to earth of stars for
the salvation of men. Lehi reports that ". . . he saw one
descending out of the midst of heaven, and he beheld that
his luster was above that of the sun at noon-day. And he
also saw twelve others . . . and their brightness did exceed
that of the stars in the firmament." (*Ibid.*, 9-10.) Ignatius
of Antioch says that when Christ was born "there shone a
star in heaven brighter than all the stars . . . and all the
other stars, with the sun and the moon made a chorus to
that star."[26] Speaking of the star of Bethlehem, an early
Apocryphon says "it was in the form of a star" that Michael
guided the magi to Christ.[27] After long ages of darkness,
says the *Testament of Judah*, "shall a star rise to you from
Jacob in peace, and a man shall arise like the sun of righteousness, and the heavens shall be opened to him."[28] Or,
as the *Testament of Levi* puts it, "Then shall the Lord raise
up a new priest; . . . His Star shall rise in heaven as of a
king . . . and the heavens shall be opened; I will bring
light to the Gentiles."[29] "The stars shone in their watches
and were glad," says *II Baruch*, speaking of God's ministers
as stars. "They shone with gladness unto him that made
them," and gladly responded when he summoned them.[30]
In the *Battle Scroll* the deliverer in war is called "the Star
from Jacob,"[31] and in the *Zadokite Fragment* the leader of

---

[25]Lucifer who fell "like a star from heaven" is the best-known example.
But the most fully documented identification of fallen angels with fallen
stars is in the ancient tradition of the Watchers, with their cult of the Morning
Star; Tha'labi, *Qissas al-Anbiyah* (1340 A. H. ed.), pp. 35-37. For the background of this tradition, G. Widengren, in S. H. Hooke (ed.) *Ritual and
Kingship* (Oxford, 1958), pp. 176f. Among the Maya "Venus, as morning
star, was feared as bringing death, famine, and destruction to man"; E. Bacon,
in S. Piggott (ed.), *Vanished Civilizations* (New York: McGraw-Hill, 1963),
p. 163.
[26]Ignatius, *Ep. ad Ephes.*, c. 19.
[27]*Book of the Mysteries of Heaven and Earth;* fol. 17, in *Patrologia
Orientalis,* 1, 28.
[28]*Testament of Judah,* 24:1.
[29]*Testament of Levi,* 18:2-3.
[30]*Book of Baruch,* 3:34.
[31]*Battle Scroll (Milhama)*, xi, 6.

the sect in its wanderings is called simply "The Star."[32] The author of the *Clementine Recognitions* resents the pirating of Christian ideas by the Zoroastrians, who call their prophet "The Living Star," and Eusebius says that Barcochebas, "the Star," who has left us a letter in his own handwriting among The Dead Sea Scrolls, was really "a fallen star."[31] In one of the early Apocrypha, Mary says to the Apostles, "Ye are shining stars."[35]

All this is imagery having nothing to do with star worship: the early Christians avoided the pitfalls of astrology into which the later churchmen fell when they abolished flesh-and-blood prophets and depersonalized God, leaving the heavenly bodies as the only means of communication between heaven and earth.[36] It is simply a conventional imagery, and the point to notice is the idea that chosen spirits which come down to minister to men upon the earth are conceived as circulating stars. This is the image behind the concept of the Seven Wise Men,[37] but the explicit situation depicted in Lehi's vision is that peculiar to the early Apocrypha.

We have mentioned the Way of Light and the Way of Darkness as an expression of man's life as a time of probation. The contrast of light and dark is, as is well known by now, an obsession with the writers of the Dead Sea Scrolls, but no more so than with the writers of the Book of Mormon.[38] But since the contrast is a perfectly natural one, a more particular instance is in order to point

---

[32]*Damascus Covenant (Zadokite Fragment)*, 7(19), 18f. A number of other such instances in the Jewish Apocrypha are cited by C. Rabin, *The Zadokite Documents* (Oxford, 1954), p. 30.
[33]*Clementine Recognitions*, IV, 38; for other references see note 10 in Migne, *Patrologia Graeca*, I, 1327.
[34]Eusebius, *Church History*, IV, 6.
[35]*Gospel of Bartholomew*, in M. R. James, *The New Testament Apocrypha* (1953), p. 171.
[36]Clement of Alexandria, in Migne, *Patrologia Graeca*, 8:96.
[37]Barkowski, in Pauly-Wissowa, *Realenzyklopädie des Altertumswissen*, IIA, 2247.
[38]See Reynolds', *op. cit.*, under "light" and "darkness"; in one verse, Alma 19:6, the word "light" occurs six times.

up the common idiom of the Apocrypha and the Book of Mormon.

"These arrayed in white." Such an instance is the image of the white garment, specifically, the "three men in white." Recently Professor E. Goodenough has pointed out that the earliest known Jewish art represents "their great heroes . . . in white garments to symbolize their 'luminous' nature. . . . Another striking element . . . is the great prominence of groups of three figures, usually in this dress. . . . the choice of three was arbitrary, and the total number of scenes which represent a group of three seems quite beyond coincidence. . . . Philo himself made the vision of the 'three men' into a vision of the essential nature of God."[39]

The "three men" is a constantly recurring motive in the Apocrypha, and Cyrus Gordon has commented on the peculiar preoccupation of the early Hebrew epic with "triads of offices," celestial and earthly.[40] Enoch is conducted to heaven by "three who were clothed in white,"[41] and in *Jubilees* when the Lord descends to see the tower he is accompanied by two others as in Genesis 18.[42] In the newly found *Sayings of Moses* we learn that the Law was delivered not by Moses alone but by Moses and his two counselors, Eleazar and Joshua.[43] When we read in the *Manual of Discipline* that "God through his Anointed One, has made us to know his holy Spirit," we are plainly dealing with three who speak to man.[44] According to the Mandaean doctrine three celestial beings assisted at the creation and occasionally visited the earth; these were not

---

[39]E. Goodenough, *Jewish Symbolism in the Greco-Roman Period* (New York: Bollingen Series, 1953), I, 2-527.

[40]C. Gordon, *Before the Bible* (New York: Harper & Row, 1962), pp. 16f.

[41]*Secrets of Enoch*, iii.

[42]*Jubilees*, 10:23.

[43]*Sayings of Moses*, I, 11f.

[44]A. Dupont-Sommer, *The Dead Sea Scrolls* (New York: Macmillan, 1952), p. 65.

the Godhead, however, but three messengers who later lived upon the earth as prophets.[45]

In a strange old writing known as the Pseudo-Philo, Samuel tells Saul that it is not the Witch of Endor who has called him up, "but the precept which God spoke to me while yet I lived, that I should come and tell thee that thou hast sinned a second time." The witch is quite overpowered and says that this is not the result of her conjuring powers, for this is no ordinary human spirit, "for he is arrayed in a white robe and hath a mantle upon it, and two angels leading him." It is the three men in white again.[46]

The Book of Mormon has a good deal to say about messengers in white. Lehi's desert vision opens with "a man, and he was dressed in a white robe," who becomes his guide. (1 Nephi 8:5.) He is shown "twelve ministers. . . . their garments . . . made white . . ." (1 Nephi 12:10), followed by three generations of men whose "garments were white, even like unto the Lamb of God." (1 Nephi 12:11.) Soon after, Nephi also in a vision "beheld a man, and he was dressed in a white robe," this being John who was to come. (1 Nephi 14:19.)

". . . there can no man be saved," says Alma, "except his garments are washed white. . . ." (Alma 5:21.) He tells how the ancient priesthood "were called after this holy order, and were sanctified, and their garments were washed white through the blood of the Lamb. Now they . . . [have] their garments made white, being pure and spotless before God. . . ." (Alma 13:11-12.) But the most moving and significant passage is his formal prayer for the city of Gideon: ". . . may the Lord bless you, and keep your garments spotless, that ye may at last be brought to sit down with Abraham, Isaac, and Jacob, and the holy

---

[45]G. Widengren, in J. Leipoldt (ed.), *Religionsgeschichte des Orients* . . . (Leiden: E. J. Brill, 1961), p. 86. Tha'labi, *op. cit.*, p. 35. According to one Mandaean text, these men later lived on the earth as apostles.

[46]*Pseudo-Philo* (M. R. James), lxiv, 5.

prophets . . . having your garments spotless even as their garments are spotless, in the kingdom of heaven to go no more out." (Alma 7:25.)

Here Abraham, Isaac, and Jacob are *the* "three men in white."[47]

2. *Desert Imagery*: We have commented before on the vivid little pictures of ancient desert life that Nephi gives us, but what we have not noted is the desert *imagery*, which is a different sort of thing. A person may employ desert imagery though he has never lived with the Beduins in his life, its inspiration being not in a real but in a literary experience. The desert imagery of Nephi's writings has been studied against the real desert background before now, but it has never been compared with the rich desert imagery in the apocryphal writings, both Jewish and Christian—which is not surprising, since *Lehi in the Desert* appeared before the Dead Sea Scrolls had been published. Take Nephi's supplication:

"O Lord, wilt thou . . . that I may walk in the path of the low valley, that I may be strict in the plain road! O Lord, wilt thou encircle me around in the robe of thy righteousness! O Lord, wilt thou make a way for mine escape before mine enemies! Wilt thou make my path straight before me! Wilt thou not place a stumbling block in my way—but that thou wouldst clear my way before me, and hedge not up my way, but the ways of mine enemy." (2 Nephi 4:32-33.)

It is all straight desert lore—the low valley, the plain road, the flight from relentless enemies, the great sheikh placing the fringe of his robe (*kuffeh*) around the shoulder of the kneeling suppliant as a sign of his protection, the open passage, and the stumbling blocks—but it is also authentic apocryphal imagery. So *Ben Sirach*: "His paths are plain for the blameless; even so they present stumbling-

---

[47]Goodenough, *op. cit.*, I, 26, notes that the identity of the three men in white varies considerably, not being confined to any particular three.

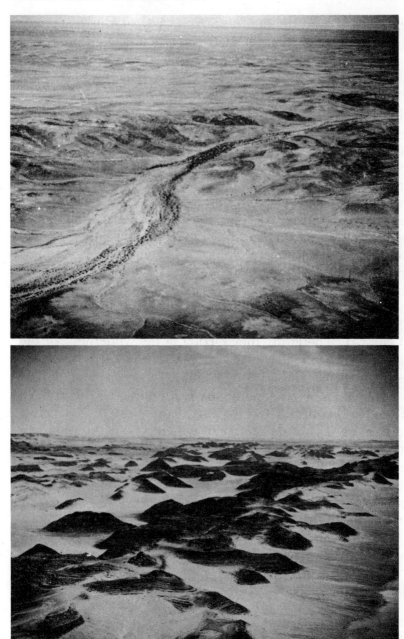

Scenes in the desert wilderness along the Gulf of Aqaba.

blocks to the offender."[48] Sirach sees in the dangerous
journey through the desert the most compelling image of
man's dependence on God, as Nephi does.[49]

The latter describes those who fall away as being led
"away into broad roads, that they perish and are lost."[50]
In our culture the broadest roads are the safest, but it was
not so in the desert. In the popular Egyptian literature of
Lehi's day "it became a very common teaching," according
to H. Grapow, "that a man should never depart from the
right path . . . but be righteous, not associate his heart
with the wicked or walk upon the path of unrighteousness."[51] Recently Couroyer has shown that there was
actually a close connection between this Egyptian concept
and the "way of life" teachings in Israel, the two stemming
from a common literary tradition.[52] "We went astray from
the way of truth," says the *Wisdom of Solomon*, ". . . and
we journeyed through trackless deserts, but the way of the
Lord we knew not."[53] This is exactly the lesson of the
Liahona: "Therefore, they tarried in the wilderness, or did
not travel a direct course . . . because of their transgressions." (Alma 37:42.)

Lehi, in "a dark and dreary wilderness" (1 Nephi 8:4),
found a wonderful tree (v. 10), and near it "a river of
water" (v. 13) at the source of which he saw the righteous
members of his family standing as they considered where
to go from there (v. 14); he called them to join him at
the tree (v. 15), and also called Laman and Lemuel to
join the rest of them, but these refused. (vs. 17-18.) While
some got to the tree by taking hold of an iron rod, "Many
were drowned in the depths of the fountain; and many
were lost from his view, wandering in strange roads."

---

[48]*Ben Sirach*, 39:24.
[49]*Ibid.*, 34:11-17.
[50]1 Nephi 12:17; cf· 8:32.
[51]H. Grapow, *Die Bildlichen Ausdrücke des Aegyptischen* (Leipzig,
1924), pp. 64f.
[52]R. P. B. Couroyer, "Le Chemin de Vie en Egypte et en Israel" *Revue
Biblique*, 56 (1949), pp. 393-411.
[53]*Wisdom of Solomon*, 5:6f.

(v. 32.) The obedient members of the family found both the waters and the tree of life. The tree and the water are often mentioned together, for the simple reason that in the desert the two necessarily occur together. (Cf: the First Psalm of David.)

Lehi's appeal to his sons must have sounded like that of the *Odes of Solomon*: "Come and take water from the living fountain of the Lord. . . . Come and drink and rest by the fountain of the Lord!"[54] ". . . he that refuses the water shall not live!" says the *Zadokite Fragment*.[55] "I saw the fountain of righteousness," says *I Enoch*, telling of *his* vision, "and around it were many springs of wisdom, and all the thirsty drank from them and were filled. . . . But woe unto ye who . . . have forsaken the fountain of life!"[56] The Thanksgiving Hymns of the Dead Sea Scrolls often refer to the knowledge of God as a fountain and declare that only the humble of broken heart and contrite spirit partake of it.[57] This theme is strongly emphasized in Lehi's story, where those who partake of the fruit are mocked for their humility. (1 Nephi 8:25-28.)

Filthy water. In the tree-and-river image the emphasis is sometimes on the fruit, sometimes on the water. Nephi gives a special interpretation to the latter when he says that his father failed to notice that the water of the river was filthy, and that it represented "the depths of hell." (1 Nephi 15:26ff., 12:16.) "This was a typical desert *sayl*," we wrote some years ago, "a raging torrent of liquid filth that sweeps whole camps to destruction."[58] The same queer and unpleasant imagery meets us in the *Odes of Solomon*: "Great rivers are the power of the Lord, and they carry headlong those who despise him: and entangle their paths; and they sweep away their fords, and catch their

[54]*Odes of Solomon*, 30:1.
[55]*Damascus Covenant* (*Zadokite Fragment*), 3:16.
[56]*I Enoch*, 96:6.
[57]*Thanksgiving Hymns*, 18:14f.
[58]H. Nibley, *An Approach to the Book of Mormon*, p. 225.

bodies and destroy their lives."[59] The foolish ones who refuse counsel are swept away in the wreckage of the flood.

The *Thanksgiving Hymns* use the same flood image in a different but related sense—the vanity of the world is the torrent; "the way of the princes of this world" is such a confused rush of water that brings only ruin and is soon dried up.[60] The early Christian *Acts of Thomas* contrasts the pure perennial water with the filthy seasonal flood: God's fountain being "never filthy, and the stream thereof never faileth," it is "the sweet spring that never ceaseth, the clear fountain that is never polluted."[61]

In the *Thanksgiving Hymns* the soul that refuses to drink of "the Wellspring of Life, even though it was yielding [life or water] everlasting" becomes "as . . . rivers in flood, for they poured forth their mire upon me."[62] Again the filthy water. The *Zadokite Fragment* speaks of the false teachers of Israel as drenching the people with "waters of falsehood," the evil counterpart of the waters of life: ". . . there arose the 'man of scoffing,' who dripped [or preached] to Israel 'waters of falsehood' and 'caused them to go astray in a wilderness without way' by 'causing eternal pride [or: pride of the world] to become low' by turning aside from the pathways of righteousness. . . ."[63]

It is not only the images but the combinations of images that are arresting here. Let us recall that Nephi saw that "many were drowned in the depths of the fountain [of filthy water]; and many were lost from his view, wandering in strange roads." (1 Nephi 8:32.) This wandering, he explains, was the direct result of "the attitude of mocking" (v. 27) of the people in the fine house that repre-

---

[59]*Odes of Solomon*, 39:1.

[60]*Thanksgiving Hymns*, 8:1-120.

[61]*Acts of Thomas*, 25 and 29. In the former section the best rendering of the Syriac word is "filthy," since *kaira* means both turbulent, muddy, and foul-smelling.

[62]*Thanksgiving Hymns*, 8:15; T. H. Gaster, *The Dead Sea Scriptures* (New York: Doubleday Anchor, 1957), p. 166.

[63]Rabin, *The Zadokite Documents*, p. 4; *Damascus Document*, 1:15.

sented "the pride of the world." (1 Nephi 11:36.) Scoffing, filthy waters, the pride of the world, and straying in the wilderness are a strange combination, but the coincidence is explained by Rabin's translation, which we are giving here; in it, almost every phrase is put in quotation marks, because almost every phrase is actually a quotation from the Bible or (usually) some old apocryphal work. Nephi's imagery meets us again in *Baruch*: "Thou hast forsaken the fountain of wisdom and wandered away from the way of God,"[64] and in a striking passage of the *Talmud*, where Rabbi Isaac says, "I will give you a likeness: Once there was one wandering hungry, weary and thirsty, in the desert, and he came to a tree with beautiful fruit and shade beside a stream of water, etc."[65]

The newly found *Apocalypse of Elijah* tells how the righteous are led to the place where "they may eat of the Tree of Life and wear a white garment . . . and they will never thirst."[66] In these instances the tree and the water go together. The two things most wonderful of all things, according to the *Acts of Thomas*, are "the incorruptible food of the tree of life and the drink of the water of life."[67]

An odd aspect of the tree in the Book of Mormon is the perfect whiteness of it (the whitest of trees, 1 Nephi 11:8) and of its fruit. (1 Nephi 8:10f.) Whiteness is not an appetizing quality in trees or fruit, and so it is impressive to learn from the *Creation Apocryphon* that though the tree of life looks like a cypress, its fruit is perfectly white.[68]

Sometimes imagery seems to get remarkably jumbled up in the Book of Mormon, as in Helaman 3:29f.: ". . . whosoever will may *lay hold* upon the word of God, . . . which

---

[64] *Book of Baruch*, 3:13f.
[65] *Tanith*, fol. 5b-6a.
[66] *Apocalypse of Elijah*, 21:8.
[67] *Acts of Thomas*, 36.
[68] *Creation Apocryphon*, 158:16-17.

shall *divide asunder* all the cunning and the *snares* and the wiles of the devil, and lead the man of Christ in a straight and *narrow course* across that everlasting *gulf.* . . . . and *land* their souls . . . at the *right hand* of God in the kingdom of heaven, to *sit down* with Abraham, and Isaac, and with Jacob . . . to go no more out." (Italics added.)

Here in a single sentence we have the image of the rod or staff ("lay hold"), the sword, the nets, the path, the yawning gulf, the ship, the throne, and the kingdom. To us this may appear rather tasteless and overdone, but it is typical. Take this from an important Mandaean writing attributed to John: "Come, come to me! I am the shepherd, whose ship soon comes . . . Who does not hearken to my call shall sink. . . . I am the fisherman . . . come, I will rescue you from the filthy birds. I will rescue my friends and bring them into my ship. I will clothe them in garments of glory and with precious light."[69]

The Land of No Return, long viewed as the fatal blunder of the Book of Mormon by the oracles of the English Department, hardly deserves mention, since there is nothing the least bit peculiar about it. It is a commonplace in the literature of the whole Near East from the earliest times to the present. We pointed out years ago that Lehi's use of the expression is strictly formulaic and did not necessarily reflect his real belief about death at all.[70] An interesting confirmation of this is to be found on early Christian and Jewish epitaphs, wherein the pious dead are described as "sleeping their last sleep," a thing which the authors of the epitaphs, as J. Frey observes, did not believe for a minute.[71] The "land of no return" is, however, a good illustration of the pitfalls of impulsive criticism. Even English majors should know that it does not have to come from Shakespeare. The most famous poem of Catullus, on the death of his lady's pet sparrow, contains a couplet that

---

[69]*Mandaean Book of John,* c. 36, ed. Lidzbarski (Giessen, 1915), **II.** 144ff.

[70]*An Approach to the Book of Mormon,* pp. 228-9.

is nearer to Lehi's language than it is to Shakespeare: *Qui nunc it per iter tenebricosum, Illuc unde negant redire quemquam.* Which Lord Byron rendered: "Now having passed the gloomy bourne from whence he never can return."

Peculiar Expressions

There are some odd expressions found in the Book of Mormon, that do not turn up in the Bible but do turn up elsewhere, notably in the Apocrypha where they go along with the strange imagery we have just mentioned.

An Identification Test

Even using the texts of present-day translations of early Apocrypha, we can mix up sentences from them with sentences from Joseph Smith's translation and defy even experts to tell which come from the Old World documents and which from the New. Let the reader decide which of the following are taken from the Book of Mormon and which from the Apocrypha. None of the translations are ours.

1. Let us prepare our souls that we may enter into possession of, and not be taken possession of.[72]

2. (In preparing for the Messiah) they have become free forever . . . to act for themselves and not to be acted upon, . . .[73]

1. But judging them little by little thou gavest them an opportunity of repentance, Thou knewest their nature was evil.[74]

2. And thus the devil cheateth their souls, and leadeth them away carefully down to hell.[75]

-----

[71] J. Frey, in *Biblica*, 13 (1932), pp. 140-145; cf· 15 (1934), pp. 265ff.
[72] *II Baruch*, 85:9. Cf. I Jeu.
[73] 2 Nephi 2:26.
[74] *Wisdom of Solomon*, 12:10, speaking of the Canaanites, Cf. 1 Nephi.
[75] 2 Nephi 28:21, 8.

1. He that diggeth a pit shall fall into it, and he that setteth a snare shall be taken in it.[76]

2. . . . that great pit which hath been digged for the destruction of men shall be filled by those who digged it, . . .[77]

1. Woe to you, ye rich, for ye have trusted in your riches, and from you your riches shall depart.[78]

2. But wo unto the rich, . . . their hearts are upon their treasures. . . . And behold, their treasure shall perish with them also.[79]

3. . . . because they have set their hearts upon their riches, I will hide up their treasures. . . .[80]

4. . . . ye are cursed because of your riches, and also are your riches cursed because ye have set your hearts upon them, . . .[81]

1. . . . may the Lord bless thee forever, for thy seed shall not utterly be destroyed.[82]

2. Fulfil my prayer, to leave me a posterity on earth, and not destroy all the flesh of man. . . .[83]

3. . . . he has promised unto us that our seed shall not utterly be destroyed, according to the flesh, . . .[84]

1. And now my children . . . how awful it is to come before the face of the ruler of heaven. . . . who can endure that endless pain?[85]

2. . . . they are consigned to an awful view of their own guilt . . . which doth cause them to shrink from the

---

[76]*Ben Sirach,* 27:26, cf. Eccles., 10:8.
[77]1 Nephi 14:3, 22:13f.
[78]*I Enoch,* 94:8.
[79]2 Nephi 9:30.
[80]Helaman 13:20.
[81]*Ibid.,* 13:21.
[82]2 Nephi 3:3.
[83]*I Enoch,* 84:5.
[84]2 Nephi 9:53.
[85]*Secrets of Enoch,* 39:8.

presence of the Lord into a state of misery and endless torment, . . .[86]

Here we seem to have a plain case of plagiarism: In a father's warning to his children the operative words are "And now my children" (And again my brethren—Mosiah 3:1), *awful*, the *face* of the ruler of heaven (the presence of the Lord), *endless pain* (endless torment), all occurring in that order. The only trouble is that the document from which the Book of Mormon is plagiarizing was not discovered until 1892.

These parallels illustrate the fact that in the preachments of the Book of Mormon we are dealing with a consciously formulaic, that is, deliberately unoriginal, type of literature. This readily explains the parallels; but if the Book of Mormon were not a genuine literary product of its age, it would not survive for an hour set against the ancient stereotypes.

There are a number of New Testament expressions which were loudly denounced as obvious anachronisms, but are now known to have gone back to times well before the New Testament was written:

Synagogue and *Church* are applied in the Book of Mormon to the institutions most closely resembling them in the Old World. The question is purely one of translation. "The origin of the Synagogue," wrote Zeitlin, "dates back to the time when local assemblies were occasionally summoned to consider the needs of a community."[87] The existence of such synagogues, he notes was by no means restricted to the times after the destruction of the Temple —the synagogue was simply the local Jewish religious assembly, in contrast to the Great Synagogue, which was an assembly "of a national character . . . to consider problems affecting the whole nation."[88] Synagogue though a Greek

---

[86]Mosiah 3:25.
[87]S. Zeitlin, in *American Academy of Jewish Research*, 1930-1, p. 79.
[88]*Ibid.*, p. 78.

word was used only by Jews to designate a Jewish assembly
in the diaspora or at Jerusalem, "the pagans, who did not
know Hebrew . . . called it a proseuche, not synagogue."
No better word, in fact no *other* word, could be found
to indicate ancient Jewish assemblies and assembly places
in any part of the world than "synagogue." The early
Christians designated their assemblies by the same Aramaic
term, *beth ha-keneseth*, as they gave to a Jewish house of
worship; but when they spoke Greek they distinguished
between the two, according to Zeitlin, by calling the Christian house an *ekklesia*—which we translate as church. Since
Zeitlin's study, however, the Dead Sea Scrolls have come
forth; in them the community is designated as a *yehad*,
which Molin, in the most careful study of the word, decided could only be translated properly as church—a pre-
Christian church![89] or as Professor Cross styled it, "a church
of anticipation." Gaster noted at the same time that the
other word used for the community at Qumran was *'edah*,
which is actually the old Syriac word for church.[90] If the
Book of Mormon used "synagogue" to designate the early
Jewish assemblies, and "church" to designate such assemblies after they had become Christian, it is hard to think
of more appropriate terms—bearing always in mind that
this is a translation, and the purpose of the words is not to
convey what the Nephites *called* their communities, but
how we are to picture them in our minds.

"*Alpha and Omega*" in the Book of Mormon is another
apparent anachronism. But here again, since it is an accepted *English* expression we may view it as the best way
of conveying the meaning of a certain Nephite expression
to English readers. The purpose of a translation is to transmit meanings, not words: the original words are already
there—they don't need to be translated. T and not long-O,
is the last letter of the old Greek as well as the old Semitic

---

[89]G. Molin, *Die Söhne des Lichts*, p. 138.
[90]Cited by A. R. C. Leaney, e. a., *Guide to the Scrolls*, p. 66f.

(including Hebrew and Phoenician) alphabets. But to say
"I am the A and the T" would be meaningless to *English*-
speaking readers, to whom the meaning of "Alpha and
Omega" is perfectly clear. In addressing Jewish communities in notoriously bad Greek, but in the peculiar idiom of
the ancient sectaries, John uses the expression in Rev. 1:8
because they too were familiar with the expression. It
remained the standard designation of Christ as Redeemer
and Judge throughout the Middle Ages among people who
knew no Greek.[91] On the other hand, in the old ritual
alphabet of the Mandaeans, a purely Semitic alphabet, "the
first and last letters, the 'alpha and omega', are the same
and represent perfection of *light and life.*" Both letters
"have their sign a circle, possibly representing the sun-disk
as a symbol of light."[92] Hence there may be more behind
3 Nephi 9:18 than a *mere* literary convention: "I am *the
light and the life.* . . . I am Alpha and Omega." (Italics
added.)

The word *"Antichrist"* in the Book of Mormon is also
a translation. In the oldest definition of the word, Polycarp
writes, "For any one who does not confess that Jesus Christ
has come in the flesh is Antichrist."[93] Such a title fits
Korihor perfectly, since the whole burden of his teaching
was that the Messiah being nothing but a myth, would
not and could not come, in the flesh. (Alma 30:6.)

The constant use of "seed" in the Book of Mormon to
designate progeny is strictly according to the Egyptian
rule, by which, according to Grapow, "seed" is *"always*
used to designate 'Son' or 'Descendant'."[94]

Helaman's "lay hold upon the word of God," while
reminding us of the iron rod, is also authentic usage. Mor-

---

[91]Discussed by F. Chatillon, in *Revue du Moyen Age Latin*, II (1955),
pp. 5-50.
[92]E. S. Drower, *The Mandaeans of Iraq and Iran* (Oxford, 1937), p. 241.
The expression "Alpha and Omega" is *not* found in any pagan writing.
[93]Polycarp, *Epistle to Philip*, vii.
[94]H. Grapow, *Ausdrücke*, p. 126.

mon wants us to "lay hold upon the gospel . . ." (Mormon
7:8), and five times Moroni speaks of laying hold on every
good thing.[95] The *Zadokite Document* deplores Israel's refusal to "grasp instruction," as Rabin translates it, noting
that the expression is found in other early Jewish Apocrypha;[96] and urges the people to "Take hold of the way of
God," another expression found in other Apocrypha.[97]

Another characteristic expression is that of failing to
heed "the mark" set by prudence and tradition. In the
Zadokite Fragment the false teachers of the Jews are
charged with having "removed the mark which the forefathers had set up in their inheritance,[98] and there is a
solemn warning to "all those of the members of the covenant who have broken out of the boundary of the Law,"
or stepped beyond the designated mark.[99] The early Christian *Gospel of Truth* says Israel turns to error when they
look for that which is beyond the mark.[100] How well
Jacob puts it in the Book of Mormon when he tells how
the clever Jews "despised the words of plainness, and
killed the prophets, and sought for things that they
could not understand. Wherefore, because of their blindness, which blindness came by looking beyond the mark,
they must needs fall . . ." (Jacob 4:14.)

Another illustration of this point is found in the
names *Christ* and *Christian* in the Book of Mormon.
These of course were also denounced as hopeless anachronisms, but today the origin of the names is no longer
regarded as the open-and-shut proposition it once was.
The newly-discovered "Gospel of Philip" has an interesting commentary on the names of Jesus and Christ.
"The name Jesus," it says, "does not exist in any other
tongue (than Hebrew), but he is always called Jesus.

95Moroni 7:19, 20, 21, 25; 10:30.
96Rabin, *op. cit.*, p. 22.
97*Ibid.*, p. 40.
98The *Damascus Document* (*Zadokite Fragment*), 1:16.
99*Ibid.*, 20B:25f.
100*Gospel of Truth*, fol. xi, line 24.

But Christ is Messiah in Syriac, while in Greek it is the Christ."[101] One and the same word must be translated as Messiah when used in one context and as Christ when used in another: Christ is the Messiah in a special and particular sense. This can be clearly seen in Arabic where the word *al-masih* must be translated Messiah if the author is a Moslem but Christ if the author is a Christian, since the Christian thinks of the Messiah in a different and special sense. "We can not, every time we meet the Hebrew term 'Messiah' assume, outside the New Testament, that it means what it means in the New Testament," H. R. C. Leaney notes.[102] Messiah is the more general term, Christ the more limited and particular. It is interesting that in the *early* parts of the Book of Mormon we read only of the Messiah, while in the later parts he is definitely Christ. When the Samaritan woman said, "I know that Messiah comes, who is called Christ," (John 4:25), she must have used two different words. Yet she was an ignorant woman who spoke no Greek but a language very close to Hebrew—what word could she possibly have used for "Christ" to distinguish it from Messiah? We must ask the same question of the Book of Mormon rather than hastily condemning it as an anachronism.

A number of studies have recently come forth dealing with the origin of the name *Christian,* all of them unsatisfied with the conventional idea that it was a term of derision first applied to the followers of Christ at Antioch. These studies are agreed that it was the Christians themselves who first took the name—as in the Book of Mormon, and that for them the mere uttering of the name was "an abbreviated confession of faith."[103] This is exactly how it is taken in the Book of Mormon.

---

[101]*Gospel of Philip,* 104:3ff.; Cf. 110:6f.
[102]H. R. C. Leaney, *Guide to the Scrolls,* pp. 90f.
[103]J. Moreau, in *Nouvelle Clio,* I-II (1949-50), pp. 190-2 and *Harvard Theological Revue* 42 (1949), pp. 109-124; H. B. Mattingly, in *Journal of Theological Studies,* 9 (1958), pp. 26-37; W. Lowie, in *Theology Today,* 8 (1951), pp. 11-19.

Proper Names

The greatest bonanza any philologist could ask for in coming to grips with the Book of Mormon is the generous supply of proper names, West Semitic and Egyptian, which the author dumps in his lap. Here is more than enough rope to hang any imposter and put an effective bridle on the well-known exuberance of people who play around with names. Let us add to our older lists a few examples that we have recently run across.

Egyptian:—We have always thought that the oddest and most disturbing name in the Book of Mormon was Hermounts, since there is nothing either Classical or Oriental about it. So we avoided it, until not long ago a student from Saudi Arabia asked point blank what the funny word was. Well, what does the Book of Mormon say it is? Hermounts in the Book of Mormon is the wild country of the borderlands, the hunting grounds, "that part of the wilderness which was infested by wild and ravenous beasts." (Alma 2:37.) The equivalent of such a district in Egypt is Hermonthis, the land of Month, the Egyptian Pan, —the god of wild places and things. Hermounts and Hermonthis are close enough to satisfy the most exacting philologist.[104] The Egyptian Month of Hermonthis was an extremely popular figure in Lehi's day, to judge by the great frequency with which his name occurs in the composition of proper names in various forms: Montu, Mendes, Menti, etc.; it is the Book of Mormon Manti, next to Ammon, the commonest name element in the Nephite onomasticon.[105] It is hard to explain bull's-eyes like Korihor, Pahoran, and Paankhi as pure accidents. Paankhi was a popular Egyptian name in the seventh century B.C., but it was not known until the end of the

---

[104]See S. V. Hermonthis in Pauly-Wissowa, Realenzyklop. der kl. Altertumswiss. VIII, 901f.; cf. Herodotus, History, II, 46.

[105]The Semitic form of Month is Manti—e.g., S. Smith, in Cambridge Ancient History, III, 381, cf. F. Bisson de la Roque, in Bull. Inst. Francais Archéol. Orient., 14 (1941), 1-49; W. K. Simpson, in Orientalia, 29 (1960), pp. 63ff.

Potsherd found in 1938 on the Gulf of Aqaba, dating from approximately the time of Lehi, and bearing the name of Lehi. (From BASOR, #80, 1940)

last century; and what American would dream of cooking up such combinations as "aa" or "kh"? Interestingly enough, there are two separate Korihors (the name is spelled variously) in the Old World, the one a genuine Egyptian name (Kherihor, Hurhor, etc., was a high priest of Ammon and chief judge who seized the throne in 1085 B.C.), and the other of Asiatic origin going back to the dawn of history.[106] This is interesting because there are also two forms of the name in the Book of Mormon, the one (Corihor) being an important Jaredite name, and the other (Korihor) the name of a Nephite chief judge.

Book of Mormon theophoric names such as Gadianhi, Korihor, Amnihor, etc., follow the proper rules of con-

---

[106]B. Hrozny, *Ancient History of Western Asia* (Prague: Artia, 1940), p. 111, on the Asiatic version. Cf. Sir Alan Gardiner, *Egypt of the Pharaohs* (Oxford: Clarendon, 1961), p. 157, for possible confusion of the two forms.

struction with the conventional employment of mimation
and nunation. The Egyptian names even fall into the Old
World statistical pattern with an absolute predominance
of the name Ammon, with Manti second in order, and
a heavy emphasis on names beginning with "Pa" and high
frequency of the elements "mor" and "hor."[107]

Zinapa, the cuneiform rendering of an Egyptian name,
certainly suggests the Book of Mormon Zeniff.[108] Since
the writing on the Anthon Transcript looks most like
Meroitic, it may be significant that Meroitic names have
a way of suggesting Book of Mormon names—to us, at
least. Thus the names Pachoras and Pakazi occur in a
short Meriotic inscription (cf. B.M. Pahoran, Pachus);[109]
others that the Book of Mormon student will recognize
are Keb or Kib (B.M. Gib),[110] Horan, Pikhas (B.M.
Pachus), Aminap (B.M. Aminadab), Anlaman, Piankhi.[111]
One easterner living in Egypt was Teumman (B.M. Teomner).[112]

Which brings us to the Hebrew names in the Book
of Mormon. A large part of the Hebrew names in the Book
of Mormon are nonbiblical, but preserve the authentic
forms of the Hebrew names of the period as attested in
newly discovered documents.[113] Some important place

[107]F. Petrie, in *Ancient Egypt* (1924), p. 79, gives a frequency list for
late Egyptian, with Ammon scoring 58, Montu (Manti) 26, and Hor 16. On
the Mor- Mer- element, P. Langlois, in *Revue Egyptologique*, N. S. I (1919),
pp. 148-162. T. Gaster, in *Ancient Egypt* (1932), p. 68, shows that Isaiah
45:15 "definitely plays on the name Amen." On the theophoric names, see
Th. Hopfner, in *Archiv Orientalni*, 15 (1946), pp. 164. On the frequencies,
F. Petrie, in *Ancient Egypt and the East*, 1924, p. 79, and P. Langlois, in
Revue Egyptologique, N.S. I (1919), pp. 148, 162.
[108]E. Edel, in *Journal of Near Eastern Studies*, 7 (1948), 11-24.
[109]F. L. Griffith, in *Journal of Egyptian Archaeology*, 11 (1925), p. 259.
[110]K. Sethe, in *Ztschr. für Aegypt. Sprache* 43 (1906), pp. 147, 149.
[111]For Horon compounds, common in Egypt and Syria, J. Gray, in *Journal
of Near Eastern Studies*, 8 (19), pp. 29, 32, 34; Pikhas, P. Martet, in
Kemi, 8 (1946), Pl. xxi-xxv; Anlaman, Animap, and Piankhy are all late forms,
see F. L. Griffith, in *Journal of Egyptian Archaeology*, 4 (1917), pp. 169,
161ff., 216f.
[112]For Teumman, Sidney Smith, in *Journal of Egyptian Archaeology* 18
(1932), p. 29.
[113]Such names are Ahimelech, Gadjahu, Jahaz, etc., in A. Reifenberg,
Ancient Hebrew Seals (London: East and West Library, 1950), Nos. 12, 13,
19, 23, etc., and Lomni, in the *Testament of Levi*, 12:1.

names we have only in translation in the Book of Mormon, the best known being Bountiful and Desolation. Bountiful is a typical colonizer's name (cf. Olbia, Euxin), while it is known that the ancient Semites gave the name Hormah, meaning Destruction or Desolation, "to any scene of defeat."[114]

Here are some interesting old West Semitic names that seem to come right out of the Book of Mormon: Matianoi Mittani (Book of Mormon, Middoni), Amminaadabbi (Edomite, cf. Book of Mormon Aminadab), Seriah, Jabish (contemporaries of Jeremiah); Lomni (Old Hebrew, cf. Book of Mormon Omni); Gadiahu Hezron, Ziph, Epher, Jalon, Ezer, Amnon, Rinnah, (Old Hebrew Seals) Jether or Ether.[115]

A surprisingly large number of studies have appeared in recent years on the subject of Egyptian names for the Red Sea, the reason being that the Egyptians had many names and were always making up others. Especially in the late period, according to a recent report, the Egyptians were fond of "evolving new names for different seas."[116] Again, the reason for the odd practice is not known, but it is entirely in keeping with Lehi's behavior: "And we beheld the sea, which *we* called Irreantum, which being interpreted, is many waters." (1 Nephi 17:5. Italics added.) "Many waters" is a typical Egyptian designation (that is the meaning of Fayyum, in fact), but what about "Irreantum"? It is not a Semitic name, and Lehi even goes to the trouble of translating it. It has recently been shown

----

[114]L. Woolley and T. E. Lawrence, *The Wilderness of Zin* (London: J. Cape, 1936), p. 107.

[115]For Mittani, R. Reinach, in *Rev. des Etudes Grecques,* 7 (1894), pp. 313-8; for Amminadabi, M. Noth, in *Zt. d. Dt. Morgenl. Ges.* 81, p. 27; Seriah and Jabish are in II *Barnabas* 5:5; for the others and many more, R. A. S. Macalister, in *Palestine Explor. Fund Quart.,* 1905, p. 333, and note 110 above.

[116]M. Copisarow, in *Vetus Testamentum,* 12 (1962), p. 1. Cf. W. Spiegelberg, in *Ztschr. f. aeg. Sprache,* 66 (1931), pp. 37-39, for a list of names and meanings, and E. Zyhlarz, in *Archiv fur aeg. Archaeol.,* 1 (1938) pp. 111-117.

that one of the more common Egytian names for the Red
Sea was Iaru, which is not Egyptian and the meaning of
which is unknown.[117] That would take care of the "Irre-"
element in Lehi's name, while "antum" can be matched by
two characteristic Egyptian forms, *iny-t* and *'anjt*, both
describing large bodies of water, the former possibly the
Gulf of Suez, and the latter the "Waters of Busiris." On the
other hand, since "Iaru" has never been explained, could it
be related to the old Indo-European word for "sea," the
Hittite form of which is *arunash*?[118] *Aru-na-sh* corresponds
closely enough with Irre-an-t (um), but we won't include
it among our more valid parallels since we throw it in
just for fun.

---

[117]J. R. Towers, in *Journal of Near Eastern Studies*, 18 (1959), pp. 150-3.
[118]Hrozny, *op. cit.*, p. 191.

CHAPTER 7

Checking on Long-forgotten Lore

Peculiar Situations

The Reverend F. S. Spaulding prefaced his elaborate and carefully-planned demonstration of the fraudulence of the Book of Mormon by the remark that "a flood of light would be thrown upon the whole question of church origins if the account of the organization of the church in the new world, described in the Book of Mormon, were similar to that in the old."[1] But the reason such a flood of light would be welcome is precisely that no description of the founding and organization of the Church in the Old World is available, as was fully demonstrated in Olaf Linton's well known study.[2] The study of the nature and organization of the early church has always been a theme of hopeless confusion and disagreement; and the present Pope has been good enough to point out how defective our knowledge of the original Christian institutions has been. Actually Bishop Spaulding hit the nail on the head: *if* the Book of Mormon gives an authentic picture of how the Lord went about setting up the church, then it gives us indeed a flood of light. But how can we tell whether the Book of Mormon account is not the purest fantasy? Today there is a way.

For in the very year in which Spaulding made his sage

---

[1]Reverend F. S. Spaulding, *Joseph Smith as a Translator* (Salt Lake City, 1912), p. 3.
[2]O. Linton, *Das Problem der Urkirche in der neueren Forschung* (Uppsala: Univ. Ersckrift, 1932, Bd. I.

observation a very early and important Christian document
was first brought forth to throw a new light on the activities of the Lord after the Resurrection.

The Forgotten Ministry of Christ

We have in the New Testament only the teachings
given by the Lord to the apostles before the resurrection.
Yet we are emphatically told that these teachings had not
been enough to give these men faith or understanding of
the resurrection, so that they flatly refused to believe the
report of the resurrection when it was given to them by
reliable persons, and when the Lord himself appeared to
them, they tried to run away in terror. Now, if we possess
only a very small part of the words of Jesus to the disciples
before his death, how can we from them alone acquire a
faith and understanding which the apostles failed to get
from the Lord himself? The standard explanation is that
the apostles re-read the things they had not understood at
first, which now in the light of the resurrection and the
effusion of the Spirit became clear: These teachings "they
now transmitted to the church—the words and deeds of
Christ, plus the intelligence which they had received
through the illuminating action of the Spirit."[3] That sounds
nice, but it is not what the record reports. The mere fact
of the resurrection, though it made everything appear in
a new light, was apparently not sufficient to give the
apostles what they needed. In an instant the doubting
Thomas accepted the resurrection, as the others had at
an earlier meeting, and yet the Lord had to spend forty
days off and on teaching the disciples "the things of the
kingdom" before they were ready to go out on their missions.[4] What he taught them was not, as is commonly

---

[3]R. Latourelle, in *Gregorianum*, 44 (1963), p. 257.

[4]Acts 1:3. ". . . the apostles . . . understood the Master only gradually
and slowly," Bo Reicke, in *Interpretation*, 16 (1962), p. 160. An extreme case
is in the *Apocryphon of James* 7:8, 10; 8:30; 11:6, where the Lord must prolong his post-resurrectional stay for eighteen days because the apostles simply
cannot learn their lesson.

maintained, simply a repetition of what they had heard before—far from it. All are agreed that at the time the apostles heard very secret things which they had never heard before; they asked questions which they had never dared ask before and cried in wonder, "These things are more marvellous than what we were taught before." Now for the first time they learned "the ultimate secrets," "the highest knowledge."[5] "Now," they cried, "he teaches us things which we had not known before, great, amazing, and real things."[6]

What were these things? If the story of Christ's return after the resurrection were only a myth or wishful thinking, we would find either total silence on the matter or else the usual gnostic-philosophic claptrap masquerading as deep mysteries. Instead of that, we find, if we bring the records together, a remarkably consistent, plain, and factual account of what the Lord did on his return. Whenever a really old Christian text is discovered today, one can be pretty sure that its subject will be what the Lord taught the apostles in secret *after* the Resurrection.[7]

In the texts from Nag Hammadi we have the library of a devout body of sectaries, preserved by the sands of the desert; but these people, instead of looking forward only to the coming of the Messiah, look both forward and back, since, as we learn from Justin's *Dialogue,* that is the basic difference between Jew and Christian. Both situations are found in the Book of Mormon, however, and the Nag Hammadi writings deal with the second phase, and more particularly with the activity of the Lord among men *after* his resurrection. This is a great stroke of luck, since

---

[5]*Apocryphon of James,* 2:33-39; *Apocryphon of John,* 19-22; *Acts of Thomas,* c. 47; *Evang. Barthol.* (fragment), in *Revue Biblique,* 10 (1931), p. 185. Jerome, *Adv. Pelag.* 2:15, says that the apostles after the resurrection asked the Lord to tell them what he had not told them before. So also in the 127 *Canons of the Apostles,* Canon No. 12; *The Discourse on the Abbaton,* Sec. 480; the *Gospel of the Twelve Apostles,* in *Patrologia Orientalia* 2:135, 160f.

[6]*Epistle of the Apostles* 3 (14), 5 (16), 11 (22).

[7]See H. Nibley in *Vigiliae Christianae* 20 (1966), pp. 5-6.

the most striking and daring part of the Book of Mormon is that dealing with the appearance of Christ to the Nephites after the crucifixion. How do the two versions compare?

Recently this writer went through all the then available early Christian writings dealing with the activities of the Lord during the forty days after the resurrection and found that with all their pseudognostic corruptions they all have four things in common, these things being demonstrably the original Christian tradition—what remains after all the speculations and embellishments and fabrications have been drained off. The four things are (1) insistence on secrecy, (2) emphasis on the limited sojourn of the Church upon the earth at that time, (3) bodies of doctrine, and (4) rites and ordinances that differ substantially from the teachings and rituals of conventional Christianity. These four things characterize Christ's post-resurrectional teaching in the Book of Mormon as well; but since we cannot here examine scores of Coptic and Syriac texts, we may take as a sampling a writer which no less an authority than Origen claims to be older than the Gospel of Luke, and which was accepted by Christians as perfectly orthodox down to the time of the Patristic writers.

This is the writing mentioned above that came forth in the very year Spaulding flung his challenge to the Book of Mormon. It is called the *Gospel of the Twelve Apostles* and survives only in Coptic, being of the same period and locale as our Nag Hammadi books.[8] It presents a characteristic confusion of events before and after the resurrection, but this presents no great problem since it is universally conceded that the Lord repeated many things as he spent forty days off and on teaching the things of the kingdom. (Cf. Acts 1:3.) The point is that there are conspicuous aspects of the story which can be confirmed by

[8]The text is discussed by E. Revillout in *Patrologia Orientalis*, 2:123-130, where the text is reproduced, pp. 131-184.

the "forty-day" literature in general and the Book of Mormon in particular.

Fragment 2 of the so-called *Gospel of the Twelve Apostles*[9] begins by informing "the brethren" who want to know "how things really were" that "as long as Jesus was upon the earth he continued to eat with his apostles on an earthly table, pointing their minds forward to the table in his kingdom, for the things of this world he counted as nothing." The language here is typically post-resurrectional. The writer tells how Jesus wanted his apostles to be one, "and used to pray to his Father for them, 'that they might be one even as we are one.'"

After a lacuna we see Thomas at the Lord's behest bringing him five loaves and two fishes, while Andrew protests the inadequacy of the fare: "Bring them to me," says the Lord in reply, "and there will be enough." As in the New Testament *and* the Book of Mormon, the people have been three days in the desert with nothing to eat—albeit under very different circumstances. Still the situation is a type and an image. Before he blesses the bread and fish, Jesus holds intimate conversation with a little child (cf. 3 Nephi 26:14 and 17:11ff.), after which he explains to the multitude that what they are about to enjoy is a special providence which they must always remember and a meal that will truly fill them. (Cf. 3 Nephi 20:8.) Next "Jesus took the bread, prayed over it, giving praise and thanks, and then divided it, giving it to the apostles that they might pass it to the multitude" (cf. 3 Nephi 18:3-4), announcing that "he to whom I have not given a share of the bread with my hands is not worthy to partake of my flesh. . . . This is a mystery of the Father with regard to the distribution of my flesh." (Cf. 3 Nephi 18:27ff.)

Note that the loaves and fishes seem to be here confused with the sacrament. The identity, it is now known,

---

[9]All the material here discussed is found *ibid.*, pp. 132-143.

is intentional: a number of scholars, especially Roman
Catholic, have recently called attention to the close connection of the loaves and fishes miracle with the sacrament,
noting that the feeding of the multitude was actually an
ordinance.[10] The passing of the sacrament by the Twelve
and their administering to the people in twelve separate
bodies (cf. 3 Nephi 19:5) is a significant detail. Recently
A. Adam has shown that this division into twelve bodies
was an essential part of the old Jewish rite of the shew-
bread of which the Christian sacrament was a continuation
—as it is in the Book of Mormon.[11]

Jesus blesses the bread that those who eat of it may
be filled, "that Thy Son might receive glory in Thee; that
those whom thou hast taken out of the world might obey
him." The reference to being taken out of the world occurs
also in the other oldest-known prayer on the sacrament—
that in the *Didache*—while the element of obedience is
important in the prayer on the bread in the Book of Mormon: ". . . that they may . . . keep his commandments
which he hath given them. . . ." (Moroni 4:3.)

Then, we are told, "all the people ate and were filled;
whereupon they praised God." (Cf. 3 Nephi 20:9: "Now,
when the multitude had all eaten . . . they were filled with
the Spirit; and they did cry out with one voice, and gave
glory to Jesus. . . .")

The next section tells how Jesus went about making
his disciples and his followers perfectly one with each
other, with him, and with the Father: "Have ye not heard,
O my beloved, the love of Jesus for his apostles; which
was so great that he withheld nothing from them in all
the works of his godhead?" This blessing was imparted in
three steps, "the first time in blessing the five barley

---

[10]G. H. Boobyer, in *Journal of Theological Studies*, N.S. 3 (1953),
pp. 161-171; A. M. Farrer in the same journal, 4 (1953), pp. 1-14; B. van
Grassi, in *Novum Teslamentum,* 7 (1964) pp 119-123; B. van Iersel, ibid
7 (1965) pp 167-195.
[11]A. Adam, in *Theologische Literaturzeitung*, 88 (1963), pp. 10-19.

loaves, the second time when he prayed and glorified the Father, the third time when he blessed the seven loaves." In 3 Nephi 19 the Lord also imparts his glory to the disciples in three steps as they prayed three times "to the Father in the name of Jesus." (verse 8.)

The main theme of both accounts is how the Lord made the disciples one with each other by making them one with himself and his Father. In founding the church, it was this oneness which according to both texts he desired of the Father more than anything else. Accordingly, in two short prayers in the Book of Mormon, one four verses long (3 Nephi 19:20-23) and the other only two verses (3 Nephi 19:28f.), we find no less than sixty-nine personal pronouns! Thus the second prayer ends: ". . . that *they* may be purified in *me*, that *I* may be in *them* as *thou*, Father, art in *me*, that *we* may be one, that *I* may be glorified in *them*." (3 Nephi 19:29). These utterances, astonishing as they seem, are actually matched and even surpassed in the Gospel of John 14-17 where the mingling of identities becomes positively overpowering. Plainly we are in the same thought-world as John, treating of matters concerning which the most persistent repetition fails to convince the Christian world. John and Nephi tell us that Father, Son, and Holy Ghost are one in exactly the same way that they want the apostles and all the other members of the church to be one with them and with each other.

After this, "Thomas says unto Jesus, Behold, O Lord, thou hast in thy goodness bestowed every grace upon us. But there yet remains one thing which we would that thou wouldst grant unto us." This is a common theme in the "forty-day" accounts, where the apostles, after having received all knowledge and enlightenment and become perfectly one with Jesus, have yet one question to ask him, but are abashed at the presumption of asking until Jesus, who knows what is in their hearts, tells them he knows what it is they desire and that they need not be ashamed for it is a worthy request. In the present text the Lord simply encourages Thomas and his brethren not to be embarrassed to ask what is in their minds, though usual commendation is lacking. It is not lacking in the Book of Mormon account:

"And it came to pass . . . he spake unto his disciples *one by one* [they always question him individually in the 'forty-day' literature], saying unto them: What is it that ye desire of me . . .?

"And when he had spoken unto them, he turned himself unto the three. . . .

"And they sorrowed in their hearts, for they durst not speak unto him the thing which they desired.

"And he said unto them: Behold, I know your thoughts, and ye have desired the thing which John, my beloved . . . desired of me.

"Therefore, more blessed are ye. . . ." (3 Nephi 28:1, 4-7, Italics added.)

Here we are directly referred to an identical situation in the Old World. And what is the special boon granted the three? That they "shall never taste of death . . . even until all things shall be fulfilled. . . .

"And . . . shall never endure the pains of death; but . . . shall be changed in the twinkling of an eye. . . ." (3 Nephi 27:7-8.)

A like request is granted in our Coptic account: "We desire, O Lord, that we may see how things are with the dead who lie in their tombs, whom thou hast raised up to be a sign of thy resurrection to take place for us. . . . We desire to see the bones which have fallen apart in the tomb, how they are reunited one to another, that the dead may speak." What follows shows that this is plainly a post-resurrectional tradition, for in answer to their request Thomas and two friends are shown the raising of Lazarus, at whose coming forth the whole cemetery revolves on its axis, and "the dead arose and came forth because of the voice of Jesus."

Such a mass resurrection could, of course, only take place after the Lord himself had been resurrected. The descriptions of the *descensus* (the visit of the Lord to the spirits in prison) and the *kerygma* (his preaching to them and liberating of them) that follow also clearly belong in a post-crucifixion setting. At the moment Jesus calls Lazarus forth, Adam also hears his voice and cries: "This voice which I hear is the voice of my Creator and my Redeemer. This is the voice of Him who was my glory when he addressed me in Paradise. . . . O my son, Lazarus, take greetings to My Creator. O when will the time come when I too may hear the voice of life calling me?"

Before he grants the wish of the apostles, Jesus says to the people, "More blessed are they who have not seen but believed than they who have seen and not believed," which is akin to the Book of Mormon, ". . . blessed are ye if ye shall believe . . . after that ye have seen me. . . .

"And again, more blessed are they who shall believe in your words . . ." (i.e., without having seen). (3 Nephi 12:1f.) Then the Coptic text adds, "You see how many miracles and signs I did among the Jews, and yet they did not believe me." This again compares with 3 Nephi 19:35: "So great faith have I never seen among all the Jews; wherefore I could not show unto them so great miracles, because of their unbelief."

It is always one to three apostles who are singled out for special blessings and manifestations after the resurrection. In the first of all our early Christian Coptic texts to be discovered, the famous *Pistis Sophia* (c. 42f.), we are told that Jesus appointed three of his disciples to keep official written records of what he said and did, conformant to the ancient order (Deut. 19:15) requiring that all things be established by three witnesses. In this case the three are Matthew, Thomas, and Philip, which accounts for the prominence of their names in the earliest Christian records. The significance of the "three witnesses" theme for the Book of Mormon needs no comment.

In the so-called *Gospel of Philip* we have another mixing of sacrament and transfiguration motifs, when Philip tells how Christ "made the disciples great, that they might be able to see him in his greatness. He said on that day in blessing the sacrament: 'Thou who hast joined the perfect, the light, with the Holy Ghost, unite with angels with us also. . . .' "[12] Compare this with the 19th chapter of Third Nephi, where ". . . they were filled with the Holy Ghost and with fire. . . . And angels did come down out of heaven and did minister unto them.

"And . . . Jesus came and stood in the midst. . . .

". . . and behold *they* were as white as the countenance and also the garments of Jesus. . . ." (Vs. 13-15, 25. Italics added.)

The great difference between the spirit and teaching of the Dead Sea Scrolls and the New Testament, according to F. F. Bruce, was that the Messiah of the New Testament "was different from any kind of Messiah expected at Qumran or elsewhere in Israel . . . and all the accompaniments of messianic expectation had their meaning transformed in the light of his messianic achievement." Moreover the Lord "fulfilled the scriptures in addition to making their meaning plain."[13] Those statements describe very well what happened in the Book of Mormon where when the Lord finally came what he said and did was marvellous and unspeakable and quite unlike anything anybody expected. He went through the scriptures and showed the Nephites how their meaning had indeed been transformed by his coming (3 Nephi 12-17, 20), and showed them how he had "fulfilled the scriptures in addition to making their meaning

[12]*Gospel of Philip*, 106:8-13.
[13]F. F. Bruce, *Second Thoughts* . . . , p. 147, 149.

clear." After that, for over 200 years Nephite society wore a completely altered countenance.

Strange Behavior

In the *Ascension of Isaiah* we read a strange story: "When Somnas the scribe and Assur the record-keeper [cf. Zoram in the Book of Mormon] heard that the great prophet Isaiah was coming up from Gilgal [near Jericho and about ten miles from Qumran] to Jerusalem, and with him 40 sons of prophets and his own son Jasum, they announced his approach to King Hezekiah. When he heard this King Hezekiah rejoiced exceedingly and went forth to meet the blessed Isaiah, taking him by the hand and conducting him into his royal dwelling, and ordered that a chair be brought for him." Then the king brought in his son Manasseh and besought the prophet to give him a blessing. When Isaiah declared this impossible because of what he could foresee, the king was so smitten with grief and dismay that he "sorrowed exceedingly and rent his garments and wept bitterly . . . and fell upon his face as one dead."

Isaiah, however, told the king that such behavior would profit him nothing since Satan would have his way with Manasseh. Later while he was sitting on the king's bed conversing, the prophet was overcome by the Spirit, "and his consciousness was carried away from this world, so that Somnas the record-keeper began to say that Isaiah was dead. But when Hezekiah the King came in and took his hand he knew that he was not dead; but they thought he had died. . . . And thus he lay upon the bed of the King in his transported state (ecstasy) for three days and three nights. Then his spirit returned to his body," and Isaiah "summoned Jasum his son and Somnas the scribe and Hezekiah the King and all those who stood about such as were worthy to hear those things he had seen." To them he delivered an ecstatic discourse on the "surpassing, indescribable, and marvellous works of God who is merciful to men, and of the glory of the Father and of his Beloved Son and of the Spirit, and of the ranks of the holy angels standing in their places. . . ." It will be recalled that Lehi was "carried away in a vision" on his bed, and when he awoke discoursed to his family on the "power, and goodness, and mercy" of God, (1 Nephi 1:14.) and that in his vision he too saw "numberless concourses of angels." (v. 8).

Here we have something very much like the story of Ammon in the court of King Lamoni (Alma 18-19), with both the king and his inspired guest being overcome and taken for dead and having visions of the glorious plan of salvation. Also in this fragment we see Isaiah at home among the pious men of the Judaean desert, the "40 sons of prophets," apparently heading some sort of religious community as Lehi and other prophets did later in the same desert, even down to the people of Qumran and the monks of the Middle Ages. Such societies, writes J. Eaton, "were essentially related to the religious communities of later Judaism and of Christianity" and were "called to a special task of guarding and witnessing to Yahweh's revelations vouchsafed in the first place to Isaiah."

In the next section, which is a fragment of the lost "Testament of Isaiah," according to R. H. Charles, we see Isaiah accused before King Manasseh by a false prophet who wins the king and the people to his side with "flattering words"—a reminder both of the opponent of the righteous teacher in the Dead Sea Scrolls and of the troubles of Zenos in the Book of Mormon. Since he cannot endure the awful wickedness of Jerusalem, Isaiah goes into the desert again with his followers, this time camping in "a quiet and pure place on a mountain" not far from Bethlehem and still very near Qumran.

Even more unusual than the story of Ammon at Lamoni's court is the tale of how that same Ammon at the waters of Sebus, where "all the Lamanites drive their flocks" discomfited a band of cattle-raiders when he "smote off as many of their arms as were lifted against him, and they were not a few." (Alma 18:26, 38.). The feat of Ammon at the waters of Sebus is easy to explain. It is very clear from what we are told that Ammon had a trick blow which his heavy-handed opponents, rough herdsmen with their clubs and stones, could never get the hang of until it was too late; he was a sort of karate expert with a sword. The cattle-stealing at the waters of Sebus is rather typical too, there is a close parallel to it in the 18th book of the Iliad where the picture on the shield of Achilles of cattle-rustlers attacking at a watering-place is described as part of a *typical* episode of everyday life:

"When they had found what they thought was a good spot to lie and wait, at a place on a river where all the cattle were watered, there they crouched bristling with their shining weapons. And they sent out a couple of scouts to give them the sign as soon as the sheep and horned cattle were in sight. Before long they turned up with a pair of herdsmen playing on their flutes and not suspecting a thing. Then the men in the ambush dashed out and in short order rounded up the herds of cattle and flocks of fine white-wooled sheep and killed the two herdsmen." The townspeople came out to rescue their animals and a lively fight ensued at the "watering place of all the cattle." (Iliad 18:520-540).

The almost supernatural power of Ammon reminds one of Judah in the Testament of Judah, where "an angel of might followed him everywhere that he should never be beaten."

Peculiar Teachings

The strange imagery and odd expressions and names found in the Book of Mormon are matched by the strangeness of the doctrines and concepts of the people—things utterly unfamiliar to the world of Joseph Smith, but now beginning to emerge as the legitimate property of the ancient saints. For example, the Book of Mormon opens with what today would be called the Testament of Lehi, parts of which are given verbatim ("in the language of my father") by Nephi. Of recent years a good many such "Testaments" have come to light, revealing the existence of a very old and established tradition of inspired writing.

Another "Testament"

We have called attention above to the existence of a special category of ancient religious writing which we designated as the "Testament" type of literature, because the writings in question purported to contain the last admonitions and prophecies of certain patriarchs and prophets to their children and disciples; what all these "Testaments" have in common, we noted, is the inclusion of a cosmological discourse in which the patriarch gives an account of a conducted tour he has just taken in the spirit to the worlds above.[14] This motif is among the oldest in literature, and the Testaments that contain it (e.g., of Enoch, Abraham, Zenez, the Twelve Patriarchs, etc.) are among the oldest of all apocryphal writings.

The visit of a pious observer to the other world, where he is allowed to look in on a great and glorious assemblage of heavenly beings in the presence of God, is familiar to all from Dante, who derived his ideas (it has recently been demonstrated) from Moslem models coming to him through Spain. At once one recalls Mohammed's journey to heaven in the 17th Sura of the Koran, which in turn harks back to a wealth of Jewish and Christian material much older than Islam. Some scholars today maintain that the Christian tradition has definite affinities with Egyptian teachings of great age,[15] and indeed the journey to heaven

---

[14]Above, pp. 42-43.
[15]For a general treatment, see H. Nibley, in *B.Y.U. Studies* VII (1965), pp. 3ff.

to behold the great ones sitting in council before the throne of dominion is made by Pharaoh in the oldest written documents, the Pyramid Texts and Coffin Texts of the Old Kingdom.

The Great Council held in heaven "at the foundation of the world" is a theme that runs like a red thread through the scriptures: the first book of the Old Testament opens with it, and the last book of the New Testament closes with it, and all the major prophets had the privilege of viewing the heavenly scene of God upon his throne surrounded by numberless concourses of angels. But the idea of a *real* council ran counter to the prevailing doctrines of the schools, especially the University of Alexandria, at the time when those doctrines were adopted as the norms of Christian and Jewish orthodoxy; ever since the victory in the 4th century of intellectualized "horizontal" Christianity and Judaism over the old "vertical" religions, the tradition of how the plan of salvation was adopted at the council in heaven at the Creation has been systematically suppressed and "demythologized."[16]

In the Book of Mormon these teachings burst forth again in their original form and splendor, sweeping us back again into a forgotten world. And now, lending their voices to its voice, we have the newly-discovered Coptic texts,[17] the growing Mandaean-Manichaean corpus, and the Dead Sea Scrolls. The singer of the Thanksgiving Hymn of the Scrolls who, as we shall see, is a close counterpart of the Book of Mormon's Zenos, found himself in the same plight as Lehi, distressed by the wickedness of the Jews at Jerusalem and their hostility to his teachings; but when the vision of the great council in heaven was brought to his mind, he was filled with joy and blessed assurance:

------

[16]*Ibid.*, pp. 22-23.
[17]Containing some vivid descriptions of the Great Council, e.g., in the fragmentary *Apocalypse of Adam.* the *1st Book of Jeu,* the *Bruce Ms. No. 96,* Bp. Timothy's *Sermon on the Abbaton,* the so-called *2nd Coptic Gnostic Work,* etc.

Thou hast caused me to mount up to an eternal height and to
walk in an inconceivable exaltation. And I know that there is a
hope for every one whom thou didst form of the dust in the presence of the Eternal Assembly . . . to be counted with the hosts
of the Saints and to enter the society of the congregation of the
Sons of Heaven. Thou didst appoint unto man an eternal share
with the spirits that know, to praise thy name in joyful unison
with them . . .[18]

No matter what befalls, all is well with the righteous,
for all is going according to God's plan: "From God is the
knowledge of all that is and all that will be: and before
they existed he established their whole plan, and when
they exist (upon earth) he prescribes the conditions of
their existence according to his glorious plan."[19] The poet
cannot contain his joy at the knowledge that "Mere man
is to be raised up to join the heavenly hosts . . . and be
among those who know in the great choir of jubilation."[20]
This was exactly Lehi's reaction to a view of the heavenly
assembly; his former anguish and distress fell from him
and, like the writer of the Hymns, "He did exclaim many
things unto the Lord; such as: Great and marvelous are
thy works, O Lord God Almighty! Thy throne is high in
the heavens, and thy power, and goodness, and mercy are
over all the inhabitants of the earth . . . And after this
manner was the language of my father in the praising of
his God; for his soul did rejoice, and his whole heart was
filled, because of the things which he had seen, yea, which
the Lord had shown unto him." (1 Nephi 1:14f.)

Lehi starts right in with the heavenly journey, a vision
in which ". . . he thought he saw God sitting upon his
throne. . . ." (1 Nephi 1:8.) Here we are taken back to
a council in heaven as a fitting prologue to a religious
history. A decision is reached in the council and hailed
with a great acclamation of joy, after which the session

---

[18]*Thanksgiving Hymn F* (No. 6), p. iii, 19ff.
[19]*Zadokite Fragment*, iii, 15.
[20]*Thanksgiving Hymn* No. 3: 22-24, cf. No. 10: 4f., 28; 12:11-12;
No. 1: 19.

breaks up, various parties going about the business of carrying out their assignments in the implementation of the plan—the plan "prepared from the foundation of the world."[21]

Here we glimpse a concept of heaven wholly alien to the conventional teachings of the Jewish and Christian doctors, who can think of nothing better than Athanasius's picture of the meeting going on and on and on forever, with the choir never ceasing its hymn and the angels never relaxing from their attitude of praise. That concept comes from the few brief glimpses of heaven reported in the scriptures, cases in which inspired men have been allowed to look in for a moment in a brief flashback on what once happened above; this was to explain to them what happens here and to console them in their distress by showing them that there is a divine plan behind everything and hence letting them know that good men should not be impatient or dismayed when things seem to go wrong. This is a lesson taught in Job, John, and the *Thanksgiving Hymns* and *Battle Scroll* of the Dead Sea documents.[22]

The interesting thing about Lehi's vision is that it carries through to the dismissal of the meeting, after which ". . . he saw one descending out of the midst of heaven, . . .

"And he also saw twelve others following him, and their brightness did exceed that of the stars in the firmament.

"And they came down and went forth upon the face of the earth. . . ." (1 Nephi 1:9-11.)

---

[21]The formula appears no less than ten times in G. Reynolds, *A Complete Concordance to the Book of Mormon* (1957), p. 563.

[22]Discussed at length in the source referred to above, note 1. Speaking of the *Battle Scroll*, Y. Yadin writes: "Its main purpose is to give courage to the Sons of Light—liable to despair because of their defeats—by telling them that this sequence of defeats and victories has been determined from time immemorial", Y. Yadin, *The Scroll of the War of the Sons of Light against the Sons of Darkness* (Oxford University Press, 1962), p. 8.

"The Plan"

We have already discussed the image of "the Star," the divine person who comes down to fulfill a special mission among men. Let us here consider another aspect of the meeting.

A search through fifty-odd apocryphal writings of recent discovery reveals the surprising fact that no theme enjoys greater prominence among them than that of the council in heaven held at the foundation of the world and the plan "laid down in the presence of the first angels" on that occasion.[22a] The word "plan" (usually as *makhshavah* or *boule*) occurs with great frequency in these writings, but though it is often found also in the Bible, it is never translated as "plan" in the King James version, where, in fact, the word "plan" does not even appear.[23] On the other hand it appears no fewer than 24 times in the Book of Mormon.

Basic to the "plan" was the provision that man's life on earth was to be a time of testing or probation (that word occurs 13 times in the Book of Mormon), in which every soul would be faced every day of his life with a choice between the two ways—the way of light and the way of darkness, or of life and death respectively.[24] This theme, as fully set forth in the Book of Mormon, enjoys

---

[22a]This was the theme of the second annual faculty lecture, given by the writer at Brigham Young University on March 17, 1965, under the title of *The Expanding Gospel*, available at the BYU Press.

[23]Almost always *makhshavah* can be rendered "plan" in Isaiah and Jeremiah *e.g.*: Isa. 55:8, 9; 59:7; 65:2; 66:18; Jer. 6:19; 18:12; 29:11; 11:19; 18:18; 49:20, 30; 50:4-5; and in some cases it definitely *should* be: Jer. 29:11; 51:29; cf. Ps. 33:11; Prov. 19:21; 20:18; 2 Sam. 14:14; Mic. 4:12.

[24]"There are two roads, one wide and one narrow," leading to two gates, where Adam sits to welcome his children into eternity, according to the *Testament of Abraham*, cited by K. Kohler, in *Jewish Quarterly Review*, 7 (1895), pp. 585f. "All things have their opposites, good and bad: it is the good which is the foil and measure of the bad, and vice versa," according to *Sefer Yeshira*, VI, 2f; cf. *Zohar*, I, 23: "If God had not given men a double inclination to good and bad, he would be capable neither of virtue nor of vice, but as it is he is endowed with a capacity for both." Early Christian writings carry on the tradition; see H. Nibley, *The World and the Prophets*, pp. 168-170; which is also familiar from the Classical writers, e.g., Cicero, *De officiis*, I, 32, 118; Hesiod, *Works and Days*, 273ff.

Torah-Shrine and symbolic tree in the ancient synagogue of Dura Europos.

almost overwhelming predominance in the newly found
apocryphal writings,[25] and yet has no place in conventional Christian and Jewish theology, having been
vigorously condemned by the doctors of both religions in
the fourth and fifth centuries, since they would not tolerate
any concepts involving preexistence of the spirit of man.[26]
Hence is found the studious avoidance of such words as
"plan" and "probation" in our translations of the Bible; to
the contemporaries of Joseph Smith, these ideas were
completely foreign, though we now know, thanks to documents discovered "since Cumorah," that they were the
very essence of early Christianity and Judaism.

Lehi's Vision and the Dura Synagogue

". . . he was carried away . . . even that he saw the
heavens open, and he thought he saw God sitting upon
his throne, surrounded with numberless concourses of
angels in the attitude of singing and praising their God."
(1 Nephi 1:8.) This is a standard theme in the apocryphal
"testaments" of other patriarchs and prophets, Enoch being
the classic example.[27] But as here described, the picture
was thought to be strictly a Christian one, until the discovery of the Dura-Europos synagogue. It seems once to
have held a central position in early Jewish imagery, enjoying a prominence that was entirely lost later on. That prominence is attested on the walls of the synagogue, discovered
just a hundred years after the coming forth of the Book of
Mormon.

------

[25]"O how great the plan of our God!" (2 Nephi 9:13) ". . . prepared for
all men from the foundation of the world, . . ." (1 Nephi 10:18.) It is "the
great and eternal plan of deliverance from death" (2 Nephi 11:5; cf. Alma
12:24, 13:29f.), opposed by the counterplan of the devil, "that cunning plan
of the evil one!" (2 Nephi 9:28.) For the Jewish parallels, see A. Aalen,
*Die Begriffe 'licht' und 'Finsterniss' im AT, in Spätjudentum und im Rabbinis-
mus*, (Videnskaps-Akad. Oslo, II, Hist.-Phil. kl., 1951, No. 1.)

[26]At that time "the familiar Two Ways were no longer the ways of light
and darkness lying before Israel or the Church, but the Way of the Church
itself . . . *versus* the way of the Opposition, whoever they might be," H. Nibley, in *Church History*, 30 (1961), p. 15.

[27]We have listed them in *Vigiliae Christianae*, Vol. 20 (1966), p. 12.

"Before the discovery of the Dura synagogue in 1932," writes Professor E. R. Goodenough, "anyone would have been thought mad who suggested that Jews could have made such a place of worship. Its discovery has maddened us all, but we do not return to sanity when we force the synagogue to conform *a priori* to Jewish literary traditions which through the centuries had never suggested to anyone that such a building could have existed."[28]

Here, then, we have something truly new and revolutionary turning up "since Cumorah" to tell us how the early Jews really thought about things—splendid murals from a synagogue that has been buried in the dust since the third century A.D. showing us things so different from the conventional and accepted concepts of ancient Judaism as to appear to be nothing less than madness to the experts. In these impressive murals we see such unexpected things as the bread and wine of the Messianic meal, reminding us of the sacrament; we see the wandering of Israel in the desert with the waters of life flowing in twelve miraculous streams, with "the head thereof a little way off" (1 Nephi 8:14) to each of the tribal tents.

But the most important representation of all is the central composition that crowns the Torah shrine, the ritual center of the synagogue. Directly above the shrine, as if springing directly from the Law itself, is depicted a splendid tree beneath whose sinuous and spreading boughs the twelve sons of Israel stand around their father Jacob; while sheltered by the branches on the other side Joseph is seen conferring his blessing upon Ephraim and Manasseh. A remarkable thing about this tree of life (for none fail to recognize it as such) is that it is both a tree and a *vine*. Here Professor Goodenough helps us out: "In an atmosphere where identification rather than distinctions, mingling rather than separation, ruled the

---

[28]E. R. Goodenough, *Jewish Symbols in the Greco-Roman Period* (New York: Pantheon, 1964), Vol. 10, pt. 2, p. 197.

thoughts of men . . . the tree-vine seems to express this
sense of identification of tree with vine to the point that
we have called it the tree-vine. Out of the Torah shrine
. . . grew the tree of life and salvation which led to the
supernal throne."[29]

Now, for whatever it is worth, the olive tree that stands
for Israel in the Book of Mormon imagery is also a vine;
it grows in a vineyard, is planted, cultivated, and owned
"by the lord of the vineyard," and is in the charge of the
workers in the vineyard. We have suggested a possible
explanation for this queer state of things by the close association of the olive and the vine in Mediterranean lands,[30]
but we may have here a better explanation. There was
nothing repugnant to "the thoughts of men" in Lehi's day
in having one and the same object both a tree and a vine
and in having it represent half a dozen different things
at the same time, with no sense of contradiction or confusion whatever.

We get the same free-and-easy identifications in the
art of Dura as in the Book of Mormon. At Dura we see
high in the branches of the tree the familiar figure of
Orpheus as he sits playing his lyre to a lion and a lamb.
The earliest Christian art is fond of the figure of Orpheus,
one of the two pagan figures admitted freely to Christian
imagery; instead of playing to all the animals as he usually
does, the Christian Orpheus usually sings to a lion and a
lamb, as in the Dura synagogue—which of course suggests
that it was Isaiah 14 that paved the way for the acceptance
of Orpheus into the Christian community.[31]

Goodenough suggests that the Dura Orpheus "was
probably called David," through whose "heavenly, saving

---

[29]*Ibid.*, p. 200. Reproductions of all the murals may be found in Vol. 11
of the series.

[30]*The Improvement Era*, Vol. 68 (October 1965), p. 876.

[31]See the discussion and reproductions in H. Leclercq's article on Orpheus
in Cabrol & Leclercq, *Dictionnaire d'archaeologie et de liturgie chretiennes,*
Vol. 12, pp. 2736ff.

music Israel could be glorified."[32] Certainly he represents the harmony of Israel throughout the world as well as the harmony of all nature; the listening animals show that. In this picture, to follow Professor Goodenough again, "the artist is trying to show the glorification of Israel through the mystic tree-vine, whose power could *also* be represented as a *divine love* which the soul purifying music of an Orpheus figure best symbolized." (Italics added). What Orpheus does, then, is to show that the tree represents divine love.

Again we turn to the Book of Mormon: there the spreading tree-vine is clearly and often stated to represent Israel but it also has another significance. When the angel asked Nephi about the tree of his vision, "Knowest thou the meaning of the tree which thy father saw?" the young man "answered him saying: Yea, it is the love of God, which sheddeth itself abroad in the hearts of the children of men; wherefore, it is the most desirable above all things." (1 Nephi 11:21-22.)

What at a later date could better express "the meaning of the tree" as that universal love for which all creatures yearn than to add the classic picture of Orpheus to it?

That the Jews at Dura had by centuries of exposure to them become quite hospitable to certain standard Greek and Persian images appears also in the Iranian character of the heavenly court that appears above the tree. Above "the tree of life and salvation which led to the supernal throne" was depicted the throne itself, in a scene in which God is shown enthroned in heaven, Persian fashion, surrounded by his heavenly hosts. Goodenough finds the idea both surprising and compelling: "The enthroned king surrounded by the tribes in such a place reminds us much more of the Christ enthroned with the saints in heaven . . . than any other figure in the history of art. Let me

---

[32]Goodenough, *op. cit.*, p. 201.

repeat, that before the discovery of the synagogue all sane scholars would have agreed that 'of course' no such synagogue paintings as these could have existed at all."[33] As this is the high point in the Dura murals, so was it also in Lehi's vision.

It is interesting how these visions seem to get around, and the Book of Mormon casts some light on that problem too when it reports that after Lehi had described his vision to his family, his son Nephi was granted the identical revelation, only with a fuller explanation, including points that Lehi had overlooked. Thus we see how the same vision, far from being reserved to one man, might be shared by others with the intent that through the preaching of those thus favored the vision might become the common property and tradition of all the people. (Moroni 7:29-32.)

Some New Scrolls

Any student of the Book of Mormon reading through some of the more recently published and less familiar Scrolls from the Dead Sea should find himself delightfully at home. These documents are a fresh reminder that the study of the Book of Mormon will always remain an open-ended operation, whether one believes the claims of the book or not. Always there are new things turning up and demanding an explanation, as if the Book of Mormon were being forced on the world against its will. Only the practiced skill and single-minded determination of the learned has to date enabled them to escape the toils of a serious involvement with the Book Nobody Wants; but that skill and determination are not to be underestimated—we cannot hope to match them, but we can call attention to some of the things like the following.

The *Florilegium* ("Bouquet"; 4Q flor. I) is so called because it is a selection of proof-texts from different prophets, all of whom look forward to the fulfilling of God's

------
[33]*Loc. cit.*

plan on earth. In this fragment 2 Samuel 7:10-11 is explained as referring to the house of the Lord that shall be built in the last days, while Exodus 15:17f. shows that only the elect of Israel "who hold sacred the Name" will be allowed to enter that house which, unlike the other temple, will never be destroyed. For 2 Samuel 7:11 makes it clear that the sons of Belial will never again prevail in their attempt to carry out "the Plan of Belial (the Evil One), to overthrow the Sons of Light . . . and make their souls captive to Belial by causing them to stray in wickedness." Compare this with 2 Nephi 9:28: "O that cunning plan of the evil one!" and with Alma 12:11: ". . . and then they are taken captive by the devil, and led by his will down to destruction." Next 2 Samuel 7:11-14 is explained as referring to "the shoot of David who will stand beside the Seeker of the Law in . . . Zion in the Last Days, as it is written" in Amos 9:11, referring to "the Ark [tent, shrine] of David that is fallen which shall rise again for the salvation of Israel." The opening line of the First Psalm is next explained as referring "to those who have strayed from the road, as it is written in the Book of the Prophet Isaiah, looking forward to the Last Days." It then cites Isaiah 8:11 as applying to "those of whom it is written in the Book of Ezekiel the Prophet," quoting Ezekiel 37:23, a significant chapter. Then there is reference to the sons of Zadok seeking their own counsel, "the counsel of the church," that is, setting up their own church; and lastly Psalm 2:1-2 is quoted as describing the rage of the opposition—the Gentiles—against "the Chosen of Israel in the Last Days."[34]

It would be hard to find in any so brief a fragment a more concise and telling description of the restoration from the Latter-day Saint point of view or a neater bouquet of Book of Mormon sentiments. The reference to David calls our attention to another newly published fragment,

---

[34]The restored text and translation, Y. Yadin, in *Israel Exploration Journal* 9 (1959), pp. 95-98.

called *The Patriarchal Blessing* (4Q patr), which reads like
a typical "testament" and is a commentary on Genesis
49:10: "The rule shall not depart from Judah. . . ."[35] This
it explains as meaning that "as long as Israel has dominion
there will always be one of the House of David on the
throne," and that the support of all Israel can be counted
on until the coming of "the true Messiah, the shoot of
David, to whom and to whose seed the covenant of the
kingship is given over his people for generations without
end." This shows that the Qumran people knew of the
Messiah of the house of David, the Messiah of the New
Testament.

The fragment labelled IQSb is the *Blessing Scroll*
and contains five blessings.[36] The first is addressed to those
"who hold fast to God's holy covenant and are perfect in
walking in the ways of truth." Such language recalls Luke
1 and clearly indicates that the gospel was indeed restored
to and through those righteous few who were looking forward to the Messiah, as is so fully set forth in the Book of
Mormon.[37] Here we are further told that God shall provide
"an eternal fountain of living water for them," that they
may receive instruction "in the congregation of the Saints."
The third blessing (the second is badly damaged) says
that God shall "set a crown of eternal glory upon thy head,
and sanctify thy seed with eternal glory . . . and give thee
kingship." The emphasis on the importance of progeny and
kingship is significant. The leaders, "the Sons of Zadok,
God's chosen priests," are blessed to be "perfect ornaments
in the midst of the congregation of the saints." The fourth
blessing is also a blessing of leadership and promises eternal

---

[35]The text is reproduced with photographs by J. M. Allegro, in *Journal
of Biblical Literature*, 75 (1956), pp. 174-6, along with a discussion of many
other "Messianic references in Qumran Literature," *ibid.*, pp. 176-187.

[36]Text and discussion in D. Barthelemy and J. T. Milik, *Discoveries in
the Judean Desert* (Oxford, 1955), I, 118-130.

[37]F. F. Bruce, *Second Thoughts*, p. 151, notes that "piety and hope link
them (the characters of Luke 1) rather with 'sectarian' Judaism than with
the main stream of national religion." Cf. Dupont-Sommer, *Manuscrits de la
Mer Morte*, p. 201.

crowns and ministration in the presence of angels and of a
time when all things shall be "discussed in common council
with the saints for time and for all eternity (lit. 'for an
eternal time and for all the ages of eternity'). The leader
is one who is "sanctified among his people . . . a light
for all the earth in knowledge . . . a diadem for the Most
High; for thou shalt bless Him and glorify His Name, and
His saints likewise." Here we get the New Testament idea
of "the light of the world."

The fifth blessing deals with the time when God
"restores [renews] the covenant of the church [congrega-
tion], that the kingdom might be established for his people
forever and that the poor might receive righteous judgment
and the meek of the earth receive instruction, that they
might walk perfectly in all his ways . . . to reestablish his
holy covenant for the solace of those who seek him." As
for the wicked world, it shall be smitten and made desolate
by the power of God's mouth at a time when they who
have received the blessing will go through the gentiles like
a young ox (?) (the text is defective) trampling them
down.

A small almost perfectly preserved fragment known
as the *Testimonia* (4Q test) contains "a collection of Old
Testament proof-texts" expressing "the Messianic expectation of the congregation."[38] Moses is told to warn the
people against apostasy, and God tells them of a Prophet
whom the Lord will "raise up from the midst of their
brethren like unto thee," with strict admonition to heed
him. (Cf. Deut. 18:18-19.) A man "whose eye is perfect"
shall converse with the Lord and see the face of the Almighty, but veiled and at a distance. Then "a star will
arise in Jacob, a scepter in Israel," to prostrate Moab and
the sons of Seth. Then there is a strange passage about
the giving of "thy Thummim and thy Urim to a man who

---

[38]Lohse, *op. cit.*, p. 249. The text is in the same handwriting as the
Manual of Discipline, according to J. Allegro, who reproduces the text in
Journal of Biblical Literature, 75 (1956), pp. 182-7.

devoutly served thee (a *hasid*), whom thou hast tested in
Massah and with whom thou hast had controversy by the
waters of controversy (Meribah)." This man, it would
seem, parted from his father and his mother, his brother
and his sons, "because he kept thy command and remained
faithful to thy covenant." Such men were the leaders of
the congregations of Qumran, who here apply the scriptures to themselves. Note how well the type of refugee
prophet fits Nephi or his father, who because of their faith
left their own people, were tested in the southern desert
and on the waters, and even received the Urim and Thummim.

The *Commentary on Nahum* (4Q pNah)[39] begins with
reference to the young lions raging unopposed as representatives of God's wrath against the gentiles and the
wicked of Israel—an image that occurs no less than four
times in 3 Nephi. Here the Qumran people apply Nahum
2:12 to their own time: the "greedy priests at Jerusalem"
are protagonists in a struggle in which the opposition of
"opposing groups is depicted as a contest between Ephraim
and Manasseh." There is a vivid description of the falling
away of Ephraim, who will "seek after smooth things in
the last days, and walk in falsehood and deceit," as a
result of which "the sword of the gentiles will not depart
from the midst of her congregation." But after Ephraim
has led many astray "through deceptive doctrine and her
lying tongue and false lips—even kings, princes, priests,
and people . . . who have joined her," in the last days there
will come a change: "Many will acknowledge their sins in
Israel," when "the evil deeds of all Israel will be made
known," and "turn away from their sins and view them
with abhorrence because of their guilty pride and the
overthrow of Judah's renown." Then at last "shall the meek
of Ephraim flee out of the midst of her congregations, and

---

[39]Complete photographs of the texts are supplied by J. Allegro, in
Journal of Semitic Studies, 7 (1962), pp. 304-8.

depart from those who have led her astray, and join themselves to Israel."

As to those who sought the smooth and flattering
things, "their counsel shall fail and their congregation be
dispersed, and they shall not continue to lead the congregations astray, and the meek and simple will no longer sustain
their counsel." Nahum 3:8—"Are thou better than No-
Amon?"—is explained as meaning that "Amon is Manasseh,
and the rivers are the great and noble ones of Manasseh."
Manasseh is to profit by the weakness of Ephraim at the
time when the humble of Ephraim begin to repent. Next
we find that Manasseh had joined "the wicked hosts, the
house of Peleg," which would imply, from the mention of
Peleg elsewhere in the Apocrypha, that Manasseh has gone
beyond the sea, where he is lost in wickedness. Nahum
3:10 is interpreted as "referring to Manasseh in the last
days, when his rule over Israel shall fall," and "his wives,
his infants, and his children shall go into captivity while
his heroes and noble ones perish by the sword." With a
reference to "the godless ones of Ephraim whose cup shall
pass to Manasseh," the fragment breaks off.

Students of the Scrolls have called attention to the
image of the cup as representing suffering and martyrdom,[40] so it can mean either that Manasseh will have to
drink the cup once forced on Ephraim or that the cup
which Ephraim forced on Manasseh will be thrust upon
him. At any rate, the clear identification of the Book of
Mormon people with Manasseh (note also the overwhelming predominance of the name Ammon in the Book of
Mormon!) should make it easy for anyone to find here all
kinds of parallels to prophecies in that book.

In the *Commentary on the 37th Psalm* (4Q pPs 37)
"the congregation at Qumran," as Lohse notes, "applied

---

[40]J. Allegro, *The Treasure of the Copper Scroll* (Garden City: Doubleday
1960), p. 72.

the Psalm to their own situation."[41] Need we refer again
to 1 Nephi 19:23? Psalm 37:8f. is explained as "the return
to the law of those who do not hesitate to depart from their
wickedness. For all who do hesitate . . . will be destroyed."
Verse 9 "refers to the congregation of the Chosen who do
his will," and verse 11 to "the congregation of the Poor,
who have accepted the time of probation and who will be
saved from all the pitfalls of Belial." Verses 14 and 15
"refer to the godless of Ephraim and Manasseh . . . in the
time of probation [testing]; but God has rescued them
[the Saints] from their hand." The righteous of verse 17
are "they who return to the wilderness, who shall dwell
a thousand generations in Israel and with their seed inherit
the whole earth forever"; they shall also be spared the
famines and plagues of the last days. Verse 20 refers both
"to his Chosen Ones who shall be the heads and leaders,"
and to the wicked leaders of the opposition "who shall
pass away as smoke and wind," while (v. 21f.) "the congregations of the Poor . . . shall inherit the earth . . . possess
the high mount of Israel and rejoice in its Temple." Next
these things are applied to the contemporary feud between
the Teacher of Righteousness and the godless priest who
sought his death but on whom God will wreak vengeance
in the end, as (v. 34) "the congregation of the Poor behold
the condemnation of the wicked, his Chosen People who
will rejoice in his inheritance."

As they increase in number and tend to be taken for
granted, we are apt to forget just how remarkable these
prophecies are, coming as they do to us *directly* "in their
purity" from the hands of Jews who lived either before
or very soon after the time of Christ.

Traditions and Legends: The Iranian Puzzle

Along with strange practices the Book of Mormon recalls a number of strange non-biblical traditions that

---

[41]For the fullest discussion, H. Stegemann in *Revue de Qumran*, 4 (1963),
pp. 235-270.

deserve attention. One of the most striking of these is the tradition of the Two Garments or rather two fragments of *the* Garment of Joseph, the one blood-stained and decayed to signify the corruption of Israel, the other freshly preserved through the centuries representing that blessed remnant of Israel which would be saved.[42] Recently Prof. Philonenko has pointed out that in the Testament of the Twelve Patriarchs "an altogether special importance" is attached to the garment of Joseph, noting that in the Testament of Zebulon, 4:10, Joseph is represented as having *two* garments, a good one and a bad one.[43] This supports Tha'labi's confirmation of Moroni's legend of the double garment of Joseph (Alma 46:23-26.)

Years ago we noted that the story of Moroni and his rent coat had strong *Iranian* affinities. This we have always found rather puzzling, and yet it is no more so than the Iranian background of the Dead Sea Scrolls, in which "Iranian influence has been especially strong," according to K. Stendahl.[44] Moroni refers to the story of the Two Garments as a well-known tale which was familiar to everybody and which the people could read about in the books that were brought over from the Old World (Alma 46:24f.). The fullest Old World account was that picked up by Tha'labi among Jews living in Iran in the Middle Ages. If we wonder why Moroni should choose to re-enact the Kawe story with his Title of Liberty, it is just as much of an enigma how we are to account for "an Iranian penetration into Qumran," among the strictest of all sectarian Jews; how does it happen that early Jewish apocrypha are "saturated with Iranian material?"[45]

The frequent association and identification of Old Testament patriarchs and prophets with Zoroaster in apoc-

---

[42]Discussed in *An Approach to the Book of Mormon* (1964 ed.), pp. 177-180.

[43]M. Philonenko, in *Revue d'Histoire et de Philosophie Religieuses*, 39 (1959), p. 33.

[44]K. Stendahl, *op. cit.*, p. 5.

[45]D. Winston, in *History of Religions*, 5 (1966), p. 186.

ryphal writings both Jewish and Christian, though very
difficult to date, shows at least that the Jews had no antipathy to the Persian prophet, who was possibly a contemporary of Lehi. And though, as D. Winston observes,
"the Jewish identification of Zoroaster in itself is no guide
whatever in our attempt to ascertain the extent of Iranian-
Jewish interpenetration,"[46] it does suggest sympathetic
contacts between the two peoples as early as the time of
Lehi. For if the original image of Zoroaster had been an
unfavorable one it would have remained such traditionally;
but the image was a favorable one, showing that Zoroaster
was not first introduced to the Jews as a legendary prophet
of an alien people. At present "investigators are as divided
as ever as to the extent of Iranian influence on Jewish
literature."[47] Hopes for an objective approach to the subject are today being sought in the Iranian affinities of
Isaiah. The main difficulty there is in deciding what is
and what is not distinctively Iranian. The Jews share
various "Iranian" ideas with other neighbors who are not
only nearer to them geographically than the Persians, but
are able to produce written sources for those ideas that are
far older than anything the Iranians can offer. In fact, Iran
is more often a clearing-house for older teachings than a
place of origin, so that which passes for "Iranian" doctrine
may well be "a fusion of Persian and Babylonian teachings."[48]

Thus if Isaiah 44-45 "shows very close resemblances
to the so-called Cyrus Cylinder . . . it has been suggested
that both are dependent on the style of the Babylonian
Court Inscriptions."[49] If the same two chapters of Isaiah
suggest ancient Iranian teachings about the creation, the
same teachings may be found at a much earlier date and
much closer to Israel in the Memphite theology of Egypt

[46]D. Winston, op. cit., p.
[47]Ibid., p. 186.
[48]S. Westphal-Hellbusch, in Sumer, 12 (1956), p. 66. The quotation is
from Winston, op. cit., p. 207.
[49]Winston, op. cit., p. 188.

—and Isaiah's use of Egyptian imagery and ideas has long been recognized.[50] The case for Iranian priorities must await some means of dating Iranian traditions, which at the moment present "insuperable chronological difficulties."[51] Since, as we have already noted, the appearance of the name of Cyrus in the Book of Isaiah does not even serve to date the verse in which it occurs, the more subjective appeals to a Persian atmosphere, such as the much-debated issue of whether chapters 40-48 were written before the Edict of Cyrus and 49-55 after, or whether they were written at the same time, can hardly be expected to settle anything. E. Jenni has pointed out that Cyrus is a "stock figure" representing the herald of salvation in ancient literature. Such stock figures when they were representative of the same ideas, were interchangeable, and could be readily substituted for each other.[52] Thus the Messianic prophets listed in 3 Nephi 10:15-17 are typical stock figures, representing the same idea regardless of the time in which they lived. A later scribe would not hesitate to put the name of Cyrus in the place of that of some earlier deliverer who was not so well known to him and his hearers. The name of Cyrus, which has formerly been taken as a sure means of dating "Second Isaiah," does *not*, however, appear in the Book of Mormon.

In trying to account for the Iranian elements in very early Jewish writings, including the Book of Mormon, we must not overlook the very real possibility that the Persians, with their notorious hospitality to the ideas and religions of other people, were borrowing from the Jews rather than the other way around. For example, the imagery of the light versus the darkness which constantly

---

[50]H. Nibley, in *BYU Studies*, 7 (1966), pp. 3-6. Whereas Assyriologists such as Widengren today derive certain royal epithets in Isaiah from Mesopotamian ritual sources, Egyptologists such as Morenz derive the same titles from Egyptian cult; both are older than the Persian traditions. See G. Fohrer, *op. cit.*, p. 72.

[51]Winston, *op. cit.*, p. 211.

[52]E. Jenni, in *Theologische Zeitschrift*, 10 (1954), pp. 241-256.

recurs in the early Jewish writings, including the Dead
Sea Scrolls, does *not* appear in the old Persian writings,
but turns up later in heretical Iranian teachings plainly
borrowed from somewhere else.[53] So all we can say at
present is that Iranian and early Jewish literature have a
good deal in common and that the connection between
them has not yet been explained. The legend of Kawe, who
became the founder of the Persian monarchy and priesthood when he put his garment on a pole and went throughout the land rousing the people to fight for liberty and
overthrow the traitor and false aspirant to the throne, is
the story of Moroni and Amalickiah even in detail, and it
is far older than Lehi or Isaiah. The presence of the Old
World legend in the Book of Mormon, where Moroni
attributes it to a very old and popular tradition, is rather
a confirmation than a weakening of that book's claims to
authenticity.

The Mystery of Joseph

The ancient apocrypha like the Book of Mormon give
a peculiar importance to the figure of Joseph, who is both
a real person and a symbol. Since Joseph is "a type and a
shadow," we find a whole line of Josephs. ". . . I have led
this people forth out of . . . Jerusalem," says the Lord
through the prophet Jacob, ". . . that I might raise up unto
me a righteous branch from the fruit of the loins of Joseph."
(Jacob 2:25.) This Jacob's younger brother was named
Joseph as a reminder that Joseph was the ancestor of the
family and that he also suffered in the desert, and also
that that same Joseph "truly saw *our* day." (2 Nephi 3:5.)
Lehi's Joseph was further told that in ages yet to come
there would be yet other Josephs: "For Joseph truly testified, saying: A seer shall the Lord my God raise up. . . .
And his name shall be called after me; and it shall be after
the name of *his* father." (2 Nephi 3:6, 15.) Finally Lehi

---

[53]Winston, *op. cit.*, p. 202.

concludes, "And now, behold, my son Joseph, after this manner did *my* father of old prophesy," for he calls the Patriarch Joseph his father. (2 Nephi 3:22.)

Dupont-Sommer has lauded the genius of R. H. Charles who forty years ago saw that much in the New Testament, "especially the Sermon on the Mount," goes back to an old Jewish apocryphal writing known as the *Testament of the Twelve Patriarchs*, which G. Molin and others have shown to be in turn perhaps the closest of all the Apocrypha to the Dead Sea Scrolls.[54] The key figure in this writing is Joseph, "the most arresting and the most mysterious figure in the Testaments," according to M. Philonenko, a specialist on the subject. "He is the central character, the pivotal figure . . . Model of all the virtues . . . object of the hatred and jealousy of his brethren."[55] "How can one explain this empassioned interest?" he asks, and he notes that Hippolytus, one of the earliest Christian writers, actually cites the *Twelve Patriarchs* to show that Joseph is a prefigurement of Christ.[56] M. de Jonge, who maintains that the Testament is actually a Christian writing, points out that "Joseph was quite commonly regarded as a type of Christ" by the earliest Christian writers.[57]

The Hebrew version of the *Testament of Naphthali*, which belongs to the *Testament of the Twelve Patriarchs*, but was discovered much later, tells of a contest between Joseph and Judah. In this account, Naphthali sees Israel as a ship at sea, "the Ship of Jacob." "As long as Joseph and Judah got along together," he reports, "the ship sailed calmly and well, but when quarreling broke out between Joseph and Judah, it would not sail in the right direction

---

[54]A. Dupont-Sommer, *Manuscrits de la Mer Morte*, p. 211; R. H. Charles, *Apocrypha & Pseudepigrapha*, II, 282, 291f. See the table of comparison at the back of G. Molin, *Die Söhne des Lichtes*.

[55]M. Philonenko, in *Revue d'Histoire et de Philosophie Religieuses*, 39 (1959), p. 28.

[56]Philonenko, *Les Interpretations Chretiennes des Test. des XIII Patriarches et les Mss. de Qumran* (Paris: Presses Universitaires, 1960), p. 50.

[57]M. de Jonge, *The Testament of the Twelve Patriarchs* (Assen: Van Gorum, 1953), p. 123.

but wandered and was wrecked."[58] The Book of Mormon
student will of course think immediately of the quarreling
of the brothers on Lehi's ship, which accordingly was
driven off its course and nearly foundered; and he is li-
censed to do so, because Alma hundreds of years after
Lehi's journey, discussed that journey as "a type and a
shadow." (Alma 37:41-45.) For Lehi and his people types
and shadows are things which reappear in certain situations, and are therefore to be considered as symptomatic
—they are symbols, but they are none the less real. Thus
when father Lehi addresses "Joseph, my last-born, whom
I have brought out of the wilderness of mine afflictions,"
(2 Nephi 3:3) he is thinking of another last-born Joseph,
and he is thinking of another wilderness, but he is thinking
of both because at the moment little Joseph is *his* last-born
and he is indeed in the midst of a very real and tangible
wilderness.

When the ship of Jacob breaks up, according to the
Testament of Naphthali, all the brothers cling to floating
planks and are thus borne away by the winds and scattered
in all directions; all except Judah and Levi, who cling to
the same board, and Joseph, who all alone is able to com-
mandeer a life-boat and escape out of sight. At once we
think of the well-known image of Joseph passing "beyond
the wall" intact, and of those descendants of Joseph who
came to the New World by ship and left us their record
in the Book of Mormon, which we call (following Ezekiel
37) "the stick of Joseph,"[59] in contrast to "the stick of
Judah," which is the Bible. It is remarkable that the quarreling in the *Testament of Naphthali* is not between Judah
and Israel but specifically between Judah and Joseph, upon
whose unity and harmony the well-being of all Israel
depends. We have also noted that it is one of the *Twelve
Patriarchs* who tells of the two garments of Joseph—another

---

[58]Philonenko, *op. cit.,* in note 2 above, p. 33.
[59]See our long discussion in the *Improvement Era,* 56 (Jan. to May, 1953).

Book of Mormon story. Tha'labi, who also tells that story, has some very interesting things to say about the pre-existent Joseph, bringing to mind many teachings in newly-published Mandaean and Coptic Gnostic sources, which, however, are much too extensive to examine here.

"Most scholars," writes Tha'labi, "say that Joseph is a Hebrew name . . . and Abu-l-Hasan . . . said that *asaf* is 'sorrow' in that language, and that *asif* is 'servant,' and that the two are combined in the name of Joseph."[60] The identification of Joseph with Asaf is indeed an authentic Hebrew tradition. Adam in a vision (this is Tha'labi again) "saw Joseph sitting in all his glory, and cried out, 'Who is that noble one sitting in such an exalted degree of glory?' (Cf. Abraham 3:22-23!) And Gabriel answered, 'O Adam, that is thy son, the envied one . . .' Then Adam clasped him to his bosom and his heart and said, O my son, do not sorrow (asaf), for thou art Joseph. Thus he first gave him his name." The writer is puzzled by the pre-existent situation and explains that "Joseph knew it all in the beginning in the preeminence of his intelligence, and he was instructed in the matter (of his future trials on earth) even as it would be, and he saw that he would be so and so before he was. But that is a thing that only God understands—how, for example, Adam knew all (his children's) names beforehand."

The mystery of Joseph appears in Benjamin's admonition to his children in *The Twelve Patriarchs*: ". . . follow the example of the holy and good man Joseph. For until death he was not willing to tell regarding himself" ("No man knows my history"); "but Jacob, having learned it from the Lord, told it to him (Benjamin)."[61] In the Dead Sea Scrolls the famous Teacher of Righteousness is also called Asaph, that being, as we have seen, another name for Joseph, which, as H. J. Schonfield observes, "thus fits

---

[60]Tha'labi, *Qissas al-Anbiyah* (1898), pp. 75f.
[61]*Testament of Benjamin*, c. 3.

in with the Joseph tradition."[62] Jacob blessed Joseph
according to Benjamin's Testament, saying, "In thee shall
be fulfilled the prophecies of heaven, which say that the
blameless one shall be defiled for lawless men, and the
sinless one shall die for godless men." According to the
Testament of Zebulon, Joseph's three days in the cistern
were the type of the descent of the Lord made to the
spirits in prison.[63] One can readily see how the Joseph
type would be applied to any suffering servant, though
the Messiah remains the archtype. Indeed, the Christian
fathers were fond of working out elaborate parallels between Joseph and Jesus.[64] The Teacher of Righteousness
was also called the Chosen One, Asaph, the Son of Bere-
chiah, Joseph the Just, and Joseph ben Joezer, so that his
given name probably was Joseph and he "appears to us as
a composite figure," just as his wicked opponent does.[65]
The Joseph tradition has been traced backwards as well
as forwards, and Bo Reicke has found significant parallels
in the Ras Shamra fragments of the fourteenth and fifteenth centuries B.C.![66]

The Mystery of John

John enjoys a special place in the Book of Mormon,
where he is the only future prophet mentioned by name.
His special office, however, is not to serve as a prophet
so much as a recorder. It is John, the man in the white
robe whom Nephi sees in a vision who is to write the
fullest record of the Lord's ministry (1 Nephi 14:19ff.),
and the accurate setting forth of his words as they proceeded out of his mouth, "plain and pure, and most pre-

---

[62]H. J. Schonfield, *Secrets of the Dead Sea Scrolls* (London: Vallentine,
Mitchell, 1956), pp. 89, 131.
[63]Test. of Zebulon, 4:1-4.
[64]See the discussion by Ruprecht in Migne, *Patrologia Latina*, 167:448f.,
518-530.
[65]Schonfield, *op. cit.*, p. 150. On the Messiah Son of Joseph, see W.
Wiesenberg, in *Vetus Testamentum*, 5 (1955), p. 306.
[66]Bo Reicke, in *Svensk Exeget. Arsbok*, 1945, pp. 5-30. See especially
V. Sadek, in *Archiv Orientalni*, 1965, pp. 27-43.

cious and easy to understand of all men" (v. 23); but his record and those of others to whom the Lord "hath shown all things" are to be "sealed up to come forth in their purity" *after* the bringing forth of the Book of Mormon—hence Nephi was forbidden to write them (v. 28). When the Book of Mormon has been brought forth and introduced to the house of Israel, then shall they "know that the work of the Father has commenced upon all the face of the land," (Ether 4:17), and when the people begin to believe "*then* shall my revelation which I have caused to be written by my servant John be unfolded in the eyes of all the people . . . the time is at hand that they shall be made manifest in very deed." (Ether 4:16.)

Now nothing is more striking about the new Jewish and Christian manuscript finds than the persistent and emphatic way in which their phrases and ideas call the writings of John to mind. Student after student has been pointing this out in the journals with steadily increasing frequency. "Thirty years ago . . . a kind of current orthodoxy" insisted that John was the latest and most un-Jewish of the Gospels,[67] written very late in Alexandria or Ephesus by a Greek of Stoic and Platonic leanings. But "under the impact of the new findings," Albright informs us, "a strong reaction has recently set in. . . . Some radical scholars now consider John as the earliest of the Gospels instead of the latest."[68] Since that was written it has come to be generally recognized that the peculiarities of John takes us back to sources definitely older than the Synoptic Gospels themselves.[69]

In 1953 H. R. Dodd, and in the following year W. Noack, showed that John was "the most Hebraic book in the New Testament, except perhaps for the Apocalypse," being a product of the desert Christians of the very earliest

[67]C. L. Mitton, in *Expository Times*, 71 (1960), p. 337.

[68]W. F. Albright, *Archaeology of Palestine*, p. 240.

[69]W. Schneemelcher, *Neutestamentliche Apokryphen* (Tübingen: Mohr, 1959), I, 48.

period.[70] As for the Apocalypse, denied a place in the
Bible by some of the most eminent doctors of the church
and denied Johannine authorship by scholars down to the
present day, "this disquieting document," as Dodd puts it,
"has caused much searching of hearts in recent criticism.
A generation ago it was still possible to regard Revelation
as a work of scissors and paste"—but no longer.[71] What
shall we make of it? Dodd assures us "that the Johannine
riddle will be solved only after the point of the entire
Johannine corpus has been discovered."

Today the uniqueness of John's record with its
"immense, unexplained dissimilarities" between it and the
Synoptic Gospels is causing much perplexity.[72] Its authentic old Messianic background now becomes apparent from
the Dead Sea Scrolls; indeed, K. G. Kuhn, one of the first
and most diligent students of the Scrolls insists that "we
get hold of the fundamental source of John's Gospel" in
the Scrolls, "and this source is Palestinian-Jewish; not,
however, Pharisaic-Rabbinic (i.e., conventional) Judaism,
but a Palestinian-Jewish pietistic Sect of gnostic structure."[73] Here again, gnostic means opposed to conventional
Jewish and Christian ideas—but not to those of the Book
of Mormon! Others would attribute the resemblance
between John and the Scrolls to their common dependence
on Deuteronomy.[74] Specifically what John has in common
with the Scrolls are such expressions as "sons of Light,"
"light of life," "Walking in darkness," "doing the truth,"
"the works of God," etc.,[75] all of which are typical Book
of Mormon expressions, though in the Book of Mormon
one acts "according to the truth." From the very beginning
"studies of the Gospel of John and the Johannine literature

[70]Mitton, op. cit., p. 339.
[71]C. H. Dodd, in Davies and Daube, op. cit., pp. 75f.
[72]Mitton, l.c.
[73]K. G. Kuhn, in Zeitsch. für Katolische Theologie, 47 (1950), p. 210.
[74]A. R. C. Leaney, Guide to the Scrolls, p. 96.
[75]F. F. Bruce, Second Thoughts on the D. S. Scrolls, p. 146; cf. K. G.
Kuhn, op. cit., 49 (1952), pp. 200-222.

(were) greatly affected by our new knowledge of sectarian Judaism gleaned" from them;[76] the new picture of sectarian Judaism exactly matches that in the Book of Mormon as we shall see. The early Christians did not get their teachings from Qumran, however; the close resemblances are explained by the way in which they favor the same prophets in their quoting. Thus Jesus is fondest of quoting "Isaiah, Deuteronomy and the Psalms—which appear to have been the favorite reading also at Qumran." And though John the Baptist went about things in a completely different way from the people at Qumran "there is much similarity in his teaching" to theirs.[77] Now Isaiah, Deuteronomy, and the Psalms are also plainly the scriptures that have the greatest influence on the writers of the Book of Mormon. The makers of the New Testament and the makers of the Dead Sea Scrolls may never have been associated; the resemblances of their writings are readily explained on the assumption that they follow a common prophetic tradition, which was quite different from that of the Rabbinical Judaism and Alexandrine Christianity which were to become the official religions. The Book of Mormon gives every evidence of drawing on that same tradition.

The World of the Jaredites

With the story of the Jaredites the Book of Mormon launches boldly forth into the shadowy half-world of the dawn of history. Here is another field in which an awful lot has been discovered "since Cumorah." We have demonstrated at great length that there is no more perfect exposition of that ancient "Epic Milieu" which produced the earliest literature of the race than is to be found in the Book of Ether.[78] But it was not until the present

[76]F. M. Goss, in *Biblical Archaeologist*, February 1954, p. 3.
[77]A. N. Gilkes, *The Impact of the D. S. Scrolls* (London: Macmillan, 1962), pp. 146-7.
[78]In *The World of the Jaredites* (Salt Lake City: Bookcraft, 1952), and "There Were Jaredites," *Improvement Era*, 59 (1956), through 60 (Feb. 1957).

century that the Chadwicks first showed the world what
an Epic Milieu was and then demonstrated its tangible
historic reality.[79] Among other things, the Book of Ether
makes much of the role played by terrific winds in the
Great Migration; for a time it was fashionable to minimize
the importance of the weather in influencing major migrations, but of recent years increasing respect has been shown
towards the role of the weather in history.[80]

In our studies of Ether we overlooked one significant
expression that deserves notice: When the human race
had defiled the earth with sin, the righteous brother of
Jared was ordered to move out and establish a righteous
foundation in the earth. His people were not saints—they
were just not quite as bad as the others. But the specific
instructions to Jared were to go with his people "into that
quarter where there never had man been." (Ether 2:5.)
Some years ago H. Gressmann, in examining the traditions
of the great natural catastrophe and moral overthrow of
the time of the Tower of Babel (when our Jaredite migration takes place), came across the ancient concept found
among the Hebrews, that when the earth was defiled by
men, it was necessary for those whom God would preserve
from the general destruction that they be sent into some
undefiled part of the earth, which could only be, as Gressmann's sources have it, "a Land of the beyond, where no
member of the human race had as yet inhabited."[81] This
is exactly the sense of God's instructions to the Brother of
Jared.

Another thing we failed to note was the odd circum-
stance that in the "proto-historic" book of Ether kings
seem to be overthrown rather regularly at the end of a

[79]In H. M. and N. K. Chadwick, *The Growth of Literature* (Cambridge, 1932), and *The Heroic Age* (Cambridge, 1912).
[80]We have supplied numerous references in *Western Political Quarterly*, 19 (1966), pp. 599f., 609-615.
[81]H. Gressman, in *Archiv für Orientgeschichte*, 3 (1926), p. 12; cf. by the same, *Der Ursprung der Israelitish-judischen Eschatologie* (1905), pp. 148-154.

42-year period. (Ether 8:10, 15, 32.) Why 42? Whatever the reason, it is interesting to find in the oldest king-lists of Mesopotamia among regnal years that are obviously symbolic and astral (most being multiples of 12, 36, or 52), a significant number of reigns that are multiples of 42—2100, 840, 420, 2310, 21.[82] The number 42 is even more significant in the Pharaonic economy, where the 42 nomes are matched by the 42 blessings of the king's coronation and by the 21 bearers of his palanquin. Recently C. Levi-Strauss in an important book has called attention to the special significance of numbers uniting 6 and 7, either by addition or multiplication, among "primitive" and ancient people all over the world.[83]

Finally we should mention the crossing of the waters in a peculiar type of ship, constructed according to the Book of Ether after the manner of the ark of Noah. The description of the ships suggests nothing in the Bible, where aside from its general dimensions (which are symbolic) nothing is said as to how the ark actually looked, but it exactly matches the description of those sacred magurboats in which, according to the oldest Babylonian stories, the hero of the Flood was saved from destruction.[84] Moreover, that particular hero was in possession of a life-giving talisman which in many legends is a stone that shines in the dark—a reminder that the Zohar itself was, according to the Palestinian Talmud, a shining stone with which Noah illuminated the ark.[85] The point here is that Jared's ships were illuminated by such shining stones. It is interesting that our friend Zenez of the *Pseudo-Philo,* "the prophet of old," experimented as did the brother of Jared with shining stones, and that in both cases a knowledge of these things was withheld from mankind in general because of their sins.

---

[82]The texts are supplied with commentary in A. Deimel, *Sumerische Grammatik* (Rome, 1924), pp. 127f., 245-7, 249ff.
[83]C. Levi-Strauss, *La Pensee Sauvage* (Paris: Plon, 1962), pp. 191ff.
[84]*An Approach to the Book of Mormon* (1964 ed.), pp. 274-281.
[85]*Ibid.,* pp. 281-291.

Part III.

Some Scientific Questions

CHAPTER 8

"Forever Tentative..."

Science in a Vacuum

From the first both Mormons and their opponents recognized the possibility of testing the Book of Mormon in a scientific way. The book described certain aspects of civilizations purported to have existed in the New World in ancient times. Very well, where were the remains? A vast amount of time, energy, and patience has been expended in arguing about the interpretations of the scanty evidence that is available, but very little has been devoted to the systematic search for more. Of course, almost any object could conceivably have some connection with the Book of Mormon, but nothing short of an inscription which could be read and roughly dated could bridge the gap between what might be called a pre-actualistic archaeology and contact with the realities of Nephite civilization.

The possibility that a great nation or empire that once dominated vast areas of land and flourished for centuries could actually get lost and stay lost in spite of every effort of men to discover its traces, has been demonstrated many times since Schliemann found the real world of the Mycenaeans. In our own generation the first scraps of physical evidence for the existence of certain great civilizations have come to light, though scholars have studied the literary and historical records of those same civilizations for centuries without possessing so much as a

button or bead that could be definitely assigned to them.[1]
Indeed, until actual remains were found, it was quite possible and respectable to regard some of those civilizations
as the invention of poetic fancy or legend.

So it is with the Nephites. All that we have to go on
to date is a written history. That does not mean that our
Nephites are necessarily mythical, since the case of those
Old World civilizations has taught us by now that the
existence of written records which no one claims the credit
of having invented, is in itself good if not the very best
evidence that a people really did exist. But as things stand
we are still in the *pre*-archaeological and *pre*-anthropologi-
cal stages of Book of Mormon study. Which means that
there is nothing whatever that an anthropologist or archaeologist as such can say about the Book of Mormon.
Nephite civilization was urban in nature, like the civilizations of Athens or Babylon, and was far more confined in
space and time than either of them. It could just as easily
and completely vanish from sight as did the worlds of
Ugarit, Ur, or Cnossos; and until some physical remnant
of it, no matter how trivial, has been identified beyond
question, what can any student of physical remains possibly have to say about it? Everything written so far by
anthropologists or archaeologists—even real archaeologists
—about the Book of Mormon must be discounted, for the
same reason that we must discount studies of the lost
Atlantis: not because it did not exist, but because it has
not yet been found.

The Bering Strait Theory

The normal way of dealing with the Book of Mormon
"scientifically" has been first to attribute to the Book of
Mormon something it did not say, and then to refute the
claim by scientific statements that have not been proven.

---

[1]Thirteen such civilizations are discussed in E. Bacon (ed.) *Vanished
Civilizations of the Ancient World* (New York: McGraw-Hill, 1963).

A good example of this is the constant attempt to blast
the Book of Mormon by assuming that it allows only one
possible origin for the blood of the Indians (a perfectly
false assumption), and then pointing out that the *real*
origin is a migration via the Alaskan land-bridge or Bering
Straits—a still unproven hypothesis. This is presented as
the confrontation of crude 19th century superstition with
the latest fruits of modern science. And that, too, is misleading. For in 1835 Josiah Priest wrote in his *American
Antiquities*: "The manner by which the original inhabitants
and animals reached here, is easily explained, by adopting
the supposition, which, doubtless, is the *most* correct, that
the northwestern and western limits of America were, at
some former period, united to Asia on the *west*, and to
Europe on the east."[2]

Therewith, for Priest, the question was settled: instead
of being a fruitful and exciting *problem*, the theory of
settlement by the Alaska land bridge was the final solution.
And as such it has been accepted by North American
anthropologists to this day, even though their colleagues
in Europe and South America may shake their heads in
wonder at such naive and single-minded devotion to a
one-shot explanation of everything. We may find it strange
that back in 1835, with no evidence to go by but the con-
figuration of the map, anyone could have settled for such
finality—the *problem* was real and wonderful, the *conclusion* premature and untested. But has the situation
changed? Yes, there has been testing, but few people
realize what dismally meager results have rewarded the
vast expenditure of time and cash that has gone into the
project. "Thus far," wrote Carleton Beals, summing up the
situation in 1961, "nothing has been discovered to indicate
human presence on or near the Bering Straits prior to five

---

[2]Josiah Priest, *American Antiquities and Discoveries in the West* (Albany,
1835), p. 62, noting that "This was partly the opinion of Buffon, and other
great naturalists."

thousand years ago."[3] It is still a problem, and very much alive, but the solution rests exactly where it did in Josiah Priest's day: on a common-sense interpretation of the map.

The Race Question

To clinch the Bering Straits argument it is usual to point out that the Indians are Mongoloid and therefore cannot possibly be of the racial stock of Lehi. Again an unproven hypothesis is set against a false interpretation of the Book of Mormon. As to the hypothesis, it is fairly well known by now that the predominant blood-type among the Mongols is B, a type which is extremely rare among the Indians, whose dominant bloodtype is O, that being found among 91.3% of the pure-blooded North American Indians. "Here is a mystery," writes Beals commenting on the disturbing phenomenon, "that requires much pondering and investigation."[4]

But if we are to take the Book of Mormon to task for its ethnological teachings, it might be well at first to learn what those teachings are. They turn out on investigation to be surprisingly complicated. There is no mention in the Book of Mormon of red skins versus white, indeed there is no mention of red skin at all. What we find is a more or less steady process over long periods of time of mixing and separating of many closely related but not identical ethnic groups. The Book of Mormon is careful to specify that the terms Lamanite and Nephite are used in a loose and general sense to designate not racial but political (e.g. Moroni 1:9), military (Alma 43:4), religious (4 Nephi 38), and cultural (Alma 53:10, 15, 3:10-11) divisions and groupings of people. The Lamanite and Nephite division was tribal rather than racial, each of the main groups representing an amalgamation of tribes that retained their identity (Alma 43:13, 4 Nephi 36f.). Our text frequently

---

[3]Carleton Beals, *Nomads and Empire Builders* (Philadelphia and New York: Chilton Co., 1961), p. 76.
[4]Beals, *op. cit.*, pp. 78-79.

goes out of its way to specify that such and such a group is only *called* Nephite or Lamanite. (2 Nephi 5:14, Jacob 1:2, Mosiah 25:12, Alma 3:10, 30:59, Helaman 3:16, 3 Nephi 3:24, 10:18, 4 Nephi 36-38, 43, Moroni 1:9.) For the situation was often very mobile, with large numbers of Nephites going over to the Lamanites (Words of Mormon 16, 4 Nephi 20, Moroni 6:15, Alma 47:35f.), or Lamanites to the Nephites (Alma 27:27, Mosiah 25:12, Alma 55:4), or members of the mixed Mulekite people, such as their Zoramite offshoot going over either to the Lamanites (Alma 43:4) or to the Nephites (Alma 35:9— not really to the Nephites, but to the Ammonites who were Lamanites who had earlier become Nephites!); or at times the Lamanites and Nephites would freely intermingle (Helaman 6:7-8), while at other times the Nephite society would be heavily infiltrated by Lamanites and by robbers of dubious background. (Moroni 2:8.) Such robbers were fond of kidnaping Nephite women and children. (Helaman 11:34.)

The dark skin is mentioned as the mark of a general way of life, it is a Gypsy or Bedouin type of darkness, "black" and "white" being used in their Oriental sense (as in Egyptian), black and loathesome being contrasted to white and delightsome. (2 Nephi 5:21-22.) We are told that when "their scales of darkness shall begin to fall from their eyes" they shall become "a white and delightsome people" (2 Nephi 30:6), and at the same time the Jews "shall also become a delightsome people." (v. 7.) Darkness and filthiness go together as part of a way of life (Jacob 3:5, 9); we never hear of the Lamanites becoming whiter, no matter how righteous they were, except when they adopted the Nephite way of life (3 Nephi 2:14-15), while the Lamanites could by becoming more savage in their ways than their brother Lamanites actually become darker, ". . . a dark, a filthy, and a loathesome people, beyond the description of that which ever hath been . . . among the

Lamanites." (Moroni 5:15.) The dark skin is but one of
the marks that God places upon the Lamanites and these
marks go together; people who joined the Lamanites were
marked like them (Alma 3:10); they were naked and their
skins were dark (Alma 3:5-6); when "they set the mark
upon *themselves* . . . the Amlicites knew not that they
were fulfilling the words of God," when he said "I will
set a mark on them. . . . I will set a mark upon him that
mingleth his seed with thy brethren . . . I will set a mark
upon him that fighteth against thee (Nephi) and thy seed."
(Alma 3:13-18.) "Even so," says Alma, "doth every man
that is cursed bring upon himself his own condemnation."
(v. 19.) By their own deliberate act they both marked
their foreheads and turned their bodies dark. Though ever
alert to miraculous manifestations, the authors of the Book
of Mormon never refer to the transformation of Lamanites
into "white and delightsome" Nephites or of Nephites into
"dark and loathesome" Lamanites as in any way miraculous
or marvelous. When they became savage "because of their
cursing" (2 Nephi 5:24), their skins became dark and they
also became "loathesome" to the Nephites. (v. 21f.) But
there is nothing loathesome about dark skin, which most
people consider very attractive: the darkness like the
loathesomeness was part of the general picture (Jacob
3:9); Mormon prays "that they may once again be a delightsome people" (Words of Mormon 8, Moroni 5:17),
but then the Jews are also to become "a delightsome
people" (2 Nephi 30:7)—are they black?

At the time of the Lord's visit, there were "neither . . .
Lamanites, nor any manner of -ites," (4 Nephi 17), so
that when the old titles of Lamanite and Nephite were
later revived by parties deliberately seeking to stir up old
hatreds, they designated religious affiliation rather than
race. (4 Nephi 38-39.) From which it would seem that
at that time it was impossible to distinguish a person of
Nephite blood from one of Lamanite blood by appearance.

Moreover, there were no pure-blooded Lamanites or Nephites after the early period, for Nephi, Jacob, Joseph, and Sam were all promised that their seed would survive mingled with that of their elder brethren. (2 Nephi 3:2, 23, 9:53, 10:10, 19f., 29:13, 3 Nephi 26:8, Moroni 7:1.) Since the Nephites were always aware of that mingling, which they could nearly always perceive in the steady flow of Nephite dissenters to one side and Lamanite converts to the other, it is understandable why they do *not* think of the terms Nephite and Lamanite as indicating race. The Mulekites, who outnumbered the Nephites better than two to one (Mosiah 25:2-4), were a mixed Near Eastern rabble who had brought no written records with them and had never observed the Law of Moses and did not speak Nephite (Omni 18); yet after Mosiah became their king they "were numbered with the Nephites, and this because the kingdom had been conferred upon none but those who were descendants of Nephi." (Mosiah 25:13.) From time to time large numbers of people disappear beyond the Book of Mormon frontiers to vanish in the wilderness or on the sea, taking their traditions and even written records with them. (Helaman 3:3-13.) What shall we call these people—Nephites or Lamanites?

And just as the Book of Mormon offers no objections whatever to the free movement of whatever tribes and families choose to depart into regions beyond its ken, so it presents no obstacles to the arrival of whatever other bands may have occupied the hemisphere without its knowledge; for hundreds of years the Nephites shared the continent with the far more numerous Jaredites, of whose existence they were totally unaware.[5] Strictly speaking the Book of Mormon is the history of a group of sectaries preoccupied with their own religious affairs, who only notice the presence of other groups when such have reason to mingle with them or collide with them. Just as the desert tribes

---

[5]The bones of the last Jaredites were still lying in the open in a state of fair preservation cir. 120 B.C. (Mosiah 8:8-9)

through whose territories Lehi's people moved in the Old World are mentioned only casually and indirectly, though quite unmistakably (1 Nephi 17:33), so the idea of other migrations to the New World is taken so completely for granted that the story of the Mulekites is dismissed in a few verses. (Omni 14-17.) Indeed the Lord reminds the Nephites that there are all sorts of migrations of which they know nothing, and that their history is only a small segment of the big picture. (2 Nephi 10:21.) There is nothing whatever in the Book of Mormon to indicate that everything that is found in the New World before Columbus must be either Nephite or Lamanite. On the contrary, when Mormon boasts, "I am Mormon and a pure descendant of Lehi," (3 Nephi 5:20), we are given to understand that being a direct descendant of Lehi, as all true Nephites and Lamanites were, was really something special. We think of Zarahemla as a great Nephite capital and its civilization as the Nephite civilization at its peak; yet Zarahemla was not a Nephite city at all: its inhabitants called themselves Nephites, as we have seen, because their ruling family were Nephites who had immigrated from the south.

There were times when the Nephites like the Jaredites broke up into small bands, including robber bands and secret combinations, each fending for itself (2 Nephi 7:2-3), and when all semblance of centralized control disappeared, "and it was one complete revolution throughout all the face of the land." (Moroni 2:8.) Who is to say how far how many of these scattered groups went in their wanderings, with whom they fought, and with whom they joined? After the battle of Cumorah the Lamanites, who had been joined by large numbers of Nephite defectors during the war, were well launched on a career of fierce tribal wars "among themselves." (Moroni 1:2.) It would be as impossible to distinguish any one race among them as it would be to distinguish two; there may have been marked "racial" types, as there are now among the Indians (for example, the striking contrast of Navaho and Hopi), but the Book of Mormon makes it clear that those Nephites who went over to live with Lamanites soon came to look like Lamanites. An anthropologist would have been driven wild trying to detect a clear racial pattern among the survivors of Cumorah. So let us not over-simplify and take the Book of Mormon to task for naive conclusions and images that are really our own.

The Plates

It is hard for us to realize today that for many years the idea of writing a sacred record on gold plates was considered just too funny for words and that the mere mention of the "Golden Bible" was enough to shock and scandalize the world. Today at least a hundred examples of ancient writing on metal plates are available, the latest discoveries being three gold plaques found in 1964 near an ancient shrine on the coast of Italy; they are covered with Punic and Etruscan writing and date from about 500 B.C. Punic, it will be recalled, is Phoenician, a language and script that flourished in Lehi's day a few miles from Jerusalem.[6] It was also in 1964 that the writing on a thin gold plate from Sicily was identified as Hebrew; though the plate has been known since 1876, Hebrew was the last thing anybody expected.[7] The golden plates of Darius, discovered in 1938, which in their form and the manner of their preservation so strikingly resemble the plates described by Joseph Smith, were augmented by new findings in the 1950's; the contents of the latter plates, a pious mixture of religious declamation and history, are as suggestive of the Book of Mormon as their outward appearance is of the plates.[8] We have already spoken of the Copper Scrolls,

---

[6]G. Colonna, in *Archaeology*, 19 (1966), p. 21.
    [7]U. Schmoll, in *Zeitschr. der dt. Morgenländ. Gesellschaft*, 113 (1964), pp. 512-4.
    [8]H. H. Paper has translated the text of the new plates in the *Jnl. of the American Oriental Society*, 72 (1953), pp. 169f.

Darius Plates.

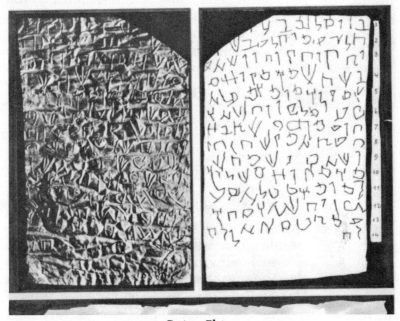

Cosimo Plates.

riveted metal sheets, and noted how the purpose and spirit as well as the method of their production and concealment matches the record-keeping practices of the Nephites in every particular. Especially interesting is the provision that treasures should be "hidden up to the Lord," that such treasures "would never be desecrated by profane use," since "to use such goods for non-religious purposes was a heinous sin," and "it was dangerous for any but priests to handle."[9] For this is a lesson that Samuel the Lamanite drives home: "For I will, saith the Lord, that they shall hide up their treasures unto me; and cursed be they who hide not up their treasures unto me; for none hideth up their treasures unto me save it be the righteous; and he that hideth not up his treasures unto me, cursed is

---

[9] J. M. Allegro, *The Treasure of the Copper Scroll* (N.Y.: Doubleday, 1960), pp. 61-62.

he, and also the treasure, and none shall redeem it because of the curse of the land. . . . I will hide up their treasures when they shall flee before their enemies; because they will not hide them up unto me, cursed be they and also their treasure. . . ." (Helaman 13:19-20.)

Steel and Cement

Through the years critics of the Book of Mormon have constantly called attention to the mention of steel in that book as a gross anachronism. But now we are being reminded that one cannot be dogmatic in dating the appearance of steel since there is more than one kind of steel with "a whole series of variants in the combination of iron and steel components" in ancient times; and when a particularly fine combination was hit upon it would be kept secret in "individual workshops" and "passed on from father to son for many generations."[10] Hence it is not too surprising to learn that "even in early European times" there is evidence for the production of steel "of very high quality" and extreme hardness.[11] Further east steel is attested even earlier.

The mention of cement in the Book of Mormon (Helaman 3:7-11), has been considered as great an anachronism as that of steel. But within the last ten years or so much has been made of the surprising extent to which the ancient Americans used cement, concrete, and gypsum in their building operations. It is now suggested that the overlavish detail, the extremely high relief, and the tendency to round off all angles in the heavy and serpentine profusion of line that is so characteristic of some early American architectural adornment, are the direct heritage of a time when the builders worked in the yielding and plastic medium of cement.[12]

---

[10]R. Pleiner, in *Archaeology*, 16 (1963), p. 242.
[11]*Ibid.*, p. 239.
[12]Discussed in T. A. Proskouriakoff, *An Album of Maya Architecture* (Norman: Univ. of Oklahoma Press, 1963), Intd.

Money

We still get lots of letters, especially from churchmen, protesting that the mention of money in the Book of Mormon is another crude anachronism. They all point out that coinage was first invented by the Lydians in the 8th century B.C. That would make coinage available to Lehi, but the Book of Mormon says nothing about coins, but only money, which is a different thing. The Egyptians and Babylonians had real money from a very early time—metal pieces of conventional shape and size whose exact value could always be determined by weighing and which often bore an official stamp or inscription.[13] This old fashioned kind of money was favored by the Jews in Egypt even after the new modern coinage had been introduced. ". . . the money," writes Prof. E. G. Kraeling, ". . . involved pieces of metal of a certain weight which had an official recognized value. . . . In many places, even after the establishment of coinage, people continued to weigh out pieces of metal."[14] Now when Alma compares the value of *different* metals he uses the expression "equal to": thus "a senum of silver was equal to a senine of gold" and they both equalled a measure of barley, though of course they did not weigh the same (Alma 11:7), and "an antion of gold is equal to three shiblons" (v. 18), shiblons being a silver measure (v. 15). But when he compares the value of the silver pieces among themselves he uses a different expression: "And an amnor of silver was as great as two senums. And an ezrom of silver was as great as four senums. And an onti was as great as them all." (v. 11-13.) Here he is referring not to value, but "greatness," i.e., weight. Naturally a senum of silver, a senine of gold, and a measure of barley would not all weigh the same, but are equal in value; whereas the comparative values of pieces of the same metal would be exactly proportional to their

[13]Ed. Meyer, *Gesch. des Altertums* (1909), I, ii, 517.
[14]E. G. Kraeling, *Brooklyn Aramaic Papyri*, p. 38.

greatness or weight. From which it would appear that the
Nephites used the old-fashioned type of money.

But what is most remarkable about the system described by Alma is its mathematical sophistication. Alma
explains that the Nephite monetary system was not based
on any conventional Old World scale, "for they did not
reckon after the manner of the Jews . . . but they altered
their reckoning and their measure according to the minds
and the circumstances of the people, in every generation.
. . . (Alma 11:4.) Thus their system had been worked
over and improved through the years until they thought
they had the most efficient system possible. And it was
just that. Professor Richard Smith has shown that "the
Nephite system was a peculiarly efficient one. The selection of 1, 2, 4, 7 for the values of the larger coins seems
particularly wise." Comparing it with other possible combinations, Prof. Smith finds that "in every case it turns out
that the '1-2-4-7' system has an edge over the other systems
from the standpoint of number of coins required for a
purchase."[15] This is thus another of those cases where
Joseph Smith promises much—and delivers. It is one thing
for a simple rustic to say that his Nephites possessed the
best monetary system their ingenuity could devise; but it
is a very different thing to produce on demand an actual
system that answers such a description.

The Animal Kingdom

The mention in the Book of Mormon of certain
domesticated animals not found in the New World at the
time of Columbus has always been taken as irrefutable
proof of Smith's folly. Elephants head the list. What happened to the elephants? The Jaredites used them, we are
told, but there is no mention of the Nephites having them.
They disappear in between the two cultures. When? The
Book of Mormon does not say, and the guesses of scientists

---

[15]R. P. Smith, in *The Improvement Era*, 57 (1954), pp. 316-7.

range all the way from hundreds of thousands to mere hundreds of years ago. Elephants have strange ways of disappearing. If it were not for written accounts of unquestionable authenticity, no one would ever have guessed that the Pharaohs of the XVIII. Dynasty hunted elephants in Syria—where are their remains? Prof. Mallowan says that the wonderful Birs Nimrud ivories which he discovered were made from the tusks of a now extinct breed of elephant that was being hunted in Mesopotamia as recently, as the 8th century B.C. Who would have guessed that ten years ago?

Extensive studies on the domestication of the horse (and the presence of a pre-Columbian horse in America is still being argued pro and con) have established that the horse was not domesticated at just one time and place but independently in various times and places. It would appear that horses were used to pull wagons in some places long before anybody thought of riding upon their backs, though to us the reverse would be the natural course of evolution. "Multiple origins of domesticates," both plant and animal, would seem to be the rule today.[16] The denizens of the barnyard come and go, and change their breed and their appearance in sometimes extreme and surprising ways. The Book of Mormon wisely leaves the names of certain animals untranslated, since there is probably no word in the language today that would accurately designate them. It is for scientists and specialists, however, to deal with such matters.

In trespassing on scientific grounds, or rather in timidly peeping over the fence, we are only seeking enlightenment. We have heard so often that "science" has disproved, nay "disemboweled," the Book of Mormon, that we are naturally curious to have a look at some of the more spectacular havoc. Where is it? We have tiptoed

---

[16]See R. S. MacNeish, in *Antiquity,* 39 (1965), pp. 87-94, on the origins of American agriculture.

into the archaeology museum and there found nothing
that could not be interpreted many ways. We have entered
the house of the anthropologists, and there found all in
confusion—and the confusion is growing. We have consulted with the more exact or authentic scientists and found
them surprisingly hesitant to commit themselves on the
Book of Mormon. A definitive refutation must rest on
definitive conclusions, and of such conclusions scientists
are becoming increasingly wary. "Observation and experiment cannot establish anything finally," writes Karl Popper. ". . . Essentially, they help us to eliminate the weaker
theories," and thus they "lend support though only for the
time being, to the surviving theory." Hence "the method
of critical discussion does not establish anything. Its verdict
is always 'not proven.' "[17] And the most hopeless task of
all is to prove a negative.

----

[17]K. R. Popper, in *Federation Proceedings of the American Societies for
Experimental Biology*, 22 (1963), p. 970.

Part IV.

The Real Background
of the Book of Mormon

CHAPTER 9

Some Fairly Foolproof Tests

Checking the Background

To the trained eye every document of considerable
length is bound to betray the real setting in which it was
produced. This can be illustrated by something Martin
Luther wrote two days before his death: "No one can
understand the Bucolics and Georgics of Virgil who has
not been a herdsman or a farmer for at least five years.
And no one can understand Cicero's letters, I maintain,
who has not been concerned with significant affairs of
state for twenty years. And no one can get an adequate
feeling for the Scriptures who has not guided religious
communities by the prophets for a hundred years."[1] What
is the world of experiences and ideas that one finds behind
the Book of Mormon? What is its real *Sitz im Leben?* We
can start with actual experiences, not merely ideas, but
things of a strictly objective and therefore testable nature;
for example, the book describes in considerable detail what
is supposed to be a great earthquake somewhere in Central
America, and another time it sets forth the particulars of
ancient olive culture. Here are things we can check up on;
but to do so we must go to sources made available by
scholars long since the days of Joseph Smith. Where *he*
could have learned all about major Central American

---

[1]H. Bonkamm, *Grundriss Zum Studium der Kirchengeschichte* (Guterslok,
1949), p. 13.

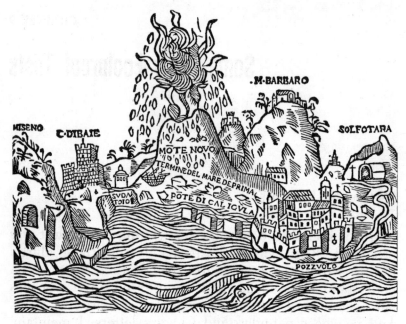

Contemporary woodcut of a mountain covering a settlement, and invasion
of the sea, 1538.

earthquakes or the fine points of Mediterranean olive culture remains a question. But the first question is, how well
does he describe them?

The Great Earthquake. Since Cumorah the earth has
done a great deal of quaking, and seismology has become
a science. Today it is possible to check step-by-step every
phenomenon described in the account of the great destructions reported in 3 Nephi 8-9 and to discover that what
passed for many years as the most lurid, extravagant, and
hence impossible part of the Book of Mormon is actually
a very sober and factual account of a first-class earthquake.
It was a terror—about XI on the Wood-Neuman scale—
but at that it is probably not the worst quake on record,
since we are expressly told that the damage was not total—
"And there were some cities which remained: . . ." (3 Nephi
8:15)—whereas in the great Assam earthquake of 1950 the

damage was total over a large area.[2] Take the Book of Mormon events in order:

First "there arose a great storm . . . and . . . also a great and terrible tempest," from which it would appear that the storm developed into a hurricane. (3 Nephi 8:5-6.) Major earthquakes are so often accompanied by "heavy rains, thunder and hailstorms, violent tempests," etc., that some specialists insist that "there is some indication that certain weather conditions may 'trigger' an earthquake,"[3] as in the Japanese earthquake of 1923, of which some Japanese seismologists maintain that "the low barometric pressure was the trigger which set off the earthquake."[4] At any rate, great earthquakes are preceded by great storms often enough to cause speculation.

Next there was a lot of noise, "terrible thunder, insomuch that it did shake the whole earth as if it was about to divide asunder." (3 Nephi 8:6.) Note that the thunder was thought to cause the shaking, obviously preceding it. This is another strange thing about earthquakes: "In accounts of earthquakes we always hear of the frightful noise which they produce. . . . But in addition, it seems that sometimes the earthquake can be heard *before* it is felt," which is "difficult to explain . . . one should feel the shock before hearing it."[5] The thunder seems to shake the earth, since "the sound always appears to come from the ground beneath the observer."[6] In the Assam earthquake of 1950 "one thing is stressed in all the reports: the awful rumble that heralded the outbreak of the earthquake . . . a deafening roar, louder than anything any of the witnesses had ever heard before."[7] The Book of Mormon aptly de-

---

[2]W. Knop, "The Day the Earth Exploded," *The Saturday Evening Post*, March 20, 1954, pp. 24f.

[3]G. A. Eiby, *About Earthquakes* (New York: Harpers, 1957), p. 25, cf. p. 107.

[4]N. H. Heck, *Earthquakes* (Princeton, N. J.: Princeton University Press, 1936), p. 118.

[5]Eiby, *Loc. cit.*

[6]J. Milne, *Earthquakes and Other Earth Movements* (London: Kegan, Paul, 1939), p. 15.

[7]Knop, *op. cit.*, pp. 114f.

scribes the continuous sounds as "the dreadful groanings
. . . and . . . tumultuous noises." (3 Nephi 10:9.)

"And there were exceeding sharp lightnings. . . ."
(3 Nephi 8:7.) According to an eyewitness account the
great earthquake that completely destroyed the old capital
of Guatemala on September 11, 1541, was preceded by
"the fury of the wind, the incessant, appalling lightning
and dreadful thunder" that were "indescribable" in their
violence.[8] One of the still unexplained phenomena of earthquakes is that "all types of lights are reported seen. . . .
there are flashes, balls of fire, and streamers."[9] The terrible
wind at Guatemala City is matched in the Book of Mormon
by high winds with occasional whirlwinds that even carried
some people away. (3 Nephi 8:12, 16; 10:13-14.) In the
Japanese earthquake of 1923 the wind reached a velocity
of 50 m.p.h., and "the fires, in turn, set up minor tor-
nadoes"; and in the Assam earthquake "strong winds raised
the dust until visibility was reduced to a few feet. . . ."[10]

"And the city of Zarahemla did take fire." (3 Nephi
8:8.) It would appear from the account of the Nephite
disaster that the main cause of destruction was fire in the
cities (3 Nephi 9:8-11), which agrees with all the major
statistics through the centuries; for "earthquakes are largely
a city problem" mainly because the first heavy shock
invariably sets fires all over town: in the Japanese experience "wind-driven flames were shown to be more dangerous than the greatest earthquake."[11]

"And the city of Moroni did sink into the depths of
the sea. . . ." (3 Nephi 8:9.) The *tsunami* or sea wave "is
the most spectacular and . . . appalling of all earthquake
phenomena" and almost invariably follows a major shake-

[8]Juarros, cited by H. J. Spinden, "Shattered Capitals of Central America,"
in *The National Geographic Magazine*, Vol. 35, No. 3 (September 1919),
p. 202.
[9]P. Byerly, *Seismology* (New York: Prentice Hall, 1942), p. 76.
[10]Heck, *op. cit.*, p. 115; Knop, *Loc. cit.*
[11]*Ibid.*, p. 118.

up on the coast.[12] Along with this, however, we have in
the Book of Mormon record what seems to be a permanent
submergence of coastal areas when "the waters . . . came
up in the stead thereof" and remain. (3 Nephi 9:7.) Such
a submergence happened on a spectacular scale in the
Chilean earthquake of 1960: "We would have taken
these flooded stretches—permanently flooded—for coastal
lagoons," a geologist reports, ". . . if here and there we
had not seen roads that ran straight towards them and into
them . . . roads that vanished, or sometimes showed under
the stagnant water, branching into what had been the
streets of a town."[13] In the New Madrid, Missouri, earthquake of 1811 two vast tracts of land were covered with
fresh water both by the damming of streams and the bursting out of numerous earthquake blows or fountains,
flooding the newly submerged areas.[14]

"And the earth was carried up upon the city of Moronihah that in the place of the city there became a great
mountain." (3 Nephi 8:10.) In September 1538 during a
tremendous storm and tidal wave a volcanic mountain
suddenly appeared and covered a town near Puzzuoli on
the Bay of Naples; ever since the mountain has been known
as *Monte Nuove*, or New Mountain.[15] The carrying *up* of
the earth upon the city suggests the overwhelming of
Pompeii by vast heaps of volcanic ash or the deep burial
of Herculaneum under lava in 79 A.D.[16] On the other
hand, other cities were "sunk, and the inhabitants thereof
. . . buried up in the depths of the earth." (3 Nephi 9:6.)
This could have been an actual engulfment: in the great

[12]*Ibid.*, p. 26.
[13]H. Tazieff, *When the Earth Trembles* (New York: Harcourt, Brace,
1964), p. 34. On a winter night of 373/2 B.C. the great city of Helice in
Greece disappeared beneath the sea: "Not a single soul survived." S. N.
Marinatos, in *Archaeology*, 13 (1960), p. 186.
[14]Heck, *op. cit.*, pp. 17, 24; Byerly, *op. cit.*, pp. 67f.
[15]A. Sieberg, *Handbuch der Erdbebenkunde* (Braunschweig: F. Vieweg,
1904), pp. 104-5.
[16]The photographs in Spinden, *op. cit.*, pp. 187-192, for cases of the earth
being carried up over the land.

earthquake of 1755, which was felt all over Europe, "the quay at Lisbon sank, with all the people on it, into a fissure, and no trace of quay or people was seen again."[17] It was a fine new breakwater, and a sizeable number of the town's inhabitants had fled to it to escape from the fire and falling houses of the city.

". . . The quakings . . . did last for about the space of three hours" (3 Nephi 8:19), though the aftershocks, correctly described as "the tremblings and groanings," continued for three days (3 Nephi 10:9), during which time the afflicted people carried on in hysterical fashion with frightful howling and lamentation. This too is a normal part of the picture, since "the incessant recurrence of aftershocks after a great earthquake is most unnerving to the populace."[18]

". . . there was thick darkness . . . the inhabitants . . . could feel the vapor of darkness; . . . neither could there be fire kindled . . . so great were the mists of darkness." (3 Nephi 8:20-22.) This, like much else in the account (e.g., that God "did *send down* fire and destroy them" [3 Nephi 9:11]), suggests nearby volcanic activity. And indeed, in many cases "earthquakes are the preparation for the volcano that follows," as in the Chilean 1960 quake, which triggered the activity of long-dormant volcanoes in the area.[19] Most of the victims of the great catastrophes of Pompeii, St. Pierre (Martinique, 1902), and Mt. Pelee (1906) died of suffocation when earthquake dust, volcanic ash, steam, and hot gasses (mostly sulfureted hydrogen gas) took the place of air. In some areas, the Book of Mormon reports, people were "overpowered by the vapor of smoke and of darkness," and so lost their lives. (3 Nephi 10:13.) Even without volcanic accompaniments, however, major earthquakes kick up a terrible dust and, according

---

[17]Milne, *op. cit.*, p. 29, giving other instances also.
[18]Byerly, *op. cit.*, p. 78.
[19]J. H. Hodgson, *Earthquakes and Earth Structure* (Englewood Cliffs, N. J.: Prentice Hall, 1964), p. 41.

to Sieberg, are accompanied by "phenomenal vapors and astonishingly thick air."[20] In the Assam earthquake such contamination "reduced visibility to a few feet and made breathing a nightmare."[21]

According to 3 Nephi 8:20-21 the "Vapor of darkness" was not only tangible to the survivors, but defeated every attempt to light candles or torches for illumination. At present intensive studies are being made of the destruction of the Greek island of Thera (today Santorini) in 1400 B.C. This catastrophe, well within historic times, is thought to have been eight times as violent as Krakatoa (!) and is described in terms exactly paralleling the account in 3 Nephi. Among other things it is pointed out that the overpowering thickness of the air must have extinguished all lamps.[22]

The Book of Mormon also mentions the rising and sinking of the land, forming new "hills and valleys" (3 Nephi 9:5-8)—with no mention of major mountain ranges! In the New Madrid earthquake of 1811-2, "over an area of 30,000 square miles the land surface was lowered by amounts of 6 to 15 feet and over a much smaller area was raised by similar amounts."[23] Hydrographic surveys after the Japanese quake of 1923 showed that over an area of 500 square miles "some areas were lowered as much as 689 feet, adjacent areas were raised 820 feet"—a difference of over 1,500 feet![24]

In the Nephite catastrophe some cities escaped total destruction, since they did not lie at the center of the earthquake zone but were south of it. (3 Nephi 8:15, 12.)

---

[20]Down to the present generation "old Indians still fix their ages and other events in relation to 'La Oscuridad Grande'—'The Great Darkness' that accompanied a great eruption and earthquake in Nicaragua in 1835; Spinden, *op. cit.*, p. 211. Sieberg, *op. cit.*, p. 123: ". . . *auffallender Nebel and wundersame dicke Luften.*"

[21]Knop, *op. cit.*, p. 25.

[22]See the long article by John Lear, in *Saturday Review*, Nov. 5, 1966, pp. 57-66. He mentions the quenching of the lamps on p. 63.

[23]Heck, *op. cit.*, p. 17.

[24]*Ibid.*, pp. 116f.

As is well known, "Central America lies in the heavy
earthquake belt,"[25] as well as being both a coastal and a
volcanic area—a perfect setup for all the disasters which
the Book of Mormon describes so succinctly and so well.
That everything looked strangely changed after the
debacle, with seams and cracks everywhere and "highways
. . . broken up, and the level roads . . . spoiled, and many
smooth places became rough" (3 Nephi 8:13, 17-18) needs
no commentary, since such are the commonest of all earthquake phenomena. The remarkable thing about such statements is their moderation. Here was a chance for the author
of the Book of Mormon to let his imagination run wild
(as too many of his followers have done), with whole
continents displaced, signs in the heavens, and monsters
emerging from the deep. Instead, we get level roads spoiled
and smooth places made rough!

We must bear in mind that what the Book of Mormon
reports are the happenings as the people experienced them
rather than as instruments would record them. Most earthquake data are of this very human nature, and exactly
match the account in 3 Nephi. The Book of Mormon description emphasizes the fact that it was not any one
particular thing but the combination of horrors that made
the experience so terrible. As N. H. Heck puts it, what
makes a major earthquake so devastating is "the combination of forces . . . into an almost irresistible source of
disaster."[26] The picture of cumulating disaster at the destruction of Guatemala City in 1541 strikingly parallels
the story in the eighth chapter of 3 Nephi: "It had rained
incessantly and with great violence . . . the fury of the
wind, the incessant, appalling lightning and dreadful
thunder were indescribable. The general terror was increased by eruptions from the volcano . . . [the following
morning] the vibrations of the earth were so violent that

[25]Byerly, *op. cit.*, p. 82.
[26]Heck, *op. cit.*, p. 118.

people were unable to stand; the shocks were accompanied by a terrible subterranean noise which spread universal dismay. . . ."[27]

We have then in the Book of Mormon a factual and sober account of a major upheaval in which by comparison with other such accounts nothing seems exaggerated. However wildly others may have chosen to interpret the Book of Mormon record, so far is it from bearing the marks of fantasy or wild imagination that it actually furnishes convincing evidence that the person who wrote it must have had personal experience of a major Meso-American quake or else have had access to authentic accounts of such.

Olive Culture. A more tranquil theme is the story of the olive tree. As we shall see below, some Book of Mormon writers were greatly concerned with the imagery of the olive tree. In setting forth its symbolism, they found it necessary to go into a description of olive culture in some detail. Now as far as the Book of Mormon is concerned, there is no sign of any cultivation of olives in the New World; the story of the olive-tree as given in the Book of Mormon is supposed to be quoted from the writings of an ancient prophet who lived in Palestine long before Lehi left the place—he is wholly concerned with describing ancient Palestinian or Mediterranean olive culture; there is no other kind mentioned in the Book of Mormon.

Jacob's (or rather Zenos's) treatise on ancient olive culture (Jacob 5-6) is accurate in every detail: Olive trees do have to be pruned and cultivated diligently; the top branches are indeed the first to wither, and the new shoots do come right out of the trunk; the olive is indeed the most plastic of trees, surpassing even the willow in its power to survive the most drastic whacking and burning; a good olive tree is greatly cherished, and no end of pains are taken to preserve it even through many centuries, for really

---

[27]Spinden, *op. cit.,* p. 202.

superior fruit is very rare and difficult to obtain and per-
petuate; the ancient way of strengthening the old trees
(especially in Greece) was to graft in the shoots of the
oleaster or wild olive; also, shoots from valuable old trees
were transplanted to keep the stock alive after the parent
tree should perish; to a surprising degree the olive prefers
poor and rocky ground, whereas rich soil produces inferior
fruit; too much grafting produces a nondescript and clut-
tered yield of fruit; the top branches if allowed to grow
as in Spain and France, while producing a good shade
tree, will indeed sap the strength of the tree and give a
poor crop; fertilizing with dung is very important, in spite
of the preference for rocky ground, and has been practised
since ancient times; the thing to be most guarded against
is bitterness in the fruit.[28] All these points, taken from a
treatise on ancient olive culture, are duly, though quite
casually, noted in Zenos's Parable of the Olive Tree.

The Axial Period. Even more difficult to fake than an
accurate description of how things really were done in a
practical way is the spiritual and cultural image of an age.
For the setting and color of life in Jerusalem in 600 B.C.
the author of the Book of Mormon could have borrowed
from the Bible. Only he goes far beyond the Bible in
describing the world of Lehi. We have discussed this picture at some length and pointed out that the author of
the Book of Mormon could have picked no better time or
place in all history for the launching of a new civilization,
and no better qualified parties to lead the enterprise than
the time, place, and characters he chose.[29] This is by no
means a rationalization of our own. Over a century ago the
French scholar, Lasaul, noted what many have since confirmed, that the years around 600 B.C. are the "Axial
Period" of world history, that is, the pivotal point or axis

---

[28]S. V. "Olive" in any good encyclopedia. We are following the article
in the 9th ed. of the *Encyclopedia Britannica.*
[29]H. Nibley, *An Approach to the Book of Mormon,* Chapters 3 through 7.

around which that whole history turns. At that time "a strange movement of the spirit passed through all civilized peoples."[30] And what historian does not recognize as a basic fact of "Geopolitics" that the pivotal region of world history, ancient, Medieval, and modern, is that point where three continents come together and where the sea reaches farthest into the great central land-mass, i.e., Palestine?

The great shift of the Axial period was from the old sacral monarchies to more free and popular forms of government, and from a religious or "mantic" orientation of thought to a scientific or "sophic" one. The swing took place quickly all over the Near East and around the Mediterranean, but mid scenes of great confusion and revolution. There is something to be said for both ways of thinking, and the great debate between them—political, religious, economic, intellectual—has been going on ever since. That debate is nowhere more clearly set forth than in the pages of the Book of Mormon. It begins with furious heat and passion, right in the household of Lehi, where the issue is clearly drawn between the defenders of the prosperous, respectable, pharisaical "Jews at Jerusalem" and the refugee father, who has turned his back on wealth and respectability to live as a righteous outcast in the desert; and the controversy continues right on down through all of Nephite history as a long line of clever and sophisticated professional preachers take issue with a long line of prophets. No Greek dramatist or philosopher ever set forth the issues with greater vigor and clarity than they are presented in the pages of the Book of Mormon.

One of the most interesting features of the Book of Mormon is the inclusion in it of long speeches by false prophets. These men are skilled Sophists who use all the stock arguments against the gospel with practised skill and great success. It is hard for a philosopher today to find

_____

[30]The problem is discussed by Karl Jaspers, *The Origin and Goal of History* (Yale Univ. Press, 1953), p. 8.

anything to add to the arguments of Sherem, Korihor, Zeezrom, or Nehor.

But are not such arguments typical of a later age, that of the schoolmen in the days when Greek thought had pervaded the East? Indeed they are, but their history goes clear back to the beginning. The split between rationalists and believers, which runs right through the Book of Mormon from the first page to the last, is what Goodenough calls the perennial conflict in Judaism between the "horizontal" and the "vertical" types of religion, that is, between the comfortable and conventional religion of forms and observances as opposed to a religion of revelations, dreams, visions, and constant awareness of the reality of the other world and the poverty of this one.[31] We have called this the conflict between the "sophic" and the "mantic," and it goes back to the earliest records of Greece and the Levant;[32] but was brought to its sharpest focus in the period just after 600 B.C.

The conflict between these two views of life and religion flared up at the time when the old sacral order of society, weakened by corruption, wars, and migrations, was attacked by a new skepticism and rationalism which suddenly became bold and outspoken. This controversy was fanned to fever-heat in the political and moral crisis of Jerusalem under Zedekiah, and was carried to the New World in the baggage of Lehi and Mulek. It begins with Laman and Lemuel, the perfect exponents of the smug "horizontal religion" with its careful concern for outward observances of the law and its utter contempt for visionary prophets of doom:

"And thou art like unto our father, led away by the foolish imaginations of his heart; . . .

"And we know that the people who were in the land of Jerusalem were a righteous people; for they kept the

---

[31]E. R. Goodenough, *Jewish Symbols*, I, 17-19.
[32]Old Babylonian literature offers a good illustration; W. G. Lambert, *Babylonian Wisdom Literature* (Oxford, 1960), pp. 4-19.

statutes and judgments of the Lord, and all his commandments, according to the law of Moses; wherefore, we know
that they are a righteous people; and our father hath judged
them. . . ." (1 Nephi 17:20, 22.) The issue is clearly
drawn and has continued to this day, as we shall see when
we consider the case of Korihor. (See pp. 416-17)

Some Strange Customs

The Book of Mormon mentions a number of strange
customs and usages not found in the Bible and only discovered in other sources in recent years.

1) The most notorious of these is *temple building.*
Ministers and other Bible students gleefully pounced on
what they thought an outrageous gaffe when they caught
Nephi telling how he and the more religious part of the
people went apart from the main body after they had been
a while in the New World, and founded their own reli-
giously oriented community, setting about to make a temple
after the manner of Solomon's Temple only not so splendid.
(2 Nephi 5:16.) In 1895 began the discovery of the writings of another group of refugees from Jerusalem, who left
about Lehi's time, settling far up the Nile at Elephantine.
The most surprising discovery to come out of this archive
was that these Jews also erected a temple in their new
home, and when it was destroyed by the hostility of a local
governor, they applied to the directors of the temple at
Jerusalem for permission to rebuild it—which permission
was granted.[33]

2) *The Order of Battle.* The so-called "Battle Scroll"
from Qumran throws a flood of light on peculiar military
practices described in the Book of Mormon especially those
of Moroni: his improvised banner with its high-sounding
patriotic inscription, and his dedicating of the enemy's land

---

[33]For recent treatments of this much-treated subject, E. G. Kraeling,
The Brooklyn Aramaic Papyrus, pp. 41, 44-46, 95; cf. B. Porten, in *Journal of
the American Oriental Society,* 81 (1961), pp. 38-42. See A. E. Cowley, *Aram
Papyri* from the Fifth Century B.C., (Oxford, 1923).

to destruction we have discussed elsewhere.[34] But we failed to take sufficient note of his consultation with a prophet before the battle to learn by divine revelation the enemy's disposition and what his own movements should be. This is standard practice in the Book of Mormon (Alma 43:23f.) and we now learn on the evidence especially of the Battle Scroll that it was also the regular practice in ancient Israel.[35] In confronting the enemy, Moroni reminds his people that they are the poor and the outcasts of the world, fittingly following a banner which was his own rent coat, representing the torn garment of their ancestor Joseph, the outcast and suffering servant. (Alma 46:18-23.) Again, the Battle Scroll described the hosts of the Children of Light as the poor and outcast of the earth, despised and now threatened with extermination by the haughty gentiles.[36]

3) Following the example of Moroni, all the people who were willing to enter his army and take the covenant rent their garments as he had his, only they went further and proceeded to *tread upon their garments*, saying as they did so, "We covenant with God, that . . . he may cast us at the feet of our enemies, even as we have cast our garments at thy feet to be trodden under foot, if we shall fall into transgression." (Alma 46:22.)

In a very recent study J. Z. Smith considers under the title of "Treading upon the Garments" an ancient ritual practice attested in the newly discovered early Christian Coptic texts in which a person upon becoming a member of the church would take off his garment and trample on it "in token" of having cast away an old way of life and as a symbol of trampling his old sins under foot, with "curses placed on the inciter" to sin.[36a] Heretofore

---

[34]An Approach to the Book of Mormon, Chapter 17.
[35]Y. Yadin, The Scroll of the War of the Sons of Light . . . (Oxford, 1962), p. 6, cf. 15, 215, IQM, Sect. 19.
[36]Ibid., pp. 311f., 323.
[36a]J. Z. Smith, "The Garments of Shame," in History of Religions, 5 (1966), pp. 224-233. Quotation is from p. 229.

the custom has been traced to Hellenistic sources, but it now appears from the newly found documents that it is an original and very old Jewish rite "probably to be traced back to Jewish exegesis of Genesis 3:21. . . ."[37] It has all the marks of being archaic and shows that peculiar blend of ritual and real-life behavior which at first made the understanding of the Battle Scroll so difficult and which puts such a distinctive stamp upon some of the historical events in the Book of Mormon.[38]

Before the battle "when he had poured out his soul to God," Moroni "named all the land which was south of the land Desolation, . . . and all the land, both on the north and on the south—a chosen land. . . ." (Alma 46:17.) Whether we punctuate this to mean that he named the enemy land Desolation and the rest "Chosen," or that he named the "chosen land" and let the rest keep its ill-omened title, the point is that we have here the practice, now attested by the Battle Scroll, of formally blessing the hosts of Israel and cursing the land of their enemy before the battle.[39]

4) The rite of the *Rameumptom* is as strange as the name:

For they had a place built up in the center of their synagogue, a place for standing, which was high above the head, and the top thereof would only admit one person. Therefore, whosoever desired to worship must go forth and stand upon the top thereof, and stretch forth his hands towards heaven, and cry with a loud voice, . . . (a long prayer follows) . . . every man did go forth and offer up the same prayers. Now the place was called by them Rameumptom, which, being interpreted, is the holy stand. (Alma 31:13-21.)

The fact that the term had to be translated into Nephite indicates that these people had their own strange dialect. And indeed they were not Nephites, but Zoramites, a

---

[37]*Ibid.*, pp. 230-233. It has special reference to the skin garment of Adam.
[38]See our discussion "Old World Ritual in the New World," ch. 23 of *An Approach to the Book of Mormon.*
[39]Yadin, *op. cit.*, pp. 15, 215, 223-5, and *IQM* Sects. 17-19.

people who preferred the old customs of the Mulekites to the discipline of the Nephites. The Mulekites, it will be recalled, were a mixed crowd of Near Eastern emigrants who took little stock in the rites and customs of the Jews. Recently Leipoldt has shown that the pillar-sitting monks of Syria, who caused such a sensation in early Christian times, were actually carrying on an ancient pagan tradition in the land, by which a man would mount on a high pillar at some important ceremonial center and from the top of it pray for the people.[40] The performance of the Christian stylites consisted of endless gyrations atop a high pillar. A large number of related Greek words describe the idea: *Remb-, ramp-, rhamph-* imply wild ecstatic circling motions, especially in the air. The word has been traced back to a Phoenician original, *raba-* (Hebrew *rab*), applied to a kind of missile launcher. Could we be here on the trail of our word Rameumptom?[41]

5) There is a peculiar rite of execution described in the Book of Mormon whose ancient background is clearly attested. When a notorious debunker of religion was convicted of murder, "they carried him upon the top of the hill Manti, and there he was caused, or rather did acknowledge, between the heavens and the earth, that what he had taught to the people was contrary to the word of God; and there he suffered an ignominious death." (Alma 1:15.) A like fate was suffered centuries later by the traitor Zemnarihah. This goes back to a very old tradition indeed, that of the first false preachers, Harut and Marut (fallen angels), who first corrupted the word of God and as a result hang to this day between heaven and earth confessing their sin. Their counterpart in Jewish tradition is the angel Shamozi, who "repented, and by way of penance hung himself up between heaven and earth."[42]

---

[40]J. Leipoldt, (ed.), *Religionsgesch, des. Orients,* (Leiden, 1961), p. 10.
[41]For various possible forms of the word, see the old Henr. Stephanus, *Thesaurus Graecae Linguae,* VII, 2337-8.
[42]See Geo. Sales's commentary in his translation of *The Koran,* II, 103; *Secrets of Enoch,* VII:1-4; Tha'labi, *Qissas al Anbiya-i,* pp. 36f.

The Copper Scrolls.

These may be only old legends, but they were legends that certain ancient people took very seriously, and the peculiar and symbolic punishment they describe is known to the author of the Book of Mormon.

6) We have said a good deal about the hiding up of sacred records, but have not noted that according to the Book of Mormon it was a prescribed practice to "hide up treasures to the Lord." The prophet Samuel the Lamanite condemns the Nephites not for hiding up treasures, but specifically for not hiding them up to the Lord:

I will, saith the Lord, that they shall hide up their treasures unto me; and cursed be they who hide not up their treasures unto me . . . I will hide up their treasure when they shall flee before their enemies; because they will not hide them up unto me, cursed be they and also their treasures. (Helaman 13:19-20.)

When they flee before their enemies, the faithful are expected to hide up their treasures to the Lord. This is exactly the lesson of the Copper Scroll, which was "intended to tell the Jewish survivors of the war . . . where this sacred material lay buried, so that . . . it would never be desecrated by profane use."[42a]

7) The Dancing Maidens are a picturesque touch in the Book of Mormon.

Now there was a place in Shemlon where the daughters of the Lamanites did gather themselves together to sing, and to dance, and to make themselves merry. (Mosiah 20:1.)

The refugee priests of Noah discovered them "having tarried in the wilderness." The custom is not Nephite but Lamanite-Zoramite, that is, not necessarily of Israelitish origin. Such a rite flourished in the same cultural complex that seems to have produced the Rameumptom, for the Sabaean women in December used to celebrate a dance and feast to Venus and the water-nymphs at some pleasant place outside the city of Harran; they would bring fruit,

---

[42a]J. M. Allegro, *The Treasure of the Copper Scroll*, pp. 61-62.

and flowers as offerings, and camp out in the country, and of course no men were allowed.[43] In Israel also the maidens would dance on the day of Atonement.[44] Asiatic legends are full of such ladies ritually disporting themselves in the woods.[45] The thing proves nothing in the Book of Mormon but it is an authentic little touch just the same.

8) Perhaps the most formidable challenge of the Book of Mormon to scholarship today is the long description of a Coronation ceremony included in it. Of all the possible ties between the Book of Mormon and the Old World, by far the most impressive in our opinion is the exact and full matching up of the long coronation rite described in the book of Mosiah with the "standard" Near Eastern coronation ceremonies as they have been worked out through the years by the "patternists" of Cambridge. Imagine a twenty-three-year-old backwoodsman in 1829 giving his version of what an ancient coronation ceremony would be like—what would be done and said, how, and by whom? Put the question to any college senior or dean of humanities today and see what you get. To the recent pronouncements of the "Cambridge school" that conform so beautifully to the long description of Mosiah's enthrone-ment, we may add another interesting bit of confirmation. In the tenth century A.D., Nathan, a Jewish scholar living in Babylon, witnessed the enthronement of the Prince of the Captivity, carried out by the Jews in exile as a reminder of the glories of their lost kingdom. Since no regular coro-nation is described in the Bible, and since the rites here depicted conform to the normal pattern of a Near Eastern coronation, we have here a pretty good picture of what a coronation in Israel would be like in Lehi's day.[46]

---

[43]E. Bacon, *Vanished Civilizations*, p. 216.
[44]R. Patai, in *Edoth*, 1 (1946), p. 186.
[45]F. A. vonSchiefner, *Tibetan Tales* (London, 1926), p. 54.
[46]Nathan Ha-Babli, "The Installation of An Exilarch," Ch. X of B. Halper, *Post-biblical Hebrew Literature* (Philadelphia: Jewish Publication Society of America, 1943), pp. 64-68; the Hebrew text in Vol. I (1946), pp. 37-40, under the same title. On "patternism" and the Book of Mormon, see our *Approach to the Book of Mormon*, Chap. 23.

The new king is set aside by the elders on the Thursday preceding his coronation. The elders are also in charge in the Book of Mormon, though they do not figure in the pre-coronation arrangements in the book of Mosiah because this was an unusual case in which the old king was still living—it is he who designates and crowns his successor. All the people "great and small" are then summoned to the royal presence, each being required to bring the most precious gift his means can afford. In return the Prince of the Captivity entertains them all at a great feast of abundance. The day before the coronation a high wooden tower (*migdol*) had been built. This was covered with precious hangings, and concealed within it was a trained choir of noble youths which under the direction of a precentor led the congregation in hymns and antiphonals preparing for the new king's appearance. This explains how at the coronation of Mosiah all the people would respond to the king in a single voice—it was the practiced and familiar *acclamatio* of the ancient world. Thus the conductor would say, "The breath of all the living . . . ," whereupon the choir would answer, ". . . shall bless thy name," and continue until they reached the passage known as the Kedusha, when the entire multitude would join in the familiar words. After this all the people sat down.

When the preliminaries were over, the king, who until then had remained invisible, appeared dramatically on the top of the tower, which until then held only three empty thrones; at the sight of him all the people stood up and remained standing while he seated himself, to be followed after a few moments by the head of the Academy of Sura, who sat on a throne to his right, though separated from him by an interval, and a little later by the head of the Academy of Pumbeditha who sat on the king's left. This of course is the image of the "three men" who represent God on earth—a Book of Mormon concept, as we have noted above.

Over the king's head alone however was the splendid *baldachin,* or royal tent—for as in the Book of Mormon the coronation rite is essentially a camp ceremony. The precentor, who has been the master of ceremonies from the first, then goes under the tent and imparts royal blessings on the new king. In the Book of Mormon the old king, who is still alive, does all this and has general charge of the meeting. Because the blessing cannot be heard by the vast multitude, the chorus of youths standing beneath the throne shout out a loud "Amen!" at the end of it to signify the universal approval.

Then comes the time for the great royal speech, the new king deferring to the head of the Academy of Sura, who in turn courteously defers to the head of the Academy of Pumbeditha, "thus showing deference to one another" and indicating their perfect oneness of mind and purpose. The speech is delivered in the manner of a message from heaven, the speaker "expounding with awe, closing his eyes, and wrapping himself up with his tallith. . . ." The people stood wrapped in silence and overwhelmed by the occasion: "There was not in the congregation one that opened his mouth, or chirped, or uttered a sound. If he (the speaker) became aware that any one spoke, he would open his eyes, and fear and terror would fall upon the congregation."

The royal speech was immediately followed by a question period, in which the king would put questions to the people, who would answer him in the person of a venerable old man "of wisdom, understanding, and experience." Then the precentor (Benjamin) would pronounce a blessing on the people with the special words, "During the life of our prince the exilarch, and during your life, and during the life of all the house of Israel." This is the typical New Year and birthday formula that always goes with a coronation. Then the precentor blesses the king and then his two counselors and makes a formal roll call of the people. This is the formal registry of the people described in Mosiah, and while the people are still standing the precentor hands the book of the Law to the new king, who reads to the people the covenant they are entering. When the book of the Law is returned to the ark, all sit down and are regaled by learned discourses on the Law, beginning with one by the king himself. After this the precentor again "blessed the exilarch by the Book of the Law," and all said amen. After a final prayer all the people departed to their homes.

The reader can see for himself how closely these rites conform to the substance and spirit of the coronation of Mosiah. But the most remarkable feature of the whole thing is the nature of the royal discourse on government. In the Book of Mormon Benjamin clearly alludes to the Old World coronation rites in which the king is treated like God on earth, receiving the rich offerings and awed acclamations reserved for divinity; and he also emphasizes the royal obligation to assure victory and prosperity for the land. While he recognizes the value of these things, Benjamin's whole speech is devoted to giving them a special twist—the homage and the offerings are very well, but they are for the heavenly King, not for Benjamin, who is only a man; victory and prosperity will surely follow, but they come not from him but from God.[47]

In a study entitled "The Refusal of the Kingship as a Characteristic of Royal Authority in the Old Testament," K. H. Bernhardt has shown at great length that part of the nomadic desert heritage of the Jews was the idea that kingship is an "unauthorized infringement of God's majesty." While in post-exilic times, Bernhardt explains, the king was no longer expected formally to disclaim his right to rule, in the days of Jeremiah and the Rechabites (Lehi's half-nomadic contemporaries) he was still felt to be something of a usurper. Thus while the Jews shared the common

---

[47]See *An Approach to the Book of Mormon* (1964 ed.), pp. 247ff.

props and protocol of the coronation rites with other Near Eastern peoples, their King's formal renunciation of absolute power put the whole thing on a different footing.[48] This is exactly what we have at the enthronement of Mosiah. Bernhardt gets most of his evidence from the Old Testament, of course; yet it took the perspicacity of a modern scholar to discover, in 1961, the institution and the idea which are so clearly set forth in the Book of Mormon.

9) *The Liahona.* We have in the Book of Mormon, a most interesting apparatus called the Liahona. Now the chances of finding a genuine Liahona are, to say the least, remote; but what if something just like it showed up in the hands of Lehi's relatives? That should certainly come as a surprise, and even provoke some thought. The Liahona has given rise to endless merriment and mockery among critics of the Book of Mormon; only the shining stones of the Jaredites can equal it as a laugh-getter. Even the present writer, for all his curiosity about Book of Mormon oddities, has always passed it by in an abashed silence— it was like nothing he ever heard or read of—until the year 1959. For it was eight years ago that an Arabic scholar by the name of T. Fahd published the hitherto scattered, scanty, and inaccessible evidence that makes it possible for the first time to say something significant about the Liahona. But before we consider his report, let us see what the Book of Mormon has to say on the subject. This is what the first edition tells about the Liahona:

(P. 38, 1 Nephi 16:10) "And it came to pass that as my father arose in the morning, and went forth to the tent door, to his great astonishment he beheld upon the ground a round ball of curious workmanship; and it was of fine brass. And within the ball were two spindles; and

---

[48]K.-H. Bernhardt, *Das Problem der Altorientalischen Konigsidealogie im Alten Testament* (Leiden: E. J. Brill, 1961), Chap. VI. Cf. G. Fohrer, in *Zeitsch. d. A.T. Wiss.* 71 (1959), pp. 1-22, and Geo. Widengren, in *Jnl. of Semit. Stud.* 2 (1957), 1-32.

the one pointed the way whither we should go into the wilderness."

(P. 40f., 1 Nephi 16:28-30) "And it came to pass that I, Nephi, beheld the pointers which were in the ball, that they did work according to the faith, and diligence, and heed, which we did give unto them. And there was also written upon them, a new writing, which was plain to be read, which did give us understanding concerning the ways of the Lord; and it was written and changed from time to time, according to the faith and diligence which we gave unto it: And thus we see, that by small means, the Lord can bring about great things.

"And it came to pass that I, Nephi, did go forth up into the top of the mountain, according to the directions which were given upon the ball. And it came to pass that I did slay wild beasts, insomuch, that I did obtain food for our families. . . ."

(P. 155, Mosiah 1:16f.) "And moreover, he also gave him charge concerning . . . the ball or director, which led our fathers through the wilderness, which was prepared by the hand of the Lord that thereby they might be led, every one according to the heed and diligence which they gave unto him. Therefore, as they were unfaithful, they did not prosper nor progress in their journey."

(P. 329f., Alma 37:38-47) "And now my son, I have somewhat to say concerning the thing which our fathers call a ball, or director or our fathers called it liahona, which is, being interpreted, a compass; and the Lord prepared it. And behold, there cannot any man work after the manner of so curious a workmanship. And behold, it was prepared to shew unto our fathers the course which they should travel in the wilderness; and it did work for them according to their faith in God; therefore if they had faith to believe that God could cause that those spindles should point the way they should go, behold, it was done; therefore they had this miracle, and also many other miracles wrought by the power of God, day by day; nevertheless, because those miracles were worked by small means, nevertheless it did shew unto them marvelous works. They were slothful, and forgot to exercise their faith and diligence, and then those marvellous works ceased, and they did not progress in their journey; therefore, they tarried in the wilderness, or did not travel a direct course, and were afflicted with hunger and thirst, because of their transgressions.

"And now, my son, I would that ye should understand that these things are not without a shadow; for as our fathers were slothful to give heed to this compass, (now these things were temporal,) they did not prosper; even so it is with things which are spiritual. For behold, it is as easy to give heed to the word of Christ, which will point to you a straight course to eternal bliss, as it was for our fathers to give heed to this compass, which would point unto them a straight course to the promised land. And now I say, Is there not a type in this thing? . . .

"O my son, do not let us be slothful, because of the easiness of the way; for so it was with our fathers; for so it was prepared for them, that if they would look, they might live; even so it is with us. The way is prepared and if we will look, we may live forever."

(P. 48f., 1 Nephi 18:12 and 21) "And it came to pass that after they had bound me insomuch that I could not move, the compass, which had been prepared of the Lord, did cease to work; wherefore, they knew not whither they should steer the ship. . . . And it came to pass that after they had loosed me, behold, I took the compass, and it did work whither I desired it."

Listing the salient features of the report we get the following:

1) The Liahona was a gift of God, the manner of its delivery causing great astonishment.

2) It was neither mechanical nor self-operating, but worked solely by the power of God.

3) It functioned only in response to the faith, diligence, and heed of those who followed it.

4) And yet there was something ordinary and familiar about it. The thing itself was the "small means" through which God worked; it was not a mysterious or untouchable object but strictly a "temporal thing." It was so ordinary that the constant tendency of Lehi's people was to take it for granted—in fact, they spent most of their time ignoring it: hence, according to Alma, their needless, years-long wanderings in the desert.

5) The working parts of the device were two spindles or pointers.

6) On these a special writing would appear from time to time, clarifying and amplifying the message of the pointers.

7) The specific purpose of the traversing indicators was "to point the way they should go."

8) The two pointers were mounted in a brass or bronze sphere whose marvelous workmanship excited great wonder and admiration. Special instructions sometimes appeared on this ball.

9) The device was referred to descriptively as a ball, functionally as a director, and in both senses as a "compass," or Liahona.

10) On occasion, it saved Lehi's people from perishing by land and sea—". . . if they would look they might live." (Alma 37:46.)

11) It was preserved "for a wise purpose" (Alma 37:2, 14, 18) long after it had ceased to function, having been prepared specifically to guide Lehi's party to the promised land. (*Idem.*, vs. 39f.) It was a "type and shadow" of man's relationship to God during his earthly journey.

We should not pass by Alma's description without noting a most remarkable peculiarity of verses 40 and 41. (chap. 37.) Let us read these verses without punctuation, as the ancients did; and as the Book of Mormon manuscript is written:

". . . therefore they had this miracle and also many other miracles wrought by the power of God day by day nevertheless because those miracles were worked by small means nevertheless it did shew unto them marvellous works they were slothful and forgot to exercise their faith and diligence and then those marvellous works ceased."

The meaning is perfectly clear: though Lehi's people enjoyed daily demonstrations of God's power, the device by which that power operated seemed so ordinary (Alma includes it among "small and simple things . . . very small means . . ." vss. 6-7) that in spite of the "marvellous works" it showed them they tended to neglect it. We could punctuate the passage accordingly:

"Therefore they had this miracle, and also many other miracles, wrought by the power of God day by day. Nevertheless, because those miracles were worked by small means (albeit it did show unto them marvellous works), they were slothful and forgot to exercise their faith and diligence. . . ."

A comparison of various editions of the Book of Mormon will show that others have tried their hand at punctuating these phrases.

But it is time to turn to Mr. Fahd's study of belomancy in the ancient Near East. Belomancy is the practice of divination by shooting, tossing, shaking, or otherwise manipulating rods, darts, pointers, or other sticks, all originally derived from arrows. Over ten years ago the present writer made a fairly exhaustive study of ancient arrow-divination, and some years later presented in the pages of the *Era* a long discourse on the ritual use of sticks and rods, especially in ancient Israel.[49] Yet it was not until he saw Fahd's study, the first full-length treatment of old Semitic arrow-divination, that it dawned upon him that these old practices might have some connection with the Liahona. For the commonest use of divination arrows, and probably their original purpose, was, according to the forgotten evidence unearthed by the diligent Fahd, the direction of travelers in the desert.

Fahd begins by pointing out that the "arrows" used in divination, called *qid-h* or *zalam,* were devoid of heads and feathers, being mere shafts or pointers.[50] Since Lane has given a fuller description of these objects from the sources, we can do no better than quote *his quotations*:

"*Zalam,* plural *azlām* [divining—] arrows by means of which the Arabs in the Time of Ignorance (i.e., before Islam) sought to know what was allotted to them: they were arrows upon which the Arabs in the Time of Ignorance wrote 'Command' and 'Prohibition'; or upon some of which was written 'My Lord hath commanded me'; and upon some, 'My Lord hath forbidden me'; or they were three arrows; upon one of which was written 'My Lord hath commanded me'; etc., . . . and the third was blank; and they put them in a receptacle, and took forth an arrow; and if the arrow upon which was 'Command' came forth, he went to accomplish his purpose; but if that upon which 'Prohibition' was written came forth, he refrained; and if the blank came forth, they shuffled the second . . . The *zilam* [were arrows that] belonged to the Kureysh, in the Time of Ignorance, upon which were written 'He hath commanded,' and 'He hath forbidden,' and 'Do thou' and 'Do thou not'; they had been well shaped and made even, and placed in the Kaabeh (the holy shrine of Meccah) . . . and when a man desired to go on a journey, or to

---

[49]"The Stick of Judah and the Stick of Joseph," *Improvement Era,* Vol. 56, Jan. 1953 to May, 1953. (5 articles).
[50]T. Fahd, "*Une Pratique cleromantique a la Ka'ba preislamique,*" *Semitica,* VIII (1958), p. 61.

marry, he came to the minister, and said, 'Take thou forth for me *zalam*'; and thereupon he would take it forth and look at it. . . . There were seven arrows thus called with the minister of the Kaabeh, having marks upon them, and used for this purpose: and sometimes there were with the man two such arrows, which he put into a sword-case; and when he desired to seek knowledge of what was allotted to him, he took forth one of them."[51]

But why arrows? Because, as we have shown elsewhere, the shooting of arrows is a universal form of divination, "as is evident in the prayers that the legendary heroes of the steppe-Finnish, Norse, Russian, Kazakh, Turkish, and Yakut—address to their three enchanted arrows before releasing them, and for instance, in the arrow-prayers of the Indian and Bedouin, all eloquently expressing the humility of men about to entrust their lives and their fate to a power beyond their control."[52] The consultation of the arrows by one about to marry was, according to Gaster, also an old Jewish custom; the parties concerned would throw rods into the air "reading their message by the manner of their fall; this, Gaster observes, is 'tantamount' to the shooting of arrows.[53] Other substitutes for shooting were shaking or drawing from a bag or quiver, balancing on the finger, or spinning on a pivot."[54]

In the New World "the autotype . . . possibly of all Indian dice games is one in which the arrows or darts are tossed or shot at an arrow tossed or shot to the ground so

[51]E. W. Lane, *Arabic-English Lexicon*, I, 1247, s.v. *zalam*.
[52]H. Nibley, "The Arrow, the Hunter, and the State," *Western Political Quarterly*, II (1949), pp. 330f.
[53]*Ibid.*, p. 335.
[54]Thus the priests at Jerusalem used to practise divination "by tossing their writing-pens," J. Wellhausen, *Reste Arabischen Heidentums* (Berlin, 1897), p. 133. G. Jacob, *Altarabisches Bedouinenleben* (Berlin, 1897), p. 110, n.2, comments on the resemblance between the shaking of Arab divination arrows and "the tossing of rune-staffs" by our own northern ancestors. In all Celtic languages divination by rods is called "throwing the wood," according to G. Dottin, in *Hastings Encyclop. of Relig. & Ethics*, IV, 788. For cases of balancing and spinning, K. F. Karjalainen, *Die Religion der Jurga-Volker*, in *Folklore Fellows Communications*, No. 63 (Helsinki, 1927), pp. 322f.

that it falls across the other. . . ." More often than not, the arrows in question were mere sticks or pointers.[55] In Arabic *sāhamahu* means both to shoot arrows with another and to draw lots or practise sortilege with one. There was no more popular form of divination among the magic-minded Babylonians than arrow-lottery, and Meissner suggests that 'casting lots' in Babylonian (*salu sha puni*) refers to an original shaking or shooting of arrows.[56]

All this shaking, tossing, and shooting emphasizes the divinatory office of arrows as *pointers;*[57] but along with that they also conveyed their message, as the passages from Lane demonstrate, by the *writing* that was upon them. Fahd notes that "on the arrows words were inscribed, determining the object of the cleromantic consultation."[58] Whenever divination arrows are described, they are invariably found to have writing on them, like the Zuni "word-painted arrows of destiny."[59] The Arabic proverb for "Know thyself!" is *absir wasma qidhika*, literally, "Examine the mark on thy divination-arrow!"[60] It has even been maintained that writing originated with the marking of arrows,[61] but whether this be so or not, it is certain that men from the earliest times have sought guidance by consulting the pointings and the inscriptions of headless and tailless arrows.

[55]S. Culin, *Games of the North American Indians* (Washington: Smithsonian Inst., 1907), pp. 383, 33, 45.

[56]B. Meissner, *Babylonien u. Assyrien* (Heidelberg, 1926), II, 65, 275, citing Ezek. 21:21ff.

[57]Abaris, the missionary who brought the cult of Apollo to Greece from the far North in prehistoric times, was guided in his travels by his patron's mantic arrow, just as later the traveling mystic Pythagoras had a special arrow "that showed him the way to go, and supplied him with substitutes for food and drink" in his wanderings; see Crusius, in Roscher's *Lexikon*, I, 2815-7, 2822; E. Bethe, in Pauly-Wissowa, *Realenzyklop. der Altertumswiss.*, I, 16. Instances of the magic arrow that shows where to find the princess, build the shrine, locate lost treasure, etc., may be found in Stith Thompson, *Motif-Index of Folk-Literature* (Bloomington, Ind., 1932-6), D 1653; H. Bachtold-Staubli, *Handwortenbuch des dt. Aberglaubens* (Leipzig, 1927ff.), 6, 1957-8; P. Sebillot, *Le Folk-Lore de France* (Paris, 1907), 4, 116, etc.

[58]T. Fahd, *op. cit.*, p. 66.

[59]This phenomenon is discussed at length by Nibley, *op. cit.*, pp. 329-339.

[60]Lane, Lexicon, *s.v. wasm*, 3053f.

[61]This was Hilprecht's theory. Nibley, *op. cit.*, pp. 338f.

The word for "divination-arrow" in the above proverb
was *qidh*, defined in Lane as one of the "two arrows used
in sortilege." The original and natural number of arrows
used in divination seems to have been two. Even when the
"magic three" were used, the third was a dud, the *manih*,
which is a blank "to which no lot is assigned."[62] It is the
other two that do the work. On the same day on which the
king of Persia shook out the divining-sticks (the *baresma*),
the Jews would draw three boxwood lots to choose the
scapegoat; but the Talmud says there were only two lots
and they were of boxwood or gold.[63]

The reason for the two basic staves is apparent from
their normal designation as "Command" and "Prohibition."
To this the priests at some shrines added a third arrow
called the "Expectative"—"Wait and see!"[64] But the original
arrangement was that *two* arrows designated the advisa-
bility or inadvisability of a journey"; they were designated
as "the *safr* (*Go ahead!*) and the *khadr* (Stay where you
are!)."[65] From passages in Lane it is clear that the regular
consultant of the arrows were those faced with travel-
problems—all others are secondary. The patron of the
caravans of the Hejaz from time immemorial was the
archer-god Abgal, "the lord of omens," in his capacity of
the master of the arrows of divination.[66] The inscriptions
on the arrows themselves give top priority to travel: typical
examples from the various systems, which employ from
two all the way to ten arrows, are "Go slow!" (*bata'*),

---

[62]Wellhausen, *op. cit.*, pp. 46f. Throughout the East three is the usual
number of arrows used in divination, G. Jacob, *op. cit.*, p. 110. F. Hommel,
Ethnologie und Geographe des alten Orients (Munich, 1926), pp. 717, 733f.,
speculates on the possible identity of the oracular arrows of Apollo, which
"appear to have resembled Zulu divining sticks," according to L. R. Farnell,
Cults of the Greek States, IV, 188. The oracular gods of the Aztecs carried
three divination arrows and an atlatl stick, E. G. Seler, *Gesammelte Abhand-
lungen* (Berlin, 1902), III, 341.
[63]Joma, Fol. 37a; Levit. 16:8.
[64]Fahd, *op. cit.*, pp. 67f.
[65]*Ibid.*, p. 68.
[66]*Ibid.*, p. 75.

"*Speed up!*" (*sari*), "Water!", "Stay where you are!" "Get moving!" "You are in the clear," etc.[67]

It would be an obtuse reader indeed who needed one to spell out for him the *resemblance* between ancient arrow-divination and the Liahona: two "spindles or pointers" bearing written instructions provide superhuman guidance for travelers in the desert. What more could you want? But what is the *relationship* between them? On this the Book of Mormon is remarkably specific. Both Nephi and Alma go out of their way to insist that the Liahona did not work itself, i.e., was not a magic thing, but worked only by the power of God and only for appointed persons who had faith in that power.

Moreover, while both men marvel at the wonderful workmanship of the brass ball in which the pointers were mounted, they refer to the operation of those pointers as "a very small thing," so familiar to Lehi's people that they hardly gave it a second glance. So contemptuous were they of the "small means" by which "those miracles were worked" for their guidance and preservation that they constantly "forgot to exercise their faith" so that the compass would work. This suggests that aside from the workmanship of the mounting, there was nothing particularly strange or mystifying about the apparatus which Alma specifies as a "temporal" thing.

Here we have an instructive parallel in the ship and the bow that Nephi made. Without divine intervention those indispensable aids to survival would never have come to the rescue of Lehi's company—their possession was a miracle. Yet what were they after all? An ordinary ship and an ordinary bow. Just so, the Liahona was "a very small thing" for all its marvelous provenience, having much the same relationship to other directing arrows that the ship and the bow did to other ships and bows. We must not forget that the ancients looked upon even ordinary *azlam*

[67]*Ibid.*, pp. 68-70.

as a means of communication with the divine: "In view of
the importance of religious sentiment in every aspect of
the activity of the Arab and of the Semite in general,"
writes Fahd, "I do not believe that one can separate these
practices (i.e., of arrow-divination) from their character
as a consultation of divinity . . . they always believed,
however vaguely, in a direct and constant intervention in
human affairs."[68]

Like the wonderful staff of Moses in Jewish history,
these things suggest remote times and occasions when,
according to popular belief, God communicates more
directly with men than he does now. Tha'labi knows of a
Hebrew tradition that Moses led the children of Israel
through the wilderness with the aid of a double arrow
mounted on the end of his staff.[69] Such a device seems
to be represented as a very ancient cult object in Egypt,
going back to the earliest migrations.[70] This is certainly
implied in the status of the ritual arrows or marked sticks
among the American Indians, regarding which Culin
writes: ". . . behind both ceremonies and games there
existed some widespread myth from which both derived
their impulse, though what this mysterious tradition is he
does not know.[71] Consistent with their holiness, "the consulting of the mantic arrows," according to one Ibn Ishaq,

---

[68]*Ibid.*, pp. 71f.

[69]Tha'labi, *Qissas al-Anbiya*, p. 123. For the latest on arrow-divination,
K. Rudolph, *Die Mandäer* (Vandenhoeck & Ruprecht, 1960), I, 173-5, 251.

[70]Massoulard, *Préhistoire et Protohistoire d'Egypte* (Paris, 1949), p. 489.
The symbol both of Min of Coptos and the lady Nieth was two arrows crossed,
sometimes mounted on the top of a pole. Can this refer to the prehistoric
migration over which these archaic deities prescribed?

[71]S. Culin, *l.c.* The Indians would learn their fortunes for the coming
year by consulting divination arrows. A. C. Fletcher & F. La Flesche, in *U.S.
Bureau of Ethnology*, XXVII (1905-6), 274. La Flesche notes, *Smithsonian
Rept.*, 1926, p. 494, that "each of the seven principal gentes (of the Omaha)
is represented by one of these mystic arrows, which are used to foretell what
will happen, good or bad, to each gens during the year following," and also
that the Indians give their sons names which "refer to the mysterious charac-
teristics of the divining arrow." A sacred arrow-bundle, the most prized
possession of the Cheyennes, is compared by Fowkes, *Bur. Ethnol.*, XIII
(1891-2), p. 116, to the Hebrew Ark of the Covenant, which also contained
divination rods, for which see Nibley, *op. cit.*, p. 337, and *Improvement Era*,
56 (Feb. 1953), p. 91.

"seems to have been reserved to questions of general public concern and to solemn occasions of life and death."[72] Which again reminds us of the Liahona, ". . . that if they would look, they might live." (Alma 37:46.)

Was the Liahona, then, just old magic? No, it is precisely here that Nephi and Alma are most emphatic—unlike magic things, these pointers worked solely by the power of God, and then, too, for only those designated to use them. *Anybody* about to make a journey could consult the mantic arrows at the shrines, and to this day throughout the world mantic arrows are still being consulted. But it is clear from Alma's words that in his day the Liahona had been out of operation for centuries, having functioned only for a true man of God and only for one special journey.

Another man of God, Lehi's great contemporary, Ezekiel, showed a remarkable interest in divinatory sticks and rods, as we have pointed out elsewhere, and he describes how the fate of certain wicked cities is sealed as God "shakes out the arrows," each one being marked with the name of a condemned city.[73]

Where, then, does one draw the line between the sacred and the profane? Religion becomes magic when the power by which things operate is transferred from God to the things themselves. As Fahd notes, the Arabs were extremely vague about the powers with which they dealt, as "primitive" people are everywhere. When men lack revelation they commonly come to think of power as residing in things. Did the staff of Moses make water come from the rock or cause the Red Sea to part? Of course not; yet in time the miraculous powers which were displayed through its agency came to be attributed by men to the

---

[72]Fahd, *op. cit.,* p. 72.

[73]Ezek. 21:21-26, discussed by Meissner, *op. cit.,* II, 275. St. Jerome, an expert in Jewish customs, says these staves bore "cut or painted upon them the names of individuals," (cited by Wellhausen, *Reste,* p. 132). Fahd, p. 73, notes that the original meaning of the Hebrew word *qesem* "divination," is "to consult the arrows." Actually it means to *cut* the arrows, being the exact equivalent of the Old Norse expression *skera or upp.*

staff itself. It became a magic thing, like Solomon's seal, which possessed *in itself* the wonder-working powers which gave Solomon his ascendancy over men and beasts.

In time the Bible became a magic book in men's eyes, conveying all knowledge by its own power, without the aid of revelation. So also after a fierce controversy on the matter, priesthood itself acquired the status of a thing that automatically bestows power and grace, regardless of the spiritual or moral qualifications of its possessor—it became a magic thing. Strangest of all, science has consistently supplanted religion by magic when dealing with final causes. When Sir Charles Sherrington, for example, after describing the incredibly complex and perfect workings of the eye, insists that it is the cells *themselves* that agree to cooperate in the miracle of seeing, following an indescribably complex plan of development which they themselves have worked out, in short, that the eye makes *itself*, he is simply appealing to the old doctrine of the magicians, that things in themselves possess wondrous powers of performance.[74]

Hunters and medicine men throughout the world who use arrows to bring them luck pray to their arrows, blow on them, and talk to them, as gamblers do to dice and cards—for at an early date "the use of divination arrows drifted down into the vulgarization of gaming cards," i.e., the practice quickly degenerated to magic.[75] That is why it is so important to understand, and why the Book of Mormon is at such pains to make perfectly clear, that the Liahona was *not* magic. It did not work itself, like other divination arrows, in any sense or to any degree.

And yet it seems to have been an ordinary and familiar object, a "temporal thing," which could also serve as "a type and a shadow," teaching us how God uses "small things" to bring about great purposes. Here we have an

[74]Sir Charles Sherrington, *Man on his Nature* (N.Y.: Doubleday Anchor, 1953), Ch. iv, "The Wisdom of the Body."
[75]W. M. F. Petrie, *Scarabs and Cylinders with Names* (Br. Mus., 1917), p. 4.

implement which, far from being the invention of a brain-sick imagination, was not without its ancient counterparts.

If we were to stop here, this would probably be the only article ever written about the Liahona that did not attempt to explain the meaning of the name. Fortunately the Book of Mormon has already given us the answer: ". . . our fathers called it Liahona, which is, being interpreted, a compass." Liahona is here clearly designated as an Old World word from the forgotten language of the fathers, which must be interpreted to present readers. But what is a compass? According to the Oxford dictionary, the derivation of the word remains a mystery; it has two basic meanings, but which has priority nobody knows: the one is "to pass or step together," referring always to a *pair* of things in motion; the other refers to the nature of that motion in a circle, "to pass or step completely," to complete a "circumference, circle, round," to embrace or enclose completely. Thus whether it refers to the ball or the arrows, "compass" is the best possible word to describe the device, though generations of Book of Mormon critics have laughed their heads off at the occurrence of the modern word in what purports to be an ancient book.

CHAPTER 10

Prophets in the Wilderness

The Desert Sectaries

It is only in our own generation that we have begun to realize the enormous importance in Judaism and Christianity of the people who flee to the desert. They are not merely a few fanatical dissenters, "outcasts of the people" (paritzim)—they are the Chosen People itself, *das wanderne Gottesvolk,* a persecuted minority ever moving apart from a once-holy nation that has become corrupted with the things of the world, to preserve the old covenants in their purity and await further light from heaven.[1] This is the main theme of the Book of Mormon as we are now beginning to realize it is of the Old and New Testaments. The people of the Testaments are the poor and outcast of the world who await the coming of the Messiah, and such were the Nephites.

The main idea is implemented in a particular way. The beliefs and practices that meet us in the Dead Sea Scrolls go back to a much earlier period than that of the sectaries of Qumran, and continue on down for many centuries after them. They are the same procedures and practices that meet us in the Book of Mormon.

A Recapitulation

Since it is normal procedure to list parallels between Qumran and this or that book or society, and since the

---

[1] E. Kaesemann, *Das wandernde Gottesvolk* (Gottingen, 1939); U. W. Mauser, *Christ in the Wilderness* (London: SCM Press, 1963).

Al Raquim Ruins.

significance of such parallels is greatly enhanced by their
cumulative effect, the following list needs no apology or
explanation.

(1) First of all, the Book of Mormon opens with a
group of pious separatists from Jerusalem moving into
the refuge of the Judaean wilderness in the hopes of
making a permanent settlement where they could live
their religion in its purity free from the persecution of
"the Jews at Jerusalem." This we pointed out in *Lehi in the
Desert* before the publication of any of the Dead Sea
Scrolls. The parallel needs no comment. (2) These people,
like those at Qumran, have a passion for writing and
reading which seems to be a long-standing family tradition;
they make records of everything, and (3) they know of an
ancient tradition of the sealing up and burying of holy
books in time of danger, to come forth "in their purity"
at a later time. (4) They themselves engage in the practice,
in which they even employ for their most valuable records
copper and gold sheets on which they laboriously engrave
their message in a cramped and abbreviated script. (5)
Both peoples apply all the scriptures to themselves in a
special way and never tire of presenting and discussing
"proof-texts." (6) Both societies held a peculiarly "open-
ended" view of scriptures and revelation and knew of no
canon of the Old Testament but accepted some of the
"Apocrypha" as inspired writings. This attitude appears
commonplace today, but we must remember that it has
been quite alien to conventional Christianity and Jewish
thinking and has been the one aspect of the Book of
Mormon which has been most loudly denounced and
ridiculed for over a century.

(7) In both the Book of Mormon and the Dead Sea
Scrolls, the peculiar and until now quite unfamiliar concept of a "church of anticipation" is very conspicuous.
(8) The religious communities in both hemispheres strove
to keep the Law of Moses in all its perfection and were

cool towards "the Jews in Jerusalem" who they felt had been false to the covenant by their worldliness. (9) They felt themselves in both cases to be the real Elect of God, the true Israel, chosen to prepare the way for the coming of the Messiah. (10) Specifically, they both think of themselves as Israel in the wilderness and consciously preserve the camp life of the desert. (11) Both have suffered persecution and expect to suffer more, being repeatedly required to seek refuge by moving from one place to another. (12) Both societies are under the leadership of inspired men (designated in both traditions as "stars")—prophets and martyrs (13) whose main message is the coming of the Messiah and (14) whose exhortation is to "righteousness" and repentance—Israel must turn away from her sins and return to the covenant. (15) In both cases a sign of the return to the covenant and to purity was baptism with water.

(16) Both societies were headed by twelve chiefs from whom were chosen a special presidency of three,[1a] and (17) both were formed into groups of fifty for instructional and administrative purposes, each group being under the direction of a priest;[2] (18) for in both societies the old priesthood was still respected and the leaders had to be legitimate priests. (19) In both societies the chief priest or leader of the whole church traveled about among the congregations giving instructions and exhortations. (20) Both societies were secret and exclusive but would admit to membership anyone in Israel who sought to live the covenant in righteousness.[3] (21) Both societies were strict observers of the Sabbath, but set aside another day of the week for their special meetings. (22) Those who joined either group were required to share their earthly wealth with all their fellow members, and (23) though both

---

[1a]This system has been examined in an article by Bo Reicke in Stendahl, *op. cit.*, pp. 143-156.
[2]Mosiah 18:18.
[3]*Ibid.*, 18:5-6.

groups were hierarchical and strictly authoritarian, a feeling of perfect equality prevailed.[4] (24) All devoted their lives to religious activity (study, preaching, discussion, prayer, and the singing and composing of hymns) and to physical labor, even the leaders working for their own support. (25) The headquarters of the societies seem to have looked remarkably alike: both were at special watering places in the desert with sheltering clumps of trees. (26) Since Alma's church shared all things in common, they probably had communal meals, like the Essenes. When Alma says to his followers: "Come unto me and . . . ye shall eat and drink of the bread and the waters of life freely" (Alma 5:34), it was plainly imagery that his hearers understood.

(27) As strict observers of the Law of Moses, both groups respected the Temple and anticipated its perfect restoration. One of the first things Nephi's community did when they went out by themselves was to build a replica of the Temple. Such an idea has been thought utterly preposterous by the critics until the discovery in the present century of other Jewish colonies in distant lands building just such duplicates of the Temple. (28) Both groups, unlike the Jews at Jerusalem, regarded the Law of Moses only as a preparation, albeit an indispensable preparation, for more light to come, it "pointing their minds forward" to a fuller revelation of salvation.

(29) Doctrinally, a fundamental teaching of both societies was the idea of a divine plan laid down in the heavens at the foundation of the world, each individual having a claim or "lot" in the knowledge and the fruits of the plan. (30) Historically this plan is unfolded apocalyptically in a series of dispensations, each divine visitation being followed by the apostasy and punishment of the people, necessitating a later restoration of the covenant. (31) This restoration is brought about through the

---

[4]Bo Reicke comments on this; *op. cit.*, pp. 154-6.

righteous Remnant, the few who remain faithful in Israel and continue to look for the Messiah and the signs of his coming. (32) The series of visitations and "ends" will be consummated with a final destruction of the wicked by fire.

(33) Meanwhile, all men are being tested: both teachings lay great stress on the dualistic nature of this time of probation in which there "must needs be . . . an opposition in all things." (2 Nephi 2:11.) (34) In this and other things both bodies of scripture show a peculiar affinity for the writings of John. (34) Both groups persistently designate themselves as "the poor," emphasizing thereby their position as outcasts. This is strikingly illustrated in the Book of Mormon in an episode from the mission of Alma.

When a large crowd gathered on a hillside outside a certain city to hear Alma preach, one of their leaders told Alma that these people were largely social outcasts, ". . . for they are despised of all men because of their poverty, yea, and more especially by our priests; for they have cast us out of our synagogues which we have labored abundantly to build with our own hands; and they have cast us out because of our exceeding poverty; and we have no place to worship our God; and behold, what shall we do?" (Alma 32:5.) It is among such people that Alma gathers recruits for his society, meeting with total rebuff at the hands of the upper classes and the priests.

The arresting point here is that a number of recent studies reach the conclusion that the mysterious demise of the Mayan civilization was brought about by just such exclusion of the masses from participation in the life of the great religious centers. The Mayan cities were not "cities in our sense of the word," we are told, but "ritual centres, where the people gathered for festivals but where nobody lived. Priests and nobility resided on the outskirts, the people in scattered settlements."[5] There came a time when "one by one the great ceremonial centres . . . were deserted. In some the end came so quickly that buildings were left half-finished. . . ." And yet "the peasants appear to have remained in their homes." What could have happened? "The most logical explanation," writes J. E. S. Thompson, "is that the old cooperation of peasant and hierarchy broke down, and that the peasant revolted and drove out or massacred the small ruling class of priest-nobles and their immediate followers."[6] In the end the poor took their revenge on the haughty priests who excluded them from the ceremonial places which had been built with the labor of their own hands. This would seem to have been an old pattern of things in the New World, by no means limited to the later Mayas. Alma describes it clearly.

And this brings us to another type of parallel. For after all, there is a good deal of secular information in the Book of Mormon.

The Tie-up

We have noted that the teachings and expressions of the Dead Sea Scrolls turn up at various times and places all over the Near East, showing that they must be seriously considered in any thorough study of Judaism or Christianity. Since the Scrolls are but "the opening of a tiny window on to the life and customs of a remarkable group of people lost to history,"[7] it is surprising when we look through other windows to find ourselves looking at much the same scene. The phenomenon is explained today

---

[5]J. E. S. Thompson, in Ed. Bacon (ed.), *Vanished Civilizations* (N.Y.: McGraw Hill, 1963), p. 146.

[6]*Ibid.*, pp. 166-8.

[7]Y. Yadin, *The Message of the Scrolls* (N.Y.: Simon & Schuster, 1957), p. 189.

by the fact that the Scrolls and other bodies of Jewish
and Christian scripture all draw on a common source.
Thus, Gilkes notes, Deuteronomy, Isaiah, and the Psalms
are Jesus' favorite sources, "which appear to have been
the favorite reading also at Qumran."[8] The windows
actually look out upon the same scene, but from different
distances and at different angles. They are "mirrors re-
flecting the same source," as Leaney puts it—offshoots of
the same trunk.[9] The Scrolls, says Father Milik, are "essentially an authentic projection of the Old Testament," with
a special brand of piety, "oriented toward intimate union
with God and the angels."[10] Each of these statements
expresses remarkably well what the Book of Mormon
claimed for itself at a time when the idea was considered
blasphemous of the mere existence of anything that could
be called "an authentic projection" of scripture. Today
the world possesses a mass of documents that not only
vindicate the idea of such writings existing and surviving
but make it possible to put various unclassified writings
to the test as they appear. The value of both the Qumran
and Nag Hammadi texts is that they are both links in a
long chain, not being at either end of it but somewhere
in the middle: the connections run forward and back.
"There is some evidence," writes F. F. Bruce, "that certain
beliefs and practices akin to those maintained at Qumran
reappeared in other communities, possibly under the influence of men of Qumran who escaped destruction."[11]
Cullmann sees such a survival in the Mandaeans, and
Schoeps in the Ebionites. In the other direction, Qumran
itself is such a survival, consciously seeking to preserve
the inspired leadership and customs of ancient Israel in

---

[8]A. N. Gilkes, *The Impact of the Dead Sea Scrolls* (London: Macmillan, 1962), p. 146.
[9]A. R. C. Leaney, *Guide to the Scrolls*, pp. 85, 95.
[10]J. T. Milik, *Ten Years of Discovery*, p. 97.
[11]F. F. Bruce, *Second Thoughts*, pp. 136f.

the desert; there, as K. Kuhn points out, "we get hold of the fundamental source of John's Gospel, and this source is Palestinian-Jewish," but not the conventional type: "Not, however, Pharisaic-Rabbinic Judaism, but a Palestinian-Jewish pietistic sect of gnostic structure."[12] Like the Coptic texts from Egypt, the designation of these writings as "gnostic" simply serves notice that their real background is still unknown. But it was certainly old. "The Qumran covenanters," writes Bruce, "bound themselves by a new covenant, but it was not so new as they thought; it was . . . a reaffirmation of the old covenant of Moses's day."[13] But no one knew that better than the covenanters themselves, the opening lines of whose *Manual of Discipline* declare the object of the society to be the carrying out of "all that he had commanded by the hand of Moses and by the hand of his servants the prophets."

We need not discuss the various points of resemblance between the New Testament and the Dead Sea Scrolls, every one of which has been warmly defended by some experts and just as warmly disputed by others. They include such things as the presence in both communities— Christian and pre-Christian—of a hierarchal organization including a council of twelve and its presidency of three, the belief in continuing revelation and the leadership of inspired prophetic men, the idea of the restoration of the covenant to the elect of Israel, the dualistic doctrine of the world as a place of probations in which all are confronted by both good and evil and obliged to make a choice, common rites and ordinances such as baptism and a sacramental meal, common ideas about the expected Messiah, common usages and expressions such as reference to the community as "the poor," a peculiar way of interpreting the scriptures and applying all the past history of Israel

---

[12]K. G. Kuhn in *Zeitschrift für Kirche u. Idealogie*, 47 (1950), p. 120.
[13]Bruce, *op. cit.*, p. 147.

to their own experiences.[14] The points of *difference,* on the other hand, are harder to find and easier to explain, since they almost invariably rest on the individual scholar's interpretation of what Christianity *should* be; the principal items are the differing attitudes of the two societies to the priesthood, the contrast between the "once-for-all" baptism of the Christians and the washings of the Essenes, the difference between the behavior of John the Baptist and the Qumran sectaries, the different attitudes towards sinners in the two churches, and above all the concept of the Messiah as one who is to come at Qumran but for the Christians has already arrived.[15] These objections to linking the New Testament with the Scrolls all rest on the basic fallacy that we know all there is to know about both societies, whereas the very purpose of studying the Scrolls is to learn more about both. But aside from that aren't the main points of difference between the pre-Christian and the early-Christian societies in the Old World precisely the same points of difference that appear in the Book of Mormon between the church as it was before the coming of Christ and as it was after? (See pp. 198-199).

There is a tantalizing link between the Old Testament, the New Testament, and the Book of Mormon in the strange sect of the Mandaeans. This ancient society, remnants of which still survive, traces its origin back to Jerusalem, whence they are said to have migrated first into

---

[14]Most popular books on the Scrolls, including all referred to so far in these notes, contain a chapter on the DS Scrolls and the New Testament. Stendahl's entire book is devoted to the subject; lists of points of resemblance may be found also in J. T. Milik, *Ten Years of Discovery in the Wilderness of Judaea* (Naperville, Ill.: A. R. Allenson, 1959), p. 98, and A. Dupont-Sommer, *The Jewish Sect of Qumran and the Essenes* (London: Vallentine, Mitchell, 1954), pp. 147-166. For a complete bibliography, H. Braun, "Qumran and das N.T." in *Theologischer Rundschau,* 28 (1962), pp. 97-234; and 29 (1963), pp. 142-176, 189-260.

[15]These points are brought up by W. F. Albright and discussed by Bruce, *op. cit.,* p. 146. Largely devoted to minimizing any resemblances between the Scrolls and the New Testament are A. R. C. Leaney, *Guide to the Scrolls* (London: SCM Press, 1958), pp. 68ff., and G. Graystone, *The Dead Sea Scrolls and the Originality of Christ* (N.Y.: Sheed and Ward, 1956), see esp. pp. 26, 63.

the desert of Judaea, where they flourished as a typical "baptist" sect for a while (they always display special devotion to John the Baptist).[16] After that they migrated to Harran and then to southern Mesopotamia where a handful of them still practice rites especially baptism, and teach secret doctrines that are at once Jewish and Christian, with a rich Iranian mixture.[17] Their departure from Judaea has been placed in the time of Isaiah, that is, even before the time of Lehi.[18] Inevitably their teachings were "sucked into the Gnostic whirlpool" and became exceedingly hard to disentangle,[19] since they "reflect theosophic theories held by certain gnostic groups scattered throughout the Middle East . . ."[20] It is typical of the Mandaeans that though "entirely independent of Christian influence, they kept Sunday as a holy day."[21] Their practices look so very Christian that Alfred Loisy could write that "Mandeism cannot be understood without reference to Christianity."[22]

Of particular interest is the great concern the Mandaeans have always had for the preparing and preservation of sacred writings. These were "wrapped, in white cloths and kept in a box, often a metal box," according to E. S. Drower.[23] One thinks at once of the practices at Qumran and among some of our Southwest Indians.[24]

---

[16]For general treatment, K. Rudolph, *Die Mandäer* (Göttingen: Vandenhoeck & Ruprecht, 1960), I, 173-5, 251; E. S. Drower, *The Mandaeans of Iraq and Iran* (Oxford, 1937).

[17]*Ibid.*, p. 252. R. Eisler, *Iesous Basileus* (Heidelberg, 1930), II, 18, 21f., 356f., 699.

[18]A. Adam, in *Ztschr. für die Neutestamentliche Wissenschaft*, Beiheft 24, p. 79.

[19]On the confusion of their doctrines with those of other groups, S. A. Pallis, *Mandaean Studies* (London: H. Milford, 1926), pp. 1-7, 188, 203-5; K. Rudolph, *op. cit.*, pp. 19-22 (relations to primitive Christianity, 36-41 (to the Sabaeans), 44 (to the Manichaeans), 253f. (to Jews, Greeks, Persians).

[20]E. Drower, *Commentary on the Alma Rishaia Rba*, p. vii.

[21]A. Adam, *loc. cit.*

[22]A. Loisy, *Le Mandeisme et les Origines Chretiennes* (Paris: Nourry, 1934), p. 142. For scholars of an earlier day, confusion was the very essence of Mandaeanism, A. J. H. W. Brandt, *Die Mandäische Religion* (Leipzig, 1889), pp. 48ff.

[23]E. S. Drower, *The Mandaeans of Iraq and Iran*, p. 23.

[24]The Scrolls were wrapped in white cloths before being put in their storage-jars. The writer has been shown sacred stones covered with glyphs which certain Indian tribes keep wrapped in cloths and stored in boxes.

There is one important difference with Qumran, however, for the Mandaean texts were never written on parchment, but only "on papyrus, metal, and stone," with special preference for metal: "The reason for using metal sheets," Mrs. Drower explains, "is that they can be purified by immersion in running water before use." Lead is used because it is cheap, but where it is available copper and even silver is used. These writings are kept very secret "because they contain mysteries that should not be shown to alien eyes." Hence it is not surprising that "during times of stress and danger, the Mandaeans 'buried the books,' and this has been done, according to them, many times."[25] Thus it would seem that the Mandaeans, among the most conservative people on earth, have preserved a tradition of record-keeping that exactly matches the Nephite practices so fully described in the Book of Mormon.

And here is another strange coincidence. It is the Mandaeans who have preserved the tradition of Ram and his brother Rud, two righteous men whose language was not confounded at the time of the Tower, and who led a migration to the east and were never heard of again. Speculation has it that Ram went back to the original site of the Garden of Eden where he spent his days writing down a history of the follies of mankind. Robert Eisler readily recognized in Ram the name of Jared.[26] One Mandaean tradition makes Ram and Rud man and wife by way of explaining how they were able to found "a race of mankind."[27] It is only to be expected that many conflicting stories should spring up about these two. Today as never before scholars are diligently searching for the kernels of historic truth that lie at the core of what has heretofore been considered purely fictitious—legendary—material. It is well known that the Mandaeans through the centuries have picked up a good deal of Persian and Babylonian

---

[25]Drower, pp. 23f., 132.
[26]R. Eisler, *Iesous Basileus* (Heidelberg, 1930), I.
[27]Drower, p. 259.

lore. So if there really was a Jared and his brother who loudly advertised their intended expedition, inviting all and sundry to accompany them (Ether 1:41), they may have made enough of an impression to leave behind them an enduring memory of their departure.

The Deepening Mystery

The Mandaeans are just another of the new enigmas that baffle the student of early Christianity, but they offer a good illustration of the sort of thing we are up against. For example, Rudolph Bultmann believes that the Gospel of John is actually adapted from certain pre-Christian teachings, a full-blown gospel, in fact, of which the Mandaean writings are a true representative.[28] In identifying John's writings as a pre-Christian myth, however, Bultmann never asks himself how it comes about that these wholesale borrowings are accompanied by John's solemn repeated asseverations that he can bear personal testimony to the literal reality of all he reports. Something is badly out of focus.

By the middle of the present century scholars had found so much of the New Testament in widely scattered writings that seemed to be definitely *older* than the New Testament, that they were forced to posit the existence of a great pre-Christian "Gnostic" church flourishing all over the Near East about the time of Christ. It was this church, it was argued, that supplied the later Christians with many of their basic concepts. But if there was such a church what was its name? where was its headquarters? its shrines? its organization? its leaders, saints, and martyrs? How did it happen that the very strictest of Jewish and Christian sects did not hesitate to borrow all their main ideas from these pagans without a word of protest from anybody? How were the Jewish sectaries and early Christians able to insist that everything they taught came to

---

[28]R. Bultmann, in *Ztschr. f. N.T. Wiss.*, 24 (1925), p. 139.

them strictly through the proper sources, with never a
dissenter or outsider to challenge the claim? If Christian
scholars cling to their impossible pre-Christian Gnostic
Church in spite of everything, it is because the alternative
is so alarming.

For if the teachings of the first Christians were, as
they insisted, authentically and completely their own and
not borrowed from anybody, then the presence of those
same teachings among other and older societies in the East
can only mean that there were people in the world in pre-
Christian times who had a much fuller knowledge of the
gospel than anyone until now had dreamed possible. This
is what the Book of Mormon teaches us to expect. Its world
differs from that of conventional ancient history in being
more free and lively in its cultural exchanges and hence
characterized by a general over-all sameness. The variety
and the sameness are equally surprising in the ancient
world and equally characteristic of the Book of Mormon
scene.

Just as the ancient cultural and religious scene was
drastically changed about 600 B.C., so it was again suddenly and radically altered in the 4th century A.D. In
each case it was as if a curtain had been dropped and the
whole stage removed from our view.

With the systematic and careful wiping out of every
trace of the old religion by the doctors of the Jews and
Christians,[31] all memory of the great prophets and teachers
of the Messianic message were diligently removed from
the record: ". . . and they despised the words of plainness,
and killed the prophets, and sought for things that they
could not understand. . . ." (Jacob 4:14.) The Book of
Mormon has a good deal to say about the line of Messianic
prophets whose work and whose very names were to be
forgotten for centuries.

---

[31]We have treated this theme in "Controlling the Past," in *The Improvement Era,* Vol. 58 (January through October, 1955).

The Forgotten Prophets

Who were the Forgotten Prophets?—Not long ago a scholar in Italy observed to this writer that if Lehi had been a real prophet living in Jerusalem, there should certainly be some record of him available. But Lehi barely began his activity before he had to leave town, and according to his account the place was swarming with prophets at the time. The Lachish Letters written in the time of Lehi and discovered in 1938, now confirm this picture; one of them, Number 8, complains that the prophets of doom are undermining the morale of the people in town and country.[32] Lehi was one of those prophets of doom. "Our father Lehi was driven out of Jerusalem because he testified of these things," wrote Helaman long after. (Helaman 8:19-22.) The teachings for which he was driven out, Helaman explains were the very teachings for which other prophets had been driven out ages before: "And now I would that ye should know, that even since the days of Abraham there have been many prophets that have testified these things; yea, behold, the prophet Zenos did testify boldly; for the which he was slain. And behold, also Zenock, and also Ezias, and also Isaiah, and Jeremiah . . . and now we know that Jerusalem was destroyed according to the words of Jeremiah (they had learned the news from the Mulekites). O then, why not the Son of God come, according to his prophecy?" It was the double teaching of the destruction of the wicked of Israel and the coming of the Messiah that got all these men into trouble, including Lehi, Zenos, Zenock, and Ezias, all heretofore unknown prophets. Lehi was not the first to be chased out of Jerusalem and not the last. Today the Scrolls can tell us about that. They, too, mention forgotten prophets, driven out of Jerusalem because they denounced

---

[32]H. Torczyner, *The Lachish Letters* (London: Oxford University Press, 1938).

King Herod's Summer Palace Ruins.

its wicked inhabitants and foretold the coming of the Messiah.

One of these was the now famous Teacher of Righteousness. Of him Father J. Danielou writes: ". . . between the great prophets of the Old Testament and John the Baptist he emerges as a new link . . . one of the great figures of Israel's prophetic tradition. It is amazing that he remained so unknown for so long. Now that he is known the question arises as to what we are to do about this knowledge. . . . Why does not this message, then, form part of the inspired Scripture?"[33] The last question was prompted by the fact, pointed out by Danielou, that the prophet in question indubitably prophesied the coming of the Messiah many years before the event. So here we

[33]J. Danielou, *The Dead Sea Scrolls and Primitive Christianity* (New York: Mentor Omega Books, 1958), p. 81.

have a major prophet foretelling the coming of Christ but completely lost to the Christian and Jewish worlds.

It has often been pointed out that the scribes and pharisees of the New Testament, the legitimate descendants of "the Jews at Jerusalem" whom Nephi so often takes to task, after they had sought the death of the Lord and the apostles, also determined to eradicate every trace of Jewish apocalyptic thought as well.[34] That is why the line of Messianic prophets disappeared.

To judge by the Dead Sea Scrolls they were closely associated with the priestly line of Zadok—"the priests who remain true to the covenant"—which was also suppressed.[35] An important name in the Zadokite tradition was that of Enos, another vanished prophet; one of the first Nephite prophets also had that name.[36] Is the Zenes or Zenos, some fragments of whose words were first published in 1893, the same as our Book of Mormon Zenos?[37] At least the names can now be confirmed, as also the existence of a suppressed line of prophets and the fact that very great prophets have actually disappeared from sight because of their Messianic teachings. Let us take the case of Zenos.

The Story of Zenos

The 33rd chapter of Alma seems to include an entire hymn by Zenos. It begins:

"Thou art merciful, O God, for thou hast heard my prayer, even when I was in the wilderness. . . ." (v. 4.)

He starts with a cry of thanksgiving, as the *Thanks-*

---

[34]How well they succeeded is shown by Goodenough, *op. cit.*, I, 20-21.

[35]*Damascus Covenant*, iv, 2; *Battle Scroll*, iii, 20f.

[36]Enos is the name which John the Baptist gave himself; it is discussed by R. Eisler, *Jesous Basileus*, II, 26, 36, 42, 76, 107, etc. According to Jewish tradition, John the Baptist was the great-great-grandson of Zadok, who in turn was the great-great-grandson of Zadok, Tha'labi, *Qissas al-Anbiyah*, p. 259.

[37]Under the title Visio Zenez (Kenaz), the fragments appear in M. R. James, *Apocrypha Anecdota*, Texts and Studies (Cambridge), II, 3 (1893), 179. The fact that this Zenes is the father of Othniel puts him right in the midst of the Qumran tradition.

giving Hymns of the scrolls do, and immediately lets us know that he has spent some time in the desert calling upon God. He mingles his praise with autobiographical material exactly as the author of said Hymns does, as he continues:

". . . yea, thou wast merciful when I prayed concerning those who were mine enemies, and thou didst turn them to me." (*Idem.*)

This takes us right into the thick of things: Zenos has had enemies, but he has been able by his piety to overcome their opposition and "turn them" again to him, the expression implying that they had been his followers before. Next we learn that Zenos was a farmer or at least engaged in the agricultural pursuits characteristic of the sectarians of the desert:

"Yea, O God, and thou wast merciful unto me when I did cry unto thee in my field. . . ." (v. 5.)

By now it is fairly certain that we are dealing with a poem, each section beginning, as in the *Thanksgiving Hymns*, with the same repeated utterance of thanks: "Thou wast merciful unto me, O God!" Zenos continues:

". . . again, O God, when I did turn to my house thou didst hear me in my prayer." (v. 6.)

Either Zenos is returning to his house from the field or (more probably) is returning from his stay in the wilderness; since he is speaking of his life's crises, this would seem to indicate that after the trouble was over the prophet went back home for a time. But soon he is on the move again:

"Yea, O God, thou hast been merciful unto me, and heard my cries in the midst of thy congregations." (v. 9.)

The word "congregations" occurs only twice in the King James Bible, both times in solemn hymns of praise,[38] confirming the poetic nature of Alma's fragment. What

---

[38]I.e., in Psalms 26:12 and 68:26.

are the "congregations" in the midst of which Zenos spent his time? In contrast to the Bible, the Dead Sea Scrolls are simply full of "congregations" (half a dozen words being translated that way), referring to various communities of saints (they use that word "saints" a lot, too) who have sought to live the Law in its purity by retreating from Jerusalem and forming independent congregations in the wilderness. Since it would appear from Alma 33:4 that it was "in the wilderness" that the showdown took place which ended in turning his enemies back into his followers, and since he could only visit congregations in the plural by moving about away from home, it would seem that Zenos was a leader among those societies of Jews which had practised the custom of occasional settlement in the desert ever since the days of Joshua. For Zenos there was more trouble ahead:

"Yea, and thou hast also heard me when I have been cast out and have been despised by mine enemies. . . ." (v. 10.)

He is now discredited, despised, and thrown out— but not for long!

". . . yea, thou didst hear my cries, and wast angry with mine enemies, and thou didst visit them in thine anger with speedy destruction." (*Idem.*)

These are serious doings indeed. The tables are completely turned; the opposition is not only discomfited but also completely overthrown, apparently by force of arms, as frequently happened to the societies in the desert. So the hymn concludes on a joyful note:

". . . I will cry unto thee in all mine afflictions, for in thee is my joy; for thou hast turned thy judgments away from me, because of thy Son." (v. 11.)

But that is not the end of the story, which we must seek in Helaman 8:19: ". . . the prophet Zenos did testify boldly; for the which he was slain."

The story of an unnamed prophet. And now let us compare the ups and downs of Zenos's career with the vicissitudes of the unnamed writer of the *Thanksgiving Hymns,* who in *Hymn* "H" or No. 8 includes in the framework of a song of thanksgiving a brief sketch of his own affairs, exactly as Zenos does:

"I thank thee, O God, that thou has illuminated my countenance by thy covenant. . . . But those who have led thy people astray, those false prophets, with their many words and their flatteries . . . I was despised by them, they esteemed me as nothing, while thou didst manifest thy power in me." (P. iv, lines 1-8.)

From the provenance of the document it is probable that this, too, took place in the wilderness; the false prophets are described in terms only too familiar to readers of the Book of Mormon, and their business here, as in Zenos's story, is to lead away the saints. "Despised" is the very word used by Zenos in a like situation—"cast out and . . . despised"—and thus our poet continues:

". . . for I was cast out of my country like a bird from its nest; and all my friends and followers were turned away from me, and considered me no more than a vessel that has passed its usefulness. While those lying teachers and vain seers who formed against me a combination of the Devil, perverted the Law which thou hast engraved on my heart against their flattering words to thy people." (iv, 8-11.)

Just so, Zenos's followers were turned against him. In *Hymn* 10 or "J" the Qumran poet tells us:

"I had become . . . a symbol of strife and discord unto my friends . . . an object of murmuring and criticism to all those whom I had gathered. . . . All spoke evil of me, with a perverse tongue, they who had been members of my congregation. . . . Because of the secret which Thou hast hidden in me, they took false reports to those seeking to make trouble."[39]

The second time, it will be recalled, Zenos did not win his enemies back, but instead they suffered violent destruction—they were the implacables. The Qumran poet's enemies met a like fate:

"For thou, O God, dost scorn the machinations of the evil one. . . . they were caught in their own schemes, they who led the people away from thy covenant. . . ."[40]

Like Zenos, our hero confronts them boldly:

"As for me, since I lean on thee, I shall arise and confront those who despise me. . . . For thou didst show me thy power at day-break, and didst not cover with shame the faces of those who supported me, who joined together in thy covenant and hearkened to my voice . . . in the congregation of the saints. Thou shalt make their cause to triumph forever." (iv, 22-25.)

As he heard the prayer of Zenos "in the midst of thy congregations," so God hearkened to the voice of this poet "in the congregation of the saints." The situations of the two men—if indeed they are not one and the same person! —are remarkably alike: It is the same story of inspiration and mighty prayer, opposition, expulsion, humiliation, and ultimate triumph, and all in the wilderness and in the midst of the congregations. As told in the *Habakkuk Commentary* of the Dead Sea Scrolls, the mysterious and much-discussed "Teacher of Righteousness" experiences much the same vicissitudes.

------

[39]*Hymn* 10 (J), v, 22-25. Those seeking trouble may have been officials in Jerusalem. As Gaster renders the next lines of the poem, they may have come right out of 1 Nephi: "Because they hemmed in my way, and because of their infamy, the fount of understanding was hidden [from them]. . . ." T. H. Gaster, *op. cit.*, p. 152. "They hedged me about with thick darkness," he continues, like Nephi in the desert, ". . . my soul was overcast. Sorrow was all about me, and the pall of shame o'er my face. . . . I was bound with unbreakable cords. . . . Over my soul swirled the torrents of hell." (*Ibid.*, p. 153. Cf. 1 Nephi 12:16!).

[40]iv, 22-25. He describes his deliverance "from the congregation of vanity and the assembly of violence" in vi, 4-7.

First of all we are told that the Teacher of Righteousness had been attacked by the wicked and that the people had been turned against him by the man of lies who led them astray from the covenant (1:4-5); then we learn that the man of lies brought false charges against the righteous teacher in a general conference, and was supported by a faction who refused to come to the teacher's defense. (1:13.)

Then we hear of a wicked priest who at first seemed to be a man of integrity but later became greedy and unscrupulous in acquiring wealth (2:5-6), and then turned against the commandments of God and as a result suffered from a horrible disease. (2:7-8.) It was this priest we are next told, who persecuted the righteous teacher and delivered him into the hands of his enemies. (2:8.)

Next we learn that the teacher of lies set up his own religious community by trickery and deceit (2:12-13) and that the wicked priest pursued the Teacher of Righteousness to the place where he had fled for refuge, apparently in the desert, and there at the meeting of a community on the Day of Atonement used his authority to try to take control of the meeting and confound the teacher. (2:15.)

The next passage tells of the overthrow of the wicked priest and his ultimate disgrace, but more as a prediction and a hope than a fact: "His loss is greater than his gain . . . the cup of the wrath of God will overcome him." (2:16.) Finally, we learn that the headquarters of the wicked priest was Jerusalem, "the City," where he defiled the temple and plundered the poor. (2:18.)

Whether or not the teacher of righteousness (as has been maintained) was the author of the *Thanksgiving Hymns*, we are obviously dealing with a situation characteristic of religious sectaries with their bitter feuding between factions and leaders.[41] But though Zenos plainly

---

[41]L. E. Toombs, in *Journal of Semitic Studies*, 1 (1956), 372f., distinguishes no less than six different teachers in the Qumran literature, all of whom suffer persecution except the Messiah in his final appearance.

has much in common with these two leaders, there is one thing that brings him so close to the writer of the *Hymns* as to suggest actual identity. This is his Parable of the Olive Tree.

The Parable of the Olive Tree

It is Jacob, whose parents had spent most of their days in Jerusalem, and who thought of himself simply as an exile from that place (Jacob 7:26), who quotes the long Parable of the Olive Tree at length from the writings of Zenos: "Behold, my brethren, do ye not remember to have read the words of the prophet Zenos. . . ." (*Ibid.*, 5:1.)

Let the reader peruse this long account in Jacob chapters 5 and 6, and then consider *Hymn* 10 (also called *Hymn 0*) of the *Thanksgiving Hymns* from Qumran:

"I thank thee, O Lord, that thou hast placed me as [or in] a fountain of running water in a desert place . . . irrigating a garden [or orchard] in the desert, where . . . stand planted for thy glory alone, the trees that never die . . . putting forth branches that never wither, taking root before they blossom, reaching out their roots to the stream . . . of living waters." (viii, 1-8.)

So far the general image of the well-watered trees represents the righteous in the desert of the world. Then, more specifically, God's law is described as a special tree, an abused and battered stump, against which the other trees vaunt their superiority, "for they spread far and wide in the vineyard, though their roots do not seek the waters of the stream [i.e., the water of life], while the tree which was planted in truth and is destined to bring to flower branches of holiness keeps its secret hidden and sealed, unesteemed and unnoticed." (viii, 9-11.) What better figure for Israel among the nations than that of the tree destined to bear fruit, but for the present a damaged stump among the proud but fruitless "fir, the pine, and the cypress?" (viii, 5, 11-13.)

God has kept the fruit of the tree, we are told next, in secret reserve as long as Israel "did not believe in the wellspring of life," though the tree remained alive. The image is familiar from some of the earliest Christian writings,[42] and Zenos, who significantly gives *no* explanation of his parable any more than our hymn writer does, has the Lord say:

". . . behold, for a long time will I lay up of the fruit of my vineyard unto mine own self against the season, which speedily cometh. . . ." (Jacob 5:76.)

On the other hand, says the hymn, "the trees of the wicked shall be felled [or hewn down] . . . and fire shall go forth, and they shall wither." (viii, 19-20.) Compare this with Jacob:

". . . and the bad [shall] be hewn down and cast into the fire. . . ." (Jacob 5:66.)

It is not only the main tree that survives, however, for in the end, as in Zenos's story, ". . . the orchard which I have planted shall bloom fair for ever, . . . its trees planted in line of the sun. . . ."[43] Note the proper technical concern as well as the happy ending. The Lord tells how, "if I relax my hand, it [the tree] becomes like a thing in the desert, its branches like weeds, like briars and brambles. . . . its leaves fade before the heat; it is not exposed to water. It suffers mishap and disease and becomes a (target) for all manner of blight." (viii, 24-26.) Just so, in Zenos's account, dire consequences followed an interval of inactivity, representing, of course, the time of Israel's distress:

"And it came to pass that a long time had passed away, and the Lord of the vineyard said . . . Come, let us

---

[42]It is the concept of the "Wintertime of the Just," according to which until the return of the Lord all trees, good and bad, alive and dead, look alike since none of them has leaves; it is only in the last days that the living trees will blossom; *Pastor of Hermas*, Similitude iii.

[43]viii, 20-22; the translation is Gaster's, *op. cit.*, pp. 166-167.

. . . labor again in the vineyard . . . and behold all sorts of fruit did cumber the tree. . . .

". . . and there [was] none of it which [was] good. . . . it profiteth me nothing. . . ." (Jacob 5:29-32.)

To restore the tree the Lord of the garden must work with a will: "When I apply my hand to dig the furrows thereof," says the *Thanksgiving Hymns*, "its roots strike even on granite, its stocks are firm-grounded in the earth. . . ." (viii, 22-23.)

Through Zenos the Lord commands: ". . . dig about the trees, both old and young, first and the last. . . .

". . . prepare the way for them, that they may grow." (Jacob 5:63f.) And when this is done, ". . . the natural branches began to grow and thrive exceedingly; . . . and they did keep the root . . . thereof equal, according to the strength thereof." (v. 73.)

Special care was taken to "pluck from the tree those branches whose fruit is most bitter. . . ."[44] See vs. 52, 57, 65, 79.) In our hymn the poet complains that what he has planted has turned to bitterness, and in another of the *Thanksgiving Hymns*, it is the tree of the wicked that bears bitter fruit: "In their every thought is a root which blossoms to wormwood and gall."[45] The tree referred to here can only be an olive.

The reader can amuse himself by working out the parallels at great length and detail. Here we have two men who write exactly the same sort of poetry including a hymn of praise in the same peculiar way, an autobiographical sketch in which they suffer the identical vicissitudes under identical conditions, and the same two men develop an elaborate parable having to do with a tree and an

---

[44]cf. Gaster, *op. cit.*, p. 167: "For that which I had planted was turned into wormwood." Dupont-Sommer, however, has the poet compare himself to an abandoned tree: ". . . there was no fountain for me. . . . I was without strength; my punishment bore fruit in bitterness . . . and I could not preserve my strength." In *Semitica*, 7 (1957), pp. 67f.

[45]iv, 14; Gaster, *op. cit.*, p. 143.

orchard or garden which they leave to others to explain. If they are the same person, the discrepancies between their accounts can be readily explained by the time gap between the Book of Mormon version and the much later Qumran version. We must remember that the Dead Sea Scrolls are full of old writings, centuries older than the manuscripts containing them, even though these are the oldest known.

The Zadok after whom the community name themselves may have been traced back as far as the Jebusite Zadok of the time of David; that shows how old their traditions are.[46] We have even suggested elsewhere that the Zenock of the Book of Mormon may have been Zadok, for not only could the "n" and the "d" have been easily confused by a scribe, but the common Arabic designation for the sectarians of the desert as "Zandokites" shows that the two could be used together.[47]

All of this, of course, is simply speculation.

Zenos—Zenez?

What can be behind the coincidence of the names Zenos and Zenez? What we propose here is not to present a solution but suggest an interesting problem.

Twelve times the Book of Mormon names the prophet Zenos, next to Isaiah the most conspicuous Old World prophetic figure in the book. The people of Lehi had brought his writings with them from Jerusalem, and they were evidently popular, for preachers living hundreds of years apart enjoin the Nephites to remember what they have read of his words. (Alma 33:3; cf. Jacob 5:1.) How, one wonders, could an important prophet like Zenos, if he ever existed, have simply dropped out of sight without leaving a trace of himself in the Bible or anywhere else?

---

[46]C. E. Haner, "Who Was Zadok?" *Jnl. Bibl. Lit.*, 82 (1963), 89-94.
[47]For Zadokite—Zandokite, see H. Nibley, in *Revue de Qumran*, 18 (1965) p. 186, n. 50.

That, as we have seen is just the question that is being asked today about certain prophets now rediscovered in the Dead Sea Scrolls.

In 1893 M. R. James published Greek and Latin versions of an ancient text entitled "The vision of Zenez the Father of Gothoniel."[48] Since the father of Othniel in the Bible is Kenaz and not Zenez, James translates the title, "The Vision of Kenaz," though the name which appears in the texts is always Zenez, and James confesses himself at a loss to explain how C or K "could have been corrupted into Z"—but there it is. The text itself he finds to be "as puzzling a document as one could well wish for," its "meaning, source, date and purpose" completely eluding him; "for at first sight there seems to be no corner of apocryphal literature into which we can fit this odd fragment, so completely without context or connexions does it come before us." For one thing, it is much older than other Apocrypha: "Thus, the Vision of Kenaz would help to attest the existence of the prophetic spirit in the dark times of the Judges." Kenaz himself is one of a mysterious prophetic line: his elder brother was Caleb, "on whom the Spirit of the Lord had rested, and who is known to have figured as a seer in the Assumption of Moses." Long since James wrote that, we have learned that the *Assumption of Moses* was a familiar writing to the Qumran people, who associate themselves with this prophetic line. Also Othniel, the son of Kenaz, prophesied by the Spirit of the Lord. According to the *Jewish Encyclopedia* (*s. v. Kenaz*), Kenaz was not the father but rather the ancestor of Othniel; but a grandson of Caleb was also a Kenaz as was a grandson of Esau. The confusion is typical, but it is not necessarily confusing: after all, family names repeat themselves in any age.

Already in 1893 James noted that "the language and

---

[48]M. R. James, *Apocrypha Anecdota* (Cambridge University, 1893), pp. 174-7, being Vol. 2, No. 3 of *Texts and Studies,* J. A. Robinson, ed.

cast of thought" in Zenez "strongly resembles that of 4 Esdras," and are even closer to "the diction and thought of Ezekiel." Today this can be taken as definitely indicating that the Vision of Zenez is old and Jewish and not, as James suggests among other possibilities, "merely a medieval attempt at imitating Old Testament prophecy."

James thought that the whole Zenez or Kenaz episode, which is contained in a longer work mistitled the "Pseudo-Philo," was the free invention of a first century Jewish scribe.[49] But today we know better; as W. Lambert writes, "The authors of ancient cosmologies [such as the Zenez story] were essentially compilers. Their originality was expressed in new combinations of old themes, and in new twists to old ideas. Sheer invention was not part of their craft."[50] The author of the Zenez story was *not* inventing but dragging out a very old tradition that had become encrusted with legend and mixed with other half-forgotten stories. That is typical of apocryphal writings; but the point is that behind all this confusion lies a real historic person: the mix-up regarding his name is a sign both of antiquity and authenticity.

The Zenez fragment begins by telling how "once when the Elders were seated together the Holy indwelling Spirit came to Zenez and he took leave of his senses and began to prophesy. . . ." We may pause here to recall how God visited the Book of Mormon Zenos "in the midst of thy congregations." Like Zenos, Zenez talks like a real prophet: "Hear now ye inhabitants of the earth [or the land]. Even as they who have dwelt therein have prophesied before me, having seen this hour, in the time before the corruption of the earth [land]. . . ." Like Zenos, Zenez is conscious of being one of a line of prophets all of whom have testified of the same things (cf. Helaman 8:22); he speaks "that all ye inhabitants therein might know the prophecies

---

[49]M. R. James, *The Biblical Antiquities of Philo* (London: SPCK, 1917) p. 34.
[50]W. Lambert, in *Journal of Theological Studies*, 16 (1965), p. 279.

according to that which hath been before appointed." Here
is the familiar motif of the appointed plan which has been
taught to the world by generations of prophets.

Turning to the specific message, Zenez recalls to his
hearers' minds the state of things at the creation of the
earth; he sees "flames of fire that did not consume and
fountains bursting forth from their slumbers when there
was as yet no foundations for men to live on. When a
foundation at last appears between the upper and lower
worlds, a voice tells Zenez, "These are the foundations
prepared for men to inhabit for seven thousand years to
come." He further sees figures like people "coming out of
the light of invisible worlds," and is told that "these are
they who shall inhabit" the foundations in the name of
Adam. "And it shall come to pass that whenever he [the
earthly Adam] shall sin against Me and the fullness of
time is come, the spark shall be extinguished and the fountain dried up, and thus will things alternate." This is
speaking of the cycles of visitation and apostasy among
the children of men, a basic theme in the early Jewish
and Christian Apocrypha. "And after Zenez had spoken
these things he awoke and his spirit returned to him, and
he remembered not what he had said and seen." Then
Zenez went forth and preached to the people saying: "If
such is to be the rest [anapausis = rest in progress] of the
righteous after they have left this life [this shows that
much of the vision is missing], it behooves them to die to
the things of this corruptible world [or age], that they
may not behold its sins. And after he had said these things
Zenez died and slept with his fathers; and the people
mourned him for thirty days." He was evidently a famous
prophet, but quite forgotten. Seventy years ago James
could find no other writing with which to compare this
one, but by now the reader should be able to recognize
familiar overtones from the Scrolls, the Nag Hammadi
writings, *and* the Book of Mormon.

The long account of Cenez-Kenaz-Zenez in the
Pseudo-Philo culminates in that prophet's Testament, given
on his death-bed to his son Phineas. He tells how the
Lord appeared to him in a vision and told him of the
apostasy of Israel to come. He comforts him, however,
with the knowledge of the divine plan laid down in the
pre-existence: "Yet I (the Lord) will remember the time
. . . when I said that the world should be . . . and I will
plant a great vineyard, and order it and call it by my
name, and it shall be mine forever. But when I have done
all that I have spoken, nevertheless my planting which is
called after me, will not know me, the planter thereof, but
will corrupt his fruit. These are the things (says Phineas)
which my father commanded me to speak unto the
people."[51]

Thus the last words of "Zenez" are a discourse on the
vineyard, telling how God planned even in the pre-
existence to plant his great vineyard and call it by his
name, and how the vineyard would go to waste and ruin.
Zenos, Zenez and the author of the Thanksgiving Hymns
all tell about this vineyard which is so oddly described as
an olive-orchard—an apparent confusion now explained as
intentional by the murals of Dura Europos. At the very
least we may now affirm that there was rumor of a prophet
named Zenez or something like that, who flourished long
before 600 B.C., and who called Israel to repentance,
describing its vicissitudes in terms of an orchard or vineyard planted and cherished by God.

Could Zenos have been the author of the Thanksgiving
Hymns? He could have, but that is not necessary—he could
have lived centuries before the Qumran poet and still resemble him very closely. After all, half a dozen Zadoks
have been identified, all related and all engaged in the
same type of activity. It is a commonplace of the apocryphal writings that two heroes who behave alike become

[51]James, *op. cit.*, p. 165.

identified in the minds of later generations. Like the religious writings of the Egyptians (to which they have genuine affinity), the documents we have been considering are wholly taken up with types and images rather than with unique historical events and personalities; ancient religious texts operate to a degree which we often fail to appreciate, with interchangeable parts, characters, and names. It is hard for the analytical-minded Westerner to understand what goes on, and a vast amount of ink has been wasted on studies attempting an exclusive pinpointing of this or that character or event in the Dead Sea Scrolls. But for the people who wrote the Scrolls, it was quite possible for John to be an Elijah, or the Teacher of Righteousness, a Messiah.

CHAPTER 11

A Rigorous Test: Military History

History With Tears

Readers of the Book of Mormon often express disgust or at least weariness and impatience at having to wade through 170 pages of wars and alarms in a religious book. This writer must confess to having suffered from the same prejudice. After surviving three years of military intelligence at every level from company to army group, with frequent visits to SHAEF on the one hand and a muddy foxhole on the other, and after reading and writing thousands of reports on enemy dispositions and tactics from company sector to army front, we have always been inclined to rush through the military parts of the Book of Mormon as painful reminders of an unpleasant past. In twenty years of writing about the Book of Mormon we have studiously ignored the war stories. But that is where we were wrong.

The whole point of Alma's (or rather Mormon's) studies in "the work of death" as he calls it, is that they are supposed to be revolting—they are meant to be painful. It is Mormon and Moroni, the tragic survivors of a nation destroyed in a senseless war, who are editing this book, and they put into it whatever they think might be useful as a warning to us. It is not their purpose to tell an entertaining or reassuring tale. War is anything but glamorous in the Book of Mormon; the campaigns and battles are described not as a writer of fiction would depict ancient warfare with all its excitement and color; all that a romantically inclined young American of the 1820's would imagine as the gaudy trappings of heroic derring-do is conspicuously missing. It is real war that we see here, a tedious, sordid, plodding, joyless routine of see-saw successes and losses—brutally expensive, destructive, exhausting, and boring, with constant marches and countermarches that end sometimes in fiasco and sometimes in intensely unpleasant engagements. The author writes as one would write—as only one *could* write—who had gone through a long war as a front-line observer with his eyes wide open. Everything is strictly authentic, with the proper emphasis in the proper place. Strategy and tactics are treated with the knowledge of an expert, logistics and supply, armaments and fortifications, recruiting and training, problems of morale and support from the home front, military intelligence from cloak and dagger to scouting and patrolling; interrogation, guarding, feeding, and exchange of war prisoners, propaganda and psychological warfare, rehabilitation and resettlement, feelers for peace and negotiations at various levels; treason, profiteering and the exploitation of the war economy by individuals and groups —it is all there.

Mormon and his son are summing up the situation after spending most of their lives in the field—and they hate it. For them war is nasty, brutalizing, wasteful, dirty, degrading, fatiguing, foolish, immoral, and above all unnecessary. It is also inevitable, as long as men are running things. But before we hear their conclusions let us hear their story. For in their long and involved surveys of the wars they have supplied us with irrefutable credentials to the authenticity of the record. Let the reader judge whether anyone writing in the peaceful world of the 1820's could have faked this complicated and swiftly-moving history.

The Distinguished Military Career of Moroni

Prologue. The Cold War

The best survey of Nephite military history is supplied by the career of the great Moroni, recorded with enthusiasm and admiration almost 500 years after by the only other Nephite general who would ever compare with him, the noble Mormon, who named his son and heir after his hero. To Mormon, Moroni was "a man of a perfect understanding. . . . yea, if all men had been . . . like unto Moroni, behold the very powers of hell would have been shaken forever." (Alma 48:11, 17.) Like most great military leaders, Moroni puts in his appearance only when he is needed in a moment of great national crisis, and gracefully retires from the scene as soon as the country is safe. The story begins with a brief introductory chapter on cold war (". . . and thus commenced a war betwixt the Lamanites and Nephites . . ." Alma 35:13) which deserves the most careful study.

Observing that "the preaching of the word . . . had had more powerful effect upon the minds of the people than the sword, or anything else," (Alma 31:5) Alma had led a very powerful missionary team (Alma 31:6-7) among the Zoramites. The Zoramites were "dissenters from the Nephites" who would not "observe the performances of the church," (Alma 31:8-10) but had gone off by themselves and, in the best Nephite tradition, founded their own community between the Nephite buffer-state of Jershon and the Lamanite-controlled wilderness. (Alma 31:3.) It was felt that the hostility of the Zoramites and their proximity to the Lamanites posed a definite threat to Nephite security, and that was why Alma, "exceeding sorrowful because of the separation of the Zoramites," (Alma 31:2) and sharing the concern of his fellow Nephites, who "greatly feared that the Zoramites would enter into correspondence with the Lamanites," (Alma 31:4) gave top priority to the Zoramite mission.

The preaching of the brethren proved highly successful among one segment of the Zoramite population and thereby greatly alarmed the rest, for there was great social unrest among the Zoramites at that time. Alma and Amulek had preached to throngs of poor people sitting on the ground, (Alma 34:1) whose leaders complained that they were "despised" and "cast out of our synagogues which we have labored abundantly to build with our own hands." (Alma 32:5.) It was among this oppressed minority that the missionaries had their success, (Alma 32:2) causing "the more popular part of the Zoramites" to take counteraction, holding angry meetings to discuss the alien teaching that "did destroy their craft." (Alma 35:3.) The authorities, "their rulers and their priests and their teachers," without letting the public know what they were doing, secretly started checking up on everybody, "therefore they found out privily the minds of all the people." (Alma 35:5.) Anyone known to have been sympathetic to the teachings of the missionaries, "those who were in favor of the words . . . spoken by Alma and his brethren were cast out of the land; and they were many. . . ." (Alma 35:6.) It will be recalled that the Nephites considered it "strictly contrary to the commands of God" that there should be any "law against a man's belief." (Alma 30:7.) But these people had dissented away from the Nephites in preference for a way of life that combined a great display of religious piety with an even more impressive display of clothes and jewelry, ". . . their costly apparel, and their ringlets, and their bracelets, and their ornaments of gold, and all their precious things . . . and behold their hearts are set upon them, and yet they cry unto thee and say—We thank thee, O God, for we are a chosen people unto thee, while others shall perish." (Alma 32:28.) Such people were in no mood to listen to "the word, for it did destroy their craft; therefore they would not hearken unto the words." (Alma 35:3.) All this is relevant to show that behind the great war that follows there is an "idealogical" conflict.

It was natural that the followers of Nephite missionaries, being expelled from their own land, should follow
their new spiritual leaders "also into the land of Jershon,"
that being the nearest territory under Nephite influence.
(Alma 35:6.) And it was also natural that the inhabitants of
Jershon, the pacifist Ammonites who were themselves
refugees from the Lamanites, should give them asylum;
"and they did nourish them, and did clothe them, and did
give unto them lands for their inheritance. . . ." (Alma
35:9.) The Zoramites promptly lodged an official protest
with the Ammonites, requesting them to deport their
Zoramite refugees, (Alma 35:8) just as the Nazis protested
the asylum given to their outcast citizens by neighboring
and other nations. And just as the Nazis issued grim warnings to those who did not heed such requests and used
the situation to stir up crises and issue ultimatums, so the
Zoramites when the people of Ammon refused to comply
"breathed out many threatenings against them" through
their "chief ruler . . . a very wicked man," (Alma 35:8-9)
and used the occasion to bring on a crisis between the
Nephites and the Lamanites. For they did just what the
Nephites had feared and "began to mix with the Lamanites
and to stir them up also to anger against them." (Alma
35:10) no doubt pointing out to them that the people of
Ammon, lately dissented from the Lamanites, were now
building up strength by receiving more dissenters into
their midst, and this with the obvious approval and assistance of the Nephites. Thus two small states, set against
each other, by each appealing to a great power set two
great powers against each other: "And thus the Zoramites
and the Lamanites began to make preparations for war
against the people of Ammon, and also against the
Nephites." (Alma 35:11.) It is a story that has become
painfully familiar in our own day.

So far there had been no military action—this is strictly
"cold war." The next step was for the Nephites to evacuate

the Ammonites from Jershon, moving them to Melek; Jershon thus returned to its old status as a defense zone, now offering the Nephites a clear field of fire as the operation "gave place in the land of Jershon for the armies of the Nephites, that they might contend with the armies of the Lamanites. . . ." (Alma 35:13.) And so with mounting tensions and threats, with each side feeling itself increasingly endangered by the other, the cold war moved into a hot war. The Ammonites being pacifists moved out of the war-zone, but the recent Zoramite refugees stayed on there and armed themselves for the event. (Alma 35:14.) The Nephites felt as insecure as the Lamanites, and with good reason: this is not going to be a war of "the good guys against the bad guys." What was worrying Alma was the decline of Nephite morality; when Nephites and Lamanites lock horns there is little to choose between them in the matter of good and bad. What grieved Alma at this time was "the wars, and the bloodsheds, and the contentions which were among them"—the Nephites themselves. (Alma 35:15.) He had visited every city in the land and found the country in a deplorable state as "the hearts of the people began to wax hard" and they refused to listen to his preaching. So he sent his sons forth on special missions to the people, and he "also, himself could not rest, and he also went forth." (Alma 43:1.)

The Trouble with Zarahemnah

The Zoramites now severed all connection with the Nephites and considered themselves as being officially Lamanite. (Alma 43:4.) They invited the Lamanite hordes to move in and occupy their country as the first major move against the Nephites. (Alma 43:5.) At their head came the Lamanite commander-in-chief, the Amalekite Zerahemnah. The Amalekites were Nephite dissenters of an earlier day, and like most dissenters were more bitter against the Nephites and "of a more wicked and murderous

disposition than the Lamanites were." (Alma 43:6.) Zerahemnah had seen to it that all the key commands in the
army had gone to Amalekites like himself or to equally
ferocious Zoramites. (Alma 34:7.) So we see the Nephites
being punished for their own wickedness in more ways
than one; in fact the Lamanites appear at times as no
more than the simple-minded tools of Nephite or ex-
Nephite wickedness. Certainly Zerahemnah was using
them as his cat's paw, "for behold, his designs were to
stir up the Lamanites to anger against the Nephites; this
he did that he might usurp great power. . . ." (Alma 43:8.)
Another familiar story—the hate campaign as a means to
personal power. Zarahemnah worked on the Lamanite
resentment of the people of Ammon, whom they regarded
as traitors (Alma 43:11)—conveniently overlooking the
fact that his own people were dissenters from the Nephites
—and in time found himself in command of a huge coalition
army against the Nephites, who understandably felt themselves desperately threatened. (Alma 43:13.)

At this moment the twenty-five year old Moroni
appears on the scene, a military genius if there ever was
one. He introduced improvements in armor to make his
people far more than a match, man for man, for the enemy
(Alma 43:19-21); he arranged the Jershon defense zone,
(Alma 43:22) and being on the defensive and greatly
outnumbered, was particularly diligent in keeping a sharp
lookout on all enemy movements, at the same time inquiring of the holy prophet Alma (after what is now known
to have been an ancient custom in Israel) regarding the
enemy's plan of battle, "whither the armies of the Nephites
should go to defend themselves against the Lamanites."
(Alma 43:23.) On the other hand, the Lamanite campaign
was directed by Amalekite and Zoramite officers, whose
knowledge of Nephite military secrets and methods would
have given them an enormous advantage over any commander but Moroni. Right at the outset his foresight had

robbed them of their first and logical objective—the buffer land of Jershon. (Alma 43:22.) He had taken up his main defensive position there, but when the messengers returned from consulting the prophet he learned that the Lamanites were planning a surprise by directing their push against the more inaccessible but weaker land of Manti, where they would not be expected. (Alma 43:24.) Immediately Moroni moved his main army into Manti and put the people there in a state of preparedness. (Alma 43:25-26.)

Informed of every Lamanite move by his spies and scouts, Moroni was able to lay a trap for the enemy, catching them off-guard as they were fording the river Sidon. (Alma 43:28-35.) Here the younger Moroni inserts an apology for the use of espionage, which he realizes is not playing fair, but since "it was only the desire of the Nephites to preserve their lands and their liberty . . . therefore he thought it no sin that he should defend them by stratagem. . . ." (Alma 43:30.) The ensuing episode shows what a stickler Moroni was for fair play.

The battle at the ford was "the work of death"—no glamor and no glory; after they had crossed the river and collided with Moroni's reserves in the "west valley" the Lamanites were at bay, but this was only their first set-back and "they did fight like dragons." (Alma 43:43f.) But the Nephites had the better cause, as Mormon explains, since they were fighting strictly on the defensive. This was no pious cant, for the Nephites in this case were really not the aggressors; they had observed the rule that God had given them, that "Inasmuch as ye are not guilty of the first offense, neither the second, ye shall not suffer yourselves to be slain. . . ." (Alma 43:46.) The Lamanites on the other hand were fighting for "monarchy and power," and made no secret of their intention of subduing and ruling. (Alma 43:45.) Even so, the ancient rule of the third offense (observed alike by the ancient Jews and Romans) rendered "preventive warfare" out of the question.

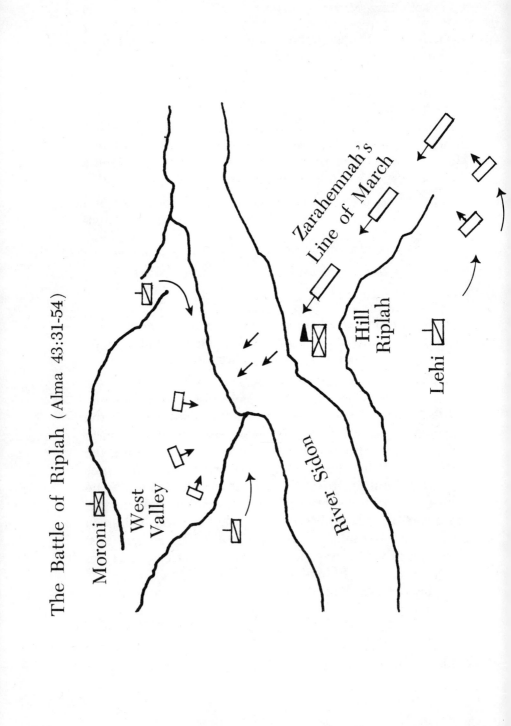

The Battle of Riplah (Alma 43:31-54)

Moroni

West
Valley

Zarahemnah's
Line of March

River Sidon

Hill
Riplah

Lehi

Phases:

    a. Zerahemnah, heading for Manti, which he thinks unde-
fended, passes the hill Riplah on the north and begins to
ford the Sidon.

    b. Lehi, concealed "on the south of the hill Riplah" attacks
Zerahemnah's rear.

    c. The main Lamanite force turns and engages Lehi.

    d. Thwarted by the superior armor of the Nephites, the La-
manites with heavy losses, seek security on the other side
of the river Sidon.

    e. Lehi accelerates their withdrawal by pressing them hotly
in the rear, but forbids any of his force to pursue them
into or beyond the river.

    f. On the other side of the river Moroni and his army have
been awaiting the Lamanites in the west Valley.

    g. The Lamanites try to break through to Manti but are met
by Moroni's reserves.

    h. Lamanite numbers begin to prevail until Moroni rallies
his forces, and the Lamanites fall back on the Sidon again.

    i. The entire Lamanite force is concentrated on the west
bank of the Sidon, where Moroni is able to encircle them.

    j. Moroni, perceiving the Lamanite perplexity, immediately
stops the battle and approaches Zerahemnah for a conference.

The sorely-pressed Lamanites by flocking together for protection, as beaten armies usually do, made it all the easier for Moroni with his carefully hoarded reserves to surround them. Then he immediately called a halt to the fighting: "Now Moroni, when he saw their terror, commanded his men that they should stop shedding their blood." (Alma 43:54.) He had his men fall back and went out to meet Zerahemnah, telling him, "We do not desire to be men of blood. Ye know that ye are in our hands, yet we do not desire to slay you." (Alma 44:1.) Here was Moroni's chance to settle the Lamanite problem once and for all on the spot; a vastly superior force had entered and ravaged a large part of his country, bent on subduing it entirely, and now he had them, as he says, completely in his power. Well might he have said, "Kill or be killed. It is either you or us!" and finished them off. But instead of that type of total victory he did not even ask for un-conditional surrender—an oxymoron, that, since everyone surrenders at least on the one condition of his life being spared. All he asked of his bloodthirsty foe was that they deliver up their weapons, and promise not to fight the Nephites any more; then they could go their way in peace without reprisals, punishment, hostages or guarantees. (Alma 44:6.) He felt perfectly secure in taking such a step, because he was aware of God's guarantees of security to the Nephites, of which he reminded Zerahemnah: "Ye see that God will support, and keep, and preserve us, so long as we are faithful unto him." (Alma 44:4.)

Zerahemnah handed over his sword to Moroni, but his hatred of Nephites was only heightened by his humili-ating defeat, and he cynically and realistically observed in so doing that there was no point in taking an oath "which ye know that we shall break." (Alma 44:8.) He recipro-cated Moroni's gallantry and humanity by accusing him of not playing fair (v. 9), and flatly refused the original terms. (v. 8.) Instead of ordering his insulting and threat-

ening adversary cut down on the spot, Moroni handed him
back his sword, with an invitation to "end the conflict"
(v. 10), but at the same time indicating his reluctance to
do so: he is forced into this position, he says—"I cannot
recall the words which I have spoken," but he again points
out to the Lamanites their hopeless position and again
invites them to accept his easy conditions. (v. 11.) He
was willing to discuss things to the end, but Zerahemnah
put an end to the conference which was so much to his
advantage by madly rushing Moroni with the sword he
had given him; he was intercepted but went down fighting
with the top of his scalp missing. (Alma 44:12.) The
guard who had cut it off put it on the end of his sword
and held it up for Zerahemnah's men to see, at the same
time repeating once again Moroni's offer of an easy peace.
(Alma 44:13-14.) By this time the Lamanites were impressed, and many accepted the offer, being forthwith
"suffered to depart into the wilderness" without prejudice
or penalty. (v. 15.)

The oath was indeed binding with these people, yet
Zerahemnah had served notice that though they might
take an oath they would not keep it. Whilst the prisoners
were being released, Zerahemnah stirred up some of his
die-hard supporters and turned savagely on the Nephites
in a wild melee. (v. 16.) This time Moroni had had enough
of the obnoxious Zoramites and gave the order to let them
have it. But very quickly Zerahemnah and his crew knew
they were beaten, and again Moroni instantly stopped the
fighting; he "caused that the work of death should cease
again . . . and after they (including Zerahemnah himself)
had entered into a covenant with him of peace they were
suffered to depart into the wilderness." (Alma 44:20.) So
they lived to fight another day (though Zerahemnah,
lacking a scalp, is never heard of again), as Moroni knew
they would. He would have been justified in view of
Zerahemnah's threats in finishing them off as a preventive

measure, by modern standards; but he would not condemn
them for a crime they had not yet committed, and in offering them a chance to sin again was also offering them a
chance to repent and become his friends, which, as we
shall see, many of them later did. The Nephites fittingly
celebrated their victory, not with getting drunk, but with
fasting and prayer. (Alma 45:1.) And yet it was at this
happy time of deliverance that Alma warned the people,
to whom he had been zealously preaching all this time,
that in the end it would be the Nephites and not the
Lamanites who would "become extinct," (Alma 45:10-14),
by their own wickedness—after which final admonition "he
departed out of the land" and "was never heard of more,"
giving rise to the tradition, which Moroni refuses to confirm
or deny, that he had been translated. (Alma 45:18-19.)

The Trouble with Amalickiah

It was not long after this that the sinister figure of
Amalickiah appeared on the scene to undo all that Moroni
had been fighting for. Amalickiah is one of a line of brilliant trouble-makers who keep things stirred up through
the turbulent pages of the Book of Mormon. Beginning
with Laman and Lemuel we meet in order Sherem,
Amulon, Nehor, Amlici, Zeezrom, Korihor, Zerahemnah,
and now, neither last nor least, Amalickiah. All of these
men had certain traits in common: all were personally
ambitious and unscrupulous, aspiring to be either king
or the religious head of the people; all were powerful
speakers and clever propagandists, skilled in the use of
"flattering words;" all sought to undermine, if they could
not seize, the highest authority of the church and state,
being particularly opposed to popular government and
drawing their support from those who sought to overthrow it.

Of these the most dangerous yet to appear was certainly Amalickiah. During the post-war boom there was

a strong tendency to ignore the admonitions of Helaman, the new spiritual head of the nation, as people "grew proud, being lifted up in their hearts, because of the exceeding great riches." (Alma 45:24.) Helaman's unyielding position became a great annoyance to those people whose hearts were set on the things of the new prosperity, and they formed an opposition party under Amalickiah. (Alma 46:1-3.) His object was to become king, and he had started out as head of the most violent of the factions, organized in high anger and out to kill, ". . . gathered together against their brethren . . . exceeding wroth . . . determined to slay them." To these, by promises of high office and power, he added a host of ambitious local officials, "lower judges of the land . . . seeking for power." (Alma 46:4-5.) These were those lawmen who had plotted against Helaman's father Alma when he had been the head of the state, and of whom he had said, ". . . the foundation of the destruction of this people is beginning to be laid by the unrighteousness of your lawyers and your judges." (Alma 10:27.) To the royalists and ambitious lawyers Amalickiah added a third force, "those people who professed the blood of nobility." (Alma 51:21.) Such would have been the great families, the "kindreds" of 3 Nephi 6:27. Finally, there were "many in the church who believed in the flattering words of Amalickiah," who obviously told them what they wanted to hear. (Alma 46:7.)

It was a dangerous coalition to be threatening a government which had barely succeeded in making a precarious peace with a foreign enemy of vastly superior forces, "and thus were the affairs of the people of Nephi exceedingly precarious and dangerous." (Alma 46:7.) "Thus we see," reflects Moroni, "how quick the children of men do forget . . . and we also see the great wickedness one very wicked man can cause." (Alma 46:8-9.)

No one saw more clearly than Moroni where this was leading—all that he had achieved with great toil and danger

was going to be thrown away if he did not act quickly.
"Angry with Amalickiah," he reacted with that speed and
decision which is the mark of the great leader in the field.
Raising his "Title of Liberty" according to the ancient
custom and as the type of the torn garment of the outcast
Joseph, and the symbol of the poor and outcast of Israel,
he announced to the people, "Surely God shall not suffer
that we, who are despised because we take upon us the
name of Christ, shall be trodden down . . . until we bring
it upon ourselves. . . ." (Alma 46:18.) Then "behold, the
people came running," arming themselves as they came
and rending their garments and casting them at Moroni's
feet in the ancient gesture of covenant and submission.
(Alma 46:21-22.) Thus Moroni rallied the people in
defense of the constitution of Mosiah, of government "by
the voice of the people," against a coalition of royalists
(for so they are called in Reynolds's *Concordance*), self-
styled nobility, and ambitious local officials who sought
to destroy it in a time of national emergency.

Things were getting hot for Amalickiah, who accordingly tried to make a break for it and join the Lamanites.
This sort of thing had happened before, and Moroni knew
that it would wreck his hard-bought peace, "for he knew
that he would stir up the Lamanites to anger . . . that he
might obtain his purposes." (Alma 46:30.) Stirring people
up to anger is the specialty of the great trouble-makers
in the Book of Mormon, who find it the surest road to
personal prominence and power. To check Amalickiah's
move, "Moroni thought it was expedient" to force a peace
on the dissenters with all possible haste. Moving with his
usual dispatch, he intercepted them before they got out of
the country, made them surrender to him, and required
them to take an oath, "a covenant to keep the peace" and
not fight against their own government. (Alma 46:35.) No
citizen could give less, and those who refused were know-
ingly accepting the status of combatants, and could expect

to be treated as such. At the time Moroni was acting with special military powers given him "by the chief judges and the voice of the people," (Alma 46:34) and accordingly put to death as an enemy in arms those who refused to lay down their arms; but these were only a few (v. 35); instead of a blanket order for the execution of all Amalickiahites as traitors, in the modern fashion, Moroni merely exacted from them a promise to support the government during a dire national emergency.

Moroni had been right about Amalickiah, for that hero escaped into the wilderness and made his way to the Lamanites, "and did stir up the Lamanites to anger against the people of Nephi," to such a degree that the Lamanite king ordered a general mobilization for war. (Alma 47:1.) Such an order to a people who had just had their fill of war was coolly received, and most of the people refused to obey it (Alma 47:2) and organized a huge protest-meeting at the main marshalling area at Onidah, electing a king for themselves on a no-war platform. (Alma 47:5-6.) Amalickiah promptly arranged a deal with the new "king," whom he later poisoned, taking over his leadership of the anti-war party. (Alma 47:10-18.) The fact that Antipus, the king-for-a-day, had to be urged four times before he would risk a secret meeting with Amalickiah shows that the latter already had something of a reputation as a smooth operator. The triumphant Amalickiah now led the obedient rebels in submission to their grateful king, whose assassination he engineered with such a show of loyalty and patriotism that he was able to marry the queen and thereby (he hoped) quiet her uncomfortable suspicions. (Alma 47:32-35.) His big problem, however, was to get the Lamanites to fight for him, and no professional public-relations office could have done a more skillful job than he did. ". . . he did appoint men to speak unto the Lamanites from their towers, against the Nephites," (Alma 48:1)—trained orators delivering set speeches from the official information centers; accusing, always accusing: "And thus he did inspire their hearts against the Nephites," until by the end of the year they were howling for blood, "for he had hardened the hearts of the Lamanites and blinded their minds, and stirred them up to anger. . . ." (Alma 48:2-3.) So now he had no trouble raising an army (v. 3), his object being "to reign over all the land . . . the Nephites as well as the Lamanites." (v. 2.)

Moroni, as you might suppose, was not idle during this time. Instead of fighting fire with fire, however, "he prepared the minds of the people to be faithful," (Alma 48:7) at the same time building up a marvelously well conceived system of defense in depth for the Nephites. Indeed all of Moroni's strategy and tactics are dictated by the necessity of meeting vastly superior numbers at all times. If his strategy was necessarily defensive, so was his psychology, "for he did not delight in bloodshed," Moroni the Younger reminds us again and again, but "did labor exceedingly for the welfare and safety of his people. . . ." (Alma 48:12.) "He had sworn to defend them," and had "taught them to defend themselves," but at the same time "never to give offense, and never to raise the sword . . . except it were to preserve their lives." (Alma 48:14.) For their part, the people "were compelled reluctantly to contend with their brethren the Lamanites," and when they took the field it was "notwithstanding their much reluctance. . . . They were sorry to take up arms against the Lamanites, because they did not delight in the shedding of blood . . . they were sorry to be the means of sending so many of their brethren out of this world." (Alma 48: 21-23.) This was Moroni's own attitude, and like Alma he insists on designating the enemy as his "brethren," and he means it. This, then, would seem to be a case of "the good people against the bad people," until we remember that the Lamanites were equally reluctant to fight the Nephites, our story being a lesson in "the great wickedness one very wicked man can cause."

Moroni's defenses were based on a series of strong-points, being a defense in depth, as modern defense-lines are; beside specially placed "small forts, or places of resort," towns and cities on the line were also converted into strong points. (Alma 48:8.) Such an arrangement can take the momentum out of any military steamroller and slow down or stop any attacking force, no matter how formidable, by forcing it to reduce one strong place after another or else bypass the fortifications and thereby leave dangerous enemy forces in its rear to disrupt communications and launch harassing counter-attacks on invading units. With this strictly defensive program (the preparation being to fight if at all only on their own grounds) an early-warning system was all-important. And it was Moroni's idea that God himself would provide such a system if the people were only faithful: ". . . if they were faithful in keeping the commandments of God, that he . . . would warn them to flee, or to prepare for war, according to their danger. And also that God would make it known unto them whither they should go to defend themselves. . . ." (Alma 48:15-16.) In short, God was their "Dew-line," their radar, and warning system, and that saved them the need of constant and costly vigilance on all fronts, to say nothing of expensive and wasteful war-plans and war-games. This was Moroni's policy of preparedness, "this was the faith of Moroni, and his heart did glory in it; not in the shedding of blood but in doing good." (Alma 48:16.) The keystone of all defense was unity at home, and for this the sons of Alma, "Helaman and his brethren were no less serviceable unto the people than was Moroni; for they did preach the word of God. . . . and the people did humble themselves . . . and thus they were free from wars and contentions among themselves," always the main source of danger in any war. (Alma 48:19-20.)

Amalickiah having worked up a war-fever among the Lamanites and carefully laid his grandiose plans of conquest, finally launched his thunderbolt. Great wars often open with nasty surprises to both sides. Von Kluck in his epic sweep into France through Belgium in 1914 did not count on Belgian resistance, British cooperation, or the amazing resilience of the French which by his own confession took him completely by surprise. The French on the other hand, insisted in the face of all the evidence that the main German attack would be to the south, while they hopelessly overestimated the effectiveness of cavalry and underestimated that of the new automatic weapons. Amalickiah's great drive ran into just such a series of nasty surprises. Moroni's system of defense in depth took all the initial momentum out of the big push: "But behold, how great was their disappointment" when they ran against his prepared "places of security," and when they found "to their utter astonishment" that the armaments of the enemy more than made up for their numerical inferiority, on which Amalickiah had been counting heavily. (Alma 49:4-8.) Generals should not be surprised that way, and yet they often have been, because of their ingrained habit of preparing for the next war in terms of the last one, exactly as the Lamanite generals had, supposing "that they should be privileged to come upon them as they had hitherto done . . . and being thus prepared . . . they should easily overpower and subject their brethren. . . ." (Alma 49:6-7.)

But Moroni was unconventional, as military geniuses must be, and his preparations had been as thorough as they were ingenious. By a complete administrative shakeup at home he had denied the Lamanites the use of certain facilities which they thought would fall into their hands, possibly through administrative incompetence or corruption: "For Moroni had altered the management of affairs among the Nephites, insomuch that the Lamanites were disappointed in their places of retreat and they could not come upon them." (Alma 49:11.)

Now when a major offensive bogs down, especially when it bogs down at the outset—the initial momentum of a Blitzkrieg being all important—exalted personages start having fits back at headquarters, and if things do not quickly improve, heads begin to roll. King Amalickiah had stayed back at his base, confident in a quick and easy victory. "He did not care for the blood of his people." (Alma 49:10.)—Moroni actually cared far more for it than he did! "His chief captains," furious at their rebuff at the city of Ammonihah, promptly lunged for the important city of Noah. They were determined to save face and retain the offensive by taking and utterly destroying a city which they believed to be unfortified and not expecting them, as the Germans did to make an object-lesson of Antwerp in 1914. The only trouble was that thanks to Moroni the city was fortified and waiting and ". . . they were again disappointed." (Alma 49:13-17.) The supreme test of generalship, we are told, is to have the enemy play your game, making just the moves you want him to make under the impression that he is being very smart on his own. Moroni did just that, and the attack on the city of Noah "was according to his desires." (Alma 49:15.) He had devised a new and ingenious type of defense for the city gate, which proved a death-trap for the Lamanites. For their desperate commanders had taken a true Prussian officers' oath to wipe out the inhabitants of the city of Noah, and their savage and repeated assaults on the impregnable gate became simply suicidal, and finally "their chief captains were all slain; yea, and more than a thousand of the Lamanites were slain." (Alma 49:21-23.)

So the great and carefully planned offensive with all its high hopes for a quick victory fizzled out, and a beaten army went back to report to the infuriated "Führer." (Alma 49:25-26.) In a towering rage, "exceedingly wroth . . . he did curse God, and also Moroni, swearing with an oath that he would drink his blood." (Alma 49:27.) At

every step in his career he had found that man Moroni
barring the way; at every step in the campaign his own
army had played into the hands of that Moroni. No wonder
Moroni began to be an obsession with him. The Nephites,
however, thanked God "because of his matchless power in
delivering them from the hands of their enemies." (Alma
48:28.)

Peace again brought prosperity, (Alma 49:30) but
Moroni was not idle. He launched out on an ambitious
program of national fortification, displaying his usual
genius in the design and disposal of the strong places.
(Alma 50:1-6.) First of all, it was necessary to remove a
dangerous bulge or salient over on the east coast. The area
was cleared of Lamanites and settled by local people and
colonists from Zarahemla. (Alma 50:7, 9.) This way
Moroni was able to shorten and straighten his defense line
(v. 8), and having determined the best possible course
for the line, he proceeded to fortify it along its entire length
from the east wilderness (north of Jershon on the coast)
to the west sea, (Alma 50:9, 11) again employing not a
single wall but a defense in depth, including even the
founding of new fortified towns at strategically located
places "by the borders." (Alma 50:13-15.) At the same
time he effected a gradual buildup of military power
within the country, (Alma 50:10) though his principal
concern was as ever to keep the peace at home, knowing
"that it had been their quarrelings, and their contentions
. . . and their abominations, which were among themselves,
which brought upon them their wars and their destructions." (Alma 50:21.)

Accordingly, when as the result of a land-squabble a
group of people under a loud and hot-tempered man
named Morianton (another of those ambitious masters of
"flattering words") decided to move out of the country,
Moroni, fearing that he would add to his supporters among
the people of Bountiful and thereby "lay a foundation for

serious consequences" (Bountiful being the most important Nephite military base), lost no time heading off the migration, sending his most mobile commander, Teancum, to stop them. Morianton was killed in the tussle that ensued, and all his people were "brought back." And upon their covenanting to keep the peace they were restored . . . and a union took place between them and the people of Lehi." (Alma 50:25-36.) Again Moroni's quick action had averted disaster but, more important, his humane policy, foregoing all reprisals and reparations, gave a happy ending to the episode with the original antagonists joined in friendship. Though the Nephites never lived in a time of greater danger, "never was there a happier time . . . than in the days of Moroni," according to the verdict of the younger Moroni at the very end of Nephite history. (Alma 50:23.) For their security was not in an absence of enemies but in the faith that they would be "delivered at all times" if they kept "the commandments of the Lord." (Alma 50:22.)

Absence of enemies? Soon Moroni had to face the most dangerous coalition of all, for the king-men were again united with "those of high birth" and all the others "who sought power and authority over the people," (Alma 51:5, 8) in a determined attempt to change the form of government, by law, to a monarchy. (Alma 51:4-5.) The opposition to this move was led by the chief judge Pahoran, who "would not alter nor suffer the law to be altered," (Alma 51:2-3): and was supported in this by a party calling themselves the Freemen (Alma 51:6.) An election was held and "the voice of the people came in favor of the Freemen" (Alma 51:7.) But the royalists had not played all their cards; their agitation had been timed to coincide with a move from the direction of their banished leader Amalickiah, who "had again stirred up the . . . Lamanites . . . and was preparing for war with all diligence." (Alma 51:9.) Counting on Amalickiah's aid, the beaten party "were glad in their hearts" of his approach, and "refused to take up arms" to resist it, being "wroth with

the chief judge, and also with the people of liberty" who
had given them a setback. (Alma 51:13.)

Again Moroni saw all his work threatened by the same
elements with whom he had been forced to deal before.
It was almost more than he could stand, "yea, he was
exceeding wroth; his soul was filled with anger against
them." (Alma 51:14.) But he knew that the people were
solidly behind him, and by popular vote received special
powers to "go up against those king-men, to pull down
their pride and their nobility" by force of arms—which he
did. (Alma 51:16-19.) Again he gave the rebels the opportunity to support the common cause without punishment
or prejudice, and used his special powers to deal summarily
with those who held out, four thousand of them, "for there
was no time for their trials at this period." (Alma 51:19.)
"And thus Moroni put an end to those king-men . . . to
the stubbornness and the pride of those people who professed the blood of nobility; but they were humbled and
were brought down to humble themselves like unto their
brethren." (Alma 51:21.) There is no talk of humbling in
the dust, but simply the restoration of equality, in which
Moroni emerges as the champion of popular government,
"beloved of all the people of Nephi." (Alma 53:2.) His
methods had been admittedly severe, and all that justified
them was an extreme national emergency.

But the emergency was very real, for even at that time
Amalickiah, made wise in the ways of war, was leading
his greatest army yet into the weakest parts of the land
and sweeping all before him. Bypassing the strongest
places, he flanked the Nephites along the coast in a lightning move that knocked out the weaker fortified places
one after another and sent the occupants fleeing like sheep
from one collapsing fortification to the next as he "went
on taking possession of many cities." (Alma 51:26-28.)
It was a well-executed operation that spread panic and
converted many of Moroni's strong places into Lamanite

bases. (v. 27.) Then the inevitable happened. The Lamanites in their forward rush having overextended themselves met an unpleasant rebuff when their spearhead was blunted by a flanking blow of the wily Teancum, who after bringing their advance guard to a halt continued to harass the army with his highly trained and highly mobile troops. (Alma 51:31.) Then on a two-man night patrol such as able and enterprising generals sometimes fancy, Teancum himself slipped into Amalickiah's tent and killed him in his sleep, after which he hurried back to his own headquarters and alerted his forces to an expected enemy attack at dawn. (Alma 51:33-36.)

The Trouble with Ammoron

The attack failed to materialize, for when the Lamanites awoke on the first day of the new year—albeit the weather was hot—showing this to be in the tropics (Alma 51:33), and found their king dead and Teancum "ready to give them battle on that day," that is, without giving them time to adjust to the new situation (Alma 52:1), they were alarmed at their position—"affrighted"—and fell back on their own strong places without a fight. (Alma 52:2.) Teancum then strengthened his own positions, digging in and awaiting reinforcements from Moroni (Alma 52:6-7), who, however, was pinned down on the west coast and could offer little assistance. The Nephites with their inferior numbers were being forced to fight that kind of a war that all commanders dread—a war on two fronts. Ammoron, the brother and successor of Amalickiah, made the most of this advantage to himself and sent a strong diversionary force to occupy Moroni and if possible split the Nephite forces even more, while harassing them everywhere and keeping them off-balance by sallies and infiltrations from the numerous former Nephite strong places now held by the Lamanites. (Alma 52:11-13.)

Things looked very bad indeed for Moroni "in those dangerous circumstances" (Alma 52:14); here was a situation that would test his skill to the utmost, and he rose to the occasion. First he ordered Teancum to sit tight on his sector while harassing the Lamanites as much as possible and keeping a sharp lookout for any chance opportunity or opening to do them real damage (Alma 52:10); at the same time he was instructed to take and keep as many prisoners of war as possible with a view to future exchange of prisoners with the Lamanites, for the addition of one man to the Nephite forces meant far more than it did to the Lamanites. (Alma 52:8.) Moroni followed up these instructions with "orders to make an attack upon the city of Mulek, and retake it if it were possible," (Alma 52:16) for Moroni was determined to get things moving. It is a neatly authentic touch, however, that Teancum after sizing up the situation decided against an attack on Mulek and sat and waited in Bountiful for Moroni to show up. (Alma 51:16-17.) When the commander-in-chief finally got through with an army a top-level "council of war" was at once convened to study the situation; at this conference it was agreed that the first thing on the agenda was for the united forces of Teancum and Moroni to take the city of Mulek, which was the eastern anchor of the main defense-line. (Alma 52:18-19.)

But how was a major city, superbly fortified by Moroni's own foresight, to be taken? The first step was a logical one. It was the ancient custom of warfare to invite the occupants of a city to come out on the open plain and engage in a fair set contest, or as the Nephites put it, "upon fair grounds";[1] the Nephite commanders in issuing such an invitation to the comfortably ensconced opposition hardly expected the Lamanites to comply with a request so disadvantageous to themselves, but they thought it was worth a try and at any rate it was the conventional thing to do. (Alma 52:19-20.) Their next move

---

[1]We have discussed this in the *Western Political Quarterly*, 19 (1966), pp. 615-619.

was to try a decoy trick. Teancum allowed the Lamanites to discover a task-force of his moving along the coast and to give it chase; Moroni then slipped into the city behind them and overpowered the defenders, characteristically sparing all who yielded up their arms. (Alma 51:22-25.) Then he too took the coast route on the heels of the Lamanites who were chasing Teancum. As a secondary diversion a small Nephite force under the terrible Lehi had issued out of the main base at Bountiful and met the Lamanites head on. (Alma 52:27.) Confused by this new development, the Lamanites sought counsel in safety by returning to Mulek, even as it occurred to them with a shock that in dashing forth they had left that city only lightly defended; and so their return to Mulek turned into a wild race with the Nephites to see who would get there first. (Alma 52:27-28.) Bent only on reaching home-base in safety, the exhausted Lamanites with Lehi hot behind them ran smack into Moroni's army coming up behind them. That was the last straw. (Alma 52:28-32.)

With his usual forbearance, Moroni waived total victory and spared all the Lamanites who would stop fighting him. (Alma 52:32.) But their leader was Jacob, a Zoramite who hated the Nephites as only a dissenter could hate; with an elite guard he tried to fight his way out of the sack but died in the attempt. (Alma 52:34.) Moroni immediately offered the usual easy terms to his followers: "Now Moroni seeing their confusion, he said unto them: If ye will bring forth your weapons of war and deliver them up, behold we will forbear shedding your blood." (Alma 52:37.) Even so, those who would not surrender were not killed but disarmed, bound, and marched off to the great central prison compound at Bountiful. (Alma 52:39.) The prisoner of war problem was now becoming a very serious one for the Nephites. Their best solution was to put their prisoners to work, which "Moroni was compelled to do" we are told, "because it was easy to guard them while at their labor," and the Nephites were frightfully short of man-power. (Alma 53:1.) The work was mainly the conversion of Bountiful into a very strong "Stalag," with ditch and breastwork—more of Moroni's ingenuity. (Alma 53:3-5.)

In the absence of Moroni from his army "on the west sea, south," an outbreak of intrigues and dissensions greatly weakened the war effort and placed the Nephites "in the most dangerous circumstances." (Alma 53:8-9.) When the Lamanites finally suggested the exchange of war prisoners that he had been waiting for, Moroni sent them a "get-tough" letter, deliberately taunting Ammoron, "a child of hell," and insisting on receiving a Nephite prisoner with his wife and children in exchange for one Lamanite soldier. (Alma 54:1-13.) This three-to-one exchange was actually to the advantage of the Lamanites, who were eager enough to transfer the feeding of non-combatants from them-selves to the Nephites, but Moroni wanted to get the best possible bargain by not appearing too eager (Alma 54:2-3) and so got tough. The result was an exchange of insults between the chiefs with mounting tempers, and in the end the deal fell through. (Alma 54-55:2.) This was not to be the last time that Moroni's hot temper ran away with him.

But Moroni knew more than one way of skinning a cat. He planned by a ruse to free the war prisoners held in the city of Gid. The trick exploited the well-known psychology of troops on permanent guard duty. Such troops must always be on the alert for what they never expect to happen and what, if they do their duty, never *will* happen. Their way of life becomes a stultifying bore, with the same dull routines from day to day and from week to week. Nothing offers a more welcome release to such misery than a little nip now and then, or better still, a party. A native Lamanite in the Nephite service answered the chal-lenge of the Lamanite guards one evening with the announcement that his little party were escapees from the Nephites who had managed to get away with some of their wine. Of course the guards insisted on sampling the stuff on the spot and on the sly; the protests of its owners that they should keep it against the day of battle "only made them more desirous to drink of the wine." (Alma 55:10.) It was a typical "G.I." binge with everybody getting happily drunk at the guard-house since the stuff was doctored, "having been prepared in its strength." (Alma 55:13.) While the guards were carousing and falling asleep weapons were being thrown over the wall at certain places under Moroni's personal supervision, and the guards even "had they awakened" would have been out of a job. (Alma 55:16-18.)

Again Moroni did the decent thing, forbidding anyone "to fall upon the Lamanites and destroy them in their drunkenness," since that would be an "injustice," and especially since "he did not delight in murder or bloodshed, but in the saving of his people from destruction." (Alma 55:19.) Note that Moroni is not only averse to shedding innocent blood, but is against the shedding of any blood at all. The guards when they came to readily handed over their weapons on order of their superiors, and pleaded for mercy; this "was the desire of Moroni," who promptly put them to work in the place of the prisoners they had just been guarding, and then had them transported to the main base at Bountiful. (Alma 55:23-26.)

After this the Lamanites hopefully experimented with some of the Nephite ruses, including the wine-trick, but the Nephites were pretty well on to them. (Alma 55:29-30.) They did succeed, however, in effecting a major buildup in the very strong city of Morianton. (Alma 55:33-34.) At this juncture, Moroni was heartened by a long letter, with an accompanying map (plainly referred to in Alma 56:13-15), from Helaman reporting improved conditions on the east front. Helaman recounted how he had organized a company of 2,000 young invincibles from, of all people, the pacifistic Ammonites. His recruits had been too young to take the oath against bloodshed when their parents took it, and so were free to join the army. (Alma 53:11.) As every commander knows, the most desirable quality in a soldier is perfect reliability, and Helaman cannot too highly praise this quality in his "2,000 Sons." They could be perfectly trusted because their parents could be trusted, having already displayed perfect integrity in refusing to take up arms even against those who were cutting them down with the sword. Moved by compassion at the sore straits of the Nephite hosts who had done so much for them, the older people had been on the verge of breaking their oaths and arming themselves to lend a helping hand in the war, when Helaman as high-priest of the land had talked them out of it, convincing them that the welfare of their souls had priority over any military expediency or emergency whatever. (Alma 53:13-15; 56:7-8.) No wonder their sons called themselves Helaman's sons and were "true at all times in whatsoever thing they were entrusted." (Alma 53:20-21.)

The intervention of the 2,000 proved a great morale-booster on the eastern front, where the exhausted Nephites had been working themselves to death fortifying by night and fighting by day with no sign of relief in sight. (Alma 56:16-17.) Their fresh and youthful vigor and the supplies they brought from home stiffened the Nephite position, but the result was a stalemate in which neither side dared move. (Alma 56:23-26.) However, the boys continued getting packages from home, and then 2,000 new recruits arrived from the capital. (Alma 56:27-28.) At this the Lamanites began to grow uneasy in the face of what looked like a Nephite buildup, and so it was possible to stage another decoy act by giving it a new twist. The 2,000 Sons of Helaman were instructed to escort a supply-train up the coast, knowing that Lamanite spies from the city of Antiparah would be sure to spot them. Naturally it was a chance not to be missed for the Lamanites, and at any rate the supplies had to be stopped. So they took a calculated risk and sent out a large force in pursuit of the 2,000, who moved briskly and kept out of reach, following instructions. Even when the Lamanites learned that another Nephite force was pursuing them they continued the chase of the 2,000, for they expected a situation like that and felt strong enough to cope with it: "Even . . . when they saw the army of Antipus pursuing them . . . they did not turn to the right nor to the left, but pursued their march in a straight course after us." (Alma 56:30-37.) In the hot pace that the three armies were setting each other nobody dared relax or turn to either side; but when the straining troops of Antipus started stepping on Lamanite heels the army turned to face them with overpowering numbers. (Alma 56:49-50.)

Then it was that Helaman up ahead asked his boys if they had had enough of running away: "What say ye, my sons, will ye go against them to battle?" (Alma 56:54.) Would they! Helaman knew the Lamanite numbers were still overwhelmingly superior to the combined Nephite forces, and suspected that this might even be a trap for him, but he was willing to risk it. (Alma 56:43.) Unleashed, the 2,000 waded in with such terrific elan that the whole Lamanite army turned to meet them (Alma 56:52); but like the young Israelis in 1948, these kids introduced a new dimension into the war: they were inspired; their strange spirit, devoid of hatred and utterly free of fear or hesitation (Alma 56:46-47) began to frighten the seasoned Lamanite troopers who had never seen anything like it. (Alma 56:56.) They started surrendering in vast numbers, and the road back to Zarahemla was soon clogged with prisoners of war. (Alma 56:57.)

When he saw that he would not be able to hold the city of Antiparah, the sly Ammoron approached Helaman with an offer to give the Nephites the city in exchange for all their prisoners; but Helaman would have no part

356   SINCE CUMORAH

of that—it would have to be on a prisoner-for-prisoner basis; so Ammoron called it off, and the Nephites took Antiparah without pains, the inhabitants having fled to Lamanite country. (Alma 57:1-4.) The success at Antiparah was rewarded by strong reinforcements from the capital; with these Helaman blockaded the city of Cumeni, intercepting all their supplies and finally forcing surrender. (Alma 57:5-12.)

By now the Nephites were simply swamped with prisoners of war, who seeing the embarrassment of their captors began to stage prison riots, "for behold, they would break out in great numbers, and would fight with stones, and with clubs . . ." (Alma 57:14), and had to be bloodily suppressed. (Alma 57:14-16.) A very large body of prisoners was being escorted back to the capital by crack Nephite troops when they collided with a Lamanite army escorting a large supply train—embarrassing moments. (Alma 57:16-17.) The guards forgot about their prisoners and high-tailed it back to Helaman's headquarters or command post to report the new danger; only just as they arrived there they found the headquarters company hotly engaged with the advanced elements of the same Lamanite army, and were able to join in the fighting just in time to turn the tide and save the command post. (Alma 57:18.) (Author's note: Shades of the dear old 101st!)

Again it was the 2,000, now augmented by 60 more boys from home, who turned the tide, for "they did obey and observe to perform every word of command with exactness." (Alma 57:19-21.) Helaman explains that their mothers had taught them that God would protect them if they were upright, and they had believed what they were taught, did what they were told, and "were firm and undaunted." And indeed, though they were all wounded in the battle, not a single one of them lost his life, proving to their simple minds "that there was a just God, and whosoever did not doubt, that they should be preserved by his marvelous power," so, Helaman explains, "their minds are firm, and they do put their trust in God continually." (Alma 57:21-27.)

Another huge prisoner contingent was sent to Zarahemla, this time under the supervision of the capable Gid. Enroute the Nephites got news of a Lamanite army marching on Cumeni, the city the Nephites had just taken by blockade. Their disturbance at the news became apparent to their prisoners who assumed that something was going badly for them and that they were in trouble, "which caused them to take courage, and they did rise up in rebellion against us," rushing in a body on the Nephite swords. Most of them were slain, but the rest escaped. (Alma 57:28-33.) However, this was not an unmixed evil, for Gid was now free to hasten to the aid of Cumeni, arriving just in time. (Alma 57:34.)

Again things settled down to a stalemate, with Helaman faced with the problem of containing greatly superior forces, who were now discouragingly familiar with the Nephite decoy tricks (58:1.) He could only appeal to the capital for aid, which was forthcoming, but was largely cancelled out by the Lamanite counter-buildup—for they too were receiving reinforcements, and had in the bargain began copying the Nephites' own tactics of harassment. (Alma 58:4-6.) As in all long wars, the two opponents in their methods, armaments, tricks and appearance had come to be more and more alike—for an enemy may not be allowed safely to monopolize any technical advantage for long. Both Nephites and Lamanites were holed up in Moroni's strong places and using his defense in depth.

So the war dragged on, and then something went wrong. Support from the capital began to fall off. "The cause of these our embarrassments . . . why they did not send more strength unto us, we knew not." But the strange turn of things stirred up the usual camp rumors and misgivings. ". . . we were grieved and also filled with fear. . . ."

(Alma 58:9.) In this tense and gloomy situation the army turned to prayer for comfort and found it. (Alma 58:10-11.) With morale somewhat restored, Helaman planned to take Manti by a ruse—and it would have to be a good one, since the Lamanites now knew all the answers. He pushed his bivouac as near to the town as he dared "by the wilderness side," (Alma 58:13) where the enemy easily discovered that his force was not a very strong one; but the insolent position he had taken, which put him in a position to cut off supplies to the city (Alma 58:15), demanded that something be done about him, even though his little army was far too weak to attempt a siege. As soon as Helaman made sure that the Lamanites were getting ready to come out and teach him a lesson, he divided his small forces into three bodies; one under Teomner went off and hid out in the wilderness in one direction, while the other under Gid moved out and lay low in the other direction. The Lamanites came out in full force and took after Helaman, who of course retreated at top speed, leading the pursuers unawares right between the forces of Gid and Teomner, who lay quietly until they had passed and then "ran to the city and fell upon the guards," for in their haste and confidence the Lamanites had left only a few to guard the town, and they were easily destroyed (Moroni not being there to prevent it). (Alma 58:16-22.) The Lamanites had to give up the chase when they found that the quarry was heading straight for Zarahemla, leading them to suspect another of those Nephite ambushes. But what they did not suspect was that their fleeing victims would double on their tracks, march around them in the nighttime while they were sleeping, and beat them back to Manti— the last place in the world they would expect to find them. So the Nephites took Manti "without the shedding of blood." (Alma 58:24-28.)

The discouraged Lamanites now began an evacuation of the area, and the Nephites began cautiously and not without risk, to resettle some of the lands they had retaken. (Alma 58:30-33.) Helaman permitted his 2,000 to go into a rest area at Manti (Alma 58:39), and waited for news from the capital, wondering what could have possibly gone wrong. We know they have more men and material than they have been sending us, he writes to Moroni; perhaps you have been having trouble and they had to send it to you, in which case we have no complaints; but "if it is not so, behold, we fear that there is some faction in the government" blocking the much-needed aid. "But, behold," he concludes, "it mattereth not—we trust God will deliver us. . . ." (Alma 58:34-37.)

The Trouble with Pahoran

Moroni had been wondering about the breakdown of communications also. At once he sat down and sent an urgent dispatch to Zarahemla, addressed directly to the chief of state, urging that help be sent to Helaman without further delay. (Alma 59:3.) Then he turned to the execution of an ambitious plan he had been working on, a grand stratagem to regain all the Nephite cities. (Alma 59:4.) It was never put into operation, however, because the Lamanites beat Moroni to the punch with a massive attack on the people of Nephihah, whose survivors came streaming into Moroni's camp. (Alma 59:5-8.) It seems that Moroni had made a serious mistake in overestimating the defensive strength of Nephihah (Alma 59:9); his grand design collapsed and he was greatly out of sorts, blaming the failure of the operation onto "the wickedness of the people" while his staff stood around nodding agreement, and berating the indifference of the government, with which he was very angry. (Alma 59:11-13.)

Heavy-hearted ("exceeding sorrowful") for the loss of Nephihah, Moroni wrote another letter to Pahoran, "the chief judge and governor over the land," in which he appears as a very tired commander indeed, following up a

serious military blunder with an equally deplorable political one. The letter seethes with the resentment of the man
at the front for the easy-living ways of the "VIP's" back
at the capital—the old misunderstandings between the
"office" and the "field." He starts out by reminding the
governor of his duty to supply the armies in the field, and
reminds him that both he and Helaman have suffered from
short supplies from the beginning. (Alma 60:2-5.) He
admits his ignorance of the situation and asks for information, and yet he cannot resist passing judgment with a
peevish and quite unjustified charge of negligence: ". . . we
desire to know the cause of this . . . neglect; yea . . . of
your thoughtless state." (Alma 60:6-7.) He goes on to
charge deliberate mismanagement: ". . . ye have withheld
your provisions," (Alma 60:9) and incompetence: ". . . for
ye ought to have stirred yourselves more diligently. . . .
ye have neglected them insomuch that the blood of thousands shall come upon your heads for vengeance." (Alma
60:10.)

This is getting serious, but there is worse to come.
Swept on by the momentum of his pent-up emotions, the
frustrated commander, who has just seen his favorite
project for ending the war go to pot, piles one accusation
on another. The government officials, he claims, in their
comfortable offices, "sitting upon their thrones in thoughtless stupor," (Alma 60:7, a wonderful expression) have
trusted in the goodness of God to justify their neglect, and
blandly attributed the calamities overtaking the soldiers in
the field not to their own high and mighty indifference but,
of all things, to the wickedness of the poor soldiers themselves and other suffering victims of the war. (Alma 60:
12.) The politicians are responsible for the disasters and
setbacks of the war, for "the wickedness . . . first commenced at our head," back in the days when the king-men
threw the nation into turmoil at the beginning of the war:
"It was the desire of power and authority which those king-

men had over us" that opened the door to the murderous Lamanites; nay, they "are *still* seeking for power and authority, yea, even those king-men." (Alma 60:15-17.) Moroni even goes so far as to hint that Pahoran himself is one of those power-seekers, and worse still, "we know not but what ye are also traitors to your country." (Alma 60: 18.) The grave charge of treason is hardly palliated by the admission, "we know not . . ." Moroni may only have suspicions, but what he suspects is the very worst. He becomes scathingly sarcastic as he describes the fat government officials complacently sitting in idleness, surrounded by hordes of lazy slackers like themselves, "tens of thousands, who do also sit in idleness, while there are thousands around about . . . who are falling by the sword." (Alma 60:22.) The picture may seem overdrawn to us, and yet it probably was not, for that is actually the way things are in wartime.

Moroni's next step was to charge the head of the state with immoral behavior and call upon him to repent. (Alma 60:24.) But now comes the height of his indiscretion, for after lecturing the governor like a "Dutch uncle," Moroni promises him a good spanking, and ends up threatening open rebellion: "And except ye grant mine epistle, and come out and show unto me a true spirit of freedom . . . I will come unto you. . . . I will stir up insurrections among you, even until those who have desires to usurp power and authority shall become extinct." (Alma 60:25-27.) This is not as bad as it sounds, for he is not attacking those in authority but those who have *usurped it*, namely that power-seeking faction he knows so well. Still, the same Moroni who had begun his letter with a profession of ignorance and a request for information can now bring the flat accusation and fling a challenge at the governor: "I do not fear your power, nor your authority, but it is my God whom I fear . . . and it is because of your iniquity that we have suffered so much loss." (Alma 60:28.) Carried along in the spate of his eloquence, he shifts from vague references to troublemakers to placing the blame squarely on the shoulders of the people to whom he is writing: ". . . and except ye do minister unto our relief, behold, I come unto you, even in the land of Zarahemla, and smite you with the sword." (Alma 60:30.)

It seems strange that this man who had deplored more than anything else the contentions and dissensions among the Nephites as the principal cause of their misfortunes in war, should now propose to add to the turmoil by stirring up insurrection. But Moroni was bursting with pent-up emotions and the accumulated memories of reverses that could have been avoided and operations that could have ended the war had the necessary support been forthcoming from home. He knows, as Helaman suspects, that someone in high places is working against him, and for his noble and idealistic nature the thought that anyone should make capital of the miseries of others was simply maddening— yet he had seen that sort of thing going on in the capital all his life. "The Lord will not suffer that ye shall live and wax strong in your iniquities," he writes to Pahoran. (Alma 60:31.) He does not blame the Lamanites—they are only doing what they think is right, "it is the tradition of their fathers that has caused their hatred;" the real enemy is as ever the private citizen or public official seeking to promote himself: ". . . your iniquity is for the cause of your love of glory, and the vain things of the world." (Alma 60:32.) Finally Moroni goes all out: the Lord has commanded him, he says, to go up in battle against the governors if they do not repent! (Alma 60:33.) He closes with what might be called Moroni's watchword: "I seek not for power, but to pull it down."

It was, to say the least, not the most tactful letter in the world, but Moroni's patience was worn out. Also it turned out, he was right—on every point but one. And that point was an important one: he had accused the wrong man. Aside from that, he had the situation correctly sized up—his long experience with the king-men had not been for nothing.

Fortunately the man thus wrongly accused was a governor worthy of his high office, as his wise, temperate, and constructive reply reveals. Instead of getting on his high horse, Pahoran reacted to Moroni's withering on-slaught by telling him that he has a right to be upset, as he himself is (Alma 61:2), and that instead of resenting such language addressed to himself he understands Moroni's intention perfectly and rejoices in his greatness of heart. (Alma 61:9.) As a matter of fact, Moroni has made a pretty good estimate of the situation, for there were indeed plenty of important people in the capital who were only too pleased to see the great Moroni in trouble— "who do joy at your afflictions;" what is more, Moroni had correctly guessed who they were—the old power-seekers, who had actually been able to take over the gov-ernment by clever propaganda, "for they have used great flattery, and they have led away the hearts of many people," and being in office had succeeded in intimidating the opposition, ". . . and have daunted our freemen. . . ." (Alma 61:2-4.) They had forced the president, Pahoran, to leave town; but in doing so he had energetically rallied as many supporters as he could (Alma 61:5), and was sure that the masses of the people, who had always followed Moroni, were still behind him, and that the ruling clique did not dare risk a test of strength in the field. (Alma 61:7.)

Who the new government were becomes apparent when we learn that upon seizing the capital they had abol-ished democratic government and set up a monarchy, and, as might be expected, immediately entered into negotia-tions with the king of the Lamanites. It was the old royalist crowd that Moroni knew so well. (Alma 61:8.) Pahoran, who was as much for popular government and as little interested in personal power as Moroni himself, proposed a plan for restoring the old government. But first of all as a civil officer he explored every possibility of avoiding violence. Like Moroni, he would, he says, gladly suffer the Lamanites if they would let him: "We should not shed the blood of the Lamanites if they would stay in their own land." (Alma 61:10.) This is no self-righteous accusing, since every battle in Moroni's time was fought on Nephite, not on Lamanite, soil. So far is Pahoran from patriotic heroics that he declares, "We would subject ourselves to the yoke of bondage, if it were requisite with the justice of God, or if he should command us," and he insists that one should only take to the sword "when words have failed." (Alma 61:14.) But "the spirit of God is the spirit of freedom," so what was he to do now? Even in this dire emergency he hesitates to use force, being "worried concerning what we should do, whether it should be just in us to go against our brethren." (Alma 61:19.) Like Moroni sparing the drunken guards, he is more concerned with doing what is *just* than anything else, and it is Moroni's letter, he says, that has made up his mind for him, since it declares that the Lord wants action. (Alma 61:20.) So, full of fight and ginger, he and his supporters join up with a small task-force of Moroni's that had marched to meet them, and as soon as Moroni raised his Title of Liberty the people flocked in ecstatic thousands to the well-known banner. Moroni and Pahoran, now fast friends, made a triumphant progress through the land, culminating in a battle in which the army of King Pachus and his supporters was quickly beaten. (Alma 62:3-8.)

Again Moroni showed his accustomed leniency. This was the third time that his Title of Liberty had been called out to put down a royalist coalition, timed to take advantage of a great national crisis; yet he pardoned without penalty or punishment all who would prove their loyalty by willingness "to take up arms in defense of their country," executing only those who still insisted on wielding the sword against it. (Alma 62:9-11.) Then, able at last to count on the help he needed, Moroni hastened back to strengthen the Nephite position on both fronts.

His first interest was to retake Nephihah, lost by his own miscalculation, and during the operation who should assist him but Pahoran, familiarizing himself with the war's problems at first hand. (Alma 62:14.) On the way to Nephihah, the two commanders ran into a special task-force of Lamanites and defeated it. (Alma 62:15.) What followed showed that the tide of war was turning and there was a new spirit in the air—Moroni's patience and humanity in dealing with the defeated was beginning to bear fruit. For instead of making prisoners of the beaten Lamanites, Moroni permitted all of them who would accept the usual covenant (about 4,000 of them did) to go off and settle peaceably among the people of Ammon! (Alma 62:17.)

At Nephihah the usual formal invitation was sent to the enemy to meet the Nephite army in the field, which invitation the Lamanites wisely declined. (Alma 62:18-19.) In a personal reconnaissance Moroni learned that the enemy were sleeping over in the area of the city's east gate, leaving the west side practically unguarded. So Moroni scaled the walls on the west side and the frightened enemy left by the opposite gate, leaving him in possession. (Alma 62:20-25.) He rounded up a lot of the fugitives and made them prisoners, but when they begged to be allowed to go and "join the people of Ammon and become a free people," he at once gave them his permission to do so. (Alma 62:27-28.) Plainly everybody was getting rather tired of war when thousands of Lamanite warriors began to see the light—that the people of Ammon were the really sensible people after all. And so the wicked Lamanites, who had made life a hell for the Nephites for as long as anyone could remember, whose territories and resources still remained intact and unravaged by war, and who still outnumbered the Nephites by an immense margin, were dismissed without even a reprimand, and in short order became model citizens of the Nephite realm. (Alma 62:29.) This also solved the vexing prisoner of war problem.

The Lamanite armies in the field, knowing that the war was going against them, drew together for mutual support, as beaten armies will, but their fighting spirit was kept up by Ammoron, the brother of that Amalickiah who had sworn undying hatred of Moroni, embracing the old philosophy of "kill or be killed," "it is either you or me," in which both the conjunctions are wrong, "kill *and* be killed . . . it is you *and* me" being the verdict of history. So Ammoron suffered the same fate as his brother when Teancum tried to repeat his former performance by stabbing the king in his tent—he succeeded but lost his own life in the attempt. (Alma 62:33-36.) With the death of their leader, the Lamanites finally withdrew. Then Moroni made a careful inspection of all the country's defenses and went into retirement. (Alma 62:38-43.)

Sequel to the War

After the war the son of the popular hero Helaman became president (chief judge) "by the voice of the people." (Helaman 2:2.) There was a great post-war boom, with its accompanying corruption and moral decline, indeed the book of Helaman is essentially a story of criminal activities which we have treated elsewhere.[2] Eight years after the long war ended, while the arch-criminal Kishkumen was plying the art of murder in an attempt to help a defeated candidate into power (Helaman 1:5-12), the Lamanites were preparing another attack. It struck with such speed and force under the leadership of the Nephite defector Coriantum, that it achieved a complete surprise

------

[2]*An Approach to the Book of Mormon,* Ch. 27 (1964 ed., Ch. 28).

and before anyone was aware of what had happened succeeded in taking and occupying Zarahemla itself! (Helaman 1:18-20.) Coriantum instantly followed up his advantage by marching through the country almost unopposed (Helaman 1:24), burning and destroying as he went, "slaying the people with great slaughter, both men, women, and children. . . ." (Helaman 1:27.) But like the Germans in Russia, Coriantum had really gotten himself into a jam: his drive had been successful because it was completely unexpected; and it had been unexpected because it was utterly foolish. The Nephite forces were stationed, of course, on the frontiers (Helaman 1:18, 26), and so Coriantum's great breakthrough which had put him in the heart of the country had also got him neatly surrounded. (Helaman 1:25, 32.) The Nephite army leaders only had to tighten the bag until Coriantum was forced to surrender. (Helaman 1:28-32.) And then what? The Nephite commander Moronihah did just as his namesake Moroni would have—he let all the Lamanites "depart out of the land in peace." (Helaman 1:33.) No reprisals or vengeance for an army that had seized the capital and devastated the land without mercy! What would the Nephites think in reading the history of some of our present-day wars?

During the post-war prosperity that followed the greatest corruption "was among those also who professed to belong to the church of God. And it was because of the pride of their hearts, because of their exceeding riches. . . ." (Helaman 4:11-12.) Because of contentions in the church many of these people went over to the Lamanites and started to stir them up (Helaman 4:1-4), and in the ensuing troubles a sudden Lamanite drive overran the entire Nephite country with the exception of the Bountiful region. (Helaman 4:5-8.) Moronihah was able to win back about half of the country, but the rest was lost to the Nephites forever (Helaman 4:9-10); from then on they had to fall back on a strategy of containment. (Helaman 4:19.) Then came the Gadianton wars which we discuss below, ending with the great earthquake, followed by the coming of the Lord. Then after about two centuries of peaceful existence, free of international or idealogical controversy of any kind (4 Nephi 15-17), the classic Nephite-Lamanite feud was resumed as people on both sides lapsed into wickedness, "one like unto another." (4 Nephi 39, 45.) The most tragic and heroic figure in the Book of Mormon is Mormon himself, whose melancholy task it was to lead the last long retreat of his people to the north, fighting a desperate rear-guard action with determined delaying tactics and gallant counter-attacks, but always in the end losing ground. The retreat begins in a scene of total confusion, "one complete revolution throughout all the face of the land," with Lamanites, robbers, and Gadiantons prowling among the Nephites who had broken up into tribes and in a last mighty effort for survival were trying to shape up into some sort of fighting force. (Mormon 2:7-8.) They fight, fall back "hunted and driven," then counterattack with the courage of despair, retake their lands and get a territorial agreement with the Lamanites and Gadiantons, after which they spend ten years in an all-out preparation for war. (Mormon 2, 3:1.) It was then that the Lord offered them a last chance to survival, but they turned it down and "did harden their hearts against the Lord their God." (Mormon 3:2-3.)

From then it was all down hill in spite of Nephite victories. Two surprise victories won a 10-year peace for the Nephites (350-360 A.D., Mor. 3:24ff.), after which a formal invitation to battle was accepted by the Lamanite king, and the Nephites in another surprising comeback won two brilliant victories in succession. (Mormon 3:7-8, 13.) In a great surge of pride and confidence "because of this great thing which . . . the Nephites had done," (Mormon 3:9) they declared themselves ready to settle the Lamanite question once and for all, swearing by God that they would avenge the blood of their brethren and cut the Lamanites off from the face of the land— "It is either them or us!" (Mormon 3:9-10.) Mormon, the author of the recent victories, reacted to this policy by at once resigning under protest: "I, Mormon, did utterly refuse from this time forth to be a commander and a leader of this people. . . . I had led them many times . . . I had loved them with all my heart . . . my soul had been poured out in prayer . . . nevertheless, it was without faith, because of the hardness of their hearts." (Mormon 3:11-12.) In taking the offensive, Mormon explains, the Nephites lost everything: "And it was because the armies of the Nephites went up unto the Lamanites that they began to be smitten. . . ." (Mormon 4:4; see especially 3 Ne. 3:20-21.)

The see-saw war raged on as each side, seeking vengeance for the war-crimes of the other, surpassed those crimes in a dismal escalation of atrocities, mostly at the expense of non-combatants. (Mormon 4:11-15.) Finally there came a day when the Nephites "began to be swept off by them even as a dew before the sun." (Mormon 4:18.) With their resistance broken, they were simply melting away; the situation so alarmed and moved Mormon that in spite of his vow to have nothing to do with the business his great heart could not resist the people's pleas for assistance, "as though I could deliver them . . . But behold I was without hope." (Mormon 5:2.) Hypnotized by the "kill or be killed" psychology, the Nephites "did struggle for their lives without calling upon that Being who created them." (Mormon 5:2.) Now it was the Lamanites who were all out for total victory, sparing nothing that was Nephite from destruction—and why not? Hadn't the Nephites planned the same fate for them?

The retreat became a rout (Mormon 5:7), until the Nephites finally decided to call a halt by requesting for the last time the ancient courtesy of stipulating the time and place for a final showdown on a fair field. (Mormon 6:2.) This was granted them, and in the last scene the Nephites are allowed the melancholy and terrifying privilege of enjoying one last tremendous spectacle—the full-dress approach of their executioners: ". . . and with that awful fear of death which fills the breasts of all the wicked, did they await to receive them." (Mormon 6:7.) The "wicked"—please note: this is no contest between good people and bad people. As for the wicked Lamanites their total victory turned out to be a cruel deception— nobody won the war, for it still went on: "The Lamanites are at war one with another," wrote Moroni after Cumorah, "and the whole face of this land is one continual round of murder and bloodshed; and no one knoweth the end of the war." (Mormon 8:8.)

Part V.

The Prophetic
Book of Mormon

CHAPTER 12

Good People and Bad People

The Supreme Test

Since it first came forth the Book of Mormon has been subjected as it were to a graded series of tests. First of all, was Joseph Smith bluffing? It was all right to tell wonderful stories to beguile the local yokels, but would the easy-going country boy back down when he found himself in real trouble? If he knew it was all a joke he certainly would. But he didn't give an inch, and to the end of his life never so much as hinted that the slightest explanation or apology was due for his youthful indiscretion. Well, he had told his story of the angel and the book: could he produce the book? He produced it. It is a surprisingly big book, supplying quite enough rope for a charlatan to hang himself a hundred times; as the work of an imposter it must unavoidably bear all the marks of fraud, it should be poorly organized, shallow, artificial, patchy, and unoriginal; it should display a pretentious vocabulary (the Book of Mormon uses only 3,000 words), overdrawn stock-characters, melodramatic situations, gaudy and overdone descriptions and bombastic diction. Assuming that it must be that kind of a book, the critics, without bothering to read it, have not hesitated to brand it, with Bernard DeVoto, "a yeasty fermentation, formless, aimless, and inconceivably absurd . . ." That is why we have just gone to the trouble in this book to glance at just

a few of the technical aspects of the Book of Mormon—
to give the reader some idea of the infinite study and pains
that would have to go into the composition of such a
complicated structure in which one slip would bring down
the whole edifice. Whether one believes its story or not,
the severest critic of the Book of Mormon if he reads it
with any care at all must admit that it is the exact opposite
to what DeVoto said it was: it is carefully organized,
specific, sober, factual, and perfectly consistent.

Ah, but this fabulous story claims to be real history
—can you prove that? No, nor can we prove that Herodotus
or Gregory of Tours or the Anglo-Saxon Chronicles are
history; but we have good reasons for believing that they
contain authentic history, and the same reasons support
our endorsement of the Book of Mormon as history—we
have indicated some of those reasons in the preceding
pages. But now comes the real test. Granted, since we
can't deny it, that Joseph Smith did give a big book to
the world and that its production was an altogether
remarkable performance—so remarkable, indeed, as to
make the problem of its authorship a very puzzling one
indeed—still, all that is beside the point or of very minor
significance in comparison with what the book actually
has to say. As we see it, if an angel took the trouble to
deliver the book to Joseph Smith and to instruct him
night after night as to just how he was to go about giving
it to the world, and if Joseph Smith bade farewell to peace
and security for the rest of his life in order to carry out
instructions (and Brigham Young informs us that we can't
imagine the threats and perils that constantly surrounded
him), that book should obviously have something of importance to convey. The question that all are now asking
of the Bible—"What does it have to say that is of relevance
to the modern world?" applies with double force to the
Book of Mormon, which is a special message to the modern
world. It claims to contain an enormously important mes-

sage for whoever is to receive it, and yet until now those few who have been willing to receive it as the authentic word of God have not shown particular interest in that message. Why is that? Because, as we shall see, the full import of the message is just beginning to materialize. What was a romance of the far away and long ago to our parents and grandparents has in our own generation become a grim reality. Suddenly the Book of Mormon has become as modern as today's newspaper. If this seems like an overstatement, let us consider a few points.

A Polarized World

One thing the reader of the Book of Mormon is never allowed to forget is that the Nephites lived in a polarized world, in which they were perpetually engaged either in hot or cold wars with the Lamanites. Their basic problem was one of survival; security was an obsession with them. Vastly outnumbered and usually surrounded by people whose way of life and whose idealogy were totally alien to their own, who nursed ancient grudges and attributed all their own setbacks and misfortunes to Nephite wickedness, with whom any communication was usually out of the question, the Nephites had by all human standards ample cause for alarm. Yet from the beginning they received full assurance that God had purposely arranged things that way, and that they had absolutely nothing to fear as long as they behaved themselves. God intended that the Nephites should have hostile Lamanites breathing down their necks: "I will curse them even with a sore curse, and they shall have *no power* over thy seed except they shall rebel against me also. And if it so be that they rebel against me, they shall be as a scourge unto thy seed, to stir them up in the ways of remembrance." (1 Nephi 2:23-24.)

So it was a blessing to the Nephites after all to have the Lamanites on their doorstep to "stir them up to re-

membrance"—"Happy is the man whom God correcteth."
No matter how wicked and ferocious and depraved the
Lamanites might be (and they were that!), no matter
by how much they outnumbered the Nephites, darkly
closing in on all sides, no matter how insidiously they
spied and intrigued and infiltrated and hatched their dia-
bolical plots and breathed their bloody threats and pushed
their formidable preparations for all-out war, *they were
not the Nephite problem.* They were merely kept there
to remind the Nephites of their real problem, which was
to walk uprightly before the Lord. That is why as soon
as the Nephites started talking about settling the Lamanite
question once for all by using their military might to "cut
them off from the face of the land," Mormon "did utterly
refuse from this time forth to be . . . a leader of this people," (Mormon 3:9-11) pointing out that God had expressly
forbidden that sort of thing, and that if there was any
avenging to be done he and he alone would do it: "But
behold, the judgments of God will overtake the wicked;
and it is by the wicked that the wicked are punished. . . ."
(Mormon 4:5.) From being a maker of history, Mormon
became its recorder—for our benefit. For he immediately
appends to the above remark: "I write unto you, Gentiles,
and also unto you, house of Israel . . . and I write also unto
the remnant of this people." (Mormon 4:17-19.)

And his theme is co-existence. At that time the
Lamanites were feeling about the Nephites exactly as the
Nephites felt about them, and so the process of polarization
had been pushed to its limit, with each side out to exter-
minate the other, obsessed with the old doctrine of "It is
either you or us." As in the days of Shiz and Coriantumr,
everybody was forced to choose either one side or the
other, at a time, of course, when there was very little to
choose between them, for "both the people of Nephi and
the Lamanites had become exceeding wicked one like unto

another." (4 Nephi 45.) Indeed Mormon says of his own people, "their wickedness doth exceed that of the Lamanites." (Mormon 9:20.)

Whenever the Nephites were truly righteous, however, the old polarization broke down or vanished completely. When things were at their best ". . . there was no contention in the land. . . . neither were there Lamanites, nor any manner of -ites; but they were in one . . . And how blessed were they!" (4 Nephi 17-18.) This happy state of things persisted until "a small part of the people had revolted . . . and taken upon them the name of Lamanites," (v. 20), reviving the old prejudices and teaching their children to hate, "even as the Lamanites were taught to hate the children of Nephi from the beginning." (v. 39.) And so the polarizing process began all over again.

In the days of their integrity the Nephites displayed singular forbearance in their dealings with the Lamanites. We have seen how Moroni time and again resolutely refused to punish the Lamanites when he was in a position to do so. The case of the Lamanite maidens is an impressive lesson in self-control. When the wicked priests of Noah carried off some Lamanite girls, the Lamanites, thinking that the people of Limhi were to blame, made war on them. In the battle the Lamanite king was wounded and taken to Limhi, who asked him to explain his hostility. The king told about the stolen girls and somebody remembered that the priests of King Noah were wandering loose in the woods—so there had probably been a mistake. At this the king not only apologized but offered to explain things to his people, "that they may be pacified." (Mosiah 20:19.) At the same time the mighty Nephite warrior Gideon urged his people to "pacify the king . . . for it is better that we should be in bondage than that we should lose our lives; therefore let us put a stop to the shedding of so much blood." (Mosiah 20:22.) But before the

Lamanite king could explain things to his people, he had
to get them to listen to him, which he did by "bowing
himself down before them, and did plead in behalf of the
people of Limhi," who had come out with him completely
unarmed. Whereupon "the Lamanites . . . had compassion
on them, and were pacified towards them, and returned
with their king in peace to their own land." (Mosiah
20:25-26.) Here was a perfect set-up for a long war; but
because Limhi took the pains to investigate, and Gideon
talked sense instead of heroic cliches, and a proud king
was willing to humble himself before his subjects, and
those subjects were willing to have compassion on a
hereditary foe, and because the people of both sides,
though both had been attacked without provocation, were
able to see that a mistake had been made, the story had
a happy ending.

Even more instructive is the experience of Ammon.
First he went among the wickedest of the Lamanites,
addressing their king with courtesy and respect and expressing his desire to live in the land and serve the king.
(Alma 17:23-25.) The people he converted in the land
absolutely refused to shed blood, even when a Lamanite
army started mowing them down. (Alma 24:21-22.) This
we might say, is coexistence carried to absurd lengths;
and yet it was wisdom, for presently the Lamanites realized
what they were doing and "did forbear from slaying them,"
and ended up joining their society in large numbers. (Alma
24:23-26.)

"Good Guys and Bad Guys"

Critics like Mr. O'Dea have told the world that the
Book of Mormon is a rather naive tale, a typical "Western,"
in which the "good guys" fight the "bad guys." Nothing
could be further from the truth. At every confrontation
of the Nephites and Lamanites in war, the Book of Mormon is at pains to point out that the conflict is to be

attributed to the wickedness of both parties. Indeed, the greatest battle before the final debacle was fought not between the Nephites and Lamanites but between Nephite armies. (3 Nephi 4:11.) ". . . they shall have no power over thy seed," the Lord promised Nephi, "except they shall rebel against me *also*." (1 Nephi 2:23f.) The "also" is important—it means that whenever the Nephites and Lamanites fight it is because *both* have rebelled against God. It is never a case of "good guys versus bad guys."

In the Book of Mormon we are constantly admonished of the folly of pinning "good" and "bad" labels on people. Father Lehi constantly took his wicked sons, Laman and Lemuel to task for murmuring against God, and yet when the going got really rough he joined them in their complaints: ". . . and also my father began to murmur against the Lord his God," (1 Nephi 16:20), as a result of which "he was brought down into the depths of sorrow." (1 Nephi 16:25.) One thinks of Peter, the first president of the church and truest of the true, who vowed that he would never deny the Lord even at the cost of his life, and within twelve hours was swearing "with an oath" that he had never known him.

Likewise the Brother of Jared, the most righteous man of his time, after all his sufferings and tribulations had to be severely rebuked "because he remembered not to call upon the name of the Lord." (Ether 2:14.) Nephi's penitential hymn was no hollow rhetoric: he too had sinned, only with transparent honesty he finds the cause of his reverses entirely within himself, and rebukes himself for wanting to take it out on others: "And why should I yield to sin, because of my flesh? . . . that the evil one have place in my heart to destroy my peace and afflict my soul? Why am I angry because of mine enemy?" (2 Nephi 4:27.)

If the good people slip in the Book of Mormon, the

bad people often surprise us no less. Laman and Lemuel, determined to murder Nephi, could still hear the voice of the Lord, and "did turn away their anger, and did repent of their sins." (1 Nephi 16:39.) There never were more noble and powerful teachers of righteousness than Alma the Elder and Mosiah, and yet their sons were perfect rotters, and deliberately went about undermining all their work; it took an angel to convert them, but almost overnight the arch-delinquents became model missionaries. (Mosiah 8:11-13, 32-35.) Another arch-enemy of the church who suddenly became a great missionary was Zeezrom. (Alma 11.) Morianton, a descendant of the wicked Riplakish, was a fierce outlaw who came to the throne by violence and was decidedly immoral in his personal life, yet once in power he was an excellent ruler who "did do justice unto the people. . . ." (Ether 10:11.) One of the keepers and transmitters of the holy record was the heroic Omni who fought gallantly to preserve his people, and yet must confess, "I of myself am a wicked man, and I have not kept the statutes and the commandments of the Lord as I ought to have done." (Omni 2.)

Were the Nephites good people? Some of the time, but by no means always. Early in their history Jarom marvels that they have not long since been destroyed because of their sins (Jarom 3), and tells how the prophets had to threaten and protest continually and how the laws had to be savagely severe to keep the people in line. In the midst of the most desperate military crises Nephite society was shot through with dissensions and intrigue. (Alma 53:8-9.) When they were on the very verge of destruction, their leaders "marvelled at the wickedness of the people." (Alma 59:12.) When they lost half their country to the Lamanites it was because "they were wicked even like unto the Lamanites." (Helaman 4:22.) In the final escalation of atrocities the Nephites were not a whit behind the Lamanites. (Moroni 9.)

If the Nephites are not all good, the Lamanites are by no means all bad. For many years it was only because Nephite dissenters stirred them up that the Lamanites came to war against the Nephites. It was hardened Lamanite troopers who had sworn vengeance upon the Nephites (Alma 25:1) who upon returning from a campaign, of their own free will went over in large numbers "and did join themselves to the people of God, who were the people of Anti-Nephi-Lehi." (Alma 25:13.) It was fierce tribesmen with a long record of savagery and bloodshed who suddenly decided to bury their weapons and became the most righteous people in the New World. (Alma 24:19.) It was also the Lamanite veterans of a long war who later went over in droves to join them, becoming overnight model Nephite citizens. (Alma 62:17, 29.)

The prophets in the Book of Mormon marvel at how soon a righteous people can become wicked, and the speed of the reverse process is even more surprising. It is a common fallacy to think of things happening very slowly in history, and especially in ancient history. But the student has only to compare *any* two consecutive decades of history to realize that things do not move slowly at all— history moves at breath-taking speed, and as far as the existing records show, always has. If, as the result of a single famine a wicked nation becomes a righteous nation (Helaman 11:18); if after the Gadianton crisis the Nephites suddenly became believers to a man (3 Nephi 5:1) and people hardened in the ways of sin "did serve God with all diligence day and night" (3 Nephi 5:3); if the Gadianton robbers themselves at that time presently became solid citizens (3 Nephi 6:3); and if the hardened criminals in a Lamanite prison could suddenly be "encircled about, yea every soul, by a pillar of fire . . . and filled with that joy which is unspeakable and full of glory" (Helaman 5:43f.) and then go forth as missionaries to convert "the more part of the Lamanites" (Helaman 5:50), if all such changes seem rather sudden, we have only to think of countless parallels in our own history. How long did it take millions of Germans and Italians, individually and collectively to change completely from one state of mind to another? As a single speech could turn thousands of mild and sober citizens into ranting fanatics, so with the disappearance of the leader dangerous men of war reverted just as quickly to well-meaning and sympathetic human beings. Does it take fifty years for great nations to change from fast friendship to bitter enmity? Twenty-four hours is enough.

The Law of the Judgment

The Book of Mormon does not leave us to draw our own conclusions from all this, even though those conclusions are rather obvious. By precept as well as example the book keeps hammering away at the great lesson summed up by Mormon and Moroni as they look back over the course of Nephite history before closing and sealing the record and sorrowfully ask: "Where did we go wrong?" Hear the magnificent words of Mormon:

For behold, the same that judgeth rashly shall be judged rashly again; for according to his works shall his wages be; therefore, he that smiteth shall be smitten again, of the Lord. Behold what the scripture says—man shall not smite, neither shall he judge; for judgment is mine, saith the Lord, and vengeance is mine also, and I will repay." (Mormon 8:19-20) . . . see that ye do not judge wrongfully; for with that same judgment which ye judge ye shall also be judged. (Moroni 7:18.)

Our own dispensation opens with the same ringing declaration that closed the book of Nephite history:

. . . the Lord shall come to recompense unto every man according to his work, and measure to every man according to the measure which he has measured to his fellow man. . . . that man should not counsel his fellow man, neither trust in the arm of flesh. (D.&C. 1:10-19.)

The opposite of judgment, vengeance, and the arm of flesh is charity, and Mormon and Moroni both end up with an impassioned plea for charity. Mormon, who had seen nothing all his life "but a continual scene of wickedness and abominations" (Mormon 2:18), has a great yearning for peace and rest (Moroni 7:3-4), but he is convinced that unregenerate men are not capable either of receiving or giving good of themselves, (Moroni 7:10), and must remain as nothing until they have charity, "the pure love of Christ." (Moroni 7:44-47.) He gives an ancient definition of charity (the same one Paul gives)— for charity there is no bookkeeping, no *quid pro quo*, no deals, interests, bargaining, or ulterior motives; charity gives to those who do not deserve and expects nothing in return; it is the love God has for us, and the love we have for little children, or whom we expect nothing but for whom we would give everything. By the Law of the Harvest, none of us can expect salvation, for "all men that are in a state of nature . . . a carnal state . . . have gone contrary to the nature of God," and if they were to be restored to what they deserve would receive "evil for evil, or carnal for carnal, or devilish for devilish." (Alma 41: 11, 13.) "Therefore, my son," says Alma in a surprising conclusion, "see that you are merciful unto your brethren." (Alma 41:14.) That is our only chance, for if God did not have mercy none of us would ever return to his presence, for we are all "in the grasp of justice" from which only "the plan of mercy" can save us. (Alma 42:14f.) But God does have mercy, and has declared that we can have a claim on it to that exact degree to which we have shown charity towards our fellow man. Man cannot be righteous before God, his wisdom is foolishness with God. (1 Corinthians 1:25), his intelligence is laughable even to himself, his courage is highly conditioned and subject to change without notice, he can be virtuous and abstemious only in the absence of temptation (2 Nephi 4:27), in short "a man being evil cannot do that which is good; neither will he give a good gift." (Moroni 7:10.)

What can man do, then, that will be to his credit? He can do two good things, according to Alma and all the other Book of Mormon prophets: he can have mercy, and he can repent—that is the theme of Alma's great discourse to his wayward son who questions the justice of God in punishing men. (Alma 42.) And charity to be charity must be "to all men," especially to those evil people who hate us, "For if ye love them which love you what reward have ye? do not even the publicans do the same?" (Matthew 5:46.) Nor should we demand or expect charity in return: "If they have not charity it mattereth not unto thee, thou hast been faithful." (Ether 12:37.) Still, we might say that the Law of the Harvest wins after all, since we must have and give charity to receive it.

We find, then, in the Book of Mormon, that the Lamanites are sometimes better than the Nephites and sometimes worse, that good people can become bad with astonishing speed (a "fall" is usually a rather sudden affair), and bad people can just as suddenly become good —the instant that the wicked Alma called upon Jesus he became a new man, "born of God." (Alma 36:19f., 23.) Thus we learn by precept and example the folly of trying to judge our fellow man. Of one thing we can be sure, however—the good people never fight the bad people: they never fight anybody: ". . . it is by the wicked that the wicked are punished; for it is the wicked that stir up the hearts of the children of men unto bloodshed." (Mormon 4:5.) We are apt to forget when we read about the heroic resistance of the Nephites to the overwhelming Lamanite power and the noble deeds of the 2,000 youths during the long war, that the gallant Nephites had brought the war upon themselves and were being punished by God for their sins. Surveying conditions throughout the entire land on the eve of that war, which he knew was coming, Alma was "exceeding sorrowful" at the wickedness and hard-heartedness of the people everywhere, who refused all counsel. And so he and his sons worked like beavers to do what good they could to stave off the increasing violence and cynicism that were leading the Nephites right into a major conflict. (Alma 35:15-16.) Whenever Nephites and Lamanites collide it is because they are both bad. Being good or bad, therefore, does not consist in being on one side or the other—that was the illusion of Nephites and Lamanites alike in the day of their wickedness, when each side sought to put off its sins on the heads of the other. One did not have to be a Nephite or a Lamanite, however, in order to be wicked or righteous: every man and woman who ever lived has been capable of doing right and wrong no matter when or where he or she lived.

Free agency, according to the Book of Mormon, belongs to everybody. Again it is Mormon who reminds us of this: "For behold, my brethren, it is given unto you to judge, that ye may know good from evil; and the way to judge is plain, that ye may know with a perfect knowledge, as the daylight is from the dark night. For behold, the Spirit of Christ is given to *every* man, that he may know good from evil; wherefore, I show unto you the way to judge. . . ." (Moroni 7:15f.) At last man is allowed to judge—himself! This free agency was given to us in the pre-existence as a basic principle of the plan of life; no mortal can give it to another or take it away from another: ". . . whosoever perisheth, perisheth unto himself," said Samuel the Lamanite to the benighted Nephites—apparently their living under a bad government deprived none of them of free agency—"and whosoever doeth iniquity, doeth it unto himself; for behold, ye are free; ye are permitted to act for yourselves; for behold God hath given unto you a knowledge and he hath made you free. He hath given unto you that ye might know good from evil, and he hath given unto you that ye might choose life or death;

and ye can do good and be restored unto that which is good . . . or ye can do evil, and have that which is evil restored unto you." (Helaman 14:30f.) This is an absolute law and operates regardless of the type of society in which one lives. (Alma 41:7-8, 42:7, 26-28.) It is true that some environments favor virtue as others do sin, that "an unrighteous king doth pervert the ways of all righteousness," (Mosiah 29:23), and sometimes "the voice of the people doth choose iniquity," (Mosiah 29:27), but that is no excuse for any individual; he is not thereby deprived of his knowledge of good and evil or his free agency: in a telling passage Alma reports how "because of the exceeding great length of the war . . . many had become hardened . . . and many were softened because of their afflictions . . ." (Alma 62:41.) The same cause produced a hardening in the one case and a softening in the other—who could blame the war for his bad behavior? No person or thing can force another to sin, for a sin is only a sin to that degree to which one participates of his own free will.

But if all have free agency in the Book of Mormon, all do not have civil liberties. The Zoramites, as we have seen, had a thought-police, "therefore they found out privily the minds of all the people," and forthwith deported "those who were in favor of the words . . . spoken by Alma. . . ." (Alma 35:5-6.) Amulon, as a vassal ruler under the supreme king of the Lamanites, kept a close watch on the Nephites under his authority, "that whosoever should be found calling upon God should be put to death." (Mosiah 24:11.) The descendants of this Amulon, "those rulers who were the remnant of the children of Amulon," (Alma 25:7), "having usurped the power and authority over the Lamanites, caused that many of the Lamanites should perish by the fire because of their belief," (Alma 25:5), that is, when they began to embrace the teachings of the missionaries and prophets. (v. 6.) Just before the birth of Christ, the unbelieving majority of the Nephites planned a coup and set a day on which "all those who believed in those traditions (of the coming of the Messiah) should be put to death. . . ." (3 Nephi 1:9.) This was illegal, of course, but then it was also illegal among the Nephites to put any individual to death "save their condemnation was signed by the governor of the land," a rule which the clever lawyers tried with some success to evade. (3 Nephi 6:22-26.) It was also the lawyers who tried to get a death-sentence against Nephi the son of Helaman for speaking against them and the laws. (Helaman 8-9.) He was saved because some ordinary Nephites still retained some sense of fair play. (Helaman 8:7.) Civil rights have never been a strong point with kings, of course, and Abinadi was burned alive for preaching what was displeasing to King Noah and his court.

By contrast, among the righteous Nephites Korihor was allowed to speak out freely against the religion and practices of the people, and though he was an embarrassment to local authorities, he was never kept in prison nor tried nor sentenced for his preaching, for "there was no law against a man's belief." (Alma 30:6, 11.) One could be punished only for specific crimes, and wrong belief was not a crime punishable by man: "If a man desired to serve God, it was his privilege," not a duty imposed by law, and if he was an atheist "there was no law to punish him." (Alma 30:9.) This was more than a sense of fair play, the Nephites being convinced that "it was strictly contrary to the commands of God that there should be a law which should bring men on unequal grounds." (Alma 30:7.) This explains why Korihor was not only free to believe what he wanted, but to teach wherever he chose, for to muzzle him would put him "on unequal grounds" with other preachers, right or wrong. In short, the Nephites shared the opinion of Joseph Smith, who said in the King Follett Discourse: "Every man has a natural, and, in our country, a constitutional right to be a false prophet, as well as a true prophet."

To guarantee such liberty, the Nephites passed and enforced laws. "King Mosiah sent a proclamation . . . that there should not any unbeliever persecute any of those who belonged to the church of God." (Mosiah 27:2.) This did not give the church unfair advantage, for at the same time there was "a strict law among the people of the church, that there should not any man, belonging to the church, arise and persecute those that did not belong to the church." (Alma 1:21.) Among the Nephites it was also "against the law . . . that there should be any slaves among them . . ." (Alma 27:9.) The law of Mosiah was the organic law of the land (Alma 1:14, 11:1, Helaman 4:22), and Mosiah had laid down its fundamental concept at his inauguration: "I desire that this inequality should be no more in this land . . . but I desire that this land be a land of liberty, and every man enjoy his rights and privileges alike." (Mosiah 29:32.) Mosiah realized that liberty and equality must go together. Even a king of the Lamanites protected by law and where necessary by the application of force the right of Ammon and other Nephite missionaries to preach freely among his people. (Alma 32:1-2.)

Some have felt that the attempt of the state to implement the ideas of liberty and equality by passing and enforcing laws repugnant to a majority or minority, i.e., laws restraining persecution, discrimination, slavery, and all violence whatever, is an infringement of free agency. But plainly the Nephites did not think so. As we have seen, they believed that no one was ever without his free agency: one can sin or do unrighteously under any form of government whatever, indeed, the *worse* the government the better the test: after all, we are all being tried and tested on this earth "under the rule of Belial" himself, "the prince of this world;" but since no one can ever make us sin or do right, our free agency is never in the slightest danger. But free institutions and civil liberties are, as history shows, in constant danger. They are even attacked by those who would justify their actions as a defense of free agency, and insist that artificial barriers erected by law to protect the rights of unpopular and weak minorities are an attempt to limit that agency.

How far can men go in "counselling" their fellow-men? God can give life and he can take it, he can judge and he can punish, he can smite the blasphemer and the unbeliever, he can heal and bless at will, he can forgive or condemn whom he will, he can curse and he can segregate, and he can put a mark on whom he pleases, and be avenged on his enemies—all of which we learn from the Book of Mormon. But *men* may *not* do these things; God has reserved judgment and punishment for himself and pronounced terrible penalties on any man who shall presume to exercise those high offices. In punishing Cain he pronounced seven-fold vengeance upon any mortal who should presume to contribute to that punishment. (Gen. 4:15.) When the Nephites decided to "avenge themselves of the blood of their brethren" the voice of the Lord pronounced their doom in awful wrath as it came to Mormon "saying: Vengeance is mine, and I will repay. . . ." (Mormon 3:14-15.) He punishes the wicked even in this life, but does not enlist the aid of the righteous in that unpleasant task, for "it is by the wicked that the wicked are punished. . . ." (Mormon 4:5.) The closing verses of the Book of Mormon remind us that the Lord alone exercises power and judgment, or, in the words of Nephi, ". . . the keeper of the gate is the Holy One of Israel; and he employeth *no servant* there . . . for he cannot be deceived, for the Lord God is his name." (2 Nephi 9:41.) When Korihor by his vicious and subversive teachings sinned grievously against God, Alma left it entirely up to God to punish him, and it was not the Nephites but the wicked and intolerant Zoramites who put him to death by mob action. (Alma 30:59.) As for the Nephites, whenever they became wicked they would also become intolerant and "scornful, one towards another, and they began to persecute those that did not believe according to their own will and pleasure." (Alma 4:8.) The Book of Mormon offers striking illustrations of the psychological principle that impatience with the wickedness of others (even when it is real wickedness and not merely imagined) is a sure measure of one's own wickedness. The Book of Mormon presents what has been called the "conspiratorial interpretation of history." People who accept such an interpretation are prone to set up their own counter-conspiracies to check the evil ones. But that is exactly what the Book of Mormon forbids above all things, since, as it constantly reminds us, God alone knows the hearts of men and God alone will repay.

Nephite Disease. The Danger Signs

When a person suffering from diabetes consults a doctor, the doctor does not prescribe a treatment for cancer, even though cancer is today considered *by far the more dangerous disease.* What we read about in the Book of Mormon is the "Nephite Disease"—and we have it! We should be glad that we do not have the much worse diseases that infect some other societies, and that there is greater hope for us. But diabetes if neglected can kill one just as dead as cancer—after all, the Nephites were terminated. We can be most grateful, therefore, regardless of how sick others may be, that God in the Book of Mormon has diagnosed our sickness for our special benefit, and prescribed a cure for us. It is into our hands that the Book of Mormon has been placed: after 140 years the Russians, Portuguese, and Turks do not even know of its existence. Plainly it is meant for us, as it reminds us many times; it is the story of what happened to the Nephites—and we are the Nephites: ". . . it must needs be that the riches of the earth are mine to give; but beware of pride, lest ye become as the Nephites of old." (D.&C. 38:39.) There it is in a nutshell: it is the fate of the Nephites, not of the Lamanites, Greeks, or Chinese, that concerns us; and that doom was brought on them by pride which in turn was engendered by the riches of the earth.

There are four portentous danger-signals in the Book of Mormon, three internal and one external. Internal and external go hand in hand; in the brief but ample exposition on cold war in the 35th chapter of Alma we see how the growing corruption in all the cities as "the hearts of the people began to wax hard," (Alma 35:15), was accompanied by steady deterioration of relations with the Lamanites and mounting danger on all the frontiers. Alma and Moroni were always convinced that the internal ills were the really dangerous ones, and that without them there would be no external threat whatever—". . . they shall have no power over thy seed except they shall rebel against me also." (1 Nephi 2:23.) The external threat is of course the Lamanites; the internal danger signals are 1) the accumulation of wealth, 2) the appearance on the scene of ambitious men, and 3) the presence in the society of "secret combinations to get power and gain." Let us consider these in order.

1. Wealth: A Fringe Benefit, Not a Goal

Wealth as such is not described as an evil in the Book of Mormon; indeed prosperity is depicted as the normal reward of righteousness. Many have asked why God would consistently reward the virtues of the Nephites with a prosperity which almost infallibly destroyed that virtue. The answer is in the "almost"—there is no paradox here; wealth need not be destructive. A person in exuberant health is certainly more likely to be tempted of the flesh than one suffering from a dire disease. And yet exuberant good health is a reward of right living. The temptations of health and the temptations of wealth are real, to be sure, but they are *not* irresistible, and they *are* necessary to test mankind in this life of probation.

The Book of Mormon starts out with Lehi in Jerusalem, a very rich and also a very righteous man—which
shows us that wealth is not in itself an evil. But almost
immediately Lehi is called upon to choose between his love
of righteousness and his comfortable circumstances by
leaving all his precious things behind him and taking to
the desert. His elder sons think this is simply insane, that
they are being led by "a visionary man . . . to leave . . .
their gold, and their silver, and their precious things, to
perish in the wilderness. . . . because of the foolish imaginations of his heart." (1 Nephi 2:11.) The difference
between Lehi and his sons was not one of wealth but of
attitude to wealth; the old man did not set his heart on
the stuff and was willing to give it up, but the boys were
very bitter: "Behold, these many years we have suffered
in the wilderness, which time we might have enjoyed our
possessions . . . yea, and we might have been happy."
(1 Nephi 17:21.) That is the situation throughout the
Book of Mormon where prosperity wears a double face.

The righteous can be entrusted with unlimited wealth
because *they do not put their hearts upon it.* To his highly
prosperous subjects King Benjamin announced, "I . . . have
not sought gold nor silver nor any manner of riches of you."
(Mosiah 2:12.) And his even more prosperous son was
never guilty of "seeking for gain, yea, for that lucre which
doth corrupt the soul." (Mosiah 29:40.) Riches are to be
accepted gratefully as a fringe benefit, in the Book of
Mormon, but never to be the object of our search: "But
the laborer in Zion shall labor for Zion; for if they labor
for money they shall perish." (2 Nephi 26:30.) The condemnation of the Nephites in the days of wickedness and
vengeance is ever that "they have set their hearts upon
riches." "Ye are cursed because of your riches," says
Samuel the Lamanite, "and also your riches are cursed
because ye have set your hearts upon them. . . ." (Helaman
13:21.) At the very beginning Nephi declares, "But wo

unto the rich . . . their hearts are upon their treasures;
wherefore their treasure is their God." (2 Nephi 9:30.)
And another Nephi at the time of Christ repeats the re-
frain: "O, how could you have forgotten your God in the
very day that he has delivered you? . . . ye have set your
hearts upon the riches and the vain things of this world
. . ." (Helaman 7:21.)

Why should we labor this unpleasant point? Because
the Book of Mormon labors it, for our special benefit.
Wealth is a jealous master who will not be served half-
heartedly and will suffer no rival—not even God: ". . . their
treasure is their God." "Ye *cannot* serve God and Mam-
mon." (Matthew 6:24.) In return for unquestioning
obedience wealth promises security, power, position,
and honors, in fact anything in this world. Above all,
the Nephites like the Romans saw in it a mark of
superiority and would do anything to get hold of it, for
to them "money answereth all things." (Ecclesiastes 10:
19.) Even the people of the church when they "began
to wax proud, because of their exceeding riches" (Alma
4:6) became fiercely competitive, full of "envyings, and
strife, and malice, and persecutions, and pride. . . ." (Alma
4:9.) "Ye do always remember your riches," cried Samuel,
". . . unto great swelling, envyings, strifes, malice, persecutions and murders, and all manner of iniquities." (Helaman 13:22.) Along with this, of course, everyone dresses
in the height of fashion, the main point being always that
the proper clothes are expensive—the expression "costly
apparel" occurs 14 times in the Book of Mormon. The
more important wealth is, the less important it is how one
gets it; in one of many enlightening passages we are told
how the Lamanites upon adopting Nephite business
methods became corrupt as a matter of course, almost as
if it were inevitable: ". . . they taught them that . . . they
might write one to another. And thus the Lamanites began

to increase in riches, and began to trade one with another and wax great, and began to be a cunning and a wise people . . . delighting in all manner of wickedness and plunder, except it were among their own brethren." (Mosiah 24:6-7.) At least they retained a spark of ethics.

Wealth and Inequality

The most calamitous effect of wealth, according to the Book of Mormon, is the inequality it begets in any society. Right at the beginning Jacob sounds the warning: ". . . many of you have begun to search for . . . precious ores, in the which this . . . land of promise . . . doth abound most plentifully. And the hand of providence hath smiled upon you most pleasingly . . . and because some of you have obtained more abundantly than that of your brethren ye are lifted up in the pride of your hearts. . . . Do ye not suppose that such things are abominable unto him who created all flesh? And the one being is as precious in his sight as the other. . . ." (Jacob 2:12f., 21.) Jacob then denounces the "grosser crime" of immorality, which in the Book of Mormon as in secular history is the infallible attendant on the pride of wealth. Inequality is not only the result of wealth-seeking: it is sometimes actually its purpose: ". . . they began to seek to get gain *that they might* be lifted up one above another. . . ." (Helaman 6:17.)

With great insight the Book of Mormon shows us how wealth-oriented societies sought moral justification in a display of religious piety, like the Zoramites, "a wicked and a perverse people . . . their hearts were set upon gold, and upon silver, and upon all manner of fine goods. . . . their hearts are set upon them, and yet they cry unto thee, and say—We thank thee, O God, for we are a chosen people unto thee. . . ." (Alma 31:24-28.) It would even seem that church people are especially susceptible to the Nephite disease; none reverence "precious things" more ardently than the priests, and yet even the people of the true church share the weakness: ". . . the people of the church began to be lifted up in the pride of their eyes, and to set their hearts upon riches and upon the vain things of the world, that they began to be scornful, one towards another, and they began to persecute those that did not believe according to their own will and pleasure. . . ." (Alma 4:8.) An aggressive and self-righteous bigotry was the best defense against uneasy consciences.

Accordingly, as Samuel the Lamanite caustically observes, any professional toady who could not only justify but sanctify the ways of the affluent Nephites could name his own price, "because he speaketh flattering words unto you, and he saith that all is well. . . ." (Helaman 13:27f.) An army of Nephite lawyers made everything legal and respectable and in the process laid "the foundation of the destruction of this people." (Alma 10.) But who would be such a churl as to speak of robbing the poor of money that went to adorning the house of God? (Mormon 8:37, 39.) For that matter, who persecutes the poor? Nobody in our time goes out of his way to oppress the poor—as Mormon puts it, you simply suffer the poor "to pass by you, and notice them not." (Mormon 9:39.) They just don't exist. The guilty conscience, or rather, the guilty subconscious, is hypersensitive to criticism in the Book of Mormon, and reacts vigorously to it, denouncing the critic as "a false prophet . . . a sinner, and of the devil," and taking immediate measures "in all manner of ways to destroy him." (Helaman 13:26.) The great Nephi when he dared criticize the lawyers was in danger of his life at their hands and was only saved because there were a few common people who still preserved a lingering sense of justice and fair play. (Helaman 8-9.) And Samuel's blast against the curse of riches was met by a righteous counter-blast: "Take this fellow and bind him, for behold he hath a devil. . . ." (Helaman 16:6.)

Champions of Equality

King Benjamin was a stickler for equality in word and deed. He labored with his own hands to make it clear that his people should "labor to serve one another." (Mosiah 2:14, 17.) He rebuked the self-made: "Can ye say aught of yourselves? I answer you, Nay . . . And I, whom ye call your king, am no better than ye yourselves are." (Mosiah 2:26.) He insisted that anyone who withheld his substance from the needy, no matter how improvident and deserving of their fate they might be, "hath great cause to repent," (Mosiah 4:16-18), explaining his position in ringing words: "For behold, are we not all beggars?" (Mosiah 4:19.) His son Mosiah wrote equality into the constitution, "that every man should have an equal chance throughout all the land. . . ." (Mosiah 29:38.) "I desire," said the king, "that this inequality should be no more in this land of liberty, and every man may enjoy his rights and privileges alike. . . ." (Mosiah 29:32.) This does not mean that some should support others in idleness, "but that the burden should come upon all the people, that every man might bear his part." (Mosiah 29:34.) This was in conformance with Benjamin's policy of taxation: "I would that ye should (this is a royal imperative) impart of your substance to the poor, every man *according to that which he hath* . . . administering to their relief, both spiritually and temporally, *according to their wants*." (Mosiah 4:26.) In the same spirit, a Lamanite king during an emergency "commanded that every man should impart to the support of the widows and their children, that they might not perish with hunger. . . ." (Mosiah 21:17.)

Here taxation appears as a means of implementing the principle of equality. Whenever taxation is denounced in the Book of Mormon, it is always because the taxer uses the funds not to help others but for his own aggrandizement. Thus Benjamin says that he has labored for his own support so that nobody will have to pay taxes to support *him*. (Mosiah 2:14.) The people of Limhi suffered under a punitive tax imposed by their conquerors, a vicious tax because it was designed to give the payers no benefit whatever, direct or indirect. (Mosiah 7:15.) King Noah levied a 20 per cent tax, which was the normal tax in ancient times (e.g., in Egypt and Greece), and was by no means ruinous; the trouble was that instead of spreading it around, Noah spent every penny of the tax on himself and his court. (Mosiah 11:4-6.) The same applies to Riplakish the Jaredite, who saw to it that all the wealth of the kingdom flowed in one direction only, until "the people did rise up in rebellion" and drove him out. (Ether 10:5-8.)

When the constitution of Mosiah was threatened by the king-men, Moroni came to the rescue and "put an end to the stubbornness and the pride of those people who professed the blood of nobility; but they were brought down to humble themselves like unto their brethren. . . ." (Alma 51:21.) This drastic enforcement of equality was justified by an extreme national emergency; but both Alma and Moroni had pointed out to the people on occasion that the worst danger their society had to fear was inequality. It was inequality that had broken up the church, according to Alma: "And . . . Alma saw the wickedness of the church . . . bringing on the destruction of the people. Yea, he saw great inequality among the people. . . . and seeing all their inequality, began to be very sorrowful. . . ." (Alma 4:11f., 15.) Commenting on the war that followed, Alma concluded: "Thus we see how great the inequality of man is because of sin and transgression, and the power of the devil. . . ." (Alma 28:13.) Four hundred years later the religious and civil society was again broken up when the people "had become exceedingly rich. . . . and from that time forth they did have their goods and their substance no more common among them. And they began to be divided into classes. . . ." (4 Nephi 24-25.) It was the beginning of the end.

2. Ambitious People

There are no -isms in the Book of Mormon—they are
an expression of our modern passion for classifying. But
there are certain irreducible constants that get down as it
were to the bedrock of history—there are things and there
are people. Put them together and you get prosperity: the
word "prosperity" occurs no fewer than 75 times in the
Book of Mormon, "riches" 46 times, "gain" 43 times,
"treasures" and "precious things" each 23 times, and
"money" 14 times. These words regularly appear in company with what may be called their derivatives, indicating
less tangible qualities: "Pride" 63 times, "power" 44 times,
the "poor" 32 times. It needs no electronic computer to tell
us in what sense these words are to be interpreted by us;
even the casual reader of the Book of Mormon cannot miss
the point, both because it is explicitly pointed out to him
and because the significant stock situations are repeated
over and over again for our benefit.

The Book of Mormon is greatly concerned with the
issue of power: the word "power" occurs over 100 times
in a good sense—when it refers to the power of God, which
is available to men through righteous living, and over 40
times in a bad sense, usually in the common formula
"power and gain," when it refers to the power which men
seek for themselves and which is available through the
possession of wealth. In the ups and downs of Nephite
history the prologue to disaster is always the accumulation
of wealth, but the evil genius of the plot is always an
ambitious and driving individual. In this history the infallible test for distinguishing good leaders from bad is the
touchstone of ambition. The greatest king, chief judge,
high-priest and general of the Nephites each retired and
yielded up his great powers to others when he felt that his
own maximum usefulness was past. Ambitious men do
not give up power—they seek it: Laman sought the kingship
that Nephi refused, and generations of Jaredites fought

and bled to seize the throne that all the righteous sons of
the Brother of Jared had wisely turned down.

It is largely the doings of ambitious seekers after
power and gain which provide the dramatic and tragic
interest of the Book of Mormon. We have already looked
in on the careers of some of these. Some, like the ancient
Sophists, had an intellectual appeal, and aspired to guide
the faith and thinking of the nation to their own glory and
renown: such were Sherem, Nehor, Amlici and his school,
and Korihor. Typical followers of such would be such
young "smart Alecs" as Alma Jr. and the sons of Mosiah,
and Alma's youngest son Corianton. Others sought power
through political manipulation and intrigue: we have already seen the deadly Amalickiah in action. What they
all had in common along with a passion to be top man was
"much power of speech"—a gift of words and a knack for
telling people what they wanted to hear. "Flattery" and
"flatter" occur 22 times in connection with their operations.
The baneful activity of ambition can best be surveyed in
the operations of those "secret combinations to get power
and gain" which we must now consider.

3. The Secret Combinations

As the type and model of secret combinations to be
avoided the Book of Mormon gives us the Gadianton
Society. Let us look at it. Gadianton history really begins
with the skilled professional killer, Kishkumen. After
Pahoran had foiled the attempt of the king-men to overthrow the "free government and to establish a king," (Alma
51:3-5), he was succeeded by his son Pahoran in a popular
election. The defeated candidates were the new judge's
brothers, and bore the good Egyptian names of Paanchi
and Pacumeni. One of them conceded the election and
"did unite with the voice of the people," but the other "was
exceeding wroth" at losing the election and "was about to
flatter away those people (his supporters) to rise up in

rebellion. . . ." Just in time he was seized, tried, and condemned to death for having "raised up in rebellion and sought to destroy the liberty of the people." (Helaman 1:6-8.) His backers, however, weren't going to take that lying down, and so "they sent forth one Kishkumen" who "murdered Pahoran as he sat on the judgment-seat." (Helaman 1:9.) Then they all took an oath, following Kishkumen's instructions (for he had "the goods" on them and they could not refuse) to support Kishkumen and preserve complete secrecy regarding their operations; after which they went forth and "did mingle themselves among the people" as respectable citizens. (Helaman 1:11-12.)

Thus they became an underground organization, the identity of whose members "was not known to those who were at the head of the government." (Helaman 3:23.) And that explains how it was possible later on, in the midst of great peace and prosperity, for the chief of state, Cezoram, and after him his son and successor to be murdered in office in such a way that the assassins were never discovered. (Helaman 6:15.) It is significant that the times of great prosperity and abundance were also the times when the secret societies flourished most vigorously and when murder and intrigue were the order of the day, "for behold, the Lord had blessed them so long with the riches of the world that . . . they began to set their hearts upon their riches; yea they began to seek to get gain that they might be lifted up one above another; therefore they began to commit secret murder . . . that they might get gain." (Helaman 6:17.) The sequence is a natural one: with easy wealth comes the feeling of superiority which makes people status-conscious; and with a feeling for status comes a desperate need to acquire the one thing that will give status; and with the recognition of the all-importance of that one thing, any scruples that may stand in the way of its acquisition are pushed aside, even murder being permissible as long as one is not found out.

Determined to "get gain" at any price, the Nephites soon learned that the quickest way to get rich with a minimum risk and the best way to avoid the inconvenience of the law was to belong to a protective society: ". . . the more part of the Nephites . . . did unite with those bands of robbers, and did enter into their covenants and their oaths, that they would protect and preserve one another. . . ." (Helaman 6:21.) With this type of insurance an individual could operate with impunity "contrary to the laws of their country and also the laws of their God," enjoying the protection and priority of another system of laws—the rules of the society or corporation. (Helaman 6:23-24.) This system, Helaman tells us, went right back to the beginning of the race, and took root among the Nephites at the time when they "did trample under their feet" the commandments of God . . . and did build up unto themselves idols of their gold and silver." (Helaman 6:31.) It was not idols, please note, but the gold and silver itself that they worshipped.

The objectives of the Gadianton society being to overthrow or gain control of the government and run things to suit themselves, in time they "did obtain the sole management of the government, insomuch that they did . . . turn their backs upon the poor and the meek. . . ." (Helaman 6:39.) None of Mosiah's or Limhi's sentimental social legislation for them! The one thing the Gadianton administration respected was money, and their policy was "to rule and do according to their wills, that they might get gain and glory of the world," naturally "letting the guilty and the wicked go unpunished because of their money." (Helaman 7:5.) To operate with impunity they needed public support: "Ye have united yourselves unto . . . that secret band established by Gadianton!" cries Nephi to his countrymen, "Yea, wo shall come unto you because of that pride which ye have suffered to enter your hearts, which has lifted you up beyond that which is good because of your exceeding great riches!" (Helaman 7:25f., cf. D.&C. 38:39.)

But wealth is a comparative thing, being pure quantity and nothing else, and the rivalry and jealousy among the elite and between various groups organized to grab the biggest share of the take became terrific, "insomuch that there were wars throughout all the land among all the people of Nephi." (Helaman 11:1.) Then it was that Nephi called for a famine and got it. (Helaman 11:4-5.) The famine brought the people to their senses, and in the poverty of hard times the Gadianton band simply disappeared, as "the more part of the people, both the Nephites and the Lamanites," began to behave themselves. (Helaman 11:10, 21.) Then came more prosperity, and gradually small groups of the revived Gadianton order began to make raids on the country from hiding-places in the mountains, assisted by tip-offs from Nephite sympathizers. (Helaman 11:24-25.) This sort of thing had a romantic and adventurous appeal to the younger generation of Nephites who went off and joined up with the bands in large numbers. (3 Nephi 1:27-29.) Finally the bands by uniting were strong enough to lay waste Nephite cities and defy whole armies until "the Nephites were threatened with utter destruction. . . ." (3 Nephi 2:11-13), not because of genius of the Gadiantons but "because of the wickedness of the people of Nephi. . . ." (3 Nephi 2:18.) The Gadianton campaign now took the form of a crusade, with the ancient and honorable society (3 Nephi 3:9) fighting, as it maintained, only to recover that rightful control of the government which had been wickedly denied it. (3 Nephi 3:10.) In a high-minded letter addressed to the Nephite chief of state, Giddianhi, the "governor of the society of Gadianton" testified to its lofty ideals and the high moral character of its leaders, its sense of fair play (3 Nephi 3:2-3), its magnanimity (3 Nephi 3:5), the indomitable courage of its members (3 Nephi 3:4), and the grievous

wrongs they had suffered, ending up with the characteristically paranoid charge, that all the present trouble was
"because of *your* wickedness in retaining from them their
rights of government. . . ." (3 Nephi 3:10.)

Lachoneus, the Nephite governor, was not intimidated.
He ordered the evacuation of vast tracts of land, which
the Gadiantons proceeded to occupy by massive infiltra-
tion. But since they were a predatory order and found no
loot but only "black earth," they were finally forced into
open battle. (3 Nephi 4:1-4.) Thoroughly beaten in spite
of their skillful psychological devices for inspiring terror
(3 Nephi 4:7-9), and cut off in their retreats (3 Nephi
4:16-26), the band again became "extinct" as it had been
in the days of the younger Nephi. (Helaman 11:10.) And
by what means were they wiped out? That is the most
surprising thing of all. The whole gang was in time rounded
up and imprisoned, and there the people of Lachoneus
"did cause the word of God to be preached unto them; and
as many as would repent of their sins and enter into a
covenant that they would murder no more were set at
liberty" (3 Nephi 5:4), and rehabilitated by being given
"lands according to their numbers, that they might have,
with their labors, wherewith to subsist upon. . . ." (3 Nephi
6:3.) Those who refused to change their ways, and "who
did still continue to have those secret murders in their
hearts," and betrayed their intentions by "breathing out
threatenings against their brethren were condemned and
punished according to the law." (3 Nephi 5:5.)

Fifty years earlier the Lamanites had "utterly destroyed" the Gadianton robbers from their lands by the
same method: ". . . the Lamanites did hunt the band of
robbers of Gadianton; and they did preach the word of
God among the more wicked part of them, insomuch that
this band . . . was utterly destroyed . . ." (Helaman 6:37.)
"If that sounds a little too idealistic," we once wrote commenting on this (*An Approach to the Book of Mormon*,

p. 321), "we must remember that we are dealing here not with a small and peculiar band of professional or congenital criminals, but with the general public gone mad after money—people not really criminal at heart, but unable to resist the appeal of wealth and the things it could buy. Among the Nephites these things actually "seduced the more part of the *righteous* until they had come down to believe . . ." in the system of the Gadiantons and to "partake of their spoils. . . ." (Helaman 6:38.)

The wave of prosperity that followed Lachoneus's victory over the Gadiantons brought "a great inequality in all the land, insomuch that the church began to be broken up." (3 Nephi 6:14.) Finally various groups of king-men, ambitious local officials, priests, judges, lawyers, and great families ("kindreds" 3 Nephi 6:27) "did enter into a covenant one with another" and "did combine against the people of the Lord," in such a strong coalition that working together they were able "to deliver those who were guilty of murder . . . and set at defiance the law and rights of their country. . . ." (3 Nephi 6:27-30.) It was the usual elements combined with the usual objectives—overthrow or seizure of the government and silencing "the voice of the people." This time the central government was indeed overthrown, for good. But when the followers of the ambitious Jacob then declared him king, the other groups resented it and regretted his baneful success, being "united in hatred of those who had entered into a covenant to destroy the government." (3 Nephi 7:11.) Too late they regretted their folly in removing a strong central government in the interests of unlimited ambition. So Jacob and his people planned to move out of the country and build up strength for a come-back. (3 Nephi 7:12.) At this point the great earthquake changed everything.

Two-hundred years later the old evil raised its head again as the people "having become exceeding rich. . . .

began to be divided into classes," (4 Nephi 24-26), built elegant churches (v. 26, 41), and "began again to build up the secret oaths and combinations of Gadianton." (v. 42.) Again "the robbers of Gadianton did spread over all the face of the land," (v. 46) while business boomed as never before—"and gold and silver did they lay up on store in abundance, and did traffic in all manner of traffic." (v. 46.) But the Gadiantons were tops at the grabbing game, and before long everybody started hiding up his possessions for security. (Mormon 1:18.) In vain—nothing could secure their valuables from gravitating into the competent hands of the society. In the end the Nephites had to settle for formal treaties with the Gadiantons as an independent power, sharing their lands with them on a permanent basis. (Mormon 2:28-29.)

The Jaredite Experience

These secret societies were already old in the time of the Jaredites, who learned about them from the records they brought with them, which told of "them of old and their secret plans for getting kingdoms and great glory." (Ether 8:9.) It was a pact "to help such as sought power to gain power," (Ether 8:16.) When the Jaredite Akish seeking to seize the throne, administered the oath to his supporters with fair promises, it was not by the devil but "by the God of heaven" that they swore. (Ether 8:13-17.) But God did not approve, "for the Lord worketh not in secret combinations, even as they of old; which combination is most abominable and wicked above all in the sight of God. For the Lord worketh not in secret combinations, neither doth he will that man should shed blood, but in all things hath forbidden it from the beginning of man." (Ether 8:19.) Every man may covenant with God, and may keep or break his covenant with God alone to judge and punish him. But men may never covenant with each other: "Swear not at all, by heaven or by earth . . ." (3 Ne.

12:33-37.) It was these secret combinations, Moroni informs us, that destroyed both the Nephites and the Jaredites, and will eventually destroy those who follow them in
the land of promise unless they "awake to a sense of your
awful situation . . ." (Ether 8:24), that is, the situation
which allows the secret combinations to arise and flourish:
the societies themselves are the symptom, not the disease.

Years later Heth "began to embrace the secret plans
again of old." (Ether 9:26.) This led to a series of troubles
and crimes that ended only with a terrible famine and
plague of serpents. After that came more prosperity and
the resumption of the "power and gain" game, with king
Shez being killed by a robber "because of his exceeding
riches." (Ether 10:3.) The general prosperity increased,
and "there began to be robbers . . . and they adopted the
old plans . . . and sought again to destroy the kingdom."
(Ether 10:33.) The result was "wars and contentions,
famine, pestilence, great destruction," as the various rival
combinations spread havoc in murderous gang-wars among
themselves. But everybody was playing the game—that is
what makes it so tragic—and "the prophets mourned and
withdrew." (Ether 11:13.) A popular uprising against
"that secret combination which was built up to get power
and gain," (Ether 11:15), put one Moron on the throne,
and he was followed by the mighty Coriantumr, who
fought plots against himself with the skill of an expert,
a master at fighting fire with fire and meeting violence
with violence. (Ether 13:15-18.) The outcome of this was
the dissolution of all semblance of organized government,
with "every man with his band fighting for what he desired." (Ether 13:24.)

But it was the next step downward that achieved the
ultimate in social dissolution. The end of the road is the
family shelter, with each family entirely preoccupied with
its own survival as it feuds off all the neighbors and guards
its own supplies: "Wherefore every man did cleave unto

that which was his own, with his hands, and would not borrow neither would he lend; and every man kept the hilt of his sword in his right hand, in the defense of his property and his own life and of his wives and children." (Ether 14:2.) In the final polarization of the society between Shiz and Coriantumr, both sides went down to extinction enjoying alike the assistance and the opposition of the "secret combinations." (Ether 14:8.)

"Gadiantonism"

Let us summarize the essential nature of what some have called "Gadiantonism":

Objectives

1) "Power and gain," the two being interactive: power wins gain and gain wins power for whoever has either. 2) Control or overthrow of the government; using political office "to rule and do according to their will, that they might get gain and glory. . . ." (Helaman 7:5.)

Methods

1) Secret agreements between individuals and groups. The Gadiantons are essentially an underground movement. 2) Assassination. These two things, "secret combinations" and "that men should shed blood" have been forbidden by God "in all things . . . from the beginning of man." (Ether 8:19.) 3) "Payola": "Akish did offer them money . . ." (Ether 9:11); ". . . letting the guilty . . . go unpunished because of their money. . . ." (Helaman 7:5.) 4) Skillful propaganda and public relations: ". . . flattering words . . ." 5) The hate campaign: a steady output of charges, accusations, and rumors, in the manner of Amalickiah: Accuse— always accuse. "Eagerness to accuse is from the devil." (Brigham Young.) 6) Intimidation: "breathing out many threatenings . . .", operating "by the hand of secrecy," wearing fearsome disguises. (3 Nephi 4:7.) 7) Showman-

ship, e.g., the picturesque uniforms and romantic appeal to the young. (3 Nephi 1:29.) 8) Tight control of members—death penalty for betrayal. (Ether 8:14, Helaman 1:11.)

Attitude

1) The Gadiantons were totally partisan, the laws and interests of the combination taking priority over all other laws and interests. 2) All were ambitious, hence the labor for power and gain: Cain is the type and model. 3) The combinations were highly competitive, feuding fiercely among themselves. 4) They sought to project a noble image, with much talk of rights and wrongs, high courage and upright character. (The letter to Lachoneus.) 5) They professed piety and religion, swearing their forbidden oaths not by the demons but "by the God of heaven . . ." (Ether 8:14), ". . . by their everlasting Maker. . . ." (Helaman 1:11.) 6) They were paranoid, always attributing their troubles to the wickedness of others; never the aggressors, they are constantly seeking to avenge their wrongs. Vengeance is their watchword.

Ecology

1) They flourish best in an affluent business society, and wither in times of poverty. 2) They crystallize around ambitious individuals. 3) They readily coalesce with kingmen, would-be nobility, great families, ambitious local officials, and rapacious Lamanite overlords, i.e., with all who are opposed to popular government among the Nephites. 4) They have destroyed every civilization in the New World in which they have been able to thrive. 5) They cannot thrive or even survive without the acceptance and encouragement of the society in general. Being predatory and non-productive, i.e., parasites, they must have a complacent society to host and support them. Such a society is one which accepts as desirable the Gadianton goals of power and gain. 6) They can become dormant

for long periods of time and then, when circumstances are favorable, suddenly appear in full strength and vigor, their plans having been buried and preserved intact against the day of opportunity.

The Gadiantons, terrible as they were, are treated more as a symptom than as a disease: the society that has them is sick, but they are like maggots that prey only on dead tissue, they simply exploit the evil situation that gives them their opportunity. We shall refer to the cure later.

CHAPTER 13

Prophecy in the Book of Mormon: the Three Periods

The prophecies of the Book of Mormon belong to the three categories of past, present, and future. The *past* prophecies cover the time from the days of Lehi to the translating of the book by Joseph Smith; the *present* prophecies are those which apply to our own dispensation from the coming forth of the Book of Mormon to the present; the *future* prophecies foretell events from now until the millennium. The first and last of these divisions cannot be rigorously controlled, of course, since what happened before 1830 could have been learned by the author of the Book of Mormon from mundane sources, while what happens after today is still in the future and cannot be checked. It is the middle phase that is really impressive, telling of things that we now look back on but which were still in the future when the Book of Mormon was published.

Past Prophecies

Though what we call "past prophecies" in the Book of Mormon all refer to times already past when that book was published, still those prophecies contain things that were not known to anyone at the time and have only been discovered "since Cumorah." Such a thing was the loss of precious things from the scriptures and the effect of that loss on the world, which we have discussed above. The scattering of the Jews as prophesied in the Book of

Mormon follows a pattern unfamiliar in Joseph Smith's day but being confirmed in our own. Until recently scholars have held that the "apocalypse of bliss" and the "apocalypse of woe" represented two totally different traditions; but the Book of Mormon shows how they have always gone together in a pattern of dispensations, ". . . and never hath any of them been destroyed save it were foretold them by the prophets of the Lord." (2 Nephi 25:9.) The scattering was to be not only more widespread than one supposed, embracing "all the face of the earth" even to the unknown "isles of the sea," (1 Nephi 22:3-4), but it goes on in installments, some of the migrations going back into early times and many of them being unknown to history: "And behold, there are many who are already lost from the knowledge of those who are at Jerusalem . . . and whither they are none of us knoweth . . ." (2 Nephi 22:4.) The Dead Sea Scrolls and other documents now attest the reality of such emigrations from Jerusalem.

Lehi prophesied a total destruction for Jerusalem and a dire scattering of the people in his own time. Biblical scholars, however, always assumed that the destruction of Jerusalem was only a superficial one and that only the more important people were carried away to Babylon; it was not until the present generation that archaeological findings showed that "all, or virtually all, of the fortified towns in Judah (were) razed to the ground."[1] The prophesied fate of the Nephites before and after Christ need not detain us here, since its fulfillment is described only in the Book of Mormon itself.

"Present" Prophecies

The Book of Mormon foretells its own reception by the world. Though the critics have always maintained that Joseph Smith expected it to be a best seller and make him a lot of money, the ancient prophets knew better—

---

[1]W. F. Albright, in *The Biblical Archaeologist* 9 (1946), p. 4.

they knew that they were not writing "the things which
are pleasing unto the world . . ." (1 Nephi 6:5); and tell
how "many of the Gentiles shall say: A Bible! A Bible!
We have got a Bible, and there cannot be any more Bible"
(2 Nephi 29:3), and refuse to believe that God can "remember one nation like unto another," and "speak the
same words unto one nation like unto another." (2 Nephi
29:8.) The book is to cause more than a local flurry;
while it may make some sensation among the outraged
gentiles, it is to go quietly and steadily forth over all the
world to seek out the chosen: ". . . and my words shall
hiss forth unto the ends of the earth, for a standard unto
my people, which are of the house of Israel." (2 Nephi
29:2.) Its appearance is not a triumphant one at all, but
only marks the first step, the very beginning, of the latter-
day work: "Therefore, when ye shall receive this record
ye may know that the work of the Father has commenced
upon all the face of the land." (Ether 4:17.) It shows
"that I may set my hand again the second time to recover
my people, which are of the house of Israel." (2 Nephi
29:1.) It is characteristic of adventist and millennialist
sects to preach a hasty and spectacular consummation of
all things. Not so the Book of Mormon, whose coming
forth is depicted only as the opening scene of a long and
eventful drama. With it, "the work of the Father has
commenced," not ended. (1 Nephi 14:17, 2 Nephi 3:13,
30:8, 3 Nephi 21:26-28, Mormon 3:17.)

But it has commenced with power; not with the
ruminations and counsels of men but with the intervention
of angels; and not in the familiar unfolding of history, but
by the exercise of special providence: ". . . all the kindreds
of the earth cannot be blessed unless he shall make bare
his arm in the eyes of the nations. Wherefore, the Lord
God will proceed to make bare his arm in the eyes of all
the nations, in bringing about his covenants and his gospel
unto those who are of the house of Israel." (1 Nephi 22:11.)

The Book of Mormon predicts the going forth and unfolding of the message and its effect in the world in terms
that no one could have foreseen. Who can tell when a
church is founded what direction, form, and consequence
its growth is going to take? Writing with special consideration for their own descendants, the Book of Mormon
prophets are especially concerned for the future of that
highly mixed people known as the Indians. In the 1820's
the Indians still held most of the continent and felt themselves a match for any invader. But Mormon forewarns
them that all their efforts to prevail by force of arms will
be hopeless. (Mormon 7:4.) In the beginning Lehi
prophesied that his descendants who would survive until
our day should see generations of "bloodsheds, and great
visitations among them" (2 Nephi 1:12), and that God
would "bring other nations unto them, and . . . give unto
them power, and . . . take away from them the lands of
their possessions, and he will cause them to be scattered
and smitten." (2 Nephi 1:11.) Nephi foretold the same:
". . . the Lord God will raise up a mighty nation among
the Gentiles, yea, even upon the face of this land; and by
them shall our seed be scattered." (1 Nephi 22:7.) This
scattering and smiting was to exceed anything the Indians
had experienced before 1830: it was to be carried to the
point of virtual extermination, ". . . driven about as chaff
before the wind. . . . led about by Satan, even as chaff is
driven before the wind, or as a vessel . . . without anything
wherewith to steer her . . . But behold, it shall come to
pass that they shall be driven and scattered by the Gentiles
who shall possess the land. . . ." (Mormon 5:15-20.)
Speaking in the present tense, Lehi sees the descendants
of Laman and Lemuel "visited by the sword, and by
famine, and are hated, and are led according to the will
and captivity of the devil." (2 Nephi 1:18.) Their blessings
are forfeit to their persecutors: "And behold, the Lord
hath reserved their blessings, which they might have re-

ceived in the land, for the Gentiles who shall possess the land." (Mormon 5:19.) And with the blessings the Gentiles inherit the risk: God now requires of them what he requires of all inheritors of the promised land: ". . . and after they have been driven and scattered by the Gentiles, behold, then will the Lord remember the covenant . . . unto all the house of Israel. . . . And then, O ye Gentiles, how can ye stand . . . except ye shall repent and turn from your evil ways?" (Mormon 5:19-22.)

The state of the world after the coming forth of the Book of Mormon and the scattering of the Indians is vividly described, right down to our own time. First we get a picture of Joseph Smith's generation, when the sacred record comes "out of the earth . . . in a day when it shall be said that miracles are done away . . . in a day when the blood of the saints shall cry unto the Lord, because of secret combinations and the works of darkness (the persecutions of the Saints); . . . in a day when the power of God shall be denied, and churches become defiled and be lifted up in the pride of their hearts; . . . in a day when there shall be heard of fires, and tempests, and vapors of smoke in foreign lands; and . . . of wars, rumors of wars, and earthquakes in divers places; . . . in a day when there shall be great pollutions upon the face of the earth . . . murders, and robbing, and lying, and deceivings, and whoredoms, and all manner of abominations; . . . in a day when . . . churches shall say: Come unto me, and for your money you shall be forgiven your sins." (Mormon 8:26-32.)

Next we are taken to a later time relative to the one just indicated, "concerning that which must shortly come, at *that* day when these things shall come forth among you" —these are events subsequent to the time of the coming forth; the prophet helpfully informs us that he is speaking in the timeless idiom of prophecy: "Behold, I speak unto you as if ye were present, and yet ye are not. But . . . I know your doing." (Mormon 8:35.) And so this is for us:

"And I know that ye do (present tense) walk in the pride of your hearts; and there are none save a few only who do not lift themselves up in the pride of their hearts, unto the wearing of very fine apparel, unto envyings and strifes, and malice, and persecutions, and all manner of iniquities . . ." (Mormon 8:36.) Here is our own fashionable, well-dressed, status-conscious and highly competitive society. The "iniquities" with which it is charged are interesting, for instead of crime, immorality, and atheism we are told of the vices of vanity, of the intolerant and uncharitable state of mind: pride, envy, strife, malice and persecution. These are the crimes of meanness; whereas libertines, bandits and unbelievers have been known to be generous and humane, the people whom Mormon is addressing betray no such weakness. They are dedicated people: "For behold, ye do love money, and your substance, and your fine apparel, and the adornment of your churches, more than ye love the poor and the needy, the sick and the afflicted." (Mormon 8:37.) These people do not persecute the poor (they are too singleminded for that), but simply ignore their existence: ". . . ye adorn yourselves with that which hath no life, and yet suffer the hungry, and the needy . . . to pass by you, and notice them not." (Mormon 8:39.)

It is important to note that these people are church builders (the unbelievers are addressed in the next chapter), and that they include the members of the true church: "O ye . . . who sell yourselves for that which will canker, why have ye polluted the holy church of God?" (Mormon 8:38.) The apostate churches were already pointed out in the earlier period (verses 32-33) along with their wresting of the Bible. (Mormon 8:33.) After the coming forth of the Book of Mormon, moreover, there is only one "holy Church of God" (1 Nephi 14:10.) The expression here, moreover, cannot refer to the primitive church, of which these latter-day Christians know nothing

—they are not in a position to pollute *it*, and pollution is necessarily an inside job. And why should the true Church be any more immune to the blandishments of money and fine clothes and beautiful churches today than it was in the days of the Nephites? Unless even these times are "cut short in righteousness" who shall be saved? If the Book of Mormon is to be trusted, the members of the Church as well as the non-members need someone to "prick their hearts with the word, continually stirring them up unto repentance." (Jarom 12.) Why should they now think that all these warnings are not meant for them, but only for the wicked outsiders? It is exactly that attitude which Nephi and Samuel the Lamanite attacked with such vigor. The Book of Mormon was given to us because it was meant for us.

But the unbelievers are bad enough in these days, and Mormon devotes his next section to them: "And now, I speak also concerning those who do not believe in Christ." (Mormon 9:1.) His warning to them is, "Wait and see!" (Mormon 9:2-4.) Their position is wholly untenable, scientifically or otherwise, as they will realize "when ye shall be brought to see your nakedness . . . it will kindle a flame of unquenchable fire upon you." (Mormon 9:5.) That position is set forth in the Book of Mormon with superb clarity and brevity in a speech attributed to Korihor. A full generation before Bentham, Mill, Darwin, and Marx, the Book of Mormon was stating the case for naturalism, materialism, and the survival of the fittest with the greatest precision.

Modern Thinking

First of all, Korihor insisted on a strictly rational and scientific approach to all problems, anything else being but "the effect of a frenzied mind" (Alma 30:13-16); he crusaded against the tyranny of ancient traditions and primitive superstitions, which led people to believe things which just "are not so," (Alma 30:16), calling for an emancipation from "the silly traditions of their fathers." (Alma 30:31.) He called for a new morality with the shedding of old inhibitions (Alma 30:17-18, 25.) He called for economic liberation from priestly exploitation (Alma 30:27), demanding that all be free to "make use of that which is their own." (Alma 30:28.) He preached a strict no-nonsense naturalism: ". . . when a man died, that was the end thereof," (Alma 30:18), and its corollary, which was a strict materialism: ". . . therefore every man fared in this life according to the management of the creature. . . ." (Alma 30:17.) From this followed a clear-cut philosophy of laissez-faire: "Therefore every man prospereth according to his genius, and . . . every man conquered according to his strength," with right and wrong measured only by nature's iron rule of success and failure: ". . . and whatsoever a man did was no crime." (Alma 30:17.) It was survival of the fittest applied to human behavior, and the removal of old moral and sentimental restraints was good news to many people, "causing them to lift up their heads in their wickedness, yea, leading many away . . . to commit whoredoms. . . ." (Alma 30:18.) Along with his attitude of emancipation Korihor cultivated a crusading zeal and intolerance of any opposition which has been thoroughly characteristic of his school of thought in modern times, calling all opposition "foolish" (Alma 30:13-14), "silly" (Alma 30:31), and the evidence of frenzied and deranged minds. (Alma 30:16.) And while for Alma a free society was one in which anybody could think and say whatever he chose (Alma 30: 7-12), for Korihor the only free society was one in which everyone thought exactly as *he* thought (Alma 30:24)— which was also the liberal gospel of Huxley, Dewey, Marx, et al.

The philosophy of Korihor with its naturalism, materialism, and moral relativism, is the prevailing phi-

losophy of our own day, as was foreseen in the Book of
Mormon: "Yea . . . there shall be great pollutions upon
the face of the earth . . . when there shall be many who
will say, Do this, or do that, and it mattereth not, for the
Lord will uphold such at the last day. But wo unto such
for they are in the gall of bitterness and in the bonds of
iniquity." (Mormon 8:31.) Enormously proud of their
accomplishments, "the Gentiles are lifted up in the pride
of their eyes, and have stumbled, because of the greatness
of their stumbling block." (2 Nephi 26:20.) Their own
expertise is the highest court of appeal, as they "preach up
unto themselves their own wisdom and their own learning,
that they may get gain and grind upon the faces of the
poor." (2 Nephi 26:20.) The theologians "set themselves
up for a light unto the world, that they may get gain and
praise of the world," (2 Nephi 20:29), as they "contend
one with another . . . teach with their learning, and deny
the Holy Ghost. . . ." (2 Nephi 28:4.)

The whole world will be caught up in the great
illusion when, "in the last days, or in the days of the
Gentiles . . . *all* nations of the Gentiles and also the Jews,
both . . . upon this land and . . . upon other lands . . .
will be drunken with iniquity and all manner of abominations." (2 Nephi 27:1.) As the upheavals of nature increase (2 Nephi 27:2), war becomes the order of the day,
caused by "secret abominations to get gain (which) cause
that widows should mourn . . . and also orphans . . . and
also the blood of their fathers and their husbands to cry
unto the Lord from the ground for vengeance" on those
combinations." (Mormon 8:40.) The selective killing
makes it clear that organized warfare is meant here. As
in the last two World Wars, the Christian nations "shall
war among themselves, and the sword of their own hands
shall fall upon their own heads, and they shall be drunken
with their own blood." (1 Nephi 22:13.) This would seem
to refer to revolution as well as war. Miraculously, the

House of Israel will be the survivor, as "every nation which shall war against thee . . . shall be turned one against another . . . And all that fight against Zion shall be destroyed," (1 Nephi 22:14), and pass away "as a dream of a night vision." (2 Nephi 27:2.) Formidable plans to destroy the upbuilding of Zion need not concern the Saints —like the Nephites, they have only their own sins to worry about. As for their enemies, "they shall fall into the pit which they digged to ensnare the people of the Lord." (1 Nephi 22:14.) Likewise "that great and abominable church" whatever it is, should be no concern of ours, for we are assured that with all its clever scheming and accumulated might it "shall tumble to the dust and great shall be the fall of it." (1 Nephi 22:14.)

Still in the Future

Using the same means of designating relative time that Mormon does, Nephi refers to a development that is to come "speedily" at some time after "the Lord God shall commence his work among the nations . . . ," namely, "that the Lord God shall cause a great division among the people," which, it is explained, will be necessary if the wicked are to be destroyed without destroying the righteous also. (2 Nephi 30:8, 10.) This may be future, though the division may be going on right now. It is not a division between the eastern and western hemispheres, since the Book of Mormon makes much of the gathering of the Jews when "the Lord will set his hand again the second time to restore his people from their lost and fallen state," as he "shall bring forth his words unto them . . . for the purpose of convincing them of the true Messiah. . . ." (2 Nephi 25:17-18.) Note that this gathering will begin before the Jews begin to believe in Christ. It is only "*after* the book (of Mormon) . . . shall come forth" and is carried to the remnant of Lehi's seed," that "the Jews which are scattered also shall begin to believe in Christ; and they shall begin to gather and . . . shall also become a delightsome people." (2 Nephi 30:3, 7.) And after the Book of Mormon has come forth "it is yet a very little while and Lebanon shall be turned into a fruitful field; and the fruitful field shall be esteemed as a forest." (2 Nephi 27:22, 26, 28.) Showing that this particular gathering will be in the Old World.

When the house of Israel "shall rend that veil of unbelief . . . then shall the great and marvellous things which have been hid up from the foundation of the world," begin to come forth (Ether 4:15), "greater things" than any yet known, that have been "hid up because of unbelief," (Ether 4:13), "things the Father hath laid up for you, from the foundation of the world . . ." (Ether 4:14); such as the lost writings of John—"when ye see these things, ye shall know that the time is at hand that *they* shall be made manifest." (Ether 4:16.) Note the relative time: when certain important events of the restoration have already been witnessed, then is the time for these other things: "Therefore, when ye shall receive this record (the Book of Mormon) ye may know that the work of the Father has *commenced* . . ." (Ether 4:17.) The future, then, holds more ancient records for the faithful.

The restoration of the Lamanites goes along with that of the Jews. With the Book of Mormon, "the gospel of Jesus Christ shall be declared among them; wherefore, they shall be restored unto a knowledge of their fathers . . ." (2 Nephi 30:5); and at the same time that the Jews "shall begin to believe . . . and . . . shall begin to gather in . . ." (2 Nephi 30:7), the Lamanites shall "rejoice . . . and their scales of darkness shall begin to fall from their eyes; and many generations shall not pass away . . . save they shall become a white and delightsome people." (2 Nephi 30:6.) It is still a matter of generations. The gentiles might as well realize that this land has been consecrated to Lehi's descendants forever (2 Nephi 10:19), and stop despising them and the Jews alike. (2 Nephi 29:4-5.) If the Gentiles in the Promised Land, having been given their chance and great blessings do not repent and turn from their evil ways (Mormon 5:22), the time will come when "a remnant of Jacob shall go forth among you as a lion, and tear you in pieces, and there is none to deliver." (Mormon 5:24.) Who is the remnant of Jacob? The Lord in person told the mixed Nephites and Lamanites that heard him in the temple, that these words of Isaiah applied to them: ". . . and ye shall be in the midst of them who shall be many; and ye shall be among them as a lion . . . and as a young lion among the flocks of sheep. . . ." (3 Nephi 20:16.) Though greatly outnumbering the Lamanites, the Gentiles will be unable to put up a resistance because the Lord will no longer be with them, "if the Gentiles do not repent after the blessing which they shall receive, after they have scattered my people." (3 Nephi 20:15.) So Lehi's descendants are to stage a comeback after the Gentiles have scattered them as chaff and had everything their own way. The second half of the story is still in the future, but the first half has been thoroughly fulfilled.

The Great Overburn

The culmination of the wars and troubles to come, according to the Book of Mormon, is the Great Overburn. The evil word "overburn," coined in our own generation, is made to order to describe the final holocaust of the Book of Mormon. This is not the end of the world, when the heavens are rolled up as a scroll, when "the elements should melt with fervent heat, and the earth should be wrapped together as a scroll, and the heavens and the earth should pass away," preceding the Last Judgment. (3 Nephi 26:3, Mormon 9:2.) This is a preliminary debacle just before the millennium, as we shall see. It is the last of the great wars, but it is a special kind of war, described not in the usual terms as "bloodshed" or the work of the "sword," but only as a burning. The Book of

Mormon prophets give this specific interpretation to the words of Isaiah, cited by Nephi: "For *every* battle of the warrior is with confused noise, and garments rolled in blood; but *this* shall be with burning and fuel of fire." (2 Nephi 19:5.) And again, "Through the wrath of the Lord of Hosts is the land darkened, and the people shall be as the fuel of the fire. . . ." (2 Nephi 19:19.)

The time of the Great Overburn is clearly stated. It is just when the nations "shall war among themselves, and . . . be drunken with their own blood," (1 Nephi 22:13), that "the day soon cometh that all the proud and they who do wickedly shall be as stubble; and the day cometh that they must be burned." (1 Nephi 22:15.) It is just when "all the nations . . . will be drunken with iniquity and all manner of abominations—And when that day shall come they shall be visited . . . with the flame of devouring fire," (2 Nephi 27:2), and become "as a dream of a night vision." (2 Nephi 27:3.) It is just when "the Messiah will set himself again the second time to recover them ("who wait for him") that "they who believe not in him shall be destroyed, both by fire, and by tempest, and by earthquakes, and by pestilence, and by famine," with fire heading the list. (2 Nephi 6:13-14.)

It will be a general destruction involving all the nations, "even blood, and fire, and vapor of smoke must come; and it must needs be upon the face of the earth. . . ." (2 Nephi 22:18.) What is this "vapor of smoke" on the face of the earth? The aftermath of the fire, or, since it is not ordinary smoke but a vapor, possibly fallout. ". . . all those who are built up to get power over the flesh, and those who are built up to become popular . . . and those who seek the lusts of the flesh and the things of the world . . . they are those who must be brought low in the dust; they are those who must be consumed as stubble; and this is according to the words of the prophet." (1 Nephi 22:23.) For God "must destroy the wicked by fire." (2 Nephi 30:

10.) Thus Nephi interprets Isaiah, and Moroni also: "At my command . . . the earth shall shake; and at my command the inhabitants thereof shall pass away, even so as by fire." (Ether 4:9.)

What makes it clear that this is not the end of the world is that it precedes the second coming of the Lord and the Millennium, and that the destruction is not a total but a selective one, with many survivors. That anyone should escape such a general holocaust is indeed miraculous, but the Lord has his ways of doing things: "Wherefore, he will preserve the righteous by his power, even if it so be that the fulness of his wrath must come, and the righteous be preserved, even unto the destruction of their enemies by fire. Wherefore, the righteous need not fear; for thus saith the prophet, they shall be saved, even if it so be as by fire." (1 Nephi 22:17.) The theme is repeated and its miraculous nature emphasized: "For behold, the righteous shall not perish . . . and the Lord will surely prepare a way for his people. . . ." (2 Nephi 22:19f.)

"And the righteous need not fear," but "all those who belong to the kingdom of the devil are they who need fear . . . they are those who must be brought low in the dust; they are those who must be consumed as stubble . . ." (1 Nephi 22:22-23.)

When the Lord is about to come to those who wait for him, "he will manifest himself unto them in power . . . unto the destruction of their enemies . . . and none will he destroy that believe in him." (2 Nephi 6:14.) Nephi prophesied the same miraculous preservation in a previous burning; that which was to be at the time of the Crucifixion: "Wherefore, all those who are proud, and that do wickedly, the day that cometh shall burn them up . . . for they shall be as stubble." (2 Nephi 26:4.) ". . . for the fire of the anger of the Lord shall be kindled against them, and they shall be as stubble, and the day that cometh shall consume them. . . . But behold, the righteous that hearken unto the words of the prophets . . . behold, they are they which shall not perish." (2 Nephi 26:8.) This, according to the Book of Mormon, was literally fulfilled.

The saving of the righteous "even if it so be as by fire" (1 Nephi 22:17), suggests some sort of a counter-fire. That there is to be a segregation between those to be spared and those to be destroyed is clearly stated: After "the Lord God shall commence his work among all nations," (2 Nephi 30:8), then "the time speedily cometh that the Lord God shall cause a great division among the people, and the wicked will he destroy; and he will spare his people, yea, even if it so be that he must destroy the wicked by fire." (2 Nephi 30:10.) This is the "cutting off" of the wicked from the rest of the people preparatory to the Great Overburn. (2 Nephi 22:19-20.)

After the great burning comes a great peace, "and all the nations that fight against Zion . . . shall be as a dream of a night vision." (2 Nephi 27:3.) It shall not be a peace of death but a millennial peace, when "the Holy One of Israel must reign. . . . And he gathereth his children . . . and there shall be one fold and one shepherd . . . And because of the righteousness of his people, Satan has no power; wherefore, he cannot be loosed for the space of many years. . . ." (1 Nephi 22:24-26.) If there shall still be nations during this period of peace, they must be all united: "But behold, all nations, kindreds, tongues, and people shall dwell safely in the Holy One of Israel if it so be that they will repent." (1 Nephi 22:28.) As soon as the wicked are destroyed by fire (2 Nephi 30:10), ". . . then shall the wolf dwell with the lamb . . ." (2 Nephi 30:12), . . . and Satan shall have power over the hearts of the children of men no more, for a long time." (2 Nephi 30:18.)

The Problem of Survival. Words of Plainness

If the Book of Mormon said only what we wanted it to we wouldn't need it. But we do need it. It is written "according to the plainness of the word of God," (Jacob 2:11), "in plainness, even as plain as word can be." (2 Nephi 32:7.) It needs no handbook (not even this one) to explain its meaning. "I glory in plainness," said Nephi (2 Nephi 33:6), ". . . for my soul delighteth in plainness; for after this manner doth the Lord God work . . . for he speaketh unto men according to their language, unto their understanding." (2 Nephi 31:3.) So that leaves us pretty much without excuse.

Now the one inescapable fact about the Nephites is that they were destroyed. They speak from the dust, and they speak to us, and the Book of Mormon is the story of just how their destruction came about. The purpose of telling the story, therefore, is not to reassure but to warn those who inherit the Promised Land after the Nephites, that they might not suffer a like fate without having been given a fair chance: "And this cometh unto you, O ye Gentiles, that ye may know the decrees of God—that ye may repent, and not continue . . . as the inhabitants of the land have hitherto done." (Ether 2:11, 3 Nephi 30: 1-2.) ". . . give thanks to God," says Moroni to our generation, "that he hath made manifest to you *our* imperfections, that ye may learn to be more wise than *we* have been." (Mor. 9:31.) Some civilizations have been destroyed by plague, some by upheavals of nature, some by invading hordes, some by exhaustion of natural resources. Whatever the ultimate cause, the decline and fall was usually accompanied by a weakening of moral and mental fibre rendering the society progressively less capable of meeting progressively mounting dangers.

The tragedy of the Nephites, who brought destruction by war upon their own heads, was not what became *of* them but what they themselves became: "A man's character is his fate," said Heracleitus. Mormon minces no words in describing for our benefit just what the Nephites had become on the eve of their destruction:

O the depravity of my people! They are without order and without
mercy. . . . And they have become strong in their perversion; and
they are alike brutal, sparing none, neither old nor young. . . .
they are without principle, and past feeling; and their wickedness
doth exceed that of the Lamanites. . . . I cannot recommend them
unto God. . . . and I pray unto God (for) . . . the return of his
people unto him, or their utter destruction. . . . And if they perish
it will be like unto the Jaredites, because of the wilfulness of their
hearts, seeking for blood and revenge. (Moroni 9:18-23.)

Please note that their wickedness does not consist in
being on the *wrong side*—in the Book of Mormon it never
does. And the same Mormon minces no words in describing
our society: "Behold, I speak unto you as if ye were present
. . . I know your doing. And I know that ye do walk in
the pride of your hearts. . . ." (Mormon 8:36.) What he
then proceeds to decry is not specific crimes but a meanness of character, a passion to dominate others, with
"envying, and strifes, and malice, and persecutions," with
the same hardness and inconsideration, in fact, that Mormon deplored in his own compatriots: ". . . ye adorn yourselves . . . with that which hath no life, and yet suffer the
hungry, and the needy . . . and the afflicted to pass by you,
and notice them not." (Mormon 8:39.) ". . . ye build up
your secret combinations to get gain, and cause . . . the
blood of . . . fathers and husbands to cry unto the Lord
from the ground, for vengeance upon your heads . . ."
(Mormon 8:40.) "Behold, the sword of vengeance hangeth
over you . . . for he will not suffer their cries any longer."
(Mormon 8:41.) "Hearken, O ye Gentiles," writes the
same prophet, "God . . . hath commanded me that I should
speak concerning you . . . that I should write, saying:
Turn, all ye Gentiles, from your wicked ways; and repent
of your evil doings, and your idolatries, and of your murders, and your priestcrafts, and your envyings, and your
strifes, and from all your wickedness and abominations.
. . ." (3 Nephi 30:2.) This applies to "all Gentiles" and
not only to those of a particular nation or party. But it

is to those in this land of promise that the Book of Mormon is particularly addressed.

The Two Promises

The Nephites and Lamanites each received a promise in the beginning, and each promise contained two parts, a promise of bliss and a promise of woe, ". . . for this is the cursing *and* the blessing of God upon the land. . . ." (Alma 45:16.) In the Dead Sea Scrolls every covenant which promises a blessing if kept promises a corresponding curse if broken, for a contract in which either party should be bound to no conditions whatever would be meaningless. (See 2 Nephi 2:5-10.) For the *Lamanites* the penalty of their backsliding is that they shall be scattered and smitten and driven by the Gentiles; the reward of their faith is that they are to survive all their afflictions and in time become the Lord's own people again. For the *Nephites* the promised reward of faith is that nothing on earth can without their own will and action in any way ever mar their liberty, security, prosperity and happiness: "And now there was nothing in all the land to hinder the people from prospering continually, except they should fall into transgression." (3 Nephi 6:5.) This tremendous guarantee is matched by a promise of total extinction in case they should fail to comply with the conditions of the contract. Since they never became fully ripe in iniquity as did the Nephites, the Lamanites were allowed to remain in the land, paying for the privilege by taking a terrible beating: "Wherefore, if ye are cursed, behold, I leave my blessing upon you . . . because of my blessing the Lord God will not suffer that ye shall perish. . . ." (2 Nephi 4:6-7.) It was an unconditional promise of survival. (Jacob 3:5-9, Helaman 7:24, 15:14-17.) *No such promise was given the Nephites,* and Enos was told that though the Nephites might perish, still the Lamanites would survive to receive his record. (Enos 13, 16.)

The two promises are held up in contrast by Nephi the son of Helaman: ". . . the Lord will lengthen out *their* days . . . when *thou* shalt be utterly destroyed except thou shalt repent." (Helaman 7:24.) And by Samuel the Lamanite: "Therefore, saith the Lord: I will *not* utterly destroy them, but . . . they shall return again unto me. And . . . the Nephites: If they will not repent . . . I *will* utterly destroy them. . . ." (Helaman 15:16-17.) And by Alma: "For behold, the promises of the Lord are extended to the Lamanites, but they are *not* unto you if ye transgress; for has not the Lord expressly promised and firmly decreed that if ye will rebel against him ye shall utterly be destroyed from off the face of the earth?" (Helaman 15:24.)

Alma explains the eminent fairness of the arrangement: "For he will not suffer that ye shall live in your iniquities, to destroy this people . . . he would rather suffer that the Lamanites might destroy all . . . the people of Nephi, if . . . they could fall into sins . . . after having had so much light . . . given unto them . . . yea, after having been favored above every other nation. . . ." (Alma 9:19-20.) And Samuel notes the difference: ". . . yea, the people of Nephi hath he loved, and . . . chastened them because he loveth them. But behold my brethren, the Lamanites, hath he hated because their deeds have been evil continually . . . But behold, salvation hath come unto them through the preaching of the Nephites; and for this intent hath the Lord prolonged their days." (Helaman 15:3-4.)

God does not rejoice in the sufferings of his children, and in his kindness has set aside places where those qualified to be happy could enjoy happiness even in this life: ". . . he leadeth away the righteous into precious lands," (1 Nephi 17:36), where "the hand of providence" pours blessings upon them in almost embarrassing abundance. (Jacob 2:13.) Those who come to the land of promise come by invitation: ". . . there shall none come unto this land save they shall be brought by the hand of the Lord." (2 Nephi 1:6.) Hence they are expected to behave themselves, "and if it so be that they shall serve him . . . it shall be a land of liberty to them." (2 Nephi 1:7.) But he will tolerate no nonsense, having "sworn in his wrath . . . that whoso should possess this land of promise . . . henceforth and forever, should serve him . . . or they should be swept off when the fulness of his wrath should come upon them;" (Ether 2:8); "for behold, there is a curse upon all this land, that destruction shall come upon all those workers of darkness, according to the power of God, when they are fully ripe. . . . Yea, and cursed be the land forever and ever unto those workers of darkness and secret combinations, even unto destruction, except they repent before they are fully ripe." (Alma 37:28, 31.) There are cultures in the Old World, such as those of the Greeks, Arabs, Egyptians, and Chinese, which were ancient when Lehi left Jerusalem, and which though altered still preserve their identity. But there are no such cultures in the New World. To keep this a land of promise, the wicked must be utterly removed from it to preserve it for the righteous. (1 Nephi 17:38.) Only the Lamanites plod on between occupants, and the Lamanites are still here and *we* now occupy the fortunate but dangerous position of the Nephites.

The Cure

Our medical analogy is not without illustrious precedent. The word "history," in fact, is simply the adaptation by Hecataeus of Miletus of a medical term to the affairs of nations. "Historia" means the progress of symptoms marking the course of a disease. It is highly applicable here, since the Book of Mormon itself uses the medical analogy when it speaks of "money, and your substance, and your fine apparel" as "that which will canker," i.e., cause cancer. (Mormon 8:37f.) Since the first step in the Nephite disease is exposure to wealth, the only sure cure or prevention would seem to be strict avoidance of wealth. But is it any pleasanter to die of anemia than of cancer? One can avoid almost any disease by giving up eating altogether, but there must be a better way.

One of Satan's favorite tricks is to send ailing souls after the wrong cure, leading them by his false diagnosis to "strain at a gnat and swallow a camel." In this he is ably abetted by those physicians who would force us to choose between their own violent, extreme, and sometimes fantastic remedies and a sure and agonizing death. Either accept the Wackleberry Cure, they say, or resign yourselves to a frightful and certain end—no other alternative is conceivable. And so by instilling fear with one hand and offering an only hope with the other such practitioners gain a following.

But the Book of Mormon is against violent remedies. It prescribes the gentlest of treatments—charity, accompanied by strong and steady doses of preaching of the gospel. The final analysis of Mormon and Moroni was that the fatal weakness of the Nephites was lack of charity. And whenever the worst epidemics of Nephite disease were brought under control and even stamped out, it was always through a marvelous display of charity and forbearance by such great souls as Alma, Ammon, Moroni, or Nephi or his father Helaman, and specifically through the preaching of the word, which Alma knew was more effective than any surgery: ". . . the preaching of the word . . . had had more powerful effect upon the minds of the people than the sword, or anything else, which had happened to them —therefore Alma thought it was expedient that they should try the virtue of the word of God." (Alma 31:5.)

It is most fortunate that the Book of Mormon not only sets before us the clear "historia" of Nephite disease, but describes for us as well the circumstances under which it has been cured and the remedies employed. Let us take the four danger-signals in order and see what was done to meet the threat indicated by each of them.

As to the external danger, since the Lamanite threat was meant by the Lord to serve a purpose, any attempt to achieve security by the removal of the Lamanites or by "total victory" over them was out of the question. They had to be accepted on a basis of permanent coexistence. Since the Lamanites were meant to serve as a "reminder" whenever the Nephites started slipping, the first line of defense against them was always to put the Nephite house in order, which was done by the preaching of the gospel and a strict enforcement of the laws. The second line of defense was to preach to the Lamanites, and some of the greatest Nephites went among the toughest and meanest of them and preached with great success. When Nephite-Lamanite relationships did deteriorate, as they were bound to do from time to time, able Nephite leaders were always willing to meet the Lamanites more than half-way, and when they had the upper hand never pressed their advantage. When there was fighting, the great Nephite commanders showed remarkable humanity and restraint, and never failed to remind the people that the enemy were their "brethren." Nephite military strategy was strictly defensive, almost all fighting being done on Nephite soil. The rule of the third offense made this unavoidable; it also rendered aggressive warfare impossible and preventive warfare utterly unthinkable. Nephite military preparations were reluctant and defensive—minimal—with God acting as their radar and warning-system. Since they depended on God, the real prevention and cure of Lamanite trouble was spiritual, the key to security being a state of mind: ". . . their minds are firm, and they do put their trust in God continually." (Alma 57:27.) Such optimism was justified by the promise of complete immunity to Lamanite infection as long as the simple rules of health were observed.

Since wealth was dangerous only when people set their hearts upon it, the preaching of the word was the best defense against its insidious inroads. However, once the infection had gained entry it spread rapidly and drastic measures were necessary. The entire society would be reduced to such a state of penury that mere survival became an objective that effectively supplanted the lust for power and gain; this was done (sometimes at the express request of holy men) through droughts, wars, upheavals of nature or the baffling melting away of wealth as God made "slippery" the treasures upon which men had foolishly set their hearts. The cure for that inequality which is the most pernicious effect of accumulated wealth, according to the Book of Mormon, was first of all preaching, then royal decrees or other laws for the support of the indigent, and, when things went too far, economic collapse. Equality was protected by the enforcement of laws guaranteeing such civil rights as freedom of religion and speech; Moroni led popular uprisings to "pull down" those who sought to over-ride "the voice of the people" and establish kingship or aristocracy. But since equality is a state of mind, the most effective remedy was always preaching.

The threat of ambitious individuals was met by public-spirited but *not* ambitious leaders backed by "the voice of the people." The common downfall of ambitious people, however, in the Book of Mormon as in other history, is provided by other ambitious people—they almost automatically produce antibodies which then act as a check on their power. Such is the regular course of Jaredite history. Indeed, Mormon lays down the general principle: ". . . it is by the wicked that the wicked are punished." (Mormon 4:5.) The conflict is costly and wasting, however, to the body politic, and may even lead to its destruction, as in the Roman Republic.

Secret combinations are formed to implement the ambitions of individuals, seeking power through gain and gain through power. Hence they produce and thrive in an atmosphere of conflict, within the groups and between them, assassination being, as the Book of Mormon makes very clear, the cornerstone of their dire economy. Local applications (police harassment) can be effective, but usually force the evil underground and make it harder than ever to deal with. Because these bodies are parasitic, however, they can be effectively starved out, as was demonstrated by Lachoneus and his general strike. Also because they are parasitic, in order to thrive or even survive they must enjoy a measure of cooperation from a willing host. Reports on the Mafia and Cosa Nostra agree that these societies cannot exist without the help of corrupt local officials and a complacent public; they receive financial aid from business men who would never be seen in a casino and yet will lend the owners money because their operations are "legal" and bring money into the community. So it was anciently: "Now the people of Akish were desirous of gain, even as Akish was desirous for power," and so his "wicked and secret society . . . had corrupted the hearts of *all* the people. . . ." (Ether 9:6, 11.)

In this particular case the disease proved fatal, and the Book of Mormon makes it very clear that the appearance of this loathesome parasite is the most dangerous symptom of all, since it has "caused the destruction of this (the Jaredite) people . . . and also the destruction of the people of Nephi. And whatsoever nation shall uphold such secret combinations, to get power and gain, until they shall spread over the nation, behold, they shall be destroyed." (Ether 8:21f.) What makes the thing so frightening is not the parasite itself but the fact that a society is willing to offer it entry and encouragement (to "uphold" it), without which it is not dangerous at all. Its presence therefore should be viewed more as a symptom than a cause: "Wherefore, the Lord commandeth you, when ye shall see these things come among you that ye shall awake

to a sense of *your* awful situation. . . ." (Ether 9:24.)
Immediate repentance, not police action, is urgently prescribed: "O ye Gentiles . . . repent of *your* sins, and suffer
not that these murderous combinations shall get above you,
which are built up to get power and gain. . . ." (Ether
9:23.)

There is good news, however, along with the bad,
for in the verse just cited we are assured of an effective
cure: ". . . it is wisdom in God that these things should
be shown unto you, that thereby ye may repent of your
sins . . ." The Lamanites actually cured a very bad case
of Gadianton infection one time; they "did hunt the band
of robbers of Gadianton . . . insomuch that this band of
robbers was utterly destroyed from among the Lamanites."
(Helaman 6:37.) But this was strange surgery indeed, for
instead of hunting them with knives, clubs and spears
"they did hunt the band . . . and they did preach the word
of God among the more wicked part of them, insomuch
that this band . . . was utterly destroyed. . . ." (Helaman
6:37.) Even for the most advanced stages of the most
dangerous disease the gentlest remedy is the most effective.

It was when he was commenting on the fate of the
Jaredites that Alma addressed his sermon to their
successors, including us: ". . . cursed be the land forever
unto those workers of darkness and secret combinations,
even unto destruction, except they repent before they are
fully ripe." (Alma 37:31.) Always there is the repentance
clause, God leaving the door open until the last moment.
Alma says that the less people know about these combinations in their intimate workings the better (Alma 37:32),
and then he tells us what we really need to defend ourselves:

Preach unto them repentance, and faith on the Lord Jesus Christ;
teach them to humble themselves and to be meek and lowly in
heart; teach them to withstand every temptation of the devil, with
their faith on the Lord Jesus Christ. Teach them to never be weary

of good works, but to be meek and lowly in heart; for such shall find rest to their souls . . . Counsel with the Lord in all thy doings, and he will direct thee for good; yea, when thou liest down at night lie down unto the Lord, that he may watch over you in your sleep; and when thou risest in the morning let thy heart be full of thanks unto God; and if ye do these things, ye shall be lifted up at the last day. (Alma 37:33-37.)

Momentary Conclusion

If the ultimate test of the Book of Mormon's validity is whether or not it really has something to say, then the closing chapters alone should be enough to silence all criticism. Those chapters are addressed explicitly to our own age (Mormon 8:34f.), and we can be the best judges of how well or ill they apply to it.

Mormon and Moroni supply the epilogue to the Book of Mormon, the son drawing freely on his father's notes and letters. The picture that these two paint of their world, which in their minds has a significant resemblance to our own, is one of unrelieved gloom. The situation is unbelievably bad and, in view of the way things are going, quite without hope. The scenes of horror and violence, culminating in the sickening escalation of atrocities by Lamanites and Nephites in the 9th chapter of Mormon, need no news-photographs to make their message convincing to the modern world. The Nephites, like the great heroes of tragedy—Oedipus, Macbeth, Achilles—as they approach their end, are hopelessly trapped by a desperate mentality in which the suppressed awareness of their own sins finds paranoid expression in a mad, ungovernable hatred of others: ". . . they have lost their love, one towards another; and they thirst after blood and revenge continually." (Moroni 9:5.) Their awful guilt leaps out in their instant resentment of any criticism of themselves: ". . . when I speak the word of God with sharpness they tremble and anger against me." (Moroni 9:4.) They have reached that point of suicidal defiance which the Greeks called Ate, the point of no return, when the sinner with a sort of fatal fascination does everything that is most calculated to hasten his own removal from the scene—he is finished, and now all that remains is to get him out of the way: "O my beloved son, how can a people like this, that are without civilization . . . expect that God will stay his hand . . . ?" (Moroni 9:11, 14.)

Nephite civilization was thus not extinguished at Cumorah. It had already ceased to exist for some time before the final house-cleaning. War had become the order of the day, "and every heart was hardened" (Mormon 4:11), with the military requisitioning the necessities of life and leaving the non-combatants "to faint by the way and die." (Moroni 9:16.) "O the depravity of my people!" cries Mormon, and he tells us in what this depravity consists: "They are without order and without mercy . . . they have become strong in their perversion; and they are alike brutal, sparing none neither young nor old . . . and the suffering of our women and our children upon all the face of this land doth exceed everything. . . . thou knowest that they are without principle and past feeling . . . I cannot recommend them unto God lest he should smite me." (Moroni 9:18-21.) Here then is the real calamity that befell the Nephites in all its tragic horror—and there is no mention whatever of enemy action or of anyone belonging to the wrong party: the ultimate catastrophe is not that people are struck down, but that they should be found in any circumstances whatever "without order and without mercy . . . without principle and past feeling."

In this crucible of wickedness the true greatness of Mormon shines like a star as he calls his son to action, telling him that no matter how bad things are, we must never stop trying to do what we can to improve matters, "for if we should cease to labor, we should be brought under condemnation; for we have a labor to perform whilst in this tabernacle of clay." (Moroni 9:6.) In this spirit

Mormon took over command of the army even when he knew that all was lost, ". . . for they looked upon me as though I could deliver them from their afflictions. But behold, I was without hope. . . ." (Mormon 5:1f.) His is the predicament of the true tragic hero: ". . . I had led them notwithstanding their wickedness . . . and had loved them . . . with all my heart; and my soul had been poured out in prayer unto my God all the day long for them; nevertheless, it was without faith, because of the hardness of their hearts." (Mormon 3:12.) However it might appeal to our own age of violence, Mormon found little consolation in the fact that his people were wonderfully tough and proud of it—"for so exceedingly do they anger that it seemeth to me that they have no fear of death." (Moroni 9:5.) ". . . they repented not of their iniquities, but did struggle for their lives without calling upon that Being who created them." (Mormon 5:2.) They could take care of themselves, thank you—and they did.

It is not surprising that their personal experience of things led both Mormon and his son to embrace a completely pessimistic view of the world. As far as the human race taken by itself in a splendid isolation is concerned both men talk like existentialists. For them the tragic isolation of man is a fact: men *have* cut themselves off from God and their state *is* hopeless. If the father can report, ". . . a continual scene of wickedness and abominations has been before mine eyes ever since I have been sufficient to behold the ways of man" (Mormon 2:18), the son could only have seen the latter and worst part of the picture. When Mormon says that "a man being evil cannot do that which is good; neither will he give a good gift" (Moroni 7:6, 8, 10), he really means it. True, "awful is the state of man" only *if* "faith has ceased"—but faith *has* ceased! If men insist that there is no redemption, then, sure enough, "they are as though there had been no redemption made." (Moroni 7:38f.) "If these things have ceased," says Moroni, speaking of gifts of the spirit (Moroni 7:37), "wo be unto the children of men, for it is because of unbelief, and all is vain." This is no mere figure of speech; if faith fulfils its own prophecies so does unbelief, and those who insist that all is vain are quite right; if men reject the gospel they will find everywhere powerful confirmation for their unbelief, and undeniable evidence to support their contention that the human predicament is hopeless. Does God cease to do miracles? Indeed he does, "and the reason why he ceaseth to do miracles among the children of men is because that they dwindle in unbelief. . . ." (Mormon 9:20.) Anyone who says there are no miracles, therefore, can quote Mormon to prove that he is right: ". . . he ceaseth to do miracles." Neither Mormon nor Moroni see the slightest hope of the human race ever pulling itself up by its own bootstraps. And thus far their message is in the bleak idiom of our own day.

But that is not the whole story. What Mormon and Moroni tell us next is that there is something much better than all this, and that we are supposed to be in on it. It is not something that we can get out of ourselves or work out for ourselves, let us hasten to observe. Our prophets spare us the usual cliches about higher spiritual values, the brotherhood of man, and how our problems would be solved if everybody only did this or that. The way out is not to be found in the self-consoling merry-go-round of philosophy, the heroic self-dramatization of literature and art, or the self-reassuring posturings of science and scholarship. Men have tried everything for a long time and the idea that their condition has improved rests entirely on an imaginary reconstruction of the past devised to prove that very proposition. Not that the theory may not be right, but at present we just don't know; and for a world in as dire a predicament as ours, that can guarantee no long centuries of quiet research ahead and seems to need some quick and definite assistance if it is to survive at all, it might pay to consider what Mormon and Moroni have to offer.

If mankind is to get any real help it must come from outside, and it does. First of all *angels*, yes angels, must come to explain and establish things (Moroni 7:29ff.); they do not come on their own, but are direct representatives from the presence of God, "subject to him, to minister according to the word of his command." Moreover these angels do not come to just anybody, but only to those possessing peculiar qualifications, "showing themselves unto them of strong faith and a firm mind in every form of godliness." (Moroni 7:30.) These ministrations, then, are not for the foolish, hysterical, over-imaginative, ambitious or posturing members of the race: to possess along with strong faith a firm mind in *every* form of godliness is to qualify for something definitely beyond the range of the ordinary run of mortals. Those so favored are expected to "prepare the way among the children of men" for passing on the important information they have received by sharing it with and entrusting it "unto the chosen vessels of the Lord," namely, those who, whether they receive the direct ministration of angels or not, are chosen by God to direct his work in the world. These in turn "bear testimony of him," and through their efforts "the Lord God prepareth the way that the *residue* of men may have faith in Christ." (Moroni 7:31-32.)

This is not a handing down of testimony, for each of these messengers calls upon the others to seek testimony for themselves by faith and prayer; there are no second- or third-hand testimonies: "Whoso believeth in me believeth in the Father also; and unto him will the *Father* bear record of me. . . ." (3 Nephi 11:35, cf. Matthew 16:19.)

Is there anything to this? You will never find out, say our prophets, if you begin by denying everything: "Deny not his power," is Moroni's final word of advice to the world. (Moroni 10:33.) All that Mormon and Moroni ask of the reader is, don't fight it, don't block it, give it a chance! If it does not work, then you can forget it; but it is not asking too much that men invest a little of their time and effort in an enterprise in which they stand to win everything and lose nothing—especially now, when so many *know* that as things are they stand to win nothing. Let the hesitant consider that the way of faith is the way of science, too: "Ye receive no witness until *after* the trial of your faith," says Moroni. (Ether 12:6.) First we "make the experiment" (Alma 32:27, 33, 36; 34:4) in which it is fair game to hope for results, since without hope nobody would go through with the thing at all (Moroni 10:22), and then we get our answers. That is the way it is done in the laboratory, what could be fairer?

What, then, is holding us back? Why are so few willing to let faith and hope lead them? There is a serious obstacle here, for "a man . . . cannot have faith and hope, save he shall be meek, and lowly of heart; and if a man be meek and lowly in heart . . . he must needs have charity; for if he have not charity he is nothing; wherefore he must needs have charity." (Moroni 7:43f.) Both Mormon and Moroni come back unerringly to charity as the key to the whole business; it was for lack of charity that their people were destroyed; charity is "the greatest of all" without which "all things must fail." (Moroni 7:47.) No demonstration of its existence is necessary; it "is the pure love of Christ," the irreducible quantity in the universe, as mysterious and undeniable as consciousness itself; without it we are impatient, unkind, envious, puffed up, self-seeking, touchy, suspicious, irritable, distrustful, skeptical, and intolerant (Moroni 7:45), in a word, incapable of seeking truth in any field.

But what is all this to an unbeliever whose chances of being visited by angels are not exactly brilliant? That is where the Book of Mormon comes into the picture. It asks to be taken as evidence—not proof, but material for

study and criticism—for *or* against the proposition that
things do come from outside; it is a standing challenge
to those who will maintain that man's little round of work
and play is all there is to his existence. The best of hypo-
theses, we are told, are those that are most testable, and
the most testable are those that have the courage to predict.
By way of providing tests, and thereby leaving even the
most skeptical without excuse, Moroni makes bold promises
"unto all, even unto the ends of the earth" (Mormon 9:21),
that God will give to him who asks in faith, believing in
Christ, "whatsoever he shall ask the Father . . ." and that
if anyone will ask God if the things in the Book of Mormon
itself "are not true . . . he will manifest the truth of it unto
you, by the power of the Holy Ghost." (Moroni 10:4.)
True, the fulfillment of the conditions requires real faith,
but so does the carrying out of any great experiment, and
it is the special concern of the Book of Mormon to help
men build up such faith, directing their feet if only in the
first cautious steps in that direction: ". . . if ye will awake
and arouse your faculties, even to an experiment upon my
words, and exercise a particle of faith, yea, even if ye can
no more than desire to believe, let this desire work in
you. . . ." (Alma 32:27.) How could one ask for less?

The Book of Mormon has a way of stirring the faculties
of those who read it to wondering about a number of
things. It is packed with minor matters that need looking
into, striking little coincidences that may be explained as
lucky hits or as marks of inspiration or in some other way
—for there is no limit to the possible explanations for any
phenomenon, and every explanation is as legitimate as any
other provided it is made with full intent of exposing it to
the full force of critical examination. Such minor matters
as we have pointed to are the riddle of the Liahona, the
story of Joseph's two garments, the perfect coinage system
of the Nephites, Lehi's *qasida* or didactic poem for his sons,
the genuine non-biblical Hebrew and Egyptian names,

such odd customs as treading on the garments, etc., etc. These all suggest testable theories as to their origins, for we now possess ancient records that may possibly confirm them. But verification is not proof, and the questions these little items raise must remain forever unsolved, the discussion forever open. Then why do we bother about them? Because one learns to understand a problem only by living with it, and by studying these things one can personally acquire those impressions and bits of information that will make it possible for him to reach his own decisions and direct his own researches. One can never prove the Book of Mormon to another, but one can go far enough to ask for a testimony for one's self, and get it.

Though none of the interesting details and minor coincidences in the Book of Mormon may be sufficient to push one this way or that, their cumulative effect can be pretty disturbing. The major issues, however, are more difficult to evade. They have to do with the way the Book of Mormon describes certain ancient institutions and situations of real dimension, things of which virtually nothing was known in Joseph Smith's day, but on which a good deal of information is available today. Ask a class of college students to describe out of their own imaginations and experience such things as the life of a family wandering in the Arabian desert, an ancient coronation rite (in detail), a major war or battle in ancient times, a first-class earthquake, the general state of the Near East *cir.* 600 B. C. Most of them will have little trouble writing at length on these subjects, because they have seen movies and some of them may even have read books, and all of them have had far better training than anyone could have got in early 19th-century America. We sometimes give such assignments to classes in ancient history—but it is strictly in fun, for the results would otherwise be most embarrassing; the efforts of even the best students are terribly inept and uninformed. It would be downright cruel to ask anyone for a serious discussion of such real blockbusters as life in the "Heroic Ages" of the great migrations, the ways of the early desert sectaries, what the activities and teachings of the Lord during his visits to the earth after the resurrection may have been, the techniques of preserving and transmitting sacred writings, or the rise, prosperity and fall of an ancient civilization (describe in detail).

But in all these matters we hold Joseph Smith to account. His book enjoys no immunity to the severest tests and asks for none. The study of forged documents is by no means in its infancy; it was in fact the principal delight of Renaissance scholarship. It has been known for centuries that the easiest of all forgeries to test and detect are long historical documents, and that it is never necessary to go beyond the inner inconsistencies of such documents to expose their fraudulence. So here is the Book of Mormon: if its title page is not telling the truth, it is a big, shallow, clumsy fraud, and there are hundreds of scholars in the world quite capable of refuting its claims within the hour. But whoever offers to undertake the job must be willing to submit his claims and arguments to the same severe criticism that it is his business to mete out. With this understanding the Book of Mormon may some day enjoy the serious critical examination it deserves.

INDEX

Isaiah question, so called, 137ff
It came to pass, 169
-ites, racial types not correlated with
culture, 248

—J—

Jasher, book of, 45
Jershon, a buffer state, 332f
Jews, restoration of, 420f
Jesus, newly discovered sayings of,
47ff
John, and the Dead Sea Scrolls, 236;
a great enigma, 29; mentioned in
the Book of Mormon, 32; the mystery of, 234ff; uniqueness of his
writings, 235ff; writings of withheld, 235
Joseph, a mysterious figure, 230f; as
the type of Christ, 233f
Joseph and Judah, 231f
Jubilees, book of, relates many writings, 42
Judgment, the law of, 382ff

—K—

Kenas, vision of, identical with Zenez?
323
King James Bible, language of in
Book of Mormon, 128f
King James, version of Isaiah com-
pared with Book of Mormon, 131ff
Kishkumen, 367
Korihor, his naturalism and material-
ism, 416ff; and Corihor, 195
—L—
Lachoneus, defeats the Gadianton so-
ciety, 403ff
Lamanite, and Nephite not biological
terms? 246ff
Lamanite maidens, a crisis avoided,
377f
Lamb of God, the Eternal Father,
6, 7
Lamoni, King, and the Ascension of
Isaiah, 207f
Language, offers clues to textual
background, 165f; prophetic not
understood by Nephites, 147f; spe-
cial for secret writings, 112f
Language, barrier to study of the Book
of Mormon, 163f
Latter-day Saints, name of ancient
church, 21
Lawyers, do great mischief, 339f
Laying hold, on the Word of God,
189ff
Lehi, the proper name identified, 60;
as one of a line of messianic proph-

ets, 311; as a typical Jewish sectary,
299
Liahona, and ancient guide arrows,
291f; described, 283ff; meaning of
the word, 296; not magical, 294f
Liberties, civil, enforced, 388f
Liberty, Title of, 340f
Liturgy, renewal of Christian, 14; Ro-
man Catholic, changes in, 15
Lion, Lamanites as a young lion, 421
Logia, of Jesus, discovery of, 26f,
74ff
Losses, of biblical writings seen to be
serious, 26
Loss of scripture, denied by Christians,
116ff; three steps, 97ff
Lost civilizations, 243f

—M—

Manasseh, in the Dead Sea Scrolls,
225
Mandaean, list of writings, 95
Mandaeans, background, 81f; relation-
ship to other groups, 306ff
Mark, going beyond the m., 190; the
people set it upon themselves, 248
Message, of the Book of Mormon. its
supreme test, 373f
Metal plates, some new examples, 63
Miracles, have ceased where they are
denied, 439
Miraculous powers, of early church
lost, 124f
Misconceptions, about what the Book
of Mormon claims to be, 161
Mistakes, in first edition of Book of
Mormon, 4, 5; in the scriptures, 4
Missionary, every member a, 16f
Mongoloid, as basic Indian stock, 246
Monetary system, of Nephites analyzed, 256
Money, Nephite, nature of, 255f
Morianton, stirs up a minor crisis,
347f
Mormon, despairs of Nephite survival,
436f; his tragic role, 368; resigns
his command, 369
Mormon, leads a lost cause, 437f
Moroni, angry letter to Pahaoran,
360ff; his leniency, 338, 341, 352;
his leniency bears fruit, 365f; loses
his temper with Ammoron, 352f;
the model soldier, 330; resumes
command in spite of his vow, 370;
his systems of defense, 334f, 342-
347
Moronihah, continues Moroni's leni-
ent policy, 367f; wins back half the
land, 368